INTERNATIONAL COMMERCIAL MEDIATION

In this comprehensive comparative study, Ronán Feehily analyses the legal and regulatory issues surrounding international commercial mediation and discusses their implications in a range of settings. While existing literature tends to cover mediation in general, Feehily places the commercial mediation process in its legal and regulatory context, offering an original contribution to the field. The book identifies the controversies that arise from the mediation process across numerous jurisdictions and discusses them in detail. Comparing the mediation process in Europe, North America and Australia, as well as other common, civil and 'mixed' jurisdictions, Feehily demonstrates where systemic differences are transcended and where they are significant. Organised systematically and written in an accessible style, Feehily offers an international, holistic guide to the commercial mediation process.

RONÁN FEEHILY is Associate Professor of Commercial Law at the University of Canterbury and an experienced commercial lawyer, arbitrator and mediator. He is a Fellow of the Chartered Institute of Arbitrators, CEDR Accredited Mediator and Member of the Mediation Committee of the International Bar Association. An award-winning researcher, he has published numerous articles covering international commercial dispute resolution, and his previous books include *An Introduction to the Law of Contract in New Zealand* (2018), *Understanding Company Law* (2019) and *Commercial Law and the Legal System* (2020).

T0371514

INTERNATIONAL COMMERCIAL MEDIATION

Law and Regulation in Comparative Context

RONÁN FEEHILY

University of Canterbury, Christchurch, New Zealand

CAMBRIDGE
UNIVERSITY PRESS

CAMBRIDGE
UNIVERSITY PRESS

University Printing House, Cambridge CB2 8BS, United Kingdom

One Liberty Plaza, 20th Floor, New York, NY 10006, USA

477 Williamstown Road, Port Melbourne, VIC 3207, Australia

314–321, 3rd Floor, Plot 3, Splendor Forum, Jasola District Centre,
New Delhi – 110025, India

103 Penang Road, #05–06/07, Visioncrest Commercial, Singapore 238467

Cambridge University Press is part of the University of Cambridge.

It furthers the University's mission by disseminating knowledge in the pursuit of
education, learning, and research at the highest international levels of excellence.

www.cambridge.org
Information on this title: www.cambridge.org/9781108835886
DOI: 10.1017/9781108869423

First published 2022

A catalogue record for this publication is available from the British Library.

ISBN 978-1-108-83588-6 Hardback
ISBN 978-1-108-79891-4 Paperback

To Hazel Alice
With love and thanks
and
Henry James Manaaki
With the earnest hope that your generation will resolve
conflict more sensibly than mine.
Le grá a mhac.

CONTENTS

PREFACE

Mediation has gathered momentum as a means of international commercial dispute resolution over the past four decades. The advent of the Singapore Convention has broken new ground by elevating international mediated settlement agreements to a new status, enabling them to be recognised and enforced within the framework of private international law. This new international basis for enforcement will serve to raise the international profile of the commercial mediation process, giving it increased credibility and visibility and the promise of greater regulatory robustness.

This book analyses the principal legal and regulatory issues in international commercial mediation and discusses the implications for the process in its several contexts. The controversies arising from the international commercial mediation process are identified and discussed in detail. This perspective on recent and emerging developments, and the insights it reveals, sets this book apart, comprising its original contribution to the field.

Commercial mediation is primarily a creature of contract and has proved most successful in those countries where it developed entirely separately from the court process. Consequently, private commercial mediation, as distinct from mandatory forms of mediation, is the primary process covered in this book. The main focus is on developments in common law jurisdictions in Europe, North America and Australia where mediation tends to be more advanced, while developments in other common, civil and 'mixed' jurisdictions are referred to in various places for comparative purposes. In view of the flexible nature of the mediation process, the principles and themes covered are comparative and international and largely transcend systemic differences.

The chapters are organised thematically, with each chapter reflecting a natural progression from the preceding one. While many of the themes and principles discussed in the book are relevant to mediation generally, the book's focus on commercial mediation means it will primarily be of interest to students, academics, practitioners, mediation service providers, judges and others with an interest in the law and regulation of the commercial mediation process. The content should also serve as a useful guide to recent developments in regulation and law for those engaged in other forms of mediation and those who have an interest in the mediation process generally.

I am grateful to my family, above all my wife Hazel, for their patience and support throughout the intensive process from draft manuscript to final production.

The staff at Cambridge University Press, particularly Finola O'Sullivan and Marianne Nield, have been encouraging and helpful through the process.

I am grateful to Professor Carrie Menkel-Meadow for writing the foreword. A founder of the dispute resolution field, Professor Menkel-Meadow is both a leading academic and practitioner. As one of modern mediation's 'pioneering pracademics', her work has resulted in theory influencing practice and practice influencing theory.

While this book has been an ongoing project for some time, it was finalised during a period of sabbatical research leave at the Commercial Law Centre, Harris Manchester College, University of Oxford. I am grateful to Professor Kristin Van Zwieten and Professor Horst Eidenmueller for making this visit fruitful and enjoyable, particularly in such challenging times.

I have attempted to state the law as at 30 June 2022.

Ronán Feehily
Christchurch, New Zealand
July 2022

FOREWORD

In recent decades many legal systems have come to the realisation that court procedures and lengthy and expensive trials may not be the best way to achieve justice (defined as including process fairness and good decisions on the merits, with efficient use of resources). The founding of the modern 'A' (alternative, appropriate, accessible) Dispute Resolution movement, first in the USA in the 1970s, and then transported and transplanted to many other regions, some of which, e.g., China and parts of Africa, had been using non-litigation or court processes like mediation for literally centuries, was based on two different values – efficiency, speed and lower cost of case processing (the quantitative rationale); and party-fashioned flexible and tailored solutions or agreements (the qualitative rationale). Many court systems throughout the world began to adopt pre-trial requirements of attempting negotiation, mediation or arbitration before litigants could get access to traditional trials (courtrooms and judges). In the private sector, beginning in the 1980s, lawyers, retired judges and other professionals (e.g., the Center for Public Resources in the USA and the Centre for Effective Dispute Resolution in the UK) began to offer 'private' dispute resolution (mediation, arbitration and hybrids) in major commercial matters (and large civil class actions in the United States).

Mediation was often touted as promising confidentiality, party-controlled rules of procedure and practice, self-determination over outcomes, choice of mediators and party-tailored outcomes that could focus on newly created relationships and recrafted commercial and contractual relations. So early on, as mediation and other forms of 'A' DR moved around the world to Europe, Asia, the Middle East, and South America, there have been competing views of the basic purposes of these processes – conformity to 'reasonable and common business practices' – the *lex mercatoria* of international arbitration or 'common customs' in mediation (with experienced neutrals, often with special industry knowledge, as in technology and intellectual property disputes helping the parties to reach agreements) for speed, efficiency and legitimacy of outcomes (and privacy), versus an approach that values communication, creativity and the crafting of purposeful solutions that the parties come up with themselves.

Now that courts all over the world like to actively encourage more consensual decision making (and some have required some form of mediation for a long time) court-annexed programmes of mediation are in competition with the private sector in the provision of dispute resolution services. There is concern that different mediators use different techniques and that some do not know the difference between mediation (which is third party-facilitated negotiation) and arbitration (a decision and award proclaimed by a third party chosen by the disputants). Some countries (less used to ambiguity and process pluralism) have now been seeking to clarify the differences in processes, define them and regulate when and how they can be used. The uses of different processes for the resolution of commercial disputes becomes especially problematic when the commercial disputes involve cross-border or 'international' matters and can also involve both private and public parties. There are legal rules, contract terms and differences of culture that may affect how the parties will deal with each other in seeking to resolve their claims.

In this new book Ronán Feehily provides a comprehensive review of the law that has been applied to the use of mediation in commercial matters, comprehensively reviewing case law and statutory law from Europe, the US, Canada, Australia, India, Hong Kong, the Caribbean, China, Singapore, Brazil, South Africa and New Zealand to focus on such important issues as enforcement of agreements to mediate, jurisdictional matters, enforcement of mediation agreements (now supported some-what by the Singapore Convention) and a myriad of other issues that may be raised in common, civil and 'mixed' legal systems and traditions. While exploring the decisional and statutory law, Feehily does not shy away from a variety of policy issues that plague mediation (such as why some countries take up mediation and others do not).

Just as the field of international arbitration now has many treatises (of theory and practice), mediation now has a comprehensive text to be consulted with respect to issues of practice, policy, ethics and theory. Its comprehensive treatment of these issues of practice, as well as ethics and professionalisation, in a variety of different legal systems provides one of the first detailed accounts of how a relatively simple process (two parties, one mediator) can be expanded and morphed into a complex process of many parties, lawyers, experts and others as parties seek greater control over their own commercial relations, especially in cross-border settings with no real civil 'world court' to determine their claims or set their rules of engagement.

This book raises the issues we will watch and study in the decades to come as we consider whether more interactive global business will result in more consensual and more 'universal' processes or whether legal nationalism and different legal traditions find different answers (both legal and practical) to the issues presented by cross-systemic dispute resolution. Mediation in different contexts is likely to be informed by the different cultures and businesses in which it is employed. This book allows us to see where we are now.

I have learned a lot in reading this book and so will you.

Carrie Menkel-Meadow
Distinguished Professor of Law and Political Science,
University of California,
A. B. Chettle Professor of Law, Dispute Resolution
and Civil Procedure, Emerita,
Georgetown University

CASES

AB *v.* CD [2013] EWHC 1376 (TCC), 259
Abriel *v.* Australian Guarantee Corp Ltd [2000] FCA 1198, 152, 251
Abriel *v.* Westpac Banking Corp [1999] FCA 50, 206
ADS Aerospace Ltd *v.* EMS Global Tracking [2012] EWHC 2904 TCC, 178
A-G *v.* Guardian Newspapers Ltd (No 2) [1988] UKHL 6, 269
Aird *v.* Prime Meridian Ltd [2006] EWCA Civ 1866, 253
Aiton Australia Pty Ltd *v.* Transfield Pty Ltd [1999] NSWSC 996, 59, 65, 72
Alassini *v.* Telecom Italia SpA [2010] 3 CMLR 17, Case C–317–320/08 (ECJ),
    66, 184
Allco Steel (Queensland) Pty *v.* Torres Strait Gold Pty Ltd (Supreme Court of
    Queensland, Master Horton, 12 March 1990), 76
AMF Inc *v.* Brunswick Corp 621 F Supp 456, 462 (ED NY 1985), 59
ARP Capita London Market Services Ltd *v.* Ross & Co [2004] EWHC 1181, 253
Arthur JS Hall & Co *v.* Simons [2000] UKHL 38, 168
Ashingdane *v.* United Kingdom (1985) 7 EHRR 528, 191
Atlas Express Ltd *v.* Kafco [1989] QB 833, 206
Attorney Grievance Commission of Maryland *v.* Steinberg 910 A 2d 429 (Md
    2006), 153
AWA Ltd *v.* Daniels (t/a Deloitte Haskins & Sells) (1992) 7 ACSR 463, 194, 249,
    250, 267
Barry *v.* City West Water Ltd [2002] FCA 1214, 200
Beattie PN *v.* Canham Consulting [2021] EWHC 1414 (TCC), 178
Beauty Star Ltd *v.* Janmohamed [2014] EWCA Civ 451, 79
Bernabei *v.* St Paul Fire & Marine Insurance Co Ohio App 5 Dist, WL 351754
    (2005), 259
Biala Pty Ltd *v.* Mallina Holdings Ltd [1989] 15 ACLR 208, 250
Bowden *v.* Weickert No S-02–017, 2003 WL 21419175 (Ohio Ct App, 6th Dist, 20
    June 2003), 16
Bowman *v.* Fels [2005] EWCA Civ 226, 271
BPC Hotels *v.* Brooke North [2014] EWHC 2367, 297
Brandsmart USA *v.* DR Lakes Inc 901 So 2d 1004 (Fla Dist Ct App 2005), 211
Brinkerhoff *v.* Campbell 994 P 2d 911 (2000), 210
Brosnan *v.* Dry Cleaning Station Inc [2008] US Dist LEXIS 44678 (ND Cal
    2008), 60
Brown *v.* Rice [2007] EWHC 625 (Ch), 90, 201, 205, 251, 254, 258, 260, 289
Brownlee *v.* Brownlee (High Court (Provisional Division), Brassey AJ, 25 August
    2009), 144, 176

STATUTES

Australia

New South Wales

Queensland

Victoria

Crimes Act 1958
  s 326, 270

Western Australia

Rules of the Supreme Court
  O 29 r 3(2), 194

Bermuda

International Conciliation and Arbitration Act 1993
  s 20, 225

Brazil

Arbitration Law
  art 21(4), 218
  art 28, 218

France

Code of Civil Procedure (*Code de procédure civile*)
  arts 127–31, 22

Hong Kong

Apology Ordinance (cap 631) 2017
  213
Arbitration Ordinance (cap 609)
  s 66(2), 225

India

Arbitration and Conciliation Act 1996
  art 30, 218

Ireland

Arbitration Act 2010
  s 9, 79
Mediation Act 2017, 275
  s 2, 20
  s 14, 176
  s 15, 176
  s 21, 176

Italy

Legislative Decree 28
  art 5, 186

People's Republic of China

Arbitration Law
  art 51, 218

Singapore

Rules of Court
  O 59 r 5(1)(c), 165

South Africa

Arbitration Act 1965
  s 13, 79
Labour Relations Act 1995
  s 115(2)(a), 128
  s 135(3)(c), 128

Sweden

Arbitration Act 1999
  s 27, 225

United Kingdom

Companies Act 1985
  s 459, 173
Crime Act 2002
  s 328, 270, 271
  s 338, 270
Housing Grants Construction and Regeneration Act 1996
  s 108, 14
  s 114(4), 14
Proceeds of Crime Act 2002, 270
  s 328
  s 338
Solicitors Regulation Authority Code of Conduct 2011
  r 1.12 143

England & Wales

Arbitration Act 1996
  s 6(1), 220
  s 7, 56

United States

California

Oregon

INTERNATIONAL CONVENTIONS, LAWS, CODES AND RULES

Table of International Conventions and Laws

Table of International Codes and Rules

Introduction to Commercial Mediation

1.1 Introduction

Disputes should be resolved by using the appropriate process, whether that be litigation or a form of alternative dispute resolution (ADR) such as mediation. Court systems in jurisdictions throughout the world are organised on the assumption that most commercial cases will settle, often at the doors of the court. Litigation consequently operates as a legal default or fallback option. Parties should be aware of the various forms of ADR available and where commercial mediation fits within the range of processes. Certain dispute resolution processes may be particularly well suited to certain types of dispute, and the parties' choice should be informed by clear criteria. Mediation has proved difficult to differentiate from other forms of ADR, in part due to the lack of a generally accepted definition. Attempts to define mediation have proved challenging, given its varied use in different contexts.

1.2 Mediation and Conventional Dispute Resolution

In common law jurisdictions such as England,[1] the USA and Australia, commercial litigants are likely to have access to a sophisticated and rigorous legal process. To achieve a judgment or court order, lengthy pleadings or statements of case will be exchanged setting out details of the dispute, document disclosure or discovery will be undertaken and pre-trial hearings will take place in front of judicial officers dealing with preliminary issues and preparing for the ensuing trial. Witness statements will be prepared and exchanged, and a full trial will follow, with a judge hearing oral evidence, examination, cross-examination and lawyers' speeches. The system is based on the assumption that

---

[1] For simplicity, the term 'England' is used throughout this book to describe the jurisdiction of England and Wales.

there is a correct way of deciding every issue in dispute and those involved in the process work within that assumption. The system is adversarial and assumes that if parties can battle in a controlled environment, the cut and thrust of the process will elicit the important facts and ensure that all relevant arguments are adduced to aid the judge in reaching a conclusion. For those whose rights are being tested or contested, the expense has become onerous. Clients have been advised for some time that even high-value disputes cannot economically be taken to trial.[2]

Arbitration[3] was originally created as a real alternative to the judicial system. Aristotle viewed it as a source of equity where arbitrators employed a broad discretion to fashion remedies. Over the past few decades, arbitration has been viewed more as a choice of forum than as an alternative process, having become 'legalised', with arbitrators effectively being asked to act as trial judges in applying statute and common law to claims.[4] The emergence of the mediation process as a viable alternative for resolving commercial conflict is perceived as transforming the goals and values of conventional legal processes. Through the parties' direct engagement with the process, mediation results in party self-empowerment and control.[5]

Over forty years ago, then US Chief Justice Warren Burger observed that the law is not an end in itself but a means to an end, that end being justice. The means, he believed, should not be exalted at the expense of the ends. Lawyers in his view had become too much like the pathologists

---

[2] See F Armstrong, 'Business Litigation and the Litigation Business: Getting to Settlement through Mediation' (2004) *Public Affairs Ireland* 4; H Brown and A Marriott, *ADR: Principles and Practice* (London, Sweet & Maxwell 2018) 18; J R Van Winkle, *Mediation: A Path for the Lost Lawyer* (Chicago, American Bar Association 2001) 1–16.

[3] Arbitration is defined in this chapter at 1.8.2.1.

[4] R A Creo, 'Business and Practice Issues of US Mediators' in C Newmark and A Monaghan (eds), *Butterworths Mediators on Mediation: Leading Mediator Perspectives on the Practice of Commercial Mediation* (Haywards Heath, Tottel Publishing 2005) 311. See D R Hensler, 'Our Courts, Ourselves: How the Alternative Dispute Resolution Movement is Re-shaping Our Legal System' (2003) 108(1) *Penn State Law Review* 165, 183–84. Due to 'legalisation', it has been suggested that arbitration has moved from being an art to a science: see N N Antaki, 'Cultural Diversity and ADR Practices in the World' in J C Goldsmith, A Ingen-Housz and G H Pointon (eds), *ADR in Business: Practice and Issues Across Countries and Cultures* (Alphen aan den Rijn, Kluwer Law International 2006) 270.

[5] It has been suggested that this presents a transformative dimension, an opportunity for parties to reconnect with their own practical wisdom and moral growth: see J Shestack, 'Introduction' in Van Winkle (n 2) vii–x.

who can say more about what caused death than what would preserve life. As a result of legal training, lawyers tended to cast all disputes into a legal framework that only legal professionals could deal with in traditional legal ways, leading to a 'vicious cycle.' He wrote:

> The notion that most people want black-robed judges, well-dressed lawyers and fine panelled courtrooms as the setting to resolve their disputes is not correct. People with problems, like people with pains, want relief, and they want it as quickly and inexpensively as possible.[6]

The emerging popularity of commercial mediation as an alternative form of dispute resolution would appear to be a realisation of this logic.

1.3   Commercial Interests and Legal Rights

When commercial parties enter into an agreement, they accept a number of legal rights and obligations. As time passes, circumstances may change. Due to unplanned and legally unforeseeable circumstances, the ability of one or more of the parties to perform their obligations may diminish, leaving them unable to comply with the contract. Litigation usually results. This in turn causes communication between the parties to shut down, the vacuum being filled by communication between lawyers, by pleadings and by other legal notices that slowly move the parties towards a future court date. Even when a judgment is ultimately made in a party's favour, it may expose other aspects of their commercial interests to criticism. This risk may be sufficient to make avoiding court the prudent commercial option.

In many cases, resolving a dispute through litigation or arbitration is unlikely to further the commercial interests of the parties. The rationale for entering into commercial contracts in the first place is to advance the parties' commercial interests and create shared wealth.[7] When a dispute arises, it seems counter-intuitive for disputing parties to move from a consensus-seeking relationship, where they focus their minds on the most appropriate way to further their commercial interests, into an adversarial relationship, which is highly unlikely to further those interests. An opportunity may arise to use a consensual rather than an adversarial approach to resolve the conflict by pursuing commercial

---

[6] W Burger, 'Our Vicious Legal Spiral' (1977) 16(4) *Judges Journal* 23–24, 48–49.
[7] See R Feehily and R Tiong, *An Introduction to the Law of Contract in New Zealand* (Wellington, Thomson Reuters 2018) 2–3.

interests rather than legal rights. Litigation brings with it a price that commercial parties must absorb, both directly through legal costs and indirectly in terms of management time. If the commercial mediation option is chosen, legal rights are not abandoned unless and until a new agreement is reached.[8]

Mediation can prove successful as it is forward focussed. While the law looks to the past to determine who was right, mediation looks to the future to find a solution both parties can move forward with. In law, the court uses its power to dictate a solution, while in mediation, parties empower themselves to find their own solution with the help, guidance and support of their lawyers. The legal system is not designed to solve people's problems; it has the more abstract goal of finding the truth. Truth finding and problem solving may not amount to the same thing; in fact, when resolving commercial disputes, the two concepts may prove to be mutually exclusive. When commercial parties have a dispute, rather than finding the truth, they are likely to want to have their problem solved – quickly, fairly and inexpensively – so they can get on with their lives.[9] Mediation facilitates this by empowering parties rather than controlling them. It provides the impetus for collaborating to develop settlement options such that parties construct and own the agreement reached.[10]

1.4 The Legal System

As already noted, litigation usually involves placing a dispute before a judge to examine a past event and determine how much money one party should pay another. Most commercial cases involve money. Even when a claim seeks more than this, there is often strong systemic pressure to reframe the dispute as a purely economic one, reflecting the limitations of the legal system and the lawyer's role in it. While courts in common

---

[8] Similar arguments have been made for some time: see M Antrobus and R Sutherland, 'Some ADR Techniques in Commercial Disputes: Prospects for Better Business' in P Pretorius (ed), *Dispute Resolution* (Cape Town, Juta 1993) 164–66.

[9] P Lovenheim and L Guerin, *Mediate, Don't Litigate: Strategies for Successful Mediation* (Berkeley, Nolo 2004) 1/3, 5/11.

[10] Traditional systems of justice do not seek to empower participants, but to apply rules that reinforce and solidify the dominant position of the rule makers. Such systems have been characterised as having their roots in modernist discourse. Conversely, mediation is viewed as a post-modern construct: see B Gray, 'Mediation as a Post-Modern Practice: A Challenge to the Cornerstones of Mediation's Legitimacy' (2006) 17(4) *Australasian Dispute Resolution Journal* 208, 212, 216.

law jurisdictions historically were divided into law and equity, this division now exists mostly in name only. Courts of equity can administer justice and order remedies beyond compensation for loss, reducing – if not eliminating – equity's distinct function. Further remedies such as apologies or changes in policies or practices, tend not to be ordered in many court cases. Even where courts retain the technical power to make such orders, it seems that they elect not to use it in claims where monetary relief is viewed as sufficient. Even when injunctive relief could provide a remedy, courts frequently focus on the compensatory aspects of a possible judgment.[11]

1.5 The Limits of Adjudication

Adjudicatory processes have not kept up with rapidly changing commercial environments. Adjudication – whether judicial or arbitral – is equipped to distinguish black and white. It is inadequate in recognising shades of grey and the importance of polycentric elements.

Conventional legal processes are grounded in the ethic of conscience (or conviction) and reflect the view that there is an absolute right or wrong in a given situation and that the 'right' decision is attainable. They are concerned with individual motive and action rather than with social or commercial consequences. Conversely, commercial mediation is based on the ethic of responsibility (or consequence) and reflects the principle of moral ambiguity. It accepts that people have to weigh the consequences of their actions and take into account the 'real world' and the deficiencies in those they rely on for a particular result. In this context it seems more relevant for decision-makers to focus on the consequences of an action, rather than its ethical 'purity', decision-making involves choosing the lesser wrong – not establishing a 'perfect right'.

Rather than being feared or avoided, conflict can be regarded as an opportunity for parties to enhance their understanding, to constructively collaborate and to move forward. Given that the vast majority of commercial disputes are settled at the doors of the court, it is regrettable that efforts for resolving disputes are left until this late and often uncomfortable stage.[12]

---

[11] See Creo (n 4) 310–11.

[12] See A T Trollip, *Alternative Dispute Resolution in a Contemporary South African Context* (Durban, Butterworths 1991) 3–4, 10–11; L Fuller and K Winston, 'The Forms and Limits of Adjudication' (1978) 92(2) *Harvard Law Review* 353, 394–404. See also Brown and Marriott (n 2) 6–8.

1.6   The Context of Alternative Dispute Resolution

It is generally acknowledged that the birth of modern ADR occurred in the USA at the 1976 Roscoe Pound Conference, where Frank Sander argued that disputes could be processed in ways other than adversarial litigation.[13] Despite significant opposition,[14] ADR has since become an embedded feature of the global legal landscape.[15] In the USA, where the focus is on the provision of faster and more efficient alternatives to court, ADR includes all forms of dispute resolution other than litigation or court adjudication. Outside the USA, in countries where the focus tends to be on the nature of the process and the possible outcome, ADR is normally not considered to include arbitration.[16]

'ADR' has been used to mean 'appropriate dispute resolution', on the basis that this phrase better conveys the concept of a method that is best suited or appropriate to resolving the relevant dispute.[17] It has also been

---

[13]   F Sander, 'Varieties of Dispute Processing: Address Before the National Conference on the Causes of Popular Dissatisfaction with the Administration of Justice' (1976) 70 *Federal Rules Decisions* 79, 111–34. This speech became the impetus for a movement to create what was called a 'multi-door courthouse', where disputants would be offered different forms of dispute resolution that they could choose from, with the objective of 'fitting the forum to the fuss': see F Sander and S Goldberg, 'Fitting the Forum to the Fuss: A User-Friendly Guide to Selecting an ADR Procedure' (1994) 10(1) *Negotiation Journal* 49. This movement attracted the attention of three groups in particular. One was a group of judges led by US Chief Justice Warren Burger and focussed on the 'efficiency' or 'quantitative' aspects of dispute processing. They believed there were too many cases in the courts and wanted to reduce court dockets and increase judicial efficiency. The second group was a more amorphous social movement, inspired by the political empowerment movements of the 1960s, whose members sought greater control and participation by the disputing parties in dispute resolution, less professionalisation of dispute resolution processes and more tailored solutions to problems. An emerging intellectual school, derived from the Legal Process School of the 1950s and called Process Pluralism, also believed that particular forms of dispute processing were appropriate for particular types of legal, political, social and economic problems: see C Menkel-Meadow, 'Roots and Inspirations: A Brief History of the Foundations of Dispute Resolution' in M Moffitt and R Bordone (eds), *The Handbook of Dispute Resolution* (San Francisco, Jossey-Bass 2005) 19.

[14]   See O Fiss, 'Against Settlement' (1984) 93(6) *Yale Law Journal* 1073. See also O Fiss 'Out of Eden' (1985) 94(4) *Yale Law Journal* 1669.

[15]   Before Sander's speech (n 13), ADR was viewed as 'nothing more than a hobbyhorse for a few offbeat scholars': see H T Edwards, 'Alternative Dispute Resolution: Panacea or Anathema?' (1985–1986) 99(3) *Harvard Law Review* 668, 668.

[16]   In England one of the leading authorities on ADR includes arbitration as part of the full range of alternatives to litigation potentially available to civil disputants: see S Blake, J Browne and S Sime, *The Jackson ADR Handbook* (2nd ed, Oxford, Oxford University Press 2016) 2.

[17]   See C Wallgren, 'ADR and Business' in Goldsmith, Ingen-Housz and Pointon (eds) (n 4) 7.

used to mean 'additional dispute resolution', as ADR processes are additional or complementary to litigation. As mediation does not involve imposing a decision that affects the parties' rights or interests,[18] the process is effectively an extension of business negotiations.[19] The tendency to refuse the title 'alternative dispute resolution' in favour of 'appropriate dispute resolution' or 'additional dispute resolution' acknowledges that ADR is about more than applying alternatives to litigation; it involves selecting and designing the process that is best suited to the relevant dispute and to the disputing parties. Critically assessing adversarial litigation relative to ADR is important in determining the most suitable process that may supplement – rather than supplant – court adjudication.[20]

All dispute resolution, whether conventional or alternative, takes place within a legal framework, in the 'shadow of the law'.[21] Most commercial

---

[18] L Street, 'Mediation and the Judicial Institution' (1997) 71(10) *Australian Law Journal* 794, 795. ADR has also been used to mean 'amicable dispute resolution', for example, it was used in the International Chamber of Commerce ADR Rules 2001: see Wallgren (n 17) 6–7. It has been suggested that the 'A' in ADR can stand for appropriate, alternative or amicable – each representing a specific approach to conflict management: 'appropriate DR' reflects complete party autonomy; 'alternative DR' excludes traditional litigation in the USA, and litigation and arbitration in other parts of the world, notably Europe; and 'amicable DR' (that is, non-hybrid) seeks simply to settle the dispute: see A Ingen-Housz (ed), *ADR in Business: Practice and Issues Across Countries and Cultures*, vol 2 (Alphen aan den Rijn, Kluwer Law International 2011) xxiii.

[19] See Sir Laurence Street, 'Commentary on Some Aspects of the Advent and Practice of Mediation in Australia' in Newmark and Monaghan (eds) (n 4) 361. In view of the breadth and diversity of activities and the wide range of approaches and strategies collectively known as 'ADR', it has been suggested that it is an outmoded, unhelpful term that survives as a matter of convenience: see T J Stipanowich, 'ADR and the "Vanishing Trial": The Growth and Impact of "Alternative Dispute Resolution"' (2004) 1(3) *Journal of Empirical Legal Studies* 843, 845.

[20] See P Pretorius, 'Introduction and Overview' in P. Pretorius (ed), *Dispute Resolution* (Cape Town, Juta 1993) 1–2. Where ADR is integrated into the formal legal system, ADR options should be made available at all stages of the dispute, parties should be incentivised to choose an appropriate process as early as possible, and ease of change between processes should be facilitated where the initial choice may not resolve the dispute at as low a cost as possible: see K Hopt and F Steffek, 'Mediation: Comparison of Laws, Regulatory Models, Fundamental Issues' in K Hopt and F Steffek (eds), *Mediation: Principles and Regulation in Comparative Perspective* (Oxford, Oxford University Press 2013) 20–53, 110.

[21] The term originated in R M Mnookin and L Kornhauser, 'Bargaining in the Shadow of the Law: The Case of Divorce' (1979) 88(5) *Yale Law Journal* 950. The shadow of the law operates on a number of levels in mediation. Parties in mediation should use their legal rights and obligations as a frame of reference when considering proposals relative to how the dispute would likely be determined by a court or tribunal, and the cost and risk associated with that outcome. The legal process may also be required if there are allegations of duress during the process, or a breach of confidentiality at any stage, or if

disputes involve a complex interaction of interests and rights. Mediation operates in the 'shadow of the law' to generate workable solutions by reconciling two partially conflicting goals: assessing the legal remedies that reflect the parties' no-agreement alternatives, and focussing on the parties' underlying interests.[22] Hence ADR processes such as mediation, in particular, do not diminish the role of judges. As disputes are settled against the backdrop of rights emerging from decided case law, success in mediation depends to some extent on the parties having the confidence to disclose their points of weakness to the mediator, whose role complements what judges do. A party cannot safely disclose its vulnerabilities to a judge who would ultimately decide the case. The mediation process consequently fits well within the framework of the court system.[23] While courts perform the essential function of creating judicial precedents,[24] they operate in a context where settlement is the norm.[25] ADR options such as mediation should not be perceived as mutually exclusive alternatives but as complementary elements within an integrated dispute resolution system.[26]

there are difficulties with enforcing the settlement. The court may also play a role in interpreting agreements to mediate or codes of conduct and determining the appropriate contours of mediator or lawyer behaviour.

[22] C Buhring-Uhle, L Kirchhoff and G Scherer, *Arbitration and Mediation in International Business* (2nd ed, Alphen aan den Rijn, Kluwer Law International 2006) 193.

[23] F Armstrong, 'Lost in Translation' (2004) August/September *Law Society Gazette* 26, 30.

[24] ADR has sometimes been derided in the USA as meaning 'attorney deficit revenue': see E V Ludwig, 'A Judge's View: The Trial/ADR Interface' (Summer 2004) *Dispute Resolution Magazine* 13.

[25] It has been suggested that litigation should now be viewed as the 'alternative' process and mediation as mainstream, and that the correct description should be 'EDR', with 'E' standing for 'efficient', 'effective' or 'expedited' dispute resolution: see M Kallipetis and S Ruttle, 'Better Dispute Resolution: The Development and Practice of Mediation in the United Kingdom between 1995 and 2005' in Goldsmith, Ingen-Housz and Pointon (eds) (n 4) 192–93.

[26] Buhring-Uhle, Kirchhoff and Scherer (n 22) 265–70. In the USA, for example, about 1 per cent of civil cases filed in the federal court system reach trial, and in state courts, the trial rate is almost as low. Allowing for cases decided without a trial, such as through motions for summary judgment, the large majority of civil cases are never adjudicated on the merits: see D Golann and J Folberg, *Mediation: The Roles of Advocate and Neutral* (3rd ed, New York, Wolters Kluwer 2016) 4. The phenomenon of only a small proportion of disputes ever becoming legal cases was characterised some time ago as the 'dispute pyramid': see M Galanter, 'Reading the Landscape of Disputes: What We Know and Don't Know (and Think We Know) About our Allegedly Contentious and Litigious Society' (1983) 31(1) *UCLA Law Review* 4. See also Chapter 10 at Section 10.2.3 for a discussion on this issue. Consequently, it has been suggested that the most appropriate benchmark for evaluating the efficiency of mediation is not adjudication, but unassisted negotiation. As most disputes settle through negotiation, the more relevant question is

1.7   Alternative Dispute Resolution and Litigation

Parties engaging in litigation will find familiar procedures specified by rules, while parties engaging in ADR processes have traditionally faced the additional responsibility of agreeing on the rules that should apply to the process; for this reason, the path of least resistance has often been to litigate.[27] Increasing concern with 'the pathology of litigation' is due to the fact that litigation has become expensive, is often inefficient and has a propensity to develop a life of its own; it is inconsistent with the real objectives of those involved and is not directed by the disputing parties, so the outcome can be unpredictable. It can be difficult to settle a court action or an arbitration halfway through and it is more likely that a settlement can be achieved either at an early stage or towards the end of the process. This is in part due to escalation of commitment, where parties continue with a course of action even though they face increasingly negative outcomes. Entrenched positions can bias subsequent decisions, hindering the resolution process.[28] As disputes are influenced by the

whether mediation is faster, cheaper and more efficient than direct negotiation between the parties: see D N Frenkel and J H Stark, *The Practice of Mediation* (2nd ed, New York, Wolters Kluwer Law & Business 2012) 10.

[27] See Trollip (n 12) 11. With regard to the relationship between mediation and court processes, three types of mediation can be distinguished: (1) private mediation, which is entirely independent from court proceedings; (2) court-annexed mediation, which is institutionally co-ordinated with a judicial proceeding but procedurally detached from the court as an institution; and (3) judicial mediation, which is connected with the court and court proceedings with regard to venue and personnel: see F Steffek, 'Mediation' in J Basedow and others (eds), *The Max Planck Encyclopedia of European Private Law*, vol 2 (Oxford, Oxford University Press 2012) 1163. A further distinction can be made between court-annexed mediation and court-connected mediation, even though the terms are often used interchangeably. While 'court-annexed mediation' involves a requirement to attend mediation as a precondition to accessing court, 'court-connected mediation' is voluntary although if the parties subsequently litigate, court rules and penalties for a failure to mediate may apply: see P Brooker, 'Mediator Immunity: Time for Evaluation in England and Wales?' (2016) 36(3) *Legal Studies* 464, 466. Context matters to the way mediation is practised. Institutionalised mediation in court-annexed programmes in the USA often diverge from the facilitative to the evaluative model, where the mediator plays a directive role in moving the parties towards settlement: see N A Walsh, 'Institutionalisation and Professionalisation' in Moffitt and Bordone (eds) (n 13) 491–92. See also R Kulms, 'Mediation in the USA: Alternative Dispute Resolution Between Legalism and Self-Determination' in Hopt and Steffek (eds) (n 20) 1251–53.

[28] M H Bazerman and M A Neale, 'Improving Negotiation Effectiveness Under Final Offer Arbitration: The Role of Selection and Training' (1982) 67(5) *Journal of Applied Psychology* 543, 547. See also B M Straw, 'The Escalation of Commitment to a Course of Action' (1981) 6(4) *Academy of Management Review* 577 for a review of the literature on the non-optimal escalation of commitment to a decision because of the focal

dynamics of personal and commercial relationships, ADR processes such as mediation seek to focus the minds of disputing parties on resolving the dispute, ideally at an early stage, rather than on preparing for trial.

The interdependence of people's goals can influence the type of dispute resolution process employed. When the goals of disputing parties are interconnected such that only one party can achieve their goal, it is a competitive, 'zero-sum' or 'distributive' situation; there is a negative correlation between the goal attainments of all parties. To the extent that one party achieves their goal, the others cannot achieve theirs. Conversely, when the goals of all parties are linked such that one party achieving their goals helps other parties to achieve their goals, it is a 'mutual-gains', 'non-zero-sum' or 'integrative' situation; there is a positive correlation between the goal attainments of all parties. To the extent that one party achieves their goal, the achievement of other parties' goals may in fact be significantly enhanced.[29]

In addition to distributive situations, commercial mediation is unlikely to be appropriate if those with authority to settle refuse to participate; if one or more parties are engaging in bad faith or stall for tactical reasons; if previous settlement attempts failed and a party is unwilling to offer anything new; or if the case involves fraud, criminal activity or requires that a legal point be tested.[30] However, mediation may be appropriate in any case that can be settled, which includes most commercial disputes. Consequently, any commercial case that is appropriate for arbitration is likely to be appropriate for mediation.[31] Mediation will have a greater prospect of success in resolving disputes if parties are clearly advised about their role in the process and what they should expect from their lawyers.[32]

---

decision-maker's previous commitment to that course of action. See also M H Bazerman and K Shonk, 'The Decision Perspective to Negotiation' in Moffitt and Bordone (eds) (n 13) 57–59.

[29] R J Lewicki, B Barry and D Saunders, *Essentials of Negotiation* (6th ed, New York, McGraw Hill 2016) 10–12. See Chapter 4 at Section 4.3 for a discussion on the mediation process.

[30] See also D Spencer and M Brogan, *Mediation Law and Practice* (Cambridge University Press, 2007) 109–20; J G Merrills, *International Dispute Settlement* (6th ed, Cambridge, Cambridge University Press 2017) 39–42.

[31] P Pretorius, 'Commercial Mediation in the Southern African Development Community', Arbitration Workshop, Mauritius, April 2007, 3–4.

[32] Such roles are distinctly different in ADR compared with litigation. See Chapter 6 for a discussion on the role of parties and lawyers in mediation.

1.8   Methods of Alternative Dispute Resolution

Negotiation, mediation and arbitration are the main ADR methods most commonly encountered in practice, and all other methods are seen as variants of these. Many disputes will move from one method to another, and the potential applicability of possible options should be kept under review to assess which may be most appropriate or effective in resolving the dispute. For example, a dispute may be partially resolved through negotiation and mediation but may require the intervention of a judge or an arbitrator to determine any unresolved issues.

While various processes exist, there are effectively three major categories of ADR available to disputing commercial parties: non-adjudicative options, adjudicative options and hybrid options. In each case the process may be paper-based, be internet-based or involve meetings.[33] The following sections outline the types and forms of alternative available in assessing commercial mediation's place in the spectrum of ADR methods.[34]

1.8.1   Non-adjudicative ADR Options

1.8.1.1   Negotiation

Negotiation is a bargaining relationship between conflicting parties who voluntarily join in a temporary relationship to educate one another about their respective needs and interests. Parties choose to negotiate rather than simply accepting what the other side will offer as they think they can get a better deal by doing so. In resolving commercial disputes, negotiations may be conducted by the parties themselves or by legal representatives on their behalf. There is an expectation that the process will involve 'give and take' – that is, both sides will modify or move from their opening statements, requests or demands in order to reach an agreement, and this movement may result in a compromise or a more creative solution that meets the objectives of all involved. The process will not usually involve a fixed or established set of rules, and the parties

---

[33] See S Blake, J Browne and S Sime, *A Practical Approach to Alternative Dispute Resolution* (5th ed, Oxford, Oxford University Press 2018) 5, 24–38, 297, 440–41; Blake, Browne and Sime, *The Jackson ADR Handbook* (n 16) 2.

[34] See Frenkel and Stark (n 26) 4–9. This is particularly important as empirical evidence from numerous jurisdictions suggests that disputing parties suffer from considerable information and decision-making deficits when choosing between dispute resolution options: see Hopt and Steffek, 'Mediation: Comparison of Laws, Regulatory Models, Fundamental Issues' (n 20) 96.

will usually invent their own solution for resolving the conflict. The success of the process will involve managing 'tangibles' (such as the price or the terms of an agreement) and resolving 'intangibles'. Intangibles are the underlying psychological motivations, often rooted in personal values and emotions, that can directly or indirectly influence the parties in a negotiation: for example, the need to be perceived in a particular way.[35]

1.8.1.2   Mediation

Mediation is an extension of the structured negotiation process involving the intervention of a third party to help disputing parties resolve their dispute. The role of the mediator is only to assist, not to render a decision. All decision-making powers regarding the dispute remain with the parties and the process is voluntary.[36] Mediation may be provided by the courts or by a private service provider. In the mediation context, the term 'commercial' incorporates various forms of business and economic activity including commerce and trade, taxation, bankruptcy and takeovers.[37] Subject to some qualifications, this category relates to all kinds of disputes that might be dealt with in commercial courts. The qualifications concern areas of overlap with other fields of mediation activity. Hence, while issues of separation and divorce would be excluded, other types of family dispute could come within the ambit of commercial mediation – for example, family business disputes or property disputes.[38]

1.8.1.3   Conciliation

Conciliation is also a structured negotiation process involving a third party, but the third party will usually make a formal recommendation to the parties to settle the dispute. The use of the term 'conciliation' has not been consistent. For example, in 2018 the United Nations Model Law on International Commercial Conciliation was renamed the Model Law on International Commercial Mediation and International Settlement Agreements Resulting from Mediation. In its previously adopted texts and relevant documents, the United Nations Commission on International Trade Law (UNCITRAL) used the term 'conciliation' with the understanding that the terms 'conciliation' and 'mediation' were interchangeable. However, in amending the Model Law,

---

[35] See Lewicki, Barry and Saunders (n 29) 8–9.
[36] See Chapter 4 at Section 4.3 for a discussion on the mediation process.
[37] L Boulle, *Mediation: Principles, Process, Practice* (3rd ed, Chatswood, NSW, LexisNexis 2011) 359.
[38] Brown and Marriott (n 2) 205.

UNCITRAL decided to use the term 'mediation' instead in an effort to adapt to the actual and practical use of the terms. In practical terms, the distinction between mediation and conciliation is one of degree. While mediation tends to be more facilitative and flexible, conciliation tends to be more directive and interventionist.[39]

1.8.1.4   Early Neutral and/or Expert Evaluation

Early neutral evaluation is a process involving a third party who, due to their expertise and/or independence and legal knowledge, is asked by the parties to assess the issues in a case and provide a view and possibly recommendations, usually in the form of a non-binding report. The evaluator's report should help the parties evaluate their own case, in turn helping them to narrow and refine the issues and reach a resolution. This can be helpful where the parties' positions on a specific issue of law or fact are far apart. The process can also prove very helpful in certain contexts, such as software copyright disputes, where the litigation or arbitration process could take longer than the expected market life of the product involved.[40]

1.8.1.5   Mini-Trial

A mini-trial is a structured settlement process where each party, or a lawyer on their behalf, presents a summary of their case before senior officials of the disputing parties who are authorised to settle the dispute. An impartial third party usually chairs the process, helps to clarify the issues and will give an advisory opinion if requested. The mini-trial process is designed to help the parties make a realistic evaluation of the dispute and the issues involved. Once the case summaries have been delivered, the officials attempt to negotiate a settlement, and this may involve the assistance of the third party who can act as mediator.

1.8.2   Adjudicative ADR Options

1.8.2.1   Arbitration

Arbitration is a process in which disputing parties present arguments and evidence to a neutral third party (or parties) who makes a determination.

---

[39] See Chapter 4 at Section 4.2 for a discussion on commercial mediation models.

[40] A related option is to employ a neutral fact-finding expert, who investigates issues of fact, technicality or law and produces a report that is usually non-binding and may be used in court or arbitration depending on the parties' agreement. The third party will usually assist with settlement and may act as a mediator.

While it is usually binding, resulting in an enforceable award, arbitration may be non-binding. It may be voluntary, where the parties agree to resolve the issues through arbitration; or it may be compulsory, where law or contract makes arbitration the exclusive means of resolving the dispute. While usually conducted on an adversarial basis, it may be conducted on an inquisitorial basis. There are numerous forms of arbitration that can be designed by the parties in their agreement to reflect their requirements, including their choice of arbitrator, and the legal rules and procedure that will govern the process. In many jurisdictions, arbitration is governed by statute.

1.8.2.2   Adjudication

Adjudication is similar to arbitration in some respects, but the adjudicator generally has less power than an arbitrator and must often reach a decision within strict timelines. Depending on the agreement of the parties, adjudication may lead to a binding decision or to a decision that will only be binding if the parties agree, or if neither party appeals the decision within a specified period. It has proved useful and more efficient than arbitration in specialist commercial fields, such as construction, where statutory schemes in some jurisdictions require disputes to be adjudicated if the parties have not agreed on a dispute resolution procedure.[41]

1.8.2.3   Expert Determination

Expert determination is a process in which the parties to a dispute present arguments and evidence to a dispute resolution practitioner (the expert), who is chosen because of their specialist qualifications or experience in the subject matter of the dispute, and who makes a determination. The expert does not necessarily have to follow adjudicatory rules, and follows procedures agreed with the parties. Expert determination can be particularly useful where the sole or main issues in the case require expert knowledge and a complete adjudication process is not required. Examples include property and share valuations. As with binding arbitration, this process produces determinations which the parties have agreed will be binding and which are enforceable in contract.

---

[41] See, for example, the UK Housing Grants, Construction and Regeneration Act 1996, ss 108 and 114(4). A variation of adjudication is the dispute board: three neutrals deal with disputes as they arise, producing either recommendations or decisions. Dispute boards are used extensively in construction and increasingly in financial services, shipping, engineering and the oil and gas industries.

1.8.3   Hybrid Options

Hybrid forms of dispute resolution using elements of both mediation and arbitration, such as 'med-arb' and 'arb-med', are also options available to disputing parties. In med-arb, the parties are assisted by a mediator to negotiate a settlement of their dispute. If the parties decide that they are unable to settle, the outstanding issues are submitted to the mediator who then takes on the role of an arbitrator to determine the dispute and issue an award that will be binding, or non-binding as agreed by the parties. In arb-med, the parties agree to arbitrate their dispute. Having prepared the award, the arbitrator, before issuing it, takes on the role of a mediator and assists the parties with settling their dispute. If the parties are unable to reach a settlement, the arbitrator issues the award to the parties.

The main benefit of the med-arb process is that the parties have certainty that the dispute will be resolved. There are also obvious efficiencies in terms of time and expense where the same person acts as both mediator and arbitrator. The corollary concern relates to the ostensible diminished impartiality and neutrality of the third party who acts as both mediator and arbitrator, as the parties may have shared confidential information with the mediator that they would never share with an arbitrator – information that may bias the third party in their decision-making should the dispute ultimately be arbitrated.[42] This concern also increases the likelihood that the award will be challenged. Conversely, it may result in parties being less forthcoming with information that could help to resolve the dispute during the mediation due to an understandable concern that it may subsequently prejudice them should the dispute progress to arbitration. This concern can be reduced if different individuals act as mediator and arbitrator, but this will inevitably increase costs and reduce the time and expense benefits mentioned above.[43] If settlement is reached in the course of the arbitration, the parties can ask the mediator to act as arbitrator for the purpose of making

---

[42] It has been suggested that the mixing of adjudication and mediation 'has produced a very dangerous confusion': see Fuller and Winston (n 12) 353, 406.

[43] As mediation and arbitration are very different processes, each requires very different skill sets and approaches: see E Sussman, 'Med-Arb: An Argument for Favouring ex parte Communications in the Mediation Phase' (2013) 7 *World Arbitration and Mediation Review* 1; E Sussman, 'Combinations and Permutations of Arbitration and Mediation: Issues and Solutions' in Ingen-Housz (ed) (n 18); E Sussman, 'Developing an Effective Med-Arb/Arb-Med Process' (2009) 2(1) *New York Dispute Resolution Lawyer* 71.

the mediated settlement a consent award – a useful mechanism that parties have used in particular for enforcement purposes.[44]

The main benefit of the arb-med process is that the parties may be more focussed on settlement since they do not know the contents of the award. The corollary concern is that some parties may view the mediation as simply a prelude to the arbitral award that will follow, and therefore fail to take the mediation process seriously. The main disadvantage of the arb-med process is the wasted time and expense of creating an arbitral award that is not used if the dispute settles through mediation. There is also a concern about the impartiality and neutrality of the third party; they may be viewed as giving an indication of the arbitral award in the course of the mediation through perceived evaluative comments.

Hence, care must be taken, and significant consideration given to determining the appropriate process to resolve the dispute before a hybrid option is chosen. At a minimum, the parties should give informed consent to the use of the hybrid process, particularly where the same individual plays both roles.[45]

---

[44] See Chapter 8 at Section 8.4 for a detailed discussion on this issue. European civil law jurisdictions appear to be more comfortable than their common law counterparts with the idea of arbitrators making settlement and mediative interventions. There is a greater risk of a negative impact on the integrity of the mediation when the third party's skill lies more in arbitration than mediation. For example, in the US case *Bowden* v. *Weickert* No S-02-017, 2003 WL 21419175 (Ohio Ct App, 6th Dist, 20 June 2003), the arbitral award was set aside as the arbitrator had exceeded his authority by basing his decision on confidential information received during the mediation. Many jurisdictions – including Australia, England, Germany, Hong Kong, India, Japan, Singapore and Taiwan – legislate for settlement opportunities or 'mediation windows' within the framework of arbitration. Third-party neutrals must remain vigilant not to use confidential information received during mediation when subsequently making determinations and drafting arbitral awards. In France, mediation windows operate alongside arbitration in the hybrid process *med-arb simultanés* developed by the Centre de Médiation et d'Arbitrage des Notaires de Paris, with different third parties acting in each process; the processes run simultaneously and have an agreed timeframe, where arbitration follows if there is no settlement: see N Alexander, *International and Comparative Mediation: Legal Perspectives* (Austin, Wolters Kluwer 2009) 119–22; N Alexander and S Chong, *The Singapore Convention on Mediation: A Commentary* (Alphen aan den Rijn, Kluwer Law International 2019) 39–40.

[45] See K M Scanlon and K A Bryan, 'Will the Next Generation of Dispute Resolution Clause Drafting Include Model Arb-Med Clauses?' in A W Rovine (ed), *Contemporary Issues in International Arbitration and Mediation: The Fordham Papers* (Leiden, Brill 2010) 429–35. For a discussion on the development of an effective med-arb/arb-med process, in light of relevant US case law, see Sussman, 'Combinations and Permutations of Arbitration and Mediation' (n 43) 383–91. For a discussion on the use of the same neutral, the influence of legal culture on perceptions of using the same neutral, an empirical study on the combined use of mediation and arbitration in international commercial dispute

1.9   Process Selection and Design

If a decision is made to use ADR, the first step is to select the type of ADR that is most appropriate for the particular dispute. The options vary in their applicability, level of participation and formality. As there are no absolute rules for selecting an ADR option, the characteristics of the dispute and the parties' and lawyers' preferences are relevant considerations when effectively 'fitting the forum to the fuss'.[46] Certain dispute resolution processes may be particularly well suited to certain types of dispute, and the parties' choice should be informed by clear criteria.[47] As already noted, the selection and design of a dispute resolution process requires both knowledge of the various processes and the ability to assess and compare the range of options. Transaction costs, satisfaction with the outcomes, effect on the relationship and recurrence are four criteria that can be used to assess the effectiveness of a dispute resolution process.[48]

1.9.1   Transaction Costs

Transaction costs include the time, money, emotional energy, resources consumed and destroyed and opportunities lost that disputing requires. For example, in commercial disputes the costs include legal fees, management time and the effect that litigating the dispute may have on the party's ability to continue operating normally.

---

resolution and proposed solutions to the issues that arise in using hybrid processes, see D Nigmatullina, *Combining Mediation and Arbitration in International Commercial Dispute Resolution* (New York, Routledge 2018).

[46] M Rosenberg, as quoted in Sander and Goldberg (n 13) 67. Other important considerations are process cost-effectiveness, speed, third-party expertise, process control, process flexibility, risk management, confidentiality, problem-solving approach, commercial objectives, possible creative outcomes and future shared interests and relations: see Blake, Browne and Sime, *The Jackson ADR Handbook* (n 16) 21–24.

[47] See F Steffek and others, 'Guide for Regulating Dispute Resolution (GRDR): Principles and Comments' in F Steffek and others (eds), *Regulating Dispute Resolution: ADR and Access to Justice at the Crossroads* (Oxford, Hart Publishing 2013) 5.

[48] These criteria were elucidated in the classic work by W Ury, J Brett and S Goldberg, *Getting Disputes Resolved: Designing Systems to Cut the Cost of Conflict* (San Francisco, Jossey-Bass 1988) 11–15. While this approach will be relevant in many commercial and other contexts, it will not be applicable in all: see N Rogers and others, *Designing Systems and Processes for Managing Disputes* (2nd ed, New York, Wolters Kluwer 2019) 27. For a discussion on practical considerations when considering the relevance and appropriateness of using ADR, see J F Guillemin, 'Reasons for Choosing Alternative Dispute Resolution' in Goldsmith, Ingen-Housz and Pointon (eds) (n 4) 25–52.

1.9.2   Satisfaction with the Outcomes

A party's satisfaction with the outcome of a particular process depends on two things: whether the outcome satisfies the interests that led that party to make or reject the claim in the first place, and the perceived fairness of the outcome and the process. In assessing fairness, many factors are relevant to a disputing party including the opportunities afforded to express themselves, their control over whether to accept or reject the outcome, their level of participation in shaping the outcome and the perceived fairness of the third party's involvement.

1.9.3   Effect on the Relationship

The effect of the process on the relationship between the disputing parties is particularly important where the parties have ongoing business deal-ings, where the process adopted may even enhance the relationship. This is frequently cited as one of the advantages of mediating commercial disputes, as commercial parties are more likely to engage in business together in the future if the process has facilitated a better understanding of each other's needs and interests. An amicable resolution through a private process is also more likely to enhance the relationship than a determinative outcome from a public court.

1.9.4   Recurrence

For the outcome of a dispute resolution process to be effective, it must endure. If there is a return to the original dispute, it may be perceived (and in fact be the case) that the process has been ineffective. The four criteria for effectiveness are interrelated: dissatisfaction with outcomes can place a strain on the relationship between the parties, which can contribute to the recurrence of the dispute, which can in turn increase transaction costs. Rather than focussing on the parties' rights or power, it is suggested that, in general, reconciling the parties' interests tends to result in lower transaction costs, greater satisfaction with outcomes, less strain on the relationship and less of a recurrence of disputes.[49]

While knowledge, understanding and experience of dispute resolution options can help in developing a method for selecting and designing dispute resolution processes, the particular circumstances of the dispute

---

[49] Ury, Brett and Goldberg (n 48) 15.

and the needs and interests of the parties should determine the nature of the process employed, and the parties should understand and accept the dispute resolution process used. For example, a dispute ripe for mediation may not be resolved unless the parties co-operate fully and understand the characteristics and requirements of the process. Parties in dispute should be conscious of what they want to achieve through engagement in the ADR process. For example, while parties may want to attempt a negotiated settlement, finality may be important, and the med-arb procedure may be appropriate. Alternatively, parties may need a deeper understanding of the respective strengths and weaknesses of their own and the other party's case, and the arb-med procedure could provide this and allow the parties the opportunity to settle once they have heard the other party's case and had the opportunity to have their own case tested. The mini-trial which uses elements of both the adversarial adjudicative procedure and the interest-based mediation or negotiation process has proved useful for some time, particularly in the USA, in settling large corporate claims.[50]

No single process is sufficient to resolve every dispute and an effective justice system will offer multiple processes, including litigation and mediation.[51] Different types of disputes and interests exist, and choosing between processes requires a clear understanding of the various qualities and characteristics of the different processes.[52] The critical point is that each dispute should be resolved by using the appropriate alternative process(es) or court adjudication. Mediation will not be suitable for every situation and an appropriate assessment of the type of dispute and the forms of alternative available should be completed before a particular option is chosen.[53]

---

[50] See Pretorius (n 20) 9–10. Part of the reason mini-trials have had greater uptake in the USA is the extensive pre-trial discovery requirements; the mini-trial process is viewed as the only way to condense the results of discovery to provide parties with an overview of the entire case: see Buhring-Uhle, Kirchhoff and Scherer (n 22) 195–97.

[51] For example, litigation is required for some disputes to serve the public interest in setting precedents and ensuring legal consistency, while mediation serves the private interests of efficiency and accessibility: see J R Sternlight, 'Creeping Mandatory Arbitration: Is it Just?' (2005) 57(5) *Stanford Law Review* 1631, 1668.

[52] See H Astor and C Chinkin, *Dispute Resolution in Australia* (2nd ed, Chatswood, NSW, LexisNexis Butterworths 2002) 51.

[53] See F Sander and L Rozdeiczer, 'Selecting an Appropriate Dispute Resolution Procedure: Detailed Analysis and Simplified Solution' in Moffitt and Bordone (eds) (n 13) 386–406. While early mediation intervention can increase the prospects of settlement, it cannot predict settlement. Research has failed to link any particular timing of mediation with prospects of settlement, as timing is one of many contextual factors, including alternative

1.10   Defining Commercial Mediation

Mediation has proved difficult to differentiate from other forms of ADR. This is in part due to the lack of a generally accepted definition and to the fact that ADR processes generally – and mediation in particular – elude static differentiation criteria due to their procedural flexibility. The voluntary nature of mediation and the mediator's lack of adjudicatory powers have provided broad guidelines for classification.[54] Similarly, the flexibility and open interpretation of terms such as 'voluntary' and 'neutrality', which are often used in the definition of mediation, make it difficult to define or codify.[55] The use of the term 'mediation' in different senses by different users – often for different purposes and in different contexts by mediators with varying backgrounds, skill sets and practices – adds to the difficulty in defining the term.

Notwithstanding the difficulties of definition, there are three basic approaches to defining the practice of mediation. The first is the *conceptualist approach* which defines the process in ideal terms, emphasising certain values, principles and objectives. The second focusses on what actually happens in practice and is referred to as the *descriptive approach*. The third is the *market approach* which leaves defining mediation to practitioners.

The strength of the conceptualist approach is that it highlights for users and practitioners the higher goals and values of mediation which differentiate it from other decision-making processes. Its main shortcoming is that it tends to pass off as *descriptive* those elements of mediation that are *prescriptive*, which makes it an ideological rather than an

---

forms of dispute resolution. While almost all cases will be suitable for mediation, all parties are not. The key point is that if a dispute is inappropriately referred to mediation, it will have low settlement prospects regardless of timing relative to court procedures: see Alexander (n 44) 153–54, 162; J R Seul, 'Litigation as a Dispute Resolution Alternative' in Moffitt and Bordone (eds) (n 13) 336.

54 See Steffek, 'Mediation' (n 27) 1163.

55 For example, if 'voluntary' is used in its general sense, it excludes mandatory forms of mediation. This approach is reflected in s 2 of the Irish Mediation Act 2017 which defines mediation as 'a confidential, facilitative and voluntary process in which parties to a dispute, with the assistance of a mediator, attempt to reach a mutually acceptable agreement to resolve the dispute'. It has consequently been suggested that any general definition of mediation that does not restrict mediation's 'voluntary' nature to continued participation in the process once it has commenced and the decision to settle, as the EU Mediation Directive (n 58) does, means that it may be conceptually inaccurate on a global basis, even if accurate in specific jurisdictions: see T Allen, *Mediation Law and Civil Practice* (2nd ed, London, Bloomsbury Professional 2019) 32, 264. See Chapter 5 at Section 5.7.3 for a discussion on the meaning of neutrality in the mediation context.

empirical approach to defining mediation. Based on actual practice, the descriptive approach finds its main strength in reflecting reality while its main shortcoming is that it proves to be superficial and unhelpful given the diversity of mediation practice. The market approach is helpful in acknowledging the potential flexibility and adaptability in the way mediation is conducted. However, it is becoming less tenable as a result of the various accreditation systems, codes of conduct and regulations that have emerged. While each approach to defining the process has strengths and weaknesses, all three may be adopted in a particular jurisdiction. In Australia, for example, while there is evidence of the conceptualist and market approaches, the conceptualist approach tends to predominate.[56]

1.10.1 The Assistance of a Definition

A comparative view of mediation definitions, both statutory and judicial, generally reveals a broad consensus across jurisdictions on the treatment of issues such as dispute, voluntary nature, communication between the parties and consensual resolution by the parties.[57]

1.10.1.1 Europe

Before the EU Mediation Directive,[58] some European countries did not have a legal definition of mediation,[59] while others distinguished mediation from

---

[56] Boulle (n 37) 12–17.

[57] See Hopt and Steffek, 'Mediation: Comparison of Laws, Regulatory Models, Fundamental Issues' (n 20) 11–13.

[58] Directive 2008/52/EC of the European Parliament and of the Council of 21 May 2008 on certain aspects of mediation in civil and commercial matters [2008] OJ L136/3 ('EU Mediation Directive').

[59] Examples are Belgium and Sweden: see P Taelman and C Van Severen, *Civil Procedure in Belgium* (Alphen aan den Rijn, Kluwer Law International 2018) para 603; European e-Justice, 'Mediation in Member States: Sweden' (18 March 2013) <https://e-justice .europa.eu> accessed 10 May 2022. See generally G De Palo and S Carmeli, 'Mediation in Continental Europe: A Meandering Path Toward Efficient Regulation' in Newmark and Monaghan (eds) (n 4) 342. The Civil Procedure Rules in England (discussed further in Chapter 7) do not provide a definition of mediation, only 'a guide to the meaning' of ADR which includes all non-adjudicative forms of dispute resolution. Conversely Austria, Denmark and Finland did have legal definitions of mediation: see C Mattl, A Prokop-Zischka and S Ferz, 'Mediation in Austria' in N Alexander (ed), *Global Trends in Mediation* (Alphen aan den Rijn, Kluwer Law International 2006) 66–68. Like most other countries, Austria has more than one definition of mediation: see T Lappi-Seppälä and A Storgaard, 'Nordic Mediation: Comparing Denmark and Finland' (2015) 27 *Neue Kriminalpolitik* 136, 139.

conciliation.[60] Outside of the differences that exist across EU member states, and unlike the English model where mediation is based on the premise that parties can achieve a better result by involving a neutral/impartial third party, the working definitions of mediation appear to have as a common element the concept of reciprocal concessions made by parties to reach an agreeable outcome.[61]

The EU Mediation Directive, which applies to cross-border disputes, provides the following descriptive definition:

> Mediation means a structured process, however named or referred to, whereby two or more parties to a dispute attempt by themselves, on a voluntary basis, to reach an agreement on the settlement of their dispute with the assistance of a mediator. This process may be initiated by the parties or suggested or ordered by a court or prescribed by the law of a Member State.

Trial judges who would hear the case should it not settle are expressly excluded from the definition – that is, from participating in judicial settlement. However, judges with no involvement in any proceedings regarding the dispute may act as mediators, providing for judicial mediation to be included within the definition.[62]

1.10.1.2 Australia

Australia does not have a national mediation Act, and there are no statutory definitions providing uniformity and consistency for the mediation process. Similarly, there are no national model laws, and there is diversity in the definitions used and in the interpretations they

---

[60] In France, the Code of Civil Procedure distinguishes conciliation from mediation. In conciliation settlement of the dispute is decided directly by the parties or with the help of a judge whose task is to conciliate parties. Mediation is a voluntary process that always involves a third-party individual or 'association' that listens to parties, compares their interests and allows them to find a solution to their dispute. Similarly, there is no exhaustive definition of either of these two methods given by the French legislature: see Code of Civil Procedure (*Code de procédure civile*), articles 127–31. In Spain, conciliation is the process that involves the parties resolving the dispute themselves, while mediation involves parties accepting a solution provided by the mediator, who is normally the judge before whom the proceeding has been introduced; this approach makes the process seem more like arbitration: see De Palo and Carmeli (n 59) 343.

[61] See De Palo and Carmeli (n 59) 343.

[62] EU Mediation Directive, art 3(a). See also Chapter 5 at Section 5.10 for a discussion on judges as mediators, and Chapter 2 at Section 2.4.7 for an overview of the EU Mediation Directive. While the neutrality of the mediator and confidentiality of the process are widely acknowledged as characteristics of mediation, some definitions exclude these terms. See Steffek, 'Mediation' (n 27) 1162.

are given.[63] Many 'official' definitions of mediation exist in Australian statutes, rules of court and codes of conduct for mediators. This is viewed as a significant development, as earlier laws used the term without clearly defining or describing the process. It seems that, in practice, widely varying forms of mediation process are being used in different jurisdictions and subject areas. The lack of a uniform clear legislative definition may mean that, in different states and subject areas, there is a tendency to adopt the process characteristics that are most used in practice in that state or subject area.[64]

1.10.1.3   USA

Various state statutes in the USA have provided a range of definitions of mediation.[65] In 2001 the Uniform Mediation Act was introduced by the National Conference of Commissioners on Uniform State Laws, also known as the Uniform Law Commission, to deal with the different provisions relating to mediation across the USA, with the principal purpose of assuring confidentiality and fostering uniformity. The Act provides a broad descriptive definition of mediation as a 'process in which a mediator facilitates communication and negotiation between parties to assist them in reaching a voluntary agreement regarding their dispute'. The inclusion of the words 'negotiation' and 'assist' in the definition is designed to exclude adjudicative processes. However, the definition appears to be limited in some ways. For example, its description of the role of the mediator fails to take account of the active role that a mediator can play to help the parties in reaching a resolution.[66]

---

[63] See L Boulle and R Field, *Mediation in Australia* (Chatswood, NSW, LexisNexis 2018) 4.

[64] T Sourdin, 'Mediation in Australia: Impacts on Litigation' in N Alexander (ed), *Global Trends in Mediation* (2nd ed, The Hague, Kluwer Law International 2006) 37–64. However, one definition used throughout Australia is provided in the National Mediator Accreditation Standards (2015): 'Mediation is a process that promotes the self-determination of participants and in which participants, with the support of a mediator: (a) communicate with each other, exchange information and seek understanding; (b) identify, clarify and explore interests, issues and underlying needs; (c) consider their alternatives; (d) generate and evaluate options; (e) negotiate with each other; and (f) reach and make their own decisions. A mediator does not evaluate or advise on the merits of, or determine the outcome of, disputes.' See Practice Standards, section 2.2 <https://msb .org.au> accessed 10 May 2022.

[65] S H Hughes, 'The Uniform Mediation Act: To the Spoiled Go the Privileges' (2001) 85 *Marquette Law Review* 9, 15–16.

[66] See J B Stulberg, 'The UMA: Some Roads Not Taken' (2003) 1 *Journal of Dispute Resolution* 221, 222–23. See Chapter 9 for a discussion on the Uniform Mediation Act.

1.10.1.4 United Nations

The UNCITRAL Mediation Model Law offers a descriptive definition of mediation, reflecting the diversity in mediation practice. It provides that:

> 'mediation' means a process, *whether referred to by the expression mediation, conciliation or an expression of similar import*, whereby parties request a third person or persons ('the mediator') to assist them in their attempt to reach an amicable settlement of their dispute arising out of or relating to a contractual or other legal relationship. The mediator does not have the authority to impose upon the parties a solution to the dispute.[67]

The Singapore Convention, which was drafted at the same time as the Mediation Model Law, also adopts a descriptive definition:

> 'Mediation' means a process, *irrespective of the expression used* or the basis upon which the process is carried out, whereby parties attempt to reach an amicable settlement of their dispute with the assistance of a third person or persons ('the mediator') lacking the authority to impose a solution upon the parties to the dispute.[68]

Both definitions make clear that it is the process, not its name, that is important. However, the words of the Singapore Convention have a wider ambit ('irrespective of the expression used') than those of the Mediation Model Law ('whether referred to by the expression mediation, conciliation or an expression of similar import'). This difference is due to the fact that the Singapore Convention definition is binding on states that ratify the convention, while the Mediation Model Law definition may be amended by the adopting state. The difference also recognises that legal systems use different terms to describe the dispute resolution processes covered by the Singapore Convention definition, and the drafters were keen to be inclusive of the various states with diverse legal systems, cultures and languages that it is hoped will ratify the convention.

The Mediation Model Law also includes the words 'arising out of or relating to a contractual or other legal relationship', words that were omitted from the Singapore Convention to remove any limits on the scope of the disputed issues that can be mediated. For example, an

---

[67] UNCITRAL Model Law on International Commercial Mediation and International Settlement Agreements Resulting from Mediation 2018, article 1.3 (emphasis added). This instrument is discussed further in Chapter 2 at Section 2.4.5 and Chapter 8 at Section 8.5.

[68] United Nations Convention on International Settlement Agreements Resulting from Mediation 2018, article 2.3 (emphasis added). This instrument is discussed further in Chapter 2 at Section 2.4.6 and Chapter 8 at Section 8.6.

international dispute could relate to breach of contract, but the break-down in relations that must initially be addressed is interpersonal. It would have been simpler had UNCITRAL adopted the same definition in the Mediation Model Law and Singapore Convention for greater uniformity.[69]

1.10.2 The Need for a Definition

It has been suggested that mediation cannot be defined, as any attempt to *define* mediation is to *confine* it, given the inherent flexibility of the process. It follows that the approach taken in a mediation should be determined by the mediator, in consultation with the parties, to suit the nature of the dispute and the parties' requirements. While it seems that mediation cannot and should not be defined, it can be meaningfully described, and three criteria characterise a process as a mediation:[70] (1) The parties request the appointment of an independent person (the mediator) who will in consultation with them, structure a process in light of the nature of the dispute, the stage it has reached and the requirements of the parties. The mediator will meet privately with each party and discuss any aspect of it in confidence and will only reveal confidential information to another party if expressly authorised; (2) The mediator does not have the authority to impose a decision; (3) The course that the process takes, and the outcome, are voluntary, permeated throughout by a consensus philosophy.

Consistent with the above description of the process, the following definition of mediation is provided by the Centre for Effective Dispute Resolution (CEDR):

> Mediation is a flexible process conducted confidentially in which a neutral person actively assists parties in working towards a negotiated agreement of a dispute or difference, with the parties in ultimate control of the decision to settle and of the terms of resolution.[71]

One of the main objectives of this definition is to emphasise that parties are in ultimate control of both the decision to settle and the terms of resolution. Regardless of how strong the influences may be to get

---

[69] See Alexander and Chong (n 44) 52–57, 64–65.
[70] See Sir Laurence Street (n 19) 361–62. See also Astor and Chinkin (n 52) 135.
[71] CEDR, *Model Mediation Procedure: 2020 Edition* <www.cedr.com> accessed 10 May 2022.

disputing parties to attend a mediation, once they are present, it is important that they have a sense of ownership and responsibility.[72]

The CEDR definition is useful as it captures the essence of the commercial mediation process and the mediator's function within it in a compact and clear form. The process is flexible as the parties, in consultation with the mediator, decide issues such as the venue, date and time, who will attend and the issues to be discussed. It is designed and can be redesigned by the parties. The parties are encouraged to be open in their communication by the confidential nature of the process. The mediator's authority largely stems from their neutrality, and their central function is to use their process skills to help the parties in their negotiations towards reaching an agreement. If the parties are to reach an agreement, it is their decision alone to do so. The parties largely own the process and they own any agreement that may result from that process.[73]

1.11   Concluding Thoughts

Dispute resolution options may be thought of as falling along a process continuum. At one end is court, where parties have no control over the dispute resolution design or the outcome, and at the other end is negotiation, where parties retain control over both design and outcome. Mediation, where parties control the outcome, falls on the negotiation side, and arbitration with its third party-imposed outcome falls on the court side of the continuum. Depending on their design, mini-trial and hybrid and other ADR options fall somewhere between these common ADR options on the continuum.[74] Each process is heavily influenced by the context and culture within which the process operates.[75] The

---

[72] E Carroll, 'The Future Belongs to Mediation and its Clients' in Newmark and Monaghan (eds) (n 4) 404. The word 'voluntary' had appeared in earlier versions of the definition but was removed. CEDR is primarily a commercial mediation provider and consequently reflects a narrower definition and narrower approach: see Allen (n 55) 30.

[73] Ideally the parties who attend the mediation will have authority to settle. Empirical research supports the widely accepted belief that the participation of parties who have authority to settle is a significant influencing factor on both the likelihood of settlement and the level of satisfaction in mediation: see Alexander (n 44) 164.

[74] This continuum would change if court-annexed mediation schemes were employed. Court-related activities would appear on one half and non-court related activities on the other: for example, court-annexed mediation would belong on the court half, while private mediation would belong on the other half of the continuum: see L E Susskind, 'Consensus Building and ADR: Why They Are Not the Same Thing' in Moffitt and Bordone (eds) (n 13) 359–60.

[75] Walsh (n 27) 490.

challenge for a lawyer is to advise their client to select the correct dispute resolution approach for their client's dispute and use that process effectively.[76]

The diversification of alternatives available has resulted in commercial dispute resolution clauses dealing with disputes sequentially. Hence the process will be preventative before it is corrective, and amicable before being contentious. For example, negotiation may be required first, followed by mediation and ultimately arbitration, or a hybrid of med-arb or arb-med, or alternatively litigation. The sequence takes into account the stage when the intervention is required, the nature and importance of the dispute, the urgency, the costs and the degree of success of the previous process. Dispute resolution processes are viewed as complementary rather than isolated or competitive, with the focus being on the effectiveness of the result rather than the purity of the process.[77] Hence a dispute may be partly resolved by negotiation and partly by mediation, with any outstanding issues submitted to an arbitrator or court for determination. There are obvious efficiencies, in terms of cost and time in particular, in parties moving from facilitative to determinative processes. It is also conceptually easier to focus on needs and interests before legal rights and positions. Once the focus shifts to the latter, a collaborative interest-based settlement is less likely to emerge.[78]

Litigation and arbitration are focussed on winning a dispute while mediation focusses on resolving it. While dissatisfaction with litigation and arbitration are primary reasons for the growth of mediation, mediation as a model has also skilfully adapted to pragmatic business demands. Most cases settle at the doors of the court or as arbitration approaches – before judgment or award – as parties focus to a greater extent on the strengths and weaknesses of their case and elect to avoid the expense and time involved in a trial. Litigation effectively operates as the legal default.[79] Mediation brings forward the time at which cases settle.

---

[76] See Golann and Folberg (n 26) 10–11.

[77] This is the case from the public perspective also, with courts, driven by changing public policy in many jurisdictions, encouraging parties to mediate: see Antaki (n 4) 271–72. See also Chapter 7. By focussing on outcome effectiveness rather than the purity of the process, contemporary developments are becoming more aligned with traditional, indigenous or pre-colonial approaches to dispute resolution in many jurisdictions: see R Feehily, 'Mediation as an Instrument of Transitional Justice', Harvard Law School Symposium on Restorative Justice, Harvard University, USA, 5–8 February 2019.

[78] See Chapter 4 at Section 4.3.3 for a discussion on interest-based negotiations.

[79] In practice, the litigation default is offset by various legal and policy initiatives favouring arbitration: see S I Strong, 'Applying the Lessons of International Commercial

This can result in significant savings of both legal costs and valuable senior management time and, in many cases, a settlement agreement that would not materialise in other settlement settings. Mediation facilitates commercial parties having difficult conversations, without which amicable resolution would not be possible.[80]

Disputes can be defining periods in people's lives.[81] It is important that they are dealt with as effectively and painlessly as possible. Mediation may be characterised as 'litigation's invaluable twin'. Employed in those cases where it would be of genuine advantage to the parties due to its informality, process flexibility and the possibility of remedies not available in litigation, mediation can also benefit the justice system by ensuring that the cases that genuinely require formal adjudication can access its limited resources.[82]

Arbitration to International Commercial Mediation: A Dispute System Design Analysis'
in C Titi and K Fach Gómez (eds), *Mediation in International Commercial and Investment Disputes* (Oxford, Oxford University Press 2019) 50.

[80] Kallipetis and Ruttle (n 25) 194–97.

[81] J R Cohen, 'A Taxonomy of Dispute Resolution Ethics' in Moffitt and Bordone (eds) (n 13) 250.

[82] Lord Neuberger, 'Equity, ADR, Arbitration and the Law: Different Dimensions of Justice', The Fourth Keating Lecture, 2010. See also Chapter 10 for a discussion on this issue.

2

Commercial Mediation in the International Context

2.1   Introduction

Mediation is neither novel nor new; variants of the process have been used for millennia to resolve disputes. Traditional forms of mediation are distinctly different from modern mediation practice; in traditional forms, the role and social standing of the mediator are central to the process, and the outcome focusses more on social harmony than on the individual rights or interests of the parties. This difference has given rise to two broad mediation cultures. Cultural differences can be reflected in different approaches to meeting needs, and shape the interests of the parties and party behaviour during the mediation process. Due to its flexibility in design and practice, mediation offers parties greater control over the process, procedural rules and outcomes; as an informal and adaptable process, it also offers the possibility of greater sensitivity to cultural differences.

A consequence of globalisation has been the increasing harmonisation of laws and practices, and the harmonisation of dispute resolution systems is an important part of this movement. This is reflected in the emergence of several regional and international instruments, the most recent of which is the Singapore Convention.[1] What matters is the potential for any new regional or international legal instrument to be effective and have a positive impact on the people and corporations involved in cross-border legal relationships.

2.2   Historical Background

Various forms of mediation have been used in different parts of the world for millennia.[2] Many traditional societies that lacked formal state systems

---

[1] United Nations Convention on International Settlement Agreements Resulting from Mediation (discussed in Section 2.4.6).

[2] For a comprehensive global overview, from mediation's genesis in historical, religious and customary practices to contemporary practices, see C W Moore, *The Mediation Process:*

29

and legal institutions used mediation to resolve conflict within clans, tribes and villages, and mediation continues to be the preferred means of resolving disputes in these societies.[3] The concept of mediation as a form of dispute resolution goes back thousands of years, notably in certain Asian countries.[4] Mediation has played an important role in Chinese history, particularly since the period of the Han Dynasty (202 BC to AD 220), when litigation was seen as commercialising and trivialising values such as human dignity, conscience, reputation and morality. Chinese society recognised that a dispute affected not just the primary disputing parties but the lives of many other people, and considered that concili-ation and consensus were the goals to be achieved. Mediation was the most frequently used mechanism for resolving disputes, and it derived much of its effectiveness from the fact that the disputants were members of interlocking social networks that also participated in the dispute resolution process with the principal aim of restoring social harmony.[5] Other Asian societies have also displayed cultural preferences for resolv-ing disputes through mediation,[6] and the process as a method of dispute resolution has more in common with traditional African methods of dispute resolution than with arbitration or litigation.[7]

Practical Strategies for Resolving Conflict (4th ed, San Francisco, Jossey-Bass 2014) 61–105. See also L Cole, 'Exploring International Mediation, Past, Present and Beyond' in A Georgakopoulos (ed), *The Mediation Handbook, Research, Theory, and Practice* (Abingdon, UK, Routledge 2017) 315–23.

[3] See L Boulle, *Mediation: Principles, Process, Practice* (3rd ed, Chatswood, NSW, LexisNexis 2011) 50; S Roberts, *Order and Dispute: An Introduction to Legal Anthropology* (2nd ed, Louisiana, Quid Pro Books 2013) 50–53.

[4] Mediation is believed to have traceable origins in the Chou Dynasty (1100 BC–256 BC), specifically in the writings of Confucius (551 BC–479 BC): see DC Clarke, 'Dispute Resolution in China' in TV Lee (ed), *Contract, Guanxi, and Dispute Resolution in China* (New York, Garland 1997) 369.

[5] J G Mowatt, 'Mediation and Chinese Legal Theory' (1989) 106(2) *South African Law Journal* 349, 351–53.

[6] See L Boulle and H H Teh, *Mediation: Principles, Process and Practice* (Singapore, Butterworths 2000) 138–46. Singapore, Indonesia, Thailand, Japan and Korea similarly embraced China's Confucian preference for resolving conflict amicably, and have recently embraced the modern Western facilitative model of commercial mediation for resolving international commercial disputes: see D McFadden, 'The Growing Importance of Regional Mediation Centres in Asia' in C Titi and K Fach Gómez (eds), *Mediation in International Commercial and Investment Disputes* (Oxford, Oxford University Press 2019) 160–76.

[7] See South African Law Commission, *Project 94: Domestic Arbitration Report* (2001) 9; N N Antaki, 'Cultural Diversity and ADR Practices in the World' in J C Goldsmith, A Ingen-Housz and G H Pointon (eds), *ADR in Business: Practice and Issues Across Countries and Cultures* (Alphen aan den Rijn, Kluwer Law International 2006) 285–88.

In the ancient Greek world, arbitration was the norm, and in arbitration the mediation element was primary. Regardless of the formality of the procedure, mediation was attempted first, and a mediated settlement was preferable, so that, where possible, an adjudication could be incorporated into an agreement. Conversely, a settlement might be converted into an award, for ease of enforcement. The processes of mediation and arbitration often intermingled, but were conceptually distinct, as demonstrated by the precise terminology used and the formal requirement of swearing an oath before proceeding to adjudication.[8]

In ancient Rome, mediation also featured centrally. The philosopher Favorinus observed in the second century AD:

> It is often asked whether it is fit and proper for a judex[9] after the case has been heard, if there seems to be a chance to settle, to postpone his adjudicatory function for a little while and play the part of a mutual friend and a kind of peacemaker.[10]

Even though European countries only began to regulate mediation in recent decades, ad hoc mediation has a long history in Europe as reflected in the preamble to the Peace of Westphalia of 1648.[11] Religious faiths including Judaism, Islam, Christianity, Hinduism and Buddhism also have historic traditions of mediation. Jewish communities, for example, use religious leaders as go-betweens in conflicts among members of their faith, even in political disputes.[12]

While there are many and varied forms of mediation, traditional forms may be distinguished from modern practice in one significant respect: the role and social standing of the mediator. While ownership of the process remains with the parties in modern mediation, in traditional mediation the mediator, usually a highly respected authoritative member of society, plays a dominant role and their suggestions carry great weight

---

[8] D Roebuck, 'The Myth of Modern Mediation' (2007) 73(1) *Arbitration* 105, 106. See also D Roebuck, *Ancient Greek Arbitration* (Oxford, Holo Books: Arbitration Press 2001).

[9] Judex refers to a judge or arbitrator, depending on the context.

[10] Aulus Gellius, *Attic Nights* paras 14.2.13–14.2.16, quoted in D Roebuck and B de Loynes de Fumichon, *Roman Arbitration* (Oxford, Holo Books: Arbitration Press 2004) 69. For an overview of the historical background to mediation from the ancient world to modern times, with particular reference to English developments, see Roebuck, 'The Myth of Modern Mediation' (n 8).

[11] See F Steffek, 'Mediation' in J Basedow and others (eds), *The Max Planck Encyclopedia of European Private Law*, vol 2 (Oxford, Oxford University Press 2012) 1163.

[12] Boulle (n 3) 53–59. See also S Ayse Kadayifci-Orellana, 'Religion and Mediation, Strange Bedfellows or Natural Allies?' in A Georgakopoulos (ed) *The Mediation Handbook, Research, Theory, and Practice* (Abingdon, UK, Routledge 2017) 369–78.

with the parties. Traditional mediation can be viewed as an institutional form of social control as well as dispute resolution, where the mediator helps to resolve the dispute but also represents the community, its values and norms, and the communal interest in restoring harmony, order and respect for the law. Hence, the focus is on social harmony rather than individual rights, and the mediator is more outcome focussed than process driven.[13]

Merchants and business people have for centuries been among the outspoken proponents of non-legal dispute settlement, and have sought to retain control over their commercial disputes.[14] It was the business community that pushed for laws to allow out-of-court arbitration, and in the USA it was among the first to use mediation to resolve commercial disputes.[15] Commercial communities identified the need for less expensive and more efficient methods of resolving disputes outside courts to minimise losses in management time, reduce opportunity costs and promote commercial goodwill. The move towards using mediation to resolve commercial disputes was reinforced by perceptions that arbitration had become over-legalised and increasingly complex and expensive, and that mediation could focus on commercial rather than legal solutions without jeopardising long-term business relationships. Hence, mediation was depicted as 'good business practice' in resolving various commercial conflicts ranging from leasing to takeover disputes.[16]

The global expansion of commercial mediation is a natural consequence of the cross-pollination of ideas and best practices for most effectively resolving conflict. Over time, increased communication

---

[13] This form of mediation is still used in countries such as China: see C Buhring-Uhle, L Kirchhoff and G Scherer, *Arbitration and Mediation in International Business* (2nd ed, Alphen aan den Rijn, Kluwer Law International 2006) 177–80.

[14] While every culture used mediation at some point in its development, it has been suggested that mediation in the commercial sphere can be traced to ancient Babylonian commerce from 2300 BC: see C Chern, *International Commercial Mediation* (London, Informa 2008) 1–11; C Chern, *The Commercial Mediator's Handbook* (London, Informa 2015) 15–29.

[15] JS Auerbach, *Justice Without Law?* (New York, Oxford University Press 1983) 5. In the early days of the International Chamber of Commerce (ICC) acting as a dispute resolution service provider, mediation was considered of equal importance as arbitration and was the more prominent of the two services. The earliest awards rendered under the auspices of the ICC reflect how arbitral proceedings adopted techniques similar to current ICC mediation, with awards that resembled amicable settlement agreements. However, mediation was eventually overshadowed by arbitration, prompted by the arrival of the New York Convention: see A Leoveanu and A Erac, 'ICC Mediation: Paving the Way Forward' in Titi and Fach Gómez (eds) (n 6) 82–83.

[16] See Boulle (n 3) 60, 359.

between countries inevitably leads to the spread of ideas and practices and, ultimately, changes to legal systems. The experience of mediation in the USA was a major source of inspiration for the development of mediation in Australia, the United Kingdom and other parts of the world.[17]

2.3   The Role of Culture

Culture informs our collective identity and behaviour, involving conscious and unconscious language, values, habits and norms. Being dynamic and organic, cultures influence each other when people interact. Individuals within a culture may vary significantly and may be consciously or unconsciously influenced by many cultures in their behaviour and attitudes.[18] Culture reflects a mix of usages and custom that develop slowly, evolve and transform over time. Cultures complement each other and overlap; through interaction with dominant cultures, sub-cultures develop. Culture derives from the social environment people live in; it reflects patterns of thinking, feeling and acting shared with others. It is learned rather than inherited. It is difficult to segregate or isolate culture in a pure state or reserve it for a specific group or enclose it within national, regional, geographical or any other type of border or boundary. Indeed, cultural issues can arise within borders in increasingly multicultural societies.[19]

Cultural differences can be reflected in different approaches to meeting needs, shaping the interests of parties and party behaviour during the mediation process. Although it is different from negotiation or mediation strategy, culture can and often does influence strategy. Understanding our own culturally shaped behaviour, in addition to the behaviour of other parties, can help in identifying less familiar needs of other parties or possible cultural differences between the parties that need to be bridged.

---

[17] See B Marsh, 'The Development of Mediation in Central and Eastern Europe' in C Newmark and A Monaghan (eds), *Butterworths Mediators on Mediation: Leading Mediator Perspectives on the Practice of Commercial Mediation* (Haywards Heath, Tottel Publishing 2005) 386; K Hopt and F Steffek, 'Mediation: Comparison of Laws, Regulatory Models, Fundamental Issues' in K Hopt and F Steffek (eds), *Mediation: Principles and Regulation in Comparative Perspective* (Oxford, Oxford University Press 2013) 9.

[18] A Wanis-St John, 'Cultural Pathways in Negotiation and Conflict Management' in M Moffitt and R Bordone (eds), *The Handbook of Dispute Resolution* (San Francisco, Jossey-Bass 2005) 120, 130.

[19] See Antaki (n 7) 269.

A failure to take account of cultural differences can result in disputants being ethnocentric, adopting a myopic perspective and viewing the dispute only through their own cultural prism. Effectively mediating international disputes involving different cultures is likely to require cultural relativism: parties knowing, understanding and accepting cultural differences.[20]

When parties from different cultures speak different languages, the linguistic differences may become the sole focus, with other cultural aspects being neglected. Translated words may not convey all of the intended meaning across cultures, leading to one kind of miscommunication, as communication is often not limited to words. More broadly, however, where cultural elements are less visible or are unconscious, aspects of behaviour or 'neuro-wiring' can lead to a breakdown in understanding, as each side assesses the other through the prism of its own cultural realities. Research reveals that culture continues to shape our thinking throughout our lives and influences how we view the world, and that people from different cultures process the same experiences differently. For example, parties from Eastern cultures tend to be 'high-context' communicators and negotiators, while parties from Western cultures tend to be 'low-context' communicators with a sharper focus.[21] Because culture permeates how we process thoughts and respond to ideas and proposals, it can be difficult for us to distinguish cultural and biological behaviour; cultural adaption is consequently a challenge. Culture informs how we perceive, identify, approach and communicate about conflict. Inextricably bound up in conflict, culture influences how parties mediate.[22] Mediators must remain mindful of this and use their

---

[20] The choice of the dispute resolution mechanism is determined by the parties' culture in addition to the time and place of the dispute: see Antaki (n 7) 266.

[21] Parties in the USA tend to be 'low-context', quite direct communicators compared with parties in Asia who tend to be 'high-context', indirect communicators. In high-context communication, most of the meaning is conveyed through the context rather than explicitly in words. Consequently, in the USA, compared to Asia, parties tend to have short-term compared to long-term orientations, use individual compared to collective decision-making, adopt competitive rather than co-operative negotiation approaches, value punctuality compared to having a relaxed time orientation, and have a contract focus compared to a relationship focus: see H Abramson, 'Mediation Representation: Representing Clients Anywhere' in A Ingen-Housz (ed), *ADR in Business: Practice and Issues Across Countries and Cultures*, vol 2 (Alphen aan den Rijn, Kluwer Law International 2011) 297–98.

[22] For example, formal apologies are common in Japan and are often the reason that litigation can be avoided, since pursuing litigation can be viewed as shameful. Conversely, in the USA, an apology is often viewed as demeaning and can be more

cultural awareness and, with experience, their cultural fluency, to adapt their interventions throughout the mediation process.[23]

The higher uptake of mediation in some common law countries compared with civil law countries reflects the fact that the legal culture of civil law countries did not create the demand for mediation to the same degree that the litigious culture of common law countries did.[24] Also, the comparatively low cost of litigation was partly the reason for the slower development of mediation in some civil law countries in Europe, for example.[25] However, there has been a significant cultural shift in such jurisdictions.[26] Inspired in part by the EU Mediation Directive,[27] by developments in common law countries and by international practice, many civil law countries in Europe have embraced mediation, though tending to centrally locate it within the justice system rather than following the decentralised, market-based approach adopted in common law countries.[28] Litigation is generally more expensive and disruptive in countries with a common law legal tradition compared with litigation in civil law countries, and these disadvantages of litigation in common law countries appear to have enhanced the acceptance and growth of

---

difficult to include in a settlement than monetary compensation: see S B Goldberg and others, *Dispute Resolution: Negotiation, Mediation, Arbitration, and Other Processes* (7th ed, New York, Wolters Kluwer 2020) 138–39.

[23] See L Boulle and N Alexander, *Mediation: A How To Guide* (Chatswood, NSW, LexisNexis Butterworths 2015) 158–65. The Western world is traditionally characterised as having a litigious culture; conversely, East Asian and Arab and Islamic societies are perceived as emphasising conciliation: see B M Cremades, 'Overcoming the Clash of Legal Cultures: The Role of Interactive Arbitration' (1998) 14(2) *Arbitration International* 157–59. Similar to mediators in China, Arab and Muslim mediators have traditionally practised an extreme form of evaluative mediation – effectively 'semi-arbitration' – where the parties feel morally bound to abide by the solution proposed: see Antaki (n 7) 276–85; see also 269.

[24] D Jones, 'Various Non-Binding (ADR) Processes' in AJ van den Berg (ed), *New Horizons in International Commercial Arbitration and Beyond* (The Hague, Kluwer Law International 2005) (ICCA Congress Series vol 12) 406.

[25] D J A Cairns, 'Mediating International Commercial Disputes: Differences in US and European Approaches' (2005) 60(3) *Dispute Resolution Journal* 62, 67.

[26] Mediation has been embraced in Austria, Belgium, Denmark, France, Germany, Italy, the Netherlands and Switzerland. In these countries, many structural measures have been adopted, including tax incentives and legal fee incentives, to encourage parties to use mediation rather than litigation. This represents a significant cultural shift.

[27] Discussed in Section 2.4.7.

[28] Mediation has also developed both within and outside mixed legal jurisdictions such as Scotland and South Africa: see Boulle (n 3) 184–85; R Feehily, 'The Development of Commercial Mediation in South Africa in View of the Experience in Europe, North America and Australia' (PhD thesis, University of Cape Town 2008).

mediation.[29] Mediation also varies significantly in common law legal cultures. In the USA, United Kingdom, Canada and Australia, mediation law tends to develop through case law, with limited formal regulation in either the private or public sphere. In contrast to this is the more formal – often dense – regulation of mediation in many civil law jurisdictions. Even within countries that have a federal system, such as the USA and Australia, there can be significant variance in the use and regulation of the process.[30]

Comparing some civil law and common law countries reveals a dichotomy in the rationale for the development of mediation. There are effectively two main motivations for the introduction of mediation across different legal cultures, one 'qualitative' and the other 'quantitative'. The qualitative rationale is that mediation improves methods of human communication and legal problem solving and facilitates more tailored outcomes in acknowledgement of a different form of 'justice'.[31] From the quantitative perspective, mediation is used to reduce the work of the courts or to make dispute processing more efficient. These different motivations for mediation have produced great variation in the desire for regulation;

---

[29] D Nigmatullina, *Combining Mediation and Arbitration in International Commercial Dispute Resolution* (New York, Routledge 2018) 69.

[30] C Menkel-Meadow, 'The Future of Mediation Worldwide: Legal and Cultural Variations in the Uptake of Resistance to Mediation' in I Macduff, *Essays on Mediation: Dealing with Disputes in the 21st Century* (Alphen aan der Rijn, Wolters Kluwer 2016) 33–39. There is also significant variance in the regulation and use of mediation across the European Union: see G De Palo and others, '"Rebooting" the Mediation Directive: Assessing the Limited Impact of its Implementation and Proposing Measures to Increase the Number of Mediations in the EU' (Luxembourg, European Parliament 2014), discussed further in Chapter 7 at Section 7.5. See also E A Filler (ed), *Commercial Mediation in Europe: An Empirical Study of the User Experience*, Global Trends in Dispute Resolution, Book 5 (Alphen aan den Rijn, Kluwer Law International 2012); A Howard, *EU Cross-Border Commercial Mediation: Listening to Disputants – Changing the Frame; Framing the Changes* (Alphen aan den Rijn, Kluwer Law International 2021).

[31] See A Nylund, K Ervasti and L Adrian, 'Introduction to Nordic Mediation Research' in A Nylund, K Ervasti and L Adrian (eds), *Nordic Mediation Research* (Cham, Springer 2018) 2. The authors discuss the ideology of modern mediation in Nordic countries such as Finland, Norway, Sweden and Denmark which is often attributed to Nils Christie and his ideas of conflict and conflict resolution presented in N Christie, 'Conflicts as Property' (1977) 17(1) *British Journal of Criminology* 1–15. Christie's main idea is that conflict should be resolved by those involved or affected by it rather than by the judicial system. In Finland, where a court backlog was not experienced as it was in the USA and elsewhere, court procedure is moving away from the ideals of material law and a substantively correct judgment and towards the ideal of negotiated and contextual law. See also K Ervasti, 'Past, Present and Future of Mediation in Nordic Countries' in Nylund, Ervasti and Adrian (eds) (n 31) 235–36.

this is evident in issues about the extent to which the use of mediation should be incentivised, the extent of controls over the parties who may engage in the process and ensuring a degree of transparency and public accountability of a private process to avoid the 'privatisation of justice'.[32]

As noted earlier, in East Asia, mediation has a long history and is central to the region's legal tradition.[33] The Western value of privacy is generally not as important in East Asian cultures, as conflict is dealt with diplomatically within the community.[34] A 'harmonious' solution that preserves the parties' relationship is often the objective.[35] Similarly, in Arab countries, mediation is also preferred to court proceedings and arbitration.[36] In Western mediation practice, conflict is often viewed as destructive and unhelpful, but in many non-Western traditions as potentially constitutive and productive. It is important to be conscious of differing perceptions of conflict and the role that these perceptions can play in cross-cultural mediations. This is particularly salient where parties are expected to resolve their dispute solely through a particular mediation model or approach that may be perceived as Western, and fails to recognise non-Western orientations to disputing.[37] Such an approach may not align with the cultural norms and values of all the parties, and a failure to consider cultural differences can lead to a lower uptake of mediation.[38] Cultural learning, including sensitivity to cultural differences, is essential to developing mediation processes that respond to different

---

[32] Menkel-Meadow (n 30) 30. See also Chapter 10 at Section 10.2.3. Transparency concerns have featured in the field of commercial arbitration also: see A Poorooye and R Feehily, 'Confidentiality and Transparency in International Commercial Arbitration: Finding the Right Balance' (2017) 22(2) *Harvard Negotiation Law Review* 275.

[33] Jones (n 24) 407.

[34] S Deekshitha and A Saha, 'Amalgamating the Conciliatory and the Adjudicative: Hybrid Processes and Asian Arbitral Institutions' (2014) 3(1) *Indian Journal of Arbitration Law* 76, 84–85; C De Vera, 'Arbitrating Harmony: Med-Arb and the Confluence of Culture and the Rule of Law in the Resolution of International Commercial Disputes in China' (2004) 18(1) *Columbia Journal of Asian Law* 149, 183.

[35] M S Donahey, 'Seeking Harmony: Is the Asian Concept of the Conciliator/Arbitrator Applicable in the West?' (1995) 50(2) *Dispute Resolution Journal* 74.

[36] J Almoguera, 'Arbitration and Mediation Combined: The Independence and Impartiality of Mediators' in M A Fernandez-Ballesteros and D Arias Lozano (eds), *Liber Amicorum Bernardo Cremades* (Madrid, Le Lay 2010) 112–13; Cremades (n 23) 159 fn 3.

[37] M Brigg, 'Mediation, Power and Cultural Difference' (2003) 20(3) *Conflict Resolution Quarterly* 287, 287–88.

[38] K Lau, 'Mediation in a Cross-Cultural Setting: What a Mediator Should Know' (2014) 25(4) *Australasian Dispute Resolution Journal* 221, 223.

approaches to resolving conflict and, in turn, elicit the commitment of participants.[39]

The distinction between non-Western traditional forms of mediation and modern Western forms points to two main mediation cultures internationally. One culture is intuitive and informal. The oldest form, it is close to being an art. With a communitarian focus, it is practised in regions such as Asia, Africa and Latin America. Safeguarding the harmony of the group to which the parties belong is an important objective. Social, moral and subjective arguments are often used to persuade the parties to settle. It is practised in its purest form only in isolated or protected societies, removed from international trade. However, an updated form of this approach remains central to dispute resolution in many parts of the world.

The other mediation culture is cognitive and formal; in its most developed form it is effectively a science. Developed in universities and based on professional organisation, it began in the USA, then spread to Western Europe and further afield. The parties' conduct and the mediation outcome depend on the parties' adherence to their mediation culture. Communications are easier and misperceptions less frequent when the parties are culturally homogenous.[40] The cognitive mediation culture is most prevalent in international trade and is being copied by countries that are reforming their justice systems.[41]

Many mediators work with disputes where the parties' cultures are different to each other and where cultural issues are either central to the dispute or become an impediment to progress. Cross-cultural training could assist in resolving such issues by equipping mediators with the skills to adapt the mediation process and use interventions optimally.[42] It

---

[39] Brigg (n 37) 288. The implementation of the advice in some seminal texts on negotiation, such as *Getting to Yes*, is heavily dependent on culture: for example, the limitations on separating the person from the problem and the methods for exchanging information and interests. Standardised conflict management advice may quickly lose its value depending on the cultural context and must be modified to take account of the recipients and their culture: see A Wanis-St John (n 18) 125.

[40] There will also be sensitivities regarding the culture of the mediator, particularly where the mediator is from the same culture as one of the parties but not the other(s). It is important that the mediator is viewed as culturally neutral and that their approach is culturally sensitive: see Antaki (n 7) 274–75.

[41] Antaki (n 7) 290.

[42] A M van Riemsdijk, 'An International Mediator Perspective' in Ingen-Housz (ed) (n 21) 64. The International Centre for Dispute Settlement, which is the international division of the American Arbitration Association, appoints mediators who have an appropriate intercultural background from a geographically diverse international dispute resolution

is important that parties involved in a cross-cultural mediation select a mediator or mediators that are both culturally trained and culturally suitable, as the mediator must recognise and deal with culturally shaped interests, impediments and resolutions that may emerge during the process.[43] Team or co-mediation can work well in cross-cultural contexts. When two mediators work together, each may bring linguistic, subject-matter and cultural traits that complement the other mediator. Team or co-mediation is often used in complex commercial disputes such as large construction projects where there are multiple parties and short time frames; it has proved successful where cross-cultural dynamics are at work.[44] While cultural differences may not give rise to conflict in themselves, cultural knowledge of the parties may improve the chance of settlement, by promoting trust and identifying values important to stake-holders in creating settlement proposals.[45]

2.4 Increasing Harmonisation

With the advance of the global economy, the limitations and inadequacy of national legal systems have become more apparent. They are tied to a specific legal regime – often incomprehensible to and inconsistent with other regimes – a specific geographic area, and a legally prescriptive and specific set of outcomes. The motivation to find an alternative system arose from the fact that none of these limitations are responsive to the

---

panel. The purpose is to ensure that the mediators understand the cultural and jurisdictional issues involved in the dispute. This helps in conducting the mediation using appropriate models that the parties select and adapting the process to their specific needs: see E Tuchmann and others, 'The International Centre for Dispute Resolution's Mediation Practice and Experience' in Titi and Fach Gómez (eds) (n 6) 118–19.

[43] See H Abramson, *Mediation Representation: Advocating as a Problem-Solver (In Any Country or Culture)* (Louisville, National Institute for Trial Advocacy 2010) 162–63. The approach adopted by lawyer representatives in cross-cultural mediation can be critically important. Abramson offers a comprehensive, culturally neutral framework to assist lawyers representing clients in mediation where the parties are from different countries or different cultural backgrounds. This framework includes assistance with identifying culturally shaped interests and how to overcome culturally shaped impediments, see generally H Abramson, *Mediation Representation: Advocating as a Problem-Solver (In Any Country or Culture)* (Louisville, National Institute for Trial Advocacy 2010).

[44] It has also worked well in cross-cultural contexts in the context of concurrent or 'shadow' mediation, where the two mediators work alongside an arbitrator or arbitrators and mediation acts as a parallel process to arbitration: see J J Coe, 'Concurrent Co-Mediation: Toward a More Collaborative Centre of Gravity in Investor-State Dispute Resolution' in Titi and Fach Gómez (eds) (n 6) 62–63, 73.

[45] See C H Brower, 'Selection of Mediators' in Titi and Fach Gómez (eds) (n 6) 310.

needs of disputing commercial parties from different systems. While arbitration has proved to be geographically flexible, it remains tied to a particular legal framework and to particular outcomes. Mediation's ability to operate independently of legal and geographical constraints – to effectively transcend systemic differences – makes it perfectly placed to serve the needs of the global economy.[46] As a flexible process that can be designed to facilitate the needs of varied commercial disputants and problems across jurisdictions, it offers a potential lingua franca for transnational disputants.[47]

Consistent with and a consequence of increasing globalisation, there has been a move towards the harmonisation of laws and practices. The harmonisation of dispute resolution systems is an essential part of this process. Globally, the trend can be seen through the United Nations. The United Nations (UN) Commission on International Trade Law (UNCITRAL), a subsidiary body of the UN General Assembly, promotes the unification and harmonisation of international trade law. UNCITRAL has developed model laws to help countries that wish to enact legislation in a particular field. These texts are negotiated and agreed by the UNCITRAL member states and contain provisions and concepts that are sufficiently well known to be understood and reflected in the legal systems of the participating countries.[48]

---

[46] See B Marsh, 'The Development of Mediation in Central and Eastern Europe' in Newmark and Monaghan (eds) (n 17) 385–86. Issues such as confidentiality (discussed in Chapter 9) and enforcement (discussed in Chapters 3 and 8) are determined primarily by national legal systems; however, the Singapore Convention should in time result in a more consistent international approach to the enforcement of mediated settlements.

[47] See C Menkel-Meadow, 'Roots and Inspirations: A Brief History of the Foundations of Dispute Resolution' in Moffitt and Bordone (eds) (n 18) 24. This is reflected in a new generation of trade treaties, such as the EU–Canada Comprehensive Economic and Trade Agreement and the Central American Free Trade Agreement (in 2004 renamed the Dominican Republic – Central American Free Trade Agreement) that refer specifically to mediation as an alternative or additional means of solving trade disputes: see F Nitschke, 'ICSID Conciliation Rules in Practice' in Titi and Fach Gómez (eds) (n 6) 143. See also J Bruneau and R Feehily, 'The Transatlantic Trade and Investment Partnership: A Threat to the International Trading System or the Panacea for the Economic Predicaments Faced by the EU and the USA?' (2017) 33(1) *Connecticut Journal of International Law* 43, 73.

[48] See Marsh (n 46) 386–87. UNCITRAL also drafts non-legislative texts, for example rules covering arbitration and mediation, that are directed at parties rather than states, and can be used during the relevant process: see N Alexander and S Chong, *The Singapore Convention on Mediation: A Commentary* (Alphen aan den Rijn, Kluwer Law International 2019) 2–6.

2.4.1   The New York Convention

There is one instrument that predates UNCITRAL and has implications for the enforcement of mediated settlement agreements when converted into arbitral awards that warrants a mention. The Convention on the Recognition and Enforcement of Foreign Arbitral Awards ('New York Convention') was adopted by a UN diplomatic conference in New York in 1958 and became effective the following year. Under the Convention, courts of contracting states must enforce private agreements to arbitrate and must recognise and enforce arbitral awards from other contracting states. The New York Convention is the principal legislative instrument that regulates international commercial arbitration; it has accomplished its drafters' aspirations, serving as a universal constitutional charter focussed on enforcement and recognition.[49] If arbitration laws or institutional rules provide for mediation to take place during the course of the arbitral process, and that any settlement reached can be made the subject of an arbitral award, then a mediated settlement may be converted into an arbitral award for ease of enforcement.[50]

2.4.2   UNCITRAL

UNCITRAL was created by the UN General Assembly in 1966 to help harmonise and modernise international trade law and commercial law. Its sixty state members are elected by the General Assembly and structured to reflect geographic regions and principal economic and legal systems. An organ of the General Assembly, it follows the General Assembly's rules of procedures for its sessions and working groups and determines its work programme based on proposals from states or organisations. It sets its own agenda, reviews the work of its working groups and prepares reports, models laws and conventions for the United Nations.

UNCITRAL Working Group II was assigned the mediation settlement initiative, which previously focussed on arbitration and has broadened its mandate to cover dispute settlement. Any recommendations from Working Group II are sent to UNCITRAL for its adoption, and any proposed conventions are sent first to UNCITRAL and then to the

---

[49] See Y Rampall and R Feehily, 'The Sanctity of Party Autonomy and the Powers of Arbitrators to Determine the Applicable Law: The Quest for an Arbitral Equilibrium' (2018) 23(2) *Harvard Negotiation Law Review* 345, 356–57.
[50] See Chapter 8 at Section 8.4 for a discussion on this issue.

General Assembly for consideration and adoption. UNCITRAL Working Group II was responsible for creating two recent significant mediation instruments: the revised Mediation Model Law (see Section 2.4.5) and the Singapore Convention (see Section 2.4.6).[51]

2.4.3 The UNCITRAL Mediation Rules

Adopted by UNCITRAL on 23 July 1980, the UNCITRAL Mediation Rules provide a comprehensive set of procedural rules covering all aspects of the process that parties can use when mediating their commercial disputes. The UN General Assembly recommended that the Rules be used 'in cases where a dispute arises in the context of international commercial relations and the parties seek an amicable settlement of that dispute by recourse to [mediation]'.[52] The Rules are frequently referred to by private and state parties in many and varied disputes and jurisdictions. They proved influential in the preparation of other rules, such as the London Court of International Arbitration Mediation Rules, the World Intellectual Property Organisation Mediation Rules and the International Chamber of Commerce ADR Rules, as well as in the drafting of the UNCITRAL Mediation Model Law. The name of the Rules was changed from Conciliation to Mediation to create consistency between the Rules, the Mediation Model Law and the Singapore Convention.[53]

2.4.4 The UNCITRAL Arbitration Model Law

The UNCITRAL Model Law on International Commercial Arbitration was adopted on 21 June 1985 and revised in 2006. Reflecting global consensus on key aspects of international arbitration practice, it is designed to help countries reform and modernise their law to reflect the needs of international commercial arbitration. It covers all stages of the arbitral process ranging from the arbitration agreement, the composition and jurisdiction of the arbitral tribunal and the extent of court intervention through to the recognition and enforcement of the arbitral

---

[51] See H Abramson, 'New Singapore Convention on Cross-Border Mediated Settlements: Key Choices' in Titi and Fach Gómez (eds) (n 6) 360–61.

[52] UN General Assembly Resolution 35/52 (4 December 1980).

[53] See E E Deason, 'What's in a Name? The Terms "Commercial" and "Mediation" in the Singapore Convention on Mediation', Singapore Convention Reference Book (2019) 20(4) *Cardozo Journal of Conflict Resolution* 1149, 1162.

award. However, the focus from a mediation perspective is on the implications of the Arbitration Model Law where a mediated settlement agreement is converted into an arbitral award for enforcement purposes.[54]

2.4.5 The UNCITRAL Mediation Model Law

The Mediation Model Law was adopted in 2002 and represented the consensus of ninety member nations. It was originally named the Model Law on International Commercial Conciliation. The Model Law was amended in 2018 as part of the discussions that also led to the Singapore Convention. A new section was added on international settlement agreements and their enforcement, and the instrument was renamed the Model Law on International Commercial Mediation and International Settlement Agreements Resulting from Mediation.[55]

The Mediation Model Law offers a template for countries considering the adoption of a law on commercial mediation. It has three sections. The first section provides general principles including the scope of application, the definitions of 'mediator' and 'mediation' and an interpretation provision. The second section focusses on mediation procedures. It contains the original (2002) provisions on the appointment of mediators, the commencement, termination and conduct of the process, communication between the mediator and other parties, disclosure of information, confidentiality and the admissibility of evidence in other proceedings as well as post-mediation issues. The third section focusses on settlement agreements. It contains the revised (2018) provisions to ensure consistency with the Singapore Convention. However, unlike the Singapore Convention, which covers only mediated settlement agreements, the Model Law covers the enforcement of all settlement agreements, regardless of whether they resulted from mediation.

UNCITRAL Working Group II prepared the amendments to the Mediation Model Law concurrently with the text of the Singapore

---

[54] See Chapter 8 at Section 8.4 for a discussion on this issue.

[55] In its previously adopted texts and relevant documents, UNCITRAL used the term 'conciliation' with the understanding that the terms 'conciliation' and 'mediation' were interchangeable. In amending the Model Law, UNCITRAL decided to use the term 'mediation' instead, to adapt to the actual and practical use of the term and with the expectation that this change would facilitate the promotion and heighten the visibility of the Mediation Model Law. However, this change in terminology does not have any substantive or conceptual implications.

Convention. Apart from ensuring consistency in the standards on the cross-border enforcement of international-mediated settlement agreements, the Working Group believed that the revised Model Law would be an alternative for countries that were not ready to ratify the Singapore Convention, due to their varied levels of experience with mediation.[56]

Article 2(1) of the Mediation Model Law provides: 'In the interpretation of this Law, regard is to be had to its international origin and to the need to promote uniformity in its application and the observance of good faith.' Hence this mandatory provision[57] encourages national courts to look to the international nature of the Mediation Model Law, which may include how other countries have interpreted it, favouring international harmony. Article 2(2) provides: 'Questions concerning matters governed by this Law which are not expressly settled in it are to be settled in conformity with the general principles on which this Law is based.' Hence the message to national courts is to think globally and look to the philosophy underlying the Model Law. The consequence has been the development of a body of mediation case law and court decisions on aspects of mediation; this tends to have a harmonising effect on the interpretation of mediation law within an applicable jurisdiction and is influential internationally.[58]

---

[56] Abramson (n 51) 369. The relevant sections of the Mediation Model Law are discussed in Chapter 8 at Section 8.6.

[57] There are two mandatory provisions in the Mediation Model Law. One is article 2 ('Interpretation'). The other is article 7(3) ('Conduct of mediation') which requires the mediator to treat parties fairly during the process.

[58] There are also systems that support harmonisation through dissemination of judicial decisions on cross-border mediation. For example, Case Law on UNCITRAL Texts (CLOUT) offers easy access to judicial decisions interpreting enactments of the Mediation Model Law. Many of the provisions in the Mediation Model Law are drawn from the UNCITRAL Mediation Rules, which were intended for use primarily within an arbitration focussed framework, and deal with procedural aspects of mediation. It has been suggested that the procedural aspects may be better covered by industry rules and that it may have been preferable had the Mediation Model Law restricted itself to rules dealing with rights and obligations that require legislative enforcement, including confidentiality, litigation, limitation provisions and enforceability of mediated settlement agreements. The UNCITRAL Mediation Rules were adopted twenty years before the Mediation Model Law was originally adopted and many of the provisions reflected in the Mediation Model Law are consequently archaic and not relevant to contemporary mediation law and practice in many jurisdictions, such as mediation confidentiality in article 9 discussed in Chapter 9 at Section 9.4.6.2 and article 7(4) that expressly permits the mediator to make settlement proposals, discussed in Chapter 5 at Section 5.9. However, the Mediation Model Law reflects the considered view that it was more acceptable to many signatories when consistent with the well-established Mediation Rules, and the procedural rules can be opted out from. It offers choice and flexibility to informed users

2.4.6 The Singapore Convention

In June 2018 UNCITRAL adopted the final draft of the Singapore Convention. This followed six sessions over three years involving over ninety UN member states and thirty-five international governmental and non-governmental organisations. In December that year, the UN General Assembly adopted the Convention, which is binding on member states pending their acceptance and ratification.

Inspired by the success of the New York Convention, six decades on, the Singapore Convention is expected to be to mediated settlement agreements what the New York Convention is to arbitral awards. It is designed to facilitate international trade and to promote mediation as an effective method of resolving commercial disputes by providing a uniform, efficient framework for the recognition and enforcement of international-mediated settlement agreements reached to resolve international commercial disputes.

A signing ceremony for the Convention was held in Singapore in August 2019, at which forty-six states signed it. Under article 14, the Singapore Convention came into force on 12 September 2020, six months after the third signatory state completed its ratification process.[59]

2.4.7 The EU Mediation Directive

The EU Mediation Directive was introduced to promote mediation as a means of alternative out-of-court settlement in the European Union.[60] It applies to civil and commercial disputes, with administrative and criminal matters excluded. While EU member states can extend the scope of its application domestically, it applies to cross-border disputes only.[61] The Directive is not an attempt to harmonise mediation law and

who have the time, resources and negotiating power to adapt it and possible unintended risks for others: see N Alexander, 'Harmonisation and Diversity in the Private International Law of Mediation: The Rhythms of Regulatory Reform' in Hopt and Steffek (eds) (n 17) 166–67, 188, 191–92.

[59] See Singapore Convention on Mediation <www.singaporeconvention.org> accessed 10 May 2022. See also Alexander and Chong (n 48) 6–7. The Singapore Convention is discussed further in Chapter 8 at Section 8.6.

[60] Directive 2008/52/EC of the European Parliament and the Council of 21 May 2008 on certain aspects of mediation in civil and commercial matters ('EU Mediation Directive'). The Directive applies to all member states of the European Union except Denmark (which opted out of the Directive). The deadline for member states to transpose the Directive into domestic law, regulations and administrative provisions was 20 May 2011.

[61] The extension of the scope of application of the EU Mediation Directive would ensure that minimum standards apply to all mediations throughout the European Union in civil

procedure in a general sense and is quite limited in scope. It regulates individual elements such as ensuring the quality of mediation services and the use of codes of conduct by mediators, the role of courts in inviting the parties to use mediation and hold mediation information sessions, the enforceability of settlement agreements, confidentiality, suspension of limitation and prescription periods and information for the general public on mediation, but is silent on issues such as the liability of mediators. The Directive also provides that national laws may make mediation compulsory, or subject to incentives or sanctions, provided access to the courts is not prohibited by such measures.

The provisions of the EU Mediation Directive are permissive rather than prescriptive, providing a floor rather than a ceiling that sets a minimum standard in key areas.[62] Member states may go much further in protecting elements such as mediation confidentiality. Inspired in part by the EU Mediation Directive, some member states such as France, Germany and Ireland introduced comprehensive laws and regulations on mediation, some of which go beyond the scope of the Directive, particularly for mediation that has no cross-border aspect.[63]

2.4.8 The US Uniform Mediation Act

The Uniform Mediation Act was introduced in the USA in 2001 with the principal purpose of assuring confidentiality and fostering uniformity. While the Act is intended to create a baseline minimum confidentiality standard, it does not supplant more stringent, state-based confidentiality requirements. It provides a mechanism for protecting mediation confidentiality and specifies limited exceptions where other policy considerations take priority. The Act seeks to ensure that mediation communications remain confidential to make mediation a fairer, more effective and more attractive means to settle disputes. However, many US states have refused to adopt the Act despite its invitation to incorporate existing state laws, largely because existing state mediation laws,

and commercial matters, regardless of where the parties are domiciled or reside: see K Vandekerckhove, 'Mediation of Cross-Border Commercial Disputes in the European Union' in Titi and Fach Gómez (eds) (n 6) 201.

[62] The relevant elements of the EU Mediation Directive are discussed in Chapters 3, 5, 7, 8 and 9.

[63] This has led to a dichotomous approach in some EU member states, with one regime for domestic mediations and another for cross-border mediations: see Hopt and Steffek, 'Mediation: Comparison of Laws, Regulatory Models, Fundamental Issues' (n 17) 5–8.

particularly those dealing with confidentiality, are already much stronger than the UMA's.[64]

2.5   Mediation Regulation

Public regulation involves laws and regulations, while private regulation involves model contracts, self-regulation of associations and codes. There has been significant regulatory diversity across jurisdictions leading to different practical outcomes. For example, some countries such as Austria have a high level of regulation. By contrast, in England, the Civil Procedure Rules contain only a number of rules governing issues such as costs,[65] leaving the design of mediation and the education and regulation of mediators to private associations and the self-regulating forces of the market.[66]

Effective dispute resolution requires that the strengths of the various dispute resolution processes are matched to the characteristics of the dispute, and that parties are incentivised to choose a process according to its appropriateness for the dispute.[67] To facilitate and support party choice, there has been a movement in many jurisdictions away from civil procedure laws and towards comprehensive dispute resolution laws.

The institutional integration of mediation into dispute resolution procedures and substantive law has taken the form of enabling and guiding rules. Enabling rules create frameworks that stakeholders – particularly parties, their lawyers and judges – can use for better resolution of disputes. Enabling regulations concern issues such as the consequences of agreements to mediate, the effect of mediation on limitation and prescription periods, mediation confidentiality, enforcement of settlement agreements and the structures that link court procedures with mediation such as court-annexed mediation programmes. Guiding regulation creates incentives or may set mandatory constraints and duties as a reaction to information and decision deficits. Such deficits may relate to issues such as the obligations of parties and lawyers regarding the treatment of disputes and the choice of resolution

---

[64] The Uniform Mediation Act is discussed further in Chapter 9 at Section 9.4.6.3.
[65] See Chapter 7 for a discussion on costs.
[66] See Steffek (n 11) 1163–64. See also Alexander (n 58) 145–57.
[67] For a discussion on process selection and design, see Chapter 1 at Section 1.9.

method; mandatory pre-action mediation; investigation, advice and orders regarding mediation by the courts; and cost incentives and sanctions.[68]

The regulation of mediation must find the right balance between the voluntariness and procedural flexibility of the process, on one side, and regulatory goals such as promoting mediation and ensuring a quality process, on the other. A comparative analysis of empirical research indicates that regulatory success does not come down to extensive or sparse regulation, but the targeted approach to the development stage of mediation, the regulatory environment of dispute resolution and the conflict resolution culture. Empirical research reflects that regulation should not only aim at creating good law, but also keep in mind the individuals who operate the law, particularly the parties, lawyers and judges. While different jurisdictions will adopt different regulatory regimes, mediation draws its procedural strength from its flexibility, and those who are at the centre of the process – such as the parties and the mediator – require freedom. Consequently, the core of the method of mediation should remain free of regulation.[69] Regulation must effectively manage the tensions between diversity and harmonisation, appreciating that both diversity and harmonisation are important values and that the tensions between them are essential to achieve responsive and sustainable mediation practice.[70]

2.6   Private International Law

Private international law, sometimes referred to as 'conflict of laws', relates to the way domestic laws of a country manage disputes containing a foreign element. The disputes may involve non-state actors or states

---

[68] See Hopt and Steffek, 'Mediation: Comparison of Laws, Regulatory Models, Fundamental Issues' (n 17) 20–43, 119–20. Another area of regulation involves the three regulatory models for the mediation profession, discussed in Chapter 5 at Section 5.4.

[69] See Hopt and Steffek, 'Mediation: Comparison of Laws, Regulatory Models, Fundamental Issues' (n 17) 109–18, 121.

[70] See Alexander (n 58) 138–45, 157–68. Legislative regulation is restricted in dealing with non-legal perspectives and the complexity, unpredictability and innovative nature of mediation. Often it only deals with specific aspects: for example, the US Uniform Mediation Act covers confidentiality and the admissibility of evidence, leaving other issues to more responsive and diverse forms of regulation. The World Bank Group also recommends a combination of private and public regulation with a high level of responsiveness to the needs of interest groups and changing circumstances. Stakeholder participation in determining regulation is considered to encourage performance beyond compliance: see Alexander (n 58) 151–52. See also World Bank Group, *Alternative Dispute Resolution Guidelines* (Washington DC, 2011).

acting as private transactors in cross-border or international disputes. The laws themselves are not international, being domestic statutes and case law. There is no single global system; each country has its own system.[71]

Private international law deals primarily with issues of jurisdiction, choice of law and forum, and the recognition and enforcement of foreign judgments. Jurisdiction relates to whether the local court or forum possesses the power to hear and decide the case or if the case has sufficient connection with a different jurisdiction to justify the local court restricting or limiting its own power. Forum clauses in commercial contracts reflect the parties' choice of court or jurisdiction in relation to disputes, while choice of law clauses reflect the law they wish to apply to disputes.[72] Issues relating to recognition and enforcement of foreign judgments arise when a judgment has been issued in another jurisdiction and recognition or enforcement is being sought in the local court.[73]

Traditionally, private international law has been viewed as a transnational extension of domestic law, a largely technical exercise in managing potential conflicts between the domestic and the foreign. An alternative perspective is to view it, through a global governance lens, as providing solutions to regulatory problems.[74] This is seen in regulatory choice in global governance, with the increasing use of soft legal instruments. In the mediation context, this includes the rules and model laws discussed earlier that are non-binding unless adopted in a legal

---

[71] The word 'international' is somewhat misleading in that the subject is just as concerned with relations between different legal systems within a country as they are with relations between different countries. This is apparent in Canada, Australia and the USA where the majority of cases concern inter-provincial or interstate conflicts: see T Hartley, *International Commercial Litigation: Text, Cases and Materials on Private International Law* (3rd ed, Cambridge University Press 2020) 3–5; S C Symeonides, *Choice of Law, The Oxford Commentaries on American Law* (New York, Oxford University Press 2016) 2–3, 7.

[72] This issue is discussed further in Chapter 3 at Section 3.3.6.3.

[73] See Alexander (n 58) 133–36. The conversion of mediated settlements into court judgments to enhance enforcement is discussed in Chapter 8, as is the Singapore Convention, which was introduced in response to the challenging nature of cross-border enforcement of mediated settlement agreements.

[74] See A Mills, 'Variable Geometry, Peer Governance, and the Public International Perspective on Private International Law' in H Muir Watt and D P Fernández Arroy (eds), *Private International Law and Global Governance* (Oxford, Oxford University Press 2014) 245–47; R Collins and M M Albornoz, 'On the Dwindling Divide Between Public and Private: The Role of Soft Law Instruments in Global Governance' in V R Abou-Nigm, K McCall-Smith and D French, *Linkages and Boundaries in Private and Public International Law* (Oxford, Hart 2018) 107.

instrument such as a statute or agreement. Soft law has dramatically changed the landscape of international legal regulation and the use of soft law instruments is becoming more prevalent. Soft law has been viewed as enhancing the flexibility of international law as a means of regulating specific legal issues in areas such as commercial mediation, and has been largely embraced as a necessary enhancement of the regulatory capacity of the international system.[75]

In the context of international commercial mediation, jurisdiction or competence includes the enforcement of agreements to mediate. Choice of law includes determining the applicable law of the contract where this is unclear or not recognised. Soft law, including mediator standards and procedural rules that govern the process, will be relevant to interpretation of the Singapore Convention.[76] Recognition and enforcement also relate to international-mediated settlement agreements across borders in light of the Singapore Convention.[77]

Viewed through a global governance prism, private international law can be understood as a regulatory system that aims at achieving the best, most consistent and just approach to the issues of jurisdiction, choice of law, recognition and enforcement and international co-operation between authorities. What matters is the potential for any new international legal instrument to be effective and to have a positive impact on the people and corporations involved in cross-border legal relationships. Viewing private international law as a form of governance means that hard and soft law can play complementary rather than conflicting roles.[78]

---

[75] See generally J Pauwelyn, R A Wessel and J Wouters (eds), *Informal International Lawmaking* (Oxford, Oxford University Press 2012). See also Collins and Albornoz (n 74) 108–13.

[76] An example of the use of soft law is using mediator standards when interpreting article 5(1)(e) and 5(1)(f) dealing with mediator misconduct as a basis for refusing relief under the Singapore Convention. This is discussed in Chapter 8 at Section 8.6.7.

[77] Given the stage of development of the process, the private international law of mediation is not as widely recognised as the private international law relevant to litigation or arbitration. However, as discussed in Chapter 8 at Section 8.6 this is likely to change under the Singapore Convention, which gives international commercial-mediated settlements similar enforcement status as a court judgment or arbitral award: see Alexander and Chong (n 48) 11–14.

[78] It is in areas left unregulated by countries that soft law instruments have proved particularly relevant. The involvement of private actors has been critical, resulting in a transfer of sovereignty in the field of regulating private commerce – giving greater discretion to private actors at the expense of sovereign control. The internationalist motivation that led to the professionalisation and systemisation of public international law towards the end of the twentieth century also shaped a desire to globally regulate private law transactions: see Collins and Albornoz (n 74) 113–18.

2.7 Concluding Thoughts

Contemporary interest in international commercial mediation may be attributed to a recognition of the alienating effects of the over-legislation of disputes, the globalisation of law and socio-cultural changes such as the decline of the culturally homogeneous nation state. Similarly, economic imperatives, the destructive features of the adversarial legal system, a strong intellectual impetus for more constructive alternatives and social commitments to participation and empowerment have been key factors in the development of modern mediation systems.[79]

Fundamental changes in dispute resolution culture take decades rather than years.[80] Mediation offers parties greater control over the process, procedural rules and outcome due to its flexibility in design and practice. As an informal and adaptable process, mediation offers the possibility of being more sensitive to cultural differences, but it also risks social and legal cultural 'colonisation', where a model or approach to mediation used in one jurisdiction or region may be inappropriately employed in another.[81] Cultural empathy and understanding is required to ensure the process is used appropriately and effectively.[82] While it is important to be mindful of cultural differences, mediators should also be wary of assuming that every difference emanates from culture.[83] Experience suggests that negotiating parties tend to overattribute problems to cultural differences. While cultural differences may cause misunderstandings, in practice it seems that culture-related conflicts can be exaggerated.[84] Nonetheless, while cultural differences may not ordinarily create conflict themselves,

---

[79] N Alexander, 'Global Trends in Mediation: Riding the Third Wave' in N Alexander (ed), *Global Trends in Mediation* (Alphen aan den Rijn, Kluwer Law International 2006) 6–7.

[80] For an evaluative comparison of mediation across many jurisdictions, juxtaposing legal data with law and conflict culture, see Hopt and Steffek, 'Mediation: Comparison of Laws, Regulatory Models, Fundamental Issues' (n 17) 93–108.

[81] Menkel-Meadow (n 30) 31–32. See also Chapter 4.

[82] See generally Antaki (n 7) 302–03.

[83] Research reveals that factors such as personality, negotiation style and professional training can have as much influence on negotiation behaviour as culture: see A Kupfer Schneider, 'Public and Private International Dispute Resolution' in Moffitt and Bordone (eds) (n 18) 439–40.

[84] This may be done to generate arguments that are unrelated to the substance of disputes. For example, a failure to fulfil a contractual obligation may be explained by the breaching party as their counterpart failing to understand local practices: see D Lax and J Sabenius, *3-D Negotiation: Powerful Tools to Change the Game In Your Most Important Deals* (Boston, Harvard Business School Press 2006) 222; A Fortún and A Iglesia, 'Mediation and Other ADR in International Construction Disputes' in Titi and Fach Gómez (eds) (n 6) 281.

cultural knowledge is more likely to improve the chances of settlement, by promoting trust and identifying values that are important to disputants in creating settlement proposals.[85]

Hard and soft law can play complementary roles in the regulation of commercial mediation. The effectiveness of international legal instruments will ultimately be determined by the positive impact they have on the people and corporations involved in cross-border legal relationships. Regulatory efforts must always strive to effectively manage the tensions between diversity and harmonisation, appreciating that both elements are important values and that the tensions between them are essential to achieve responsive and sustainable mediation practice.

[85] See Brower (n 45).

3

Agreements for Future Mediation

3.1   Introduction

Commercial contracts frequently contain mediation clauses, either as stand-alone provisions or contained within dispute resolution clauses. Mediation clauses usually require the parties to mediate as part of a sequence of dispute resolution methods, where they progress from consensus to evaluative methods until resolution is reached. Careful drafting is required to ensure such clauses are effective and enforceable. The primary issues relevant to the enforceability of mediation clauses include severability, certainty, completeness, attempts to oust the court's jurisdiction, additional policy considerations, certainty, waiver and remedies for breach of mediation clauses. While compliance with mediation clauses is not easy to determine, only the narrowest of requirements has proven to be workable in practice. Regional and international instruments covering mediation tend not to provide for the enforcement of mediation clauses. There is an international trend towards obligating legal advisors to discuss with their clients whether their commercial disputes are suitable for mediation, and policy in many jurisdictions is moving towards penalising parties (and in some cases, their advisors) where mediation is not given due consideration. Similar to mediation clauses, agreements to mediate require careful drafting to ensure they are enforceable.

3.2   Mediation Clauses

Many commercial contracts include mediation clauses that require the parties to mediate their disputes or to consider the use of mediation when disputes arise. The optimal time for commercial parties to agree to mediate their disputes is before a dispute arises, at a time when their relationship is positive and constructive. Including mediation clauses in commercial contracts is a good corporate governance practice as they can help solve disputes that could affect the company's reputation and performance.[1]

The clauses may cover particular types of dispute or any contractual conflict of varying complexity and intensity that may arise between the parties. Mediation service providers have produced standard mediation clauses for use in agreements. These generally stipulate that contractual disputes will be referred to mediation before the parties commence legal proceedings or go to arbitration. Such clauses vary in complexity: some provide for the appointment of a mediator who will design and control all aspects of the process; others detail features of the process or refer to a prescribed mediation procedure contained in a separate document.

Many commercial contracts contain dispute resolution provisions that comprise a tiered or escalation clause tailored to meet the parties' needs. The clause provides a sequence of dispute resolution methods, such as negotiation, followed by mediation, followed by arbitration. The parties progress through the steps from consensus to evaluative methods until resolution is reached. Careful drafting is required to ensure such clauses are effective and enforceable.[2] To determine the most appropriate

---

[1] See E Runesson and M L Guy, *Mediating Corporate Governance Conflicts and Disputes* (International Finance Corporation, World Bank Group 2007) 44, available at <www .ifc.org>. Where mediated solutions result in the best possible use of company assets and enhance the potential for future value creation, mediation assists in ensuring that management's fiduciary duties to the company are discharged, contributing to effective corporate governance. See A J A J Eijsbouts, 'Mediation as a Management Tool in Corporate Governance' in A Ingen-Housz (ed), *ADR in Business: Practice and Issues Across Countries and Cultures*, vol 2 (Alphen aan den Rijn, Kluwer Law International 2011) 67–80 for a discussion on this issue, and on the theme of mediation as a necessary tool of management in adequately managing corporate risk through effective conflict management, making it a core element of corporate governance.

[2] L A Mistelis, 'ADR in England and Wales: A Successful Case of Public Private Partnership' in N Alexander (ed), *Global Trends in Mediation* (Alphen aan den Rijn, Kluwer Law International 2006) 162. See K Hopt and F Steffek, 'Mediation: Comparison of Laws, Regulatory Models, Fundamental Issues' in K Hopt and F Steffek (eds), *Mediation: Principles and Regulation in Comparative Perspective* (Oxford, Oxford University Press 2013) 29–31; S Blake, J Browne and S Sime, *The Jackson ADR Handbook* (2nd ed, Oxford, Oxford University Press 2016) 101–03. For an analysis of seminal case law and a discussion on the need for overall clarity, specificity with regard to the procedure to be adopted in each tier and the point at which one process terminates and the next begins, see M Pryles, 'Multi-Tiered Dispute Resolution Clauses' (2001) 18(2) *Journal of International Arbitration* 159. See also A Leoveanu and A Erac, 'ICC Mediation: Paving the Way Forward' in C Titi and K Fach Gómez (eds), *Mediation in International Commercial and Investment Disputes* (Oxford, Oxford University Press 2019) 92–97. The World Intellectual Property Organization (WIPO) has developed the WIPO Clause Generator,

wording, drafters should consider the nature of the contract to assess the types of disputes that may arise during its life. Mediation clauses have evolved over time, become more complex and responded to judicial direction; while it is now uncommon for their validity to be legally assessed, the principles gleaned from established jurisprudence have resulted in more careful and detailed drafting.[3]

3.3   Enforceability of Mediation Clauses

Compliance with mediation clauses tends not to be a major issue in practice. Where a party fails to comply, it is likely that the courts will determine these clauses' enforceability under general contractual principles in the absence of a legislative basis for enforcing them.[4]

There has been some analogous reasoning with the law on the enforceability of arbitration clauses. Arbitration legislation has been enacted in many jurisdictions and interpreted by the courts and is well established. Yet there are many reasons why the differences between arbitration and mediation limit the relevance of the law on arbitration clauses. Arbitration is regulated by statute that provides for its enforceability. Modelled on litigation, arbitration follows a clear process and enjoys a certain outcome in the form of an award. By contrast, mediation has traditionally not enjoyed the same statutory support or been as well defined, and there is no certainty about the outcome of the process. Consequently, compliance has traditionally been relatively easy to assess with an arbitration clause, but difficult to assess with a mediation clause. As a result, the courts originally displayed reluctance over the enforcement of mediation clauses compared to arbitration clauses. Despite these

---

an online tool that offers assistance based on WIPO case experience, where parties need to modify WIPO standard multi-tier dispute resolution clauses to meet specific needs: see H Wollgast and I de Castro, 'WIPO Mediation: Resolving International Intellectual Property and Technology Disputes Outside the Courts' in Titi and Fach Gómez (eds) 266–68.

[3] See L Boulle, *Mediation: Principles, Process, Practice* (3rd ed, Chatswood, NSW, LexisNexis 2011) 614–16; N Alexander, *International and Comparative Mediation: Legal Perspectives* (Austin, Wolters Kluwer 2009) 171–73.

[4] For example, in the USA there is no federal statute covering the enforcement of agreements to mediate, unlike the protection provided to enforce arbitration agreements under the Federal Arbitration Act. The enforceability of agreements to mediate is generally a matter of state law: see C H Crown, 'Are Mandatory Mediation Clauses Enforceable?' (2010) 29(2) *Litigation Journal* 3, 3. Empirical evidence indicates that many jurisdictions have not enacted statutory rules for agreements to mediate; instead, the general rules of substantive and procedural laws apply: see Hopt and Steffek (n 2) 30.

differences, similar policy considerations influenced the courts' approach to both types of clauses: these involved balancing the parties' autonomy to agree on their own dispute resolution method with the constitutional right to have matters judicially determined.[5]

The primary issues relevant to the enforceability of mediation clauses include severability, certainty, completeness, attempts to oust the jurisdiction of the courts, other policy considerations, providing the required certainty, waiver and remedies for breach of mediation clauses.[6]

3.3.1   Severability

While contracts can be terminated in many ways, such as through repudiation, an issue that arises is whether an otherwise valid mediation clause survives the termination of the contract. Although further performance is not required from the parties following termination, general contractual principles – in particular, the principle of severability – appear to result in the contract remaining effective for the purpose of enforcing the mediation clause.[7] Another issue may arise where one party wants to enforce a mediation clause and the other party claims that the contract, including the mediation clause, was void *ab initio* (from the beginning). It is well established in England[8] that where a contract is void *ab initio*, an arbitration clause can still be severed from the main contract and be enforceable.[9]

---

[5]   See Boulle (n 3) 617–18. Under the principle of competence-competence, which relates to an arbitral tribunal's right to decide whether it has jurisdiction, in some jurisdictions arbitral tribunals have the power to determine whether a mediation clause has been complied with, and to stay arbitral proceedings pending compliance in appropriate cases. This may arise under a med-arb or stepped dispute resolution clause: see Alexander (n 3) 181–84.

[6]   For a detailed discussion on the seminal Australian jurisprudence in this area, see D Spencer, 'Uncertainty and Incompleteness in Dispute Resolution Clauses' (1995) 2 *Commercial Dispute Resolution Journal* 23–40. See also Boulle (n 3) 618–49; Alexander (n 3) 174–209; R Feehily, 'Commercial Mediation Agreements and Enforcement in South Africa' (2016) 49(2) *Comparative and International Law Journal of Southern Africa* 305; R Feehily, 'The Contractual Certainty of Commercial Agreements to Mediate in Ireland' (2016) 6(1) *Irish Journal of Legal Studies* 59.

[7]   While not as well established globally in the mediation field, it is well established in the field of arbitration: see R Feehily, 'Separability in International Commercial Arbitration: Confluence, Conflict and the Appropriate Limitations in the Development and Application of the Doctrine' (2018) 34(3) *Arbitration International* 355.

[8]   For simplicity the term 'England' is used throughout this book to describe the jurisdiction of England and Wales.

[9]   See *Harbour Assurance Co (UK) Ltd* v. *Kansa General International Insurance Co Ltd* [1993] QB 701 (CA). This is now provided for in statute under the Arbitration Act 1996 (UK) s 7.

Despite allegations that the underlying contract is void, the parties are presumed to have wanted their disputes to be resolved by arbitration and the underlying principle is that the agreement to arbitrate is collateral to the main agreement and therefore stands on its own. This principle could be extended to mediation clauses on the basis that they derive their authority from the agreement of the parties, are severable from the main contract and should be enforced by courts even where the main contract is void.[10]

However, where the mediation clause is contained within a multi-tiered dispute resolution provision, and aspects of the provision are found to be invalid and unenforceable, the entire provision would be likely to fail. Hence, severability is unlikely to save the mediation stage of a dispute resolution clause if the clause is otherwise invalid and unenforceable. As the Supreme Court of New South Wales held in *New South Wales* v. *Banabelle Electrical Pty Ltd*, 'severance of the offending section of the clause is inappropriate as the remainder, after the severance, would not reflect the intention of the parties'.[11]

3.3.2 Certainty

Contract provisions are void where it is difficult to assess the rights or obligations of the parties. Also, the law may decline to enforce them if they are vague about certain matters to be agreed in the future. It is therefore important that mediation clauses satisfy the legal standards of certainty to ensure they are enforceable. Where a mediation clause makes the occurrence of the mediation dependent on the future wishes of one or both parties, it is effectively an 'agreement to agree' and will not provide sufficient certainty to be enforceable.

English courts originally viewed agreements to negotiate as 'agreements to agree' and denied their enforcement.[12] Agreements to mediate are different from agreements to agree. The validity of the latter depends on the parties agreeing on an essential term; the former comprises an

---

[10] France and Germany are two jurisdictions that appear to have adopted this approach: see Alexander (n 3) 189.

[11] (2002) 54 NSWLR 503, [70] (Einstein J). The clause dealt with the submission of disputes for expert determination. As the nomination procedure was uncertain, the court concluded that the nomination procedure could not be severed and consequently the clause failed in its entirety. See also Boulle (n 3) 618–19, 640; Alexander (n 3) 188–90.

[12] See the English cases *Courtney & Fairbairn Ltd* v. *Tolaini Bros (Hotels) Ltd* [1975] 1 WLR 297; *Paul Smith Ltd* v. *H & S International Holding Inc* [1991] 2 Lloyd's Rep 127; *Walford* v. *Miles* [1992] 2 WLR 174.

agreement to resolve issues through a recognised process and the involvement of a neutral third party who facilitates the parties' negotiations. The jurisprudence of the courts in New South Wales builds on these differences.[13]

In *Hooper Bailie Associated Ltd* v. *Natcon Group Pty Ltd*,[14] the plaintiff claimed that the defendants had not complied with the conciliation requirement under the contract and sought a stay of the arbitration proceedings instituted by the defendants. The Court granted the stay, finding that the agreement to conciliate was sufficiently certain about the conduct required of the parties. Justice Giles held that an agreement to conciliate (or mediate) was more than an agreement to negotiate in good faith: it was a commitment to participate in a process that may result in an agreed settlement which would make the need for further proceedings redundant. Refusing to follow 'uncompromising' English precedents, Giles J distinguished between reaching an agreement and participating in a process which, despite the parties' initial reluctance, may result in an agreement.[15]

The *Hooper Bailie* decision in Australia became a watershed case for the enforcement of mediation clauses where the clause provides a sufficiently certain procedural framework in which the parties can operate. The requirements in that case included the procedure for the appointment of the conciliator, other procedural matters, the possibility of legal representation, information exchange and evidential matters, and the Court held that a solicitor's letter setting out the procedure established a 'clear structure' for the mediation.[16]

---

[13] See Boulle (n 3) 619–21. It has been suggested that, due to the differences between negotiation and mediation, mediation as a process exists to some extent as a structure that is independent of the parties themselves: see T Allen, *Mediation Law and Civil Practice* (2nd ed, Haywards Heath, Bloomsbury Professional 2019) 197.

[14] [1992] 28 NSWLR 194.

[15] ibid 206–8. This decision may be contrasted with *Elizabeth Bay Developments Pty Ltd* v. *Boral Building Services Pty Ltd* (1995) 36 NSWLR 709, also a decision of the Supreme Court of New South Wales. In it, Giles J, the same judge, found that the mediation clause in question lacked sufficient certainty to be enforceable as it provided that the parties should attempt to settle disputes by mediation 'administered by' a particular ADR organisation, but neither set out the procedure for the mediation in the clause nor clearly incorporated the rules or guidelines for mediation issued by that organisation. The clause also failed to identify the agreement that the parties were required to sign when a dispute arose. For a critique of the case, see Boulle (n 3) 621–22; Alexander (n 3) 195–96. See also *Con Kallergis* v. *Calshonie* [1998] 14 BCL 201, where Hayne J believed that an agreement to negotiate would be enforceable if the process contained within it has an identifiable end, rather than a contractual requirement to negotiate in order to achieve agreement.

[16] *Hooper Bailie* (n 14) 209.

The decision in *Hooper Bailie* was considered in *Aiton Australia Pty Ltd v. Transfield Pty Ltd*,[17] where a stay of proceedings was sought on the basis of a mediation clause. While there was no legislative basis for enforcing dispute resolution clauses other than those that provided for arbitration, Einstein J believed that an agreement to conciliate or mediate was enforceable, provided it was expressed as a condition precedent to litigation or arbitration. Consequently, the clause, like the arbitration clause considered in *Scott* v. *Avery*,[18] did not attempt to oust the jurisdiction of the Court. The plaintiff argued that the dispute resolution clause was unenforceable because it was merely an agreement to negotiate, rather than an agreement to conciliate and/or mediate, and because it contained a good faith requirement. Justice Einstein rejected the plaintiff's argument, holding that, as the concept of good faith depends on the context and factual circumstances of each case, the provision of a framework would ensure sufficient certainty and ensure that the clause was not an agreement to reach agreement. He held that the reason for the unenforceability of the mediation clause was the uncertainty about the allocation of the mediator's costs.[19]

The absence of a sufficient degree of certainty has also proved fatal to the enforcement of mediation clauses in the USA.[20] In *Cumberland & York Distributors* v. *Coors Brewing Co*,[21] a distributorship agreement provided that mediation was a condition precedent to binding arbitration, but did not set any limit on the duration of mediation. The Court refused to stay the proceedings, holding that the absence of a time limit on mediation could result in a delay of the final resolution of the dispute.[22]

---

[17] [1999] NSWSC 996.

[18] [1856] 10 ER 1121. The case held that arbitration was a condition precedent, rather than an alternative, to litigation. In a mediation context, the parties effectively covenant that no right of court action will accrue until mediation is attempted.

[19] *Aiton Australia* (n 17) [153], [174].

[20] See E M Weldon and P W Kelly, 'Prelitigation Dispute Resolution Clauses: Getting the Benefit of your Bargain' (2011) 31(1) *Franchise Law Journal* 28. See also *AMF Inc* v. *Brunswick Corp* 621 F Supp 456, 462 (ED NY 1985), a watershed precedent where a US court recognised and enforced an advisory dispute resolution clause.

[21] [2002] US Dist LEXIS 1962 (D Me 2002).

[22] See *Re Orkin Exterminating Co Inc* No 01-00-00730-CV, 2000 WL 1752900 (Tex App 30 November 2000) where the court order required compliance with a dispute resolution clause that specified four hours of mediation as a condition precedent to arbitration. See also *HIM Portland LLC* v. *Devito Builders Inc* 317 F 3d 41 (1st Cir 2003) and *Kemiron Atlantic Inc* v. *Aguakem International Inc* 290 F 3d 1287 (11 Cir 2002) where mediation appeared as a condition precedent to arbitration in the relevant contracts, and the courts confirmed that mediation must take place before arbitration. See also *Lakeland Fire District* v. *East Area General Contractors Inc* 791 NYS 2d 594 (App Div NY 2005)

In *Fluor Enterprises Inc* v. *Solutia Inc*,[23] the Court held that the plaintiff had fulfilled a pre-litigation mediation requirement by simply selecting a mediator; consequently, filing an action after that was appropriate, despite the mediation not having commenced. The contract provided that the parties should attempt to resolve the dispute in accordance with the Centre for Public Resources Model Procedure for Mediation of Business Disputes. If the matter was not resolved within thirty days of the commencement of the procedure, then either party could initiate litigation. The Court held that mediation 'procedure' rather than mediation 'proceeding' referred to the first step of the procedure, which was selecting a mediator.[24]

However, numerous US courts have taken a more supportive approach to the enforcement of mediation clauses. In *Brosnan* v. *Dry Cleaning Station Inc*,[25] a franchise agreement required that disputes be mediated for a minimum of four hours before the initiation of any legal action. Enforcing the mediation provision, the Court ordered a dismissal without prejudice of the court action.[26] The Court adopted an even stricter approach in *Tattoo Art Inc* v. *TAT International LLC*,[27] where mediation appeared in the contract as a condition precedent to court action. While Tattoo Art sought to negotiate the dispute, it did not seek mediation before filing the action. The Court granted the motion to dismiss even though Tattoo Art requested mediation after filing the action. The mediation did not happen as the defendant did not respond to the request to mediate.

A similarly strict approach was adopted in *DeValk Lincoln Mercury Inc* v. *Ford Motor Co*,[28] where the defendants requested summary judgment,

---

    where the court upheld a stay of arbitration, concluding that mediation was a contractual condition precedent to arbitration that had been complied with.

[23] 147 F Supp 2d 648 (SD Tex 2001).

[24] ibid 650.

[25] [2008] US Dist LEXIS 44678 (ND Cal 2008). See also *Fe-Ri Construction Inc* v. *Intelligroup Inc* 218 F Supp 2d 168 (DPR 2002) where the action was dismissed without prejudice to enforce the dispute resolution clause that included the option of either mediation or arbitration.

[26] While a stay of proceedings effectively suspends the proceeding until the mediation clause is complied with, 'without prejudice' results in the legal claim being dismissed such that parties must file a new claim if mediation fails to result in a comprehensive settlement. The latter approach is similar to that in France and Germany, where courts may reject the initiation of legal proceedings as 'temporarily inadmissible' where the litigants are in breach of a mediation clause, requiring them to file a new claim. Hence, a stay of proceedings may be more efficient in terms of time and costs: see Alexander (n 3) 203–6.

[27] 711 F Supp 2d 645 (ED Va 2010).

[28] 811 F 2d 326 (7th Cir 1987).

in part due to the plaintiffs' failure to comply with the pre-litigation mediation clause. The District Court granted summary judgment, and this was affirmed by the Seventh Circuit. The appellate court held that this mediation clause was straightforward and required the parties to appeal any protest, controversy or claim to mediation, and further stated that mediation was a condition precedent to any other remedy available at law. It also rejected the plaintiffs' argument that they substantially complied with the mediation clause because the clause specifically stated that it was a condition precedent to litigation. Although the plaintiffs fulfilled some of the purposes of mediation, such as making Ford aware of their claims by sending four separate letters to Ford and spending several months negotiating with them, they did not actually mediate and, therefore, did not fulfil the condition precedent. Similarly, in *Philadelphia Housing Authority* v. *Dore & Associates Contracting Inc*,[29] the Federal District Court of Eastern Pennsylvania granted summary judgment and a stay of proceedings where the Housing Authority failed to comply with the dispute resolution clause that included mediation.

While some US courts have adopted the extreme measure of dismissing actions for a failure to comply with a mediation clause, others have taken a 'middle ground' approach, such as staying the action. In *CB Richard Ellis Inc* v. *American Environmental Waste Management*,[30] the US District Court for the Eastern District of New York held that it was appropriate to stay the proceedings and compel the mediation because the mediation clause in the disputed agreement was sufficient to manifest the parties' intention to attempt to settle any dispute by reference to mediation.

Similarly, in *N-Tron Corp* v. *Rockwell Automation Inc*,[31] the contract required that disputes relating to a co-operative marketing programme be mediated before court action. When a dispute arose, N-Tron filed a court action without complying with the pre-litigation dispute resolution provision to negotiate, then mediate the dispute. The Court agreed that compliance with the provision was a condition precedent but believed that dismissal would unfairly prejudice the plaintiff, as it would essentially be a dismissal with prejudice,[32] prohibiting the parties from ever litigating the

---

[29] 111 F Supp 2d 663 (ED Pa 2000).
[30] [1998] US Dist LEXIS 20064.
[31] [2010] US Dist LEXIS 14130 (SD Ala 2010).
[32] However, some US courts have dismissed actions with prejudice for failure to comply with a dispute resolution clause. See *Gray & Associates LLC* v. *Ernst & Young LLP* No 24-C-02-002963, 2003 WL 23497702 (Md Cir Ct 11 June 2003), where the complaint was

issues due to an expired statute of limitations period. It effectively enforced the dispute resolution provision but simultaneously protected the plaintiff's right to have its claims ultimately heard in court.

3.3.2.1   A Certain Process

A failure to unambiguously define the process has proved fatal to the enforcement of mediation clauses in the USA. In *Ex parte Mountain Heating & Cooling Inc*,[33] the provision was unenforceable as the clause provided that disputes were to be settled by arbitration under the Construction Industry Mediation Rules of the American Arbitration Association. In *Forte* v. *Ameriplan Corp*,[34] the Court refused to enforce a clause that provided that mediation was a precondition to court action but that also incorporated by reference an employee manual that made disputes subject to arbitration. In some instances, the use of the word 'mediation' with 'binding' and 'mandatory' has led to decisions that parties intended to arbitrate their disputes.[35] However, some courts have refused to interpret the clause in this way.[36]

When considering the process to be followed by the parties, Australian courts have largely reflected the view that there should be no stage in the process that requires the parties to come to an agreement regarding a course of action, such as the appointment of the third party, before the process can continue.[37] However, a more liberal, or ADR-friendly, approach was adopted by the Victorian Supreme Court in *Computershare Ltd* v. *Perpetual Registrars Ltd (No 2)*.[38] In this case, a stay of proceedings was

---

dismissed, and the parties ordered to comply with their mediation/arbitration contractual provisions. See also J R Coben and P N Thompson, 'Disputing Irony: A Systematic Look at Litigation About Mediation' (2006) 11 *Harvard Negotiation Law Review* 43, 109.

[33] 867 So 2d 1112 (Ala 2003).

[34] No 05-01-00921-CV, 2002 WL 576608 (Tex App 18 April 2002).

[35] *High Valley Homes* v. *Fudge*, No. 03-01-00726-CV (Tex App April 17 2003).

[36] In *Oliver Design Group* v. *Westside Deutscher Frauen-Verein* No 81120, 2002 WL 31839158 (Ohio App 19 December 2002), the trial court decision was reversed and a stay on the action pending arbitration was refused, as the Court did not believe 'binding mediation' should be equated with arbitration. See also Coben and Thompson (n 32) 125–26.

[37] See *Banabelle Electrical* (n 11); *Heart Research Institute Ltd* v. *Psiron Ltd* [2002] NSWSC 646.

[38] [2000] VSC 233. The clause provided, with clear timelines, that the parties' representatives would attempt to settle any disputes, failing which the parties' CEOs would attempt to settle any disputes. Should this prove unsuccessful, the parties must endeavour in good faith to resolve any disputes, or to agree on a process to resolve all or at least part of the dispute without arbitration or court proceedings (e.g. mediation, conciliation or expert

granted to comply with an alternative dispute resolution (ADR) clause before litigation proceeded, despite the fact that the actual ADR process was left to be agreed upon by the parties when a dispute occurred.

The English view that agreements to agree or to negotiate are unenforceable for lack of certainty was diminished by the House of Lords in *Channel Tunnel Group Ltd* v. *Balfour Beatty Construction Ltd.*[39] In this case, a clause provided that disputes should be referred to a panel and if either party was dissatisfied with the outcome, it could have the panel's decision reviewed and revised by arbitration. The Court held that such a clause can only operate if it is well defined and if reasonable time limits for the completion of each stage of dispute resolution are set, otherwise the parties may be involved in a process that is too lengthy and uncertain. The Court exercised its discretionary power to stay proceedings to give effect to the clause which was 'nearly an immediately effective agreement to arbitrate, albeit not quite'.[40]

Cable & Wireless v. *IBM United Kingdom Ltd*[41] was a significant judgment in England following the introduction of the Civil Procedure Rules. An ADR clause that specifically referred disputes to mediation was vague about the nature of the procedure that should be used, referring broadly to rules of the Centre for Effective Dispute Resolution. The claimant argued that the ADR clause was unenforceable because it lacked certainty, imposing no more than an agreement to negotiate. The Court believed that the dispute resolution structure contained in the agreement left no doubt that it was the mutual intention of the parties that litigation should be engaged in as a last resort. It concluded that the mere issuing of proceedings was not inconsistent with the simultaneous conduct of an ADR procedure, or with a mutual intention to have the issue ultimately decided by the courts if the ADR procedure failed to resolve the dispute. The clause was held to be contractually enforceable, and a stay of the proceedings was granted while the parties complied with the ADR clause. Justice Colman stated:

> ... I would wish to add that contractual references to ADR which did not include provision for an identifiable procedure would not necessarily fail to

determination). This included the selection and payment of any third party and the involvement of any dispute resolution organisation, any procedural rules, the timetable, including any exchange of relevant information and documents, and the place where meetings would be held: see at [3]. See also the commentary of D Spencer, 'Uncertainty and ADR Clauses: The Victorian View' (2001) 12(4) *Australasian Dispute Resolution Journal* 214–18; Boulle (n 3) 626–27.

[39] [1993] AC 334, [1993] 1 All ER 664.
[40] [1993] 1 All ER 664, 678 (Mustill LJ).
[41] [2002] 2 All ER (Comm) 1041.

be enforceable by reason of uncertainty. An important consideration would
be whether the obligation to mediate was expressed in unqualified and
mandatory terms ... In principle however, where there is an unqualified
reference to ADR, a sufficiently certain and definable minimum duty of
participation should not be hard to find. ... The reference to ADR is
analogous to an agreement to arbitrate. As such, it represents a free standing
agreement ancillary to the main contract and capable of being enforced by
a stay of the proceedings or by injunction absent any pending proceedings.[42]

Justice Colman insisted that this was a reasonable case to mediate and
that parties entering into an ADR agreement must recognise that mediation as a tool for dispute resolution is not designed to achieve solutions
which reflect the precise legal rights and obligations of the parties, but
solutions that are mutually commercially acceptable at the time of the
mediation. If the Court declined to enforce contractual references to
ADR on the grounds of intrinsic uncertainty, he believed it would fly in
the face of public policy as expressed in the Civil Procedure Rules.

In the subsequent English case of *Sulamerica CIA Nacional de Seugros SA
v. Enesa Enenharia SA*,[43] it was argued that the mediation clause in an
insurance contract was a condition precedent to arbitration, which the
insured claimed was breached by the insurer by instituting arbitral proceedings without attempting mediation. The Court of Appeal agreed with the
trial judge, Cooke J, that the provisions did not give rise to a binding
obligation to mediate. Comparing the facts to *Cable & Wireless*,[44] the
Court said the clause did not set out any defined mediation process or
refer to the procedure of a specific mediation provider.[45] There was no
obligation to commence or participate in a mediation process. The clause
merely contained an undertaking to seek to have the dispute resolved
amicably by mediation and did not provide for the process by which that
was to be undertaken. At most, the Court believed it may amount to an
obligation to invite the other party to join in an ad hoc mediation where
a party is contemplating referring a dispute to arbitration, but even this
obligation was uncertain and impossible to enforce.

While the Court was unwilling to 'define the minimum ingredients
necessary'[46] for an enforceable mediation clause, believing that each case
must be considered on its own terms, it is clear that clauses that purport to

---

[42] ibid 1051.
[43] [2012] EWCA Civ 638.
[44] *Cable & Wireless* (n 41).
[45] The Court also referred to *Holloway* v. *Chancery Mead Ltd* [2007] EWHC 2495 (TCC);
Sulamerica (n 43) [36] (Moore-Bick LJ).
[46] *Sulamerica* (n 43) [35] (Moore-Bick LJ).

require the parties to engage in ad hoc mediation are likely to fail due to uncertainty. Special care must be taken when drafting mediation clauses to ensure they are effective and enforceable. Three elements are needed: first, a sufficiently certain process ensuring that there should not be a need for agreement at any stage before matters can proceed; second, a defined administrative process for selecting and remunerating the mediator; and third, sufficiently certain details of the mediation process, such as the model to be followed.[47]

3.3.3 Completeness

The issue of completeness is closely related to the issue of certainty (incompleteness effectively being a form of uncertainty) but has been of less practical significance. Contractual completeness requires that the contract comprise all the important parts of the transaction. Consistent with general contractual principles, an agreement will be void for incompleteness where it does not refer to an important part of the transaction. In *Triarno Pty Ltd* v. *Triden Contractors Ltd*,[48] an Australian court held that it had no jurisdiction to create procedures to be followed where a dispute resolution clause provided for binding expert determination but failed to refer to procedures to follow or to the rights the parties were to have in the process. The traditional view seems to be that courts are not inclined to imply into contracts terms about procedures to be followed; however, increased use of and familiarity with mediation may result in courts being less concerned with the issue of incompleteness.[49]

The greater the parties' control over the procedure, the choice of mediator and the content and the effect of the result, the less need there is to restrict and police the validity of mediation clauses and agreements to mediate.[50] In many jurisdictions where mediation is well established, it is likely that courts would treat them as fully enforceable as a matter of public policy, if for no other reason.[51]

---

[47] *Holloway* (n 45) [81] (Ramsay J), following Einstein J in *Aiton Australia* (n 17).
[48] (1992) 10 BCL 305.
[49] Provided this does not amount to substantial incompleteness: see Boulle (n 3) 633–34; Alexander (n 3) 191–92.
[50] See F Steffek and others, 'Guide for Regulating Dispute Resolution (GRDR): Principles and Comments' in F Steffek and others (eds), *Regulating Dispute Resolution: ADR and Access to Justice at the Crossroads* (Oxford, Hart Publishing 2013) 20–21.
[51] See Allen (n 13) 38. In Australia, before mediation clauses were deemed insufficiently certain and complete in cases such as *Elizabeth Bay Developments* (n 15), such clauses had

3.3.4   Attempts to Oust the Jurisdiction of the Courts

It is a basic constitutional principle in modern democracies that courts are accessible to people where a dispute is appropriate for adjudication by a court. It is not possible to 'contract out' of this right. If a contract provision were to declare that mediation is the exclusive alternative to litigation, the clause would be deemed unenforceable due to it conflicting with public policy in attempting to oust the jurisdiction of the courts.[52]

A recurring theme of some of the jurisprudence that has emanated from England, and an issue that practitioners and judiciaries in other jurisdictions should remain mindful of, is concern that the more vigilant the judiciary becomes in encouraging mediation, the more it may appear that mediation is becoming compulsory. The more obligatory mediation appears to be, the greater the likelihood of allegations that it violates constitutional and human rights.[53]

Lord Justice Dyson, in delivering the *Halsey v. Milton Keynes NHS Trust* judgment, remarked:

> [T]o oblige truly unwilling parties to refer their disputes to mediation would be to impose an unacceptable obstruction on their right of access to the courts ... and, therefore, a violation of article 6 [of the European Convention of Human Rights].[54]

He subsequently refined his remarks on the issue of compulsion. He conceded that 'in and of itself compulsory mediation does not breach article 6',[55] based on the judgment of the European Court of Justice in *Alassini v. Telecom Italia SpA.*[56] In that case, the Court determined that a provision in Italian law that required parties to submit their disputes to a form of out-of-court settlement, or they would lose their right to bring

---

been effectively used in hundreds of disputes, as they carried moral and commercial force, even if they were not legally effective: see Alexander (n 3) 172.

[52] See L Boulle and M Nesic, *Mediation: Principles, Process, Practice* (London, Butterworths Law 2001) 477; Alexander (n 3) 184–87.

[53] See R Feehily, 'Creeping Compulsion to Mediate: The Constitution and the Convention' (2018) 69(2) *Northern Ireland Legal Quarterly* 127.

[54] [2004] EWCA Civ 576 [9].

[55] See Lord Dyson, 'A Word on Halsey v Milton Keynes' (2011) 77(3) *Arbitration* 337, 338–39 (3rd Annual Mediation Symposium of the Chartered Institute of Arbitration, London, October 2010). See also Lord Dyson, 'Halsey 10 Years On: The Decision Revisited' in *Justice: Continuity and Change* (Oxford, Hart Publishing 2018) 381–83.

[56] Case C–317-320/08 *Alassini* v. *Telecom Italia SpA* [2010] 3 CMLR 17. See Chapter 7 at Section 7.5.

judicial proceedings, was not in breach of article 6 of the European Convention on Human Rights.

Other leading English jurists, such as Lightman J, Lord Phillips CJ and Lord Justice Clarke MR, have also commented that the basis for an order for mediation does not interfere with the right to trial, as it does not propose mediation in lieu of a trial, but merely imposes a delay. Lord Phillips, a former head of the judiciary in England and Wales and founding President of the UK Supreme Court, referred specifically to Dyson LJ's judgment in *Halsey*[57] and proceeded to say:

> Parties should be given strong encouragement to attempt mediation before resorting to litigation. And if they commence litigation, there should be built into the process a stage at which the court can require them to attempt mediation.[58]

Sir Anthony Clarke supports this view, pointing to the fact that compulsory mediation occurs in other jurisdictions, such as Germany, Belgium and Greece, with no successful article 6 challenges.[59]

Lord Justice Jackson rejected compulsory mediation in his *Review of Civil Litigation Costs: Final Report*, although, consistent with the rationale in *Halsey*, he supported sanctions against those who unreasonably refuse to mediate.[60] Despite such judicial clarification, some contend that the courts in England do in fact compel mediation surreptitiously. While the official position is that mediation is England is not, and should not be made, compulsory, it seems that judges, supported by the Civil Procedure Rules, are making it clear to parties that they expect them to engage in mediation; and parties, mindful of the potential adverse cost consequences, feel compelled to engage in the process.[61]

---

[57] *Halsey* (n 54).

[58] See Lord Phillips, 'Alternative Dispute Resolution: An English Viewpoint' (2008) 74 *Arbitration* 406, 418. Justice Lightman was one of the harshest critics of aspects of the *Halsey* judgment, in particular, the suggestion that a requirement to mediate would be a breach of article 6 of the ECHR, which he described as 'clearly wrong and unreasonable': see Sir Gavin Lightman, 'Mediation: An Approximation to Justice' (2007) 73(4) *Arbitration* 400.

[59] See Lord Justice Clarke, 'The Future of Civil Mediation' (2008) 74(4) *Arbitration* 419, 421.

[60] See Lord Justice Jackson, *Review of Civil Litigation Costs: Final Report* (Ministry of Justice, December 2009) ('Jackson Report') xxiii.

[61] This issue was exacerbated by austerity and the pressure on court resources: see M Ahmed, 'Implied Compulsory Mediation' (2012) 31(2) *Civil Justice Quarterly* 151, 164–70. Some view mediation as a new prerequisite to trial: see L Mulcahy, 'The Collective Interest in Private Dispute Resolution' (2012) 33(1) *Oxford Journal of Legal Studies* 59, 69. See also Chapter 7 at Section 7.5 for a discussion on conduct, costs and compulsion.

A contractual obligation to attempt mediation to resolve a dispute would consequently not be an attempt to oust the jurisdiction of the courts. It is important in this context that mediation clauses are drafted to ensure that mediation is reflected as a condition precedent to and not an alternative to litigation, so that if mediation fails to resolve the dispute, the parties are free to go to court.[62]

3.3.5   Other Policy Considerations Affecting the Enforceability of Mediation Clauses

A mediation clause can potentially be challenged on the basis that it fails to uphold the requirements of procedural fairness: for example, where the parties are unable to prepare or access essential information or where the nominated mediator has a conflict of interests.[63] It seems that in circumstances where mediation is combined with arbitration and the same person acts in both (med-arb),[64] the possibility of a successful challenge is greater, even though the focus of such a claim is likely to be on the arbitral aspect of the process. As noted in Section 3.3.3, public policy in many jurisdictions has moved towards favouring the enforcement of mediation clauses. Courts must essentially engage in a balancing exercise between ensuring there is an acceptable level of certainty to satisfy legal policy and facilitating a degree of flexible uncertainty to satisfy mediation practice. In light of this there are policy considerations other than legal factors that favour the enforceability of mediation clauses that could prove influential when courts consider enforcement. In *Computershare*,[65] an Australian court granted a stay of proceedings to facilitate the enforcement of an ADR clause, even though the procedures to be followed for any of the ADR processes mentioned in the clause had yet to be agreed between the parties. According to Warren J: 'Logically, parties cannot stipulate principles upon which mediation processes must

---

[62] See *Scott* v. *Avery* (n 18). In some jurisdictions such as Australia, where there is doubt about the meaning of a clause that purports to oust the court's jurisdiction, the courts will interpret the clause narrowly to give effect to the parties' intentions: see Boulle (n 3) 634–37.

[63] In the US case *Garrett* v. *Hooters-Toledo* 295 F Supp 2d 774 (ND Ohio 2003), the restrictive mediation clause requirements were deemed unenforceable due to unconscionability. They required employees to request mediation within ten days, failure to do so foreclosed the claim, and mediation was required in Kentucky rather than Ohio where the employees worked: see Coben and Thompson (n 32) 125.

[64] See Chapter 1 at Section 1.8.3 for an overview of hybrid dispute resolution options.

[65] *Computershare* (n 38).

produce an outcome. Of its very nature, the parties must negotiate and hold discussions to find their own solution'.[66] Such cases show that there are instances where the certainty requirement should be relaxed in favour of a policy supporting party autonomy and the progressive principle of contractual freedom.[67]

3.3.6   Providing the Required Certainty

While public policy in many jurisdictions has developed in favour of upholding mediation clauses where possible, some guidance can be gleaned from the cases discussed to help ensure mediation clauses have the required certainty.

3.3.6.1   Avoiding 'Agreements to Agree'

Parties should not leave any element in the clause to be agreed on in the future unless there is a fallback arrangement, as this will amount to an 'agreement to agree'. For example, if parties agree that they will select their mediator if a dispute arises, they should allow for the possibility that they may not agree by providing that a mediation service provider will make the appointment in the absence of agreement. The method for selecting other participants in the mediation, such as experts, could also be specified. Provisions requiring participation 'in good faith' should be viewed cautiously to avoid the suggestion that they amount to an agreement to reach agreement.

3.3.6.2   External Documents

Where terms are imported into the contract from an external document, such as mediation procedures, codes of conduct or service provider standards, the document should be annexed to the agreement or a specified document should be referenced, and there should be no inconsistency between this document and the mediation clause. Clarity and certainty should be apparent, or able to be readily derived, from such extrinsic documents expressly referred to in the mediation clause and the contractual provisions should be comprehensive and complete. For example, there should be no ambiguity about the scope of application such as the types of claims covered or those that are carved out. The timing of mediation efforts (such as the minimum or maximum time that

---

[66] ibid [14].
[67] See Boulle (n 3) 637–39; Alexander (n 3) 196–97.

parties should attempt to mediate the dispute) should be made clear along with how and when the mediation will be initiated.[68]

3.3.6.3   Mediation Costs, Venue, Timetables, Procedures, Law and Language

The mediation clause should specify who is responsible for payment of the costs of mediation (including the mediator's fees), the place and venue of the mediation (or a method to select it), and the procedures to be followed by the parties when setting up and undertaking the mediation. The timetable should also be referred to in the agreement. This should have some inbuilt flexibility to provide for mediator discretion where the mediator believes that variations to the timetable may prove useful as the mediation progresses, as with the use of caucus sessions, where the mediator meets each party privately in an effort to move the process along. As an alternative to detailing how the process will work in the mediation clause, the contract could incorporate by reference the mediation procedure of an organisation providing mediation services. Such a procedure is likely to have been legally tested and consequently to be effective. The applicable procedural and substantive law should also be included, particularly for cross-border mediation clauses. In an international cross-cultural context, the language of the mediation should be specified.[69]

3.3.6.4   Non-ouster Principle, Emergency Provisional Relief and Limitation Periods

The non-ouster principle should be observed by requiring that the parties first submit their dispute to mediation before instituting court proceedings or proceeding to arbitration. The provision should refer explicitly and unambiguously to mediation as a condition precedent to litigation or arbitration. This will help to ensure that the mediation clause cannot be perceived as ousting the jurisdiction of the courts. It also makes it clear and certain that the parties have agreed that they will attempt mediation before court proceedings or arbitration. As mediation is to be a condition precedent to obtaining relief in court or proceeding to arbitration, issues such as the possible need for emergency provisional relief and the

---

[68] See also Weldon and Kelly (n 20) 32–33.
[69] See Boulle (n 3) 639; Alexander (n 3) 172–74, 199–200. See also C Jarrosson, 'Legal Issues Raised by ADR' in Ingen-Housz (ed) (n 1) 163–78.

possible suspension of the statute of limitations[70] during mediation should be considered.[71]

3.3.6.5   Comprehensive Signed Writing Provision

In addition to providing that settlement terms reached will only be binding when set out in writing and signed by the parties, the mediation clause should provide that any variations, waivers or collateral agreements extending or amending this requirement must also be in writing and signed by the parties in order to be enforceable.[72]

3.3.6.6   Penalty Clause

The contract could also include a penalty (such as the forfeiture of lawyers' fees, and costs) for not engaging in mediation. This would serve as a deterrent to a party who may opt to litigate rather than mediate first by clearly stating the consequences for a failure to comply.[73]

---

[70] Also known as 'litigation limitation periods' and 'prescription periods'.

[71] This would be subject to national law finding such a provision enforceable: see Crown (n 4) 5. Many legal systems provide that the commencement of mediation results in a suspension or interruption of limitation periods. A suspension means that the limitation period does not run for the duration of the mediation and resumes once the mediation is terminated. An interruption means that the limitation period will run again from the beginning once the interruption is over. Some jurisdictions are more prescriptive in limiting the time frame available. Such rules are helpful where the parties are too far apart to agree on this issue: see Hopt and Steffek (n 2) 34–37; Alexander (n 3) 294–300. For example, article 8(1) of the EU Mediation Directive (n 89) provides: 'Member States shall ensure that parties who choose mediation in an attempt to settle a dispute are not subsequently prevented from initiating judicial proceedings or arbitration in relation to that dispute by the expiry of limitation or prescription periods during the mediation process'. A footnote to article 5 of the Mediation Model Law (n 92), covering the commencement of mediation proceedings, suggests the following text for states wishing to adopt a provision on the suspension of limitation periods: '1. When the mediation proceedings commence, the running of the limitation period regarding the claim that is the subject matter of the mediation is suspended. 2. Where the mediation proceedings have terminated without a settlement agreement, the limitation period resumes running from the time the mediation ended without a settlement agreement.' Hence, suspension of limitation periods is preferred over interruption. The text was included as a footnote, rather than a provision, in the Mediation Model Law so as not to interfere with existing procedural rules regarding the suspension or interruption of limitation periods: see P Binder, *International Commercial Arbitration and Mediation in UNCITRAL Model Law Jurisdictions* (4th ed, Alphen aan den Rijn, Kluwer Law International 2019) 585–89. Identifying the commencement and termination of mediation can prove critical where the end of the limitation period is imminent. See Chapter 4 at Section 4.3.2 for a discussion on the temporal contours of the mediation process.

[72] See *Universal Satspace (North America) LLC* v. *Republic of Kenya* (High Court (QB), Teare J, 20 December 2013) discussed further in Section 3.6.

[73] See also Weldon and Kelly (n 20) 32–33.

3.3.7   The Certainty of Compliance

No firm authority exists on what is required from parties to comply with the obligations in an enforceable mediation clause. Criteria could include attendance at the mediation, disclosure of information to the other side, compliance with the procedural directions of the mediator, engagement in constructive negotiations until there is good reason to conclude them and participation at every stage with reason and in a spirit of good faith. However, assessing compliance with such requirements would involve difficult subjective judgments by outsiders to the mediation and there would also be difficulties in defining the obligations of the parties clearly.

In the Australian case *Elizabeth Bay Developments Pty Ltd* v. *Boral Building Services Pty Ltd*,[74] Giles J expressed difficulties with the 'good faith' requirement in a mediation clause. He considered that the presence or absence of good faith was not the main difficulty; rather, it was the tension between negotiation – in which a party is self-interested – and the maintenance of good faith.[75] However, this approach overlooks the differences between unassisted, adversarial negotiations and mediated negotiations where a trained mediator can help the parties with collaborative, interest-based bargaining. It may be easier to construe that parties had acted in bad faith or unreasonably (for example, by sitting silent throughout the mediation) than that they had acted in good faith and reasonably; there are also practical difficulties in establishing proper compliance with mediation clauses given the private and confidential nature of the process.[76]

Experience from England suggests that few inherently unreasonable parties restrain their unreasonableness to circumstances where mediation confidentiality restricts judicial access to what transpired at the

---

[74] *Elizabeth Bay Developments* (n 15). See also the English case *Halifax Financial Services Ltd* v. *Intuitive Systems Ltd* [1999] 1 All ER 303, 305, where the Court was unwilling to enforce a contract provision which provided that, in the event of a dispute arising, the parties 'would meet in good faith and attempt to resolve the dispute without recourse to legal proceedings' and provided for structured negotiations with the assistance of a neutral or a mediator. Such decisions can be characterised as anachronistic and inconsistent with the approach of the English courts – and the trend internationally – of giving effect to dispute resolution mechanisms agreed by the parties. This case was decided before the adoption of the Civil Procedure Rules and would likely be decided differently now: see Mistelis (n 2) 163.

[75] (1995) 36 NSWLR 709 (Giles J). However, as Einstein J remarked in *Aiton Australia* (n 17), 'maintenance of good faith in a negotiating process is not inconsistent with having regard to self-interest': at [81]. See also *United Group Rail Services Ltd* v. *Rail Corporation (NSW)* [2009] NSWCA 177.

[76] See Boulle and Nesic (n 52) 483.

mediation. Consequently, there can be sufficient evidence of unreasonable conduct available to a court without needing to intrude into the confidentiality of the mediation. In terms of assessing behaviour, the US experience suggests that only the narrowest of good faith requirements, such as compulsory attendance at the mediation, proves workable in practice.[77]

3.3.8   Waiver and Remedies for Breach of Mediation Clauses

Parties may agree to waive their pre-existing agreement to mediate and proceed directly to court or arbitration. Where a mediation clause is not properly complied with, the issue of breach of contract arises as does, ultimately, how the breach can be remedied.

3.3.8.1   Waiver

It is open to parties to agree to bypass a pre-existing mediation clause and proceed directly to court or arbitration. This may be done, for example, where mediation is not deemed suitable by them because a judicial precedent is required, or the relationship has become acrimonious. Although there are no formal requirements for waiver, where the parties agree to waive compliance with a mediation clause, they should document this in a written agreement for clarity and evidential purposes. Once the clause has been waived it cannot be enforced.[78]

3.3.8.2   Dismissal of Court Actions, Injunctions and Summary Judgment

As noted in Section 3.3.2, some US courts have gone so far as to dismiss court actions for a failure to comply with a mediation clause. Dismissing court actions would appear to be the most common way to try to enforce a mediation clause at a federal level. US courts are divided between those that will dismiss an action and those that will grant a stay of proceedings.[79] A prudent approach is to suggest seeking dismissal and, in the alternative, should the court not grant this, a stay of proceedings until there is compliance with the clause. While in most cases a dismissal or stay will be sought because the non-compliant party has issued

---

[77] See Chapter 7 at Section 7.6.1.

[78] In France, for example, parties may waive mediation clauses by conduct, provided the conduct is clear; the mere failure to implement a clause is insufficient: see Alexander (n 3) 201.

[79] See Section 3.3.8.5 for a discussion on stay of proceedings.

proceedings, an injunction may be an option in circumstances where proceedings are not pending.[80]

As noted in Section 3.3.2 summary judgment has also been granted to enforce a mediation clause in the USA. For reasons of cost, it is often in a party's interest to seek a dismissal of the action or a stay rather than waiting for summary judgment. However, if the issue was not raised at an earlier stage and costs are not a significant factor, summary judgment may be an option.[81]

3.3.8.3   Specific Performance

Another possible remedy involves specific performance, effectively an order to perform the contractual obligation contained within the mediation clause. However, the issue arises whether a court could compel participation in a mediation. There have traditionally been difficulties in granting this discretionary equitable remedy for breach of a mediation clause: it will not be ordered in circumstances where a close personal relationship exists between the parties, where it would be difficult for the court to supervise performance, and equitable principles require that courts do not issue futile orders or orders that they cannot enforce.[82] Although US courts have granted orders of specific performance of mediation clauses, the general trend is against enforcement.[83]

3.3.8.4   Damages

An award of damages is a common remedy for a contractual breach. The award is usually intended to put plaintiffs into the position they would have been in had the defendants complied with their contractual obligations.

---

[80] See *Cable & Wireless* (n 41) 1051 (Colman J).

[81] See Weldon and Kelly (n 20) 32–33.

[82] Equity will not order specific performance of a dispute resolution clause, notwithstanding that it may satisfy the legal requirements necessary for the court to determine that the clause is enforceable. This is because supervision of performance pursuant to the clause would be untenable: see *Hooper Bailie* (n 14); *Banabelle Electrical* (n 11) [29] (Einstein J).

[83] See, e.g., *Fisher v. GE Medical Systems* 276 F Supp 2d 891 (MD Tenn 2003), where a motion to compel mediation under a tiered resolution process in an employment contract was granted. Given the increasing public policy in support of mandatory mediation in many jurisdictions, it has been suggested that courts should order specific performance of mediation clauses in appropriate circumstances. This contention is strengthened by the difficulty of awarding damages for a breach of a mediation clause (discussed in Section 3.3.8.4): see Boulle (n 3) 646; Alexander (n 3) 201–2.

In a mediation context, it can only be estimated what position the plaintiff would have been in had there been compliance with the mediation clause. It is uncertain whether there would have been a successful outcome, and if there was, what the terms would have been. The injury resulting from the breach could also be so unique that damages would not be an adequate remedy. A claim for damages may be limited to recovering the expenditure incurred where the party on the other side refused to participate in the process; in many cases this would be minimal or difficult to measure. A mediation clause could include a genuine pre-estimate of damages that would be suffered by either party if a breach occurred. The damages amount would have to be proportionate to the breach, which would be difficult to assess, and the courts could construe disproportionate liquidated damages clauses as unenforceable penalties. Despite such hypothetical endeavours, there would be difficulties in obtaining an award of damages from a court for breach of a mediation clause.[84]

3.3.8.5   Stay of Proceedings

In a stay of proceedings, a court declines to accept a matter for trial because the defendant has raised special circumstances: for example, the proceedings are vexatious, frivolous, amount to an abuse of process or lack a probable cause of action. This has proved to be an effective remedy. The court effectively achieves enforcement of the mediation clause by default by staying proceedings until the clause is complied with.[85] While courts are cautious about granting stays and exercise the power sparingly, as noted in Section 3.3.2, these general principles have been applied where a plaintiff commenced legal proceedings without first complying with an enforceable mediation clause.

In arbitration, a stay of proceedings is specifically legislated for in many jurisdictions. Mediation does not usually have this statutory remedy; consequently, it must be sought in terms of the principles outlined and the respective court's jurisdiction in relation to remedies. The defendant must establish grounds for the stay and the court must decide whether the plaintiff's actions constituted an abuse of process. In

---

[84] See Boulle (n 3) 646; Alexander (n 3) 208–9; Hopt and Steffek (n 2) 31.

[85] 'The court may, however, effectively achieve enforcement of the clause by default, by ordering that proceedings commenced in respect of a dispute subject to the clause be stayed or adjourned until such time as the process referred to in the clause is completed': *Banabelle Electrical* (n 11) [29] (Einstein J).

determining whether to grant the stay, the court will consider the validity and enforceability of the mediation clause, the practical effect of the order, and the likelihood that mediation would have led to a resolution of the dispute.[86]

A stay of proceedings is the most feasible option where one party is in breach of a valid mediation clause and there are no overriding considerations of public interest or private harm. As reflected in the jurisprudence discussed, this remedy has been supported in appropriate circumstances by courts in the USA, Australia and England. The granting of stays also seems to be supported by policy considerations, particularly in a commercial context, where parties have freely consented to a mediation clause.[87]

3.3.8.6   Denial of Lawyers' Fees

An alternative remedy may be provided for in the mediation clause itself. Some US courts have enforced provisions that deny an ultimate award of lawyers' fees if the party did not comply with a mediation clause. This is effectively a means of contractually sanctioning a party for non-compliance with a mediation clause rather than a means of ensuring compliance with it. In *Frei v. Davey*,[88] the Court considered a residential purchase agreement that contained a pre-litigation mediation provision. The clause provided if a party commenced an action without first attempting to resolve the matter through mediation or refused to mediate after a request had been made, then that party would not be entitled to recover lawyers' fees. The Daveys succeeded on appeal in the matter and sought lawyers' fees. The trial court granted the lawyers' fees motions, but the appellate court reversed the decision on the basis that the Daveys had not complied with the pre-litigation mediation provision.

---

[86] See the Australian cases *Hyslop* v. *Liverpool Hospital* (1998) 25 IR 280 and *Allco Steel (Queensland) Pty* v. *Torres Strait Gold Pty Ltd* (Supreme Court of Queensland, Master Horton, 12 March 1990) where a stay was refused in part because the court did not believe that the relevant ADR process would lead to a resolution: see Boulle and Nesic (n 52) 485. In some jurisdictions, where mediation clauses are deemed unenforceable, courts may still refer the matter to mediation: see Alexander (n 3) 203.

[87] See Boulle (n 3) 642–47; Alexander (n 3) 202–8.

[88] 124 Cal App 4th 1506, 1508 (2004). Some US states provide for the non-recovery of lawyers' fees where a party has failed to make reasonable efforts to settle the dispute. For example, Oregon statute OR Rev Stat 20.075 provides that 'the diligence of the parties in pursuing settlement of the dispute' is one of the factors that the court should consider in awarding attorney fees: see Crown (n 4) 5.

3.4 Regional and International Instruments

The EU Mediation Directive[89] and the Singapore Convention[90] do not include provisions covering the enforcement of mediation clauses.[91] The Mediation Model Law does not directly refer to the enforceability of mediation clauses and agreements to mediate, but it recognises their validity in article 14, which covers accessibility to judicial and arbitral proceedings before mediation is completed.[92]

Under article 5(2) of the Mediation Model Law, where a party who invited another party to mediate does not receive an acceptance of the invitation within thirty days or an alternative period specified in the invitation, the inviting party can treat this as a rejection of the invitation to mediate. There is a concern that this provision could be abused by parties who reject an invitation to mediate despite having a mediation clause in their agreement. The intention of the provision is to provide certainty in a situation where it is unclear whether a party is willing to mediate, rather than to disregard contractual commitments to mediate.[93] However, it could potentially deprive a mediation clause or agreement to mediate of any real meaning if a party could refuse to engage in mediation when a dispute arises.[94] Where the Mediation Model Law acts as a framework for a mediation statute in a particular jurisdiction, article 5(2) would require revision to support the enforcement of mediation clauses.

---

[89] Directive 2008/52/EC of the European Parliament and of the Council of 21 May 2008 on certain aspects of mediation in civil and commercial matters [2008] OJ L136/3 (discussed in Chapter 2 at Section 2.4.7).

[90] United Nations Convention on International Settlement Agreements Resulting from Mediation (discussed in Chapter 2 at Section 2.4.6).

[91] Nor does the US Uniform Mediation Act (discussed in Chapter 2 at Section 2.4.8).

[92] UNCITRAL Model Law on International Commercial Mediation and International Settlement Agreements Resulting from Mediation: 'Article 14. Resort to arbitral or judicial proceedings: Where the parties have agreed to mediate and have expressly undertaken not to initiate during a specified period of time or until a specified event has occurred arbitral or judicial proceedings with respect to an existing or future dispute, such an undertaking shall be given effect by the arbitral tribunal or the court until the terms of the undertaking have been complied with, except to the extent necessary for a party, in its opinion, to preserve its rights. Initiation of such proceedings is not of itself to be regarded as a waiver of the agreement to mediate or as a termination of the mediation proceedings.' See also Alexander (n 3) 173.

[93] A failure to comply with a mediation clause would be dealt with under the relevant law of obligations: see Binder (n 71) 586.

[94] See also P Sanders, 'UNCITRAL's Model Law on International Commercial Conciliation' (2007) 23(1) *Arbitration International* 105, 106–12.

3.5   An Obligation to Advise on the Mediation Option

The Civil Procedure Rules encourage the use of mediation in England
with the support of various measures, including costs sanctions for
parties who win at trial but who unreasonably refused an offer to mediate
a dispute that could have settled.[95] This view was supported by the Court
of Appeal in *Halsey* when it cautioned the legal profession in England to
consider the mediation option with disputing clients: 'All members of the
legal profession who conduct litigation should now routinely consider
with their clients whether their disputes are suitable for ADR.'[96]

The requirement to advise on the mediation option has been put on
a statutory footing in some jurisdictions and the South African High
Court has imposed a costs sanction on parties' lawyers for failing to
advise their clients on the mediation option. These developments are
discussed in the context of costs sanctions and the duty to advise in
Chapter 7 at Section 7.4.3.

3.6   Agreements to Mediate

Mediation service providers usually require parties to sign an agreement
to mediate before commencement of the process. The agreement deals
with many practical issues such as the appointment, roles and functions
of the mediator; the rights and responsibilities of the parties, including
that representatives with authority to settle attend the mediation; how the
process will work, including conduct and procedure or the incorporation
of institutional rules including a code of conduct; the scope of the
mediation; confidentiality; conflicts of interest; the mediator's fee and
ancillary charges; matters of liability and immunity; the consequences of
mediation for other processes running concurrently such as litigation;
the law of the contract and the forum for later dispute resolution; and the
requirement that any settlement reached will be reduced to writing and
signed by the parties. It may also provide that the mediator will not be
called as a witness in any subsequent proceedings relating to the dispute
or the mediation.

The agreement is signed by the parties, the mediator and possibly the
parties' lawyers and other representatives. The terms should be

---

[95] See Civil Procedure Rules 1998, rule 1.1(1). As discussed in Section 3.6, the Rules were
amended in light of the Jackson Report (n 60).

[96] *Halsey* (n 54) [11] (Dyson LJ). See also *Burchell* v. *Bullard* [2005] EWCA Civ 358 [43]
(Ward LJ). See also Chapter 7 at Section 7.4.3.

consistent with the mediation clause in the commercial contract. If the parties wish to modify their pre-existing agreement contained in the mediation clause, they should expressly state this in the agreement to mediate. Signatories to the agreement are open to being sued if they breach the agreement. Where a mediator fails to comply with an agreement to mediate, either party can take an action for breach of contract. However, this requires issuing legal proceedings, which is what the parties were attempting to avoid in the first place, and would not help resolve the original dispute. Arbitration legislation in various jurisdictions allows parties to apply for an arbitrator's removal on specified grounds.[97] In the absence of comparable legislation regarding mediators, the grounds and procedures for the removal of a mediator could be provided in the agreement to mediate.[98]

The case of *Beauty Star Ltd* v. *Janmohamed*[99] illustrated the policy in favour of enforcing agreements to mediate in England. Under a court order, the parties appointed a firm of accountants to prepare a report pursuant to an agreement to mediate into which they had entered. The mediator was an experienced barrister. The Court of Appeal held that as the appointment was made under the contract and was not a court appointment, it was not entitled to re-examine the accountant's approach. Even if the report contained mistakes, it was binding, as that is what the parties had agreed.[100]

While in practice fewer difficulties have been experienced with the enforcement of agreements to mediate compared with mediation clauses, the English case *Universal Satspace (North America) LLC* v. *Republic of Kenya*[101] demonstrates that such agreements are not always as certain as parties and advisors might believe. In this case, the agreement to mediate provided that no settlement reached in mediation would be binding

---

[97] See, e.g., in Australia, the Commercial Arbitration Act 2010 (NSW), s 14; in Ireland, the Arbitration Act 2010, s 9; and in South Africa, the Arbitration Act 1965, s 13.

[98] Boulle (n 3) 648. In jurisdictions such as the USA and Australia, basic requirements that agreements to mediate would normally include are enshrined in statute law, reducing the need for such agreements, though many parties may wish to tailor their own agreements to avoid default legal provisions or to fill gaps left by mediation laws: see Alexander (n 3) 209–13. See also Hopt and Steffek (n 2) 55–56. While an agreement to mediate could be in oral form, for clarity and evidential purposes written form is preferable: see Hopt and Steffek (n 2) 30.

[99] [2014] EWCA Civ 451.

[100] ibid [39], [40].

[101] *Universal Satspace* (n 72).

unless it was reduced to writing and signed by all parties. Neither the facts nor the settlement terms were in dispute.

Following a request from the Government of Kenya for a delay in signing the settlement for 'administrative' reasons, the parties orally agreed to sign the settlement within twenty-one days; subsequently, only Satspace did so. Satspace sought to have the defence and counter-claim struck out on the basis that the proceedings would be an abuse of process as they were effectively settled, requiring only Kenya's agreed signature to the mediated settlement agreement. The High Court held that the oral agreement to sign the written settlement gave rise to a collateral contract, which the agreement to mediate the underlying dispute was not concerned with.

There are different perspectives on whether the decision in *Universal Satspace* encourages parties to enter agreements to mediate or discourages them from doing so. It clearly demonstrates that the High Court will be reluctant to let a claim continue after it has been settled, even if the agreement is not reduced to writing as provided for in the agreement to mediate. Hence, if the terms of settlement are agreed and the parties unequivocally agree to sign up to them, the Court will give effect to that agreement in support of the outcome of the mediation process.

Conversely, it can be observed that the High Court enforced a settlement agreement that was contrary to an express provision in the agreement to mediate. As there were no written terms signed by the parties, as required, it is difficult to see how any collateral agreement, with sufficient certainty, could take effect. It is problematic to have a collateral contract in the absence of a main contract to which it purports to be collateral; the existence of the collateral contract was seemingly not possible, as a required contractual formality was not fulfilled.

Whatever perspective one chooses to take, as with mediation clauses, it is important to view agreements to mediate as organic and to draft them carefully in the light of decisions such as *Universal Satspace*. Where parties do not want oral agreements to be enforceable in similar circumstances, the language of any provision providing that no agreement is reached until reduced to writing and signed by the parties should be widened: it should require signed writing to confer validity on any collateral contract or effective waiver of formality requirements in agreements to mediate.[102]

---

[102] For a comprehensive discussion of this case, including the negative implications of this decision for the legal framework of mediation and for mediators, see T Allen, 'A Binding

The 2013 decision in *Universal Satspace* is also surprising because the Civil Procedure Rules, introduced following Lord Woolf's *Access to Justice* report, had been in effect for fourteen years. The Rules encourage the use of mediation with the support of various measures – including costs sanctions for parties who win at trial but who unreasonably refused an offer to mediate a dispute that could have settled.[103] The culture change reflected in the Rules was, at the time of the decision, ostensibly well embedded in the civil justice system in England. The changes to the Civil Procedure Rules prompted by the Jackson Report have been joined by an initiative to train and educate all judges about the mediation process and how and why it can achieve workable settlements for commercial disputants.[104] These training and education initiatives have in turn led to senior judicial support for the process that has played an instrumental role in the growth of commercial mediation in England over the past two decades.[105] It seems then that, even in a jurisdiction that has made significant endeavours to ensure that mediation is both used and understood, courts can make unexpected decisions that materially impact the enforceability of material terms in agreements to mediate.

Settlement (or Not?): The Mediator's Dilemma' (Blog Archive: Mediation Law Developments, CEDR Publications 2014) <www.cedr.com/a-binding-settlement-or-not-the-mediators-dilemma> accessed 10 May 2022. See also Blake, Browne and Sime (n 2) 206–7. It seems that similar cases, should they arise, are likely to be decided differently in view of *MWB Business Exchange Centres* v. *Rock Advertising* [2018] UKSC 24, where the UK Supreme Court ruled, overturning a decision of the Court of Appeal, that full force and effect will be given to a 'No Oral Modification Clause': see Allen (n 13) 46. See also Chapter 7 at Section 7.4.4.

[103] Civil Procedure Rules 1998, rule 1.1(1) provides: 'These Rules are a new procedural code with the overriding objective of enabling the court to deal with cases justly.' This was later amended to include 'and at proportionate cost' with the added explanation that includes 'enforcing compliance with rules, practice directions and orders'. The Rules were amended in light of the Jackson Report: see Jackson (n 60) 31. They are discussed further in Chapter 7.

[104] See E Carroll, 'The Future Belongs to Mediation and its Clients' in C Newmark and A Monaghan (eds), *Butterworths Mediators on Mediation: Leading Mediator Perspectives on the Practice of Commercial Mediation* (Haywards Heath, Tottel Publishing 2005) 401.

[105] See Lightman J, 'In My Opinion … CEDR Mediation Training for a Judge' (CEDR Publications, 27 November 2007), where the English High Court judge remarked that the more he learned about mediation, the more enthusiastic an advocate he became of the process. The Jackson Report has also focussed on continuing education efforts for judges on mediation: see Jackson (n 60) 363. See also A K C Koo, 'Ten Years after Halsey' (2015) 34(1) *Civil Justice Quarterly* 77, 81. Such initiatives are particularly important as many senior judges would never have experienced commercial mediation when in practice, as it would not have been a widely available dispute resolution process: see Allen (n 13) 112.

3.7 Concluding Thoughts

Public policy in jurisdictions throughout the world has moved in favour of supporting the enforcement of mediation clauses. In balancing certainty and flexibility, cases such as *Computershare* demonstrate the willingness of courts to relax the certainty requirement in favour of supporting party autonomy and contractual freedom. However, *Universal Satspace* provides a stark reminder that legal advisors must remain cognisant of the organic nature of agreements to mediate and the need to revise their drafting of such agreements as new jurisprudence emerges.

4

Approaches to Mediation

4.1 Introduction

Various models of mediation have been developed, reflecting mediation practice. In a commercial context, the most important distinction is between evaluative (or substance-oriented) mediation and facilitative (or process-oriented) mediation. However, in practice, a purely facilitative approach to mediation is rare, and experience suggests that a successful mediation results from using a clearly identified 'mixed process'. Pre-mediation considerations are important in laying the groundwork for a successful mediation. The temporal contours of the mediation process are also important to bear in mind, particularly when considering issues such as limitation periods, confidentiality protection and costs. The mediation process develops through stages and phases during which the mediator helps the parties towards resolution. Free from the constraint of viewing the dispute in terms of legal rights and obligations, the parties create an opportunity to empower themselves to resolve the dispute and essentially determine the future. The process offers them the opportunity to emerge from commercial conflict stronger – personally and contractually – with an outcome that better reflects their needs and interests.

4.2 Commercial Mediation Models

Four separate mediation approaches or models have been identified in an effort to conceptualise different tendencies in mediation practice. The four approaches are referred to as 'settlement', 'facilitative', 'transformative' and 'evaluative' mediation. In each approach the objective and approach are different. In settlement mediation, the objective is to reach a compromise. In facilitative mediation, it is to promote a negotiation in terms of underlying needs and interests rather than legal rights and obligations. In a transformative (or therapeutic) model of mediation, underlying causes of behaviour may be considered. In evaluative mediation, legal rights and entitlements and the anticipated range of court outcomes serve as a guide in reaching a settlement. These are not discrete forms of mediation practice but ways of conceptualising the different tendencies in practice, as a mediation may start in one mode and then adopt characteristics of another: for example, it may become evaluative after a facilitative opening.[1]

As every dispute and each mediator is unique, every mediation to some extent differs from every other mediation.[2] Even where disputes are relatively similar, there is variation in mediator practices as different mediators have different approaches.[3] Some mediators define problems in narrow terms, for example by concentrating on how much money is owed; others define the problem in broader terms, for example by assessing what is going on between two former business partners in dispute.[4] Some mediators work transparently by sharing their observations with the parties; others conduct the mediation without revealing their inner thinking.[5]

4.2.1   Facilitative Mediation and Evaluative Mediation

A prominent example of differences in mediator approaches is reflected in the distinction between 'facilitative' and 'evaluative' practices. These two approaches are the most relevant to commercial mediation. They are also described as process-oriented (facilitative) and substance-oriented

---

[1] See L Boulle, *Mediation: Principles, Process, Practice* (3rd ed, Chatswood, NSW, LexisNexis 2011) 43–48; R Feehily, 'The Role of the Commercial Mediator in the Mediation Process: A Critical Analysis of the Legal and Regulatory Issues' (2015) 132(2) *South African Law Journal* 372, 374–78. Many authors have proposed mediation model variants: see, e.g., N Alexander, 'The Mediation Metamodel: Understanding Practice' (2008) 26(1) *Conflict Resolution Quarterly* 97. See also C W Moore, *The Mediation Process* (4th ed, San Francisco, Jossey-Bass 2014) 46–59; C W Moore 'Mediation Within and Between Organisations' in A Georgakopoulos (ed), *The Mediation Handbook: Research, Theory, and Practice* (Abingdon, UK, Routledge 2017) 139–152.

[2] K K Kovach, 'Mediation' in M Moffitt and R Bordone (eds), *The Handbook of Dispute Resolution* (San Francisco, Jossey-Bass 2005) 306.

[3] ibid 310.

[4] See L Riskin, 'Understanding Mediators' Orientations, Strategies and Techniques: A Grid for the Perplexed' (1996) 1 *Harvard Negotiation Law Review* 7, 19.

[5] See M Moffitt, 'Casting Light on the Black Box of Mediation: Should Mediators Make Their Conduct More Transparent?' (1997) 13(1) *Ohio State Journal on Dispute Resolution* 1.

(evaluative) mediation. In the process-oriented approach, the parties, rather than the mediator, provide the solution to their dispute; the mediator is the facilitator of the process rather than an authority figure providing substantive advice or pressure to settle. Substance-oriented mediation is at the other end of the spectrum; the mediator is often viewed as an authority figure who evaluates the case based upon his or her experience and provides recommendations for how the case should be resolved. If the basic philosophy of mediation requires that the process is empowering, some commentators have suggested that substance-oriented mediation cannot be defined as mediation. They argue that the only 'true' form of mediation is 'facilitative' mediation.[6]

A facilitative mediator helps disputing parties search for a resolution that reflects their underlying interests and maximises joint gains and does not suggest what the resolution should be. A facilitative mediator might suggest, for example, that the parties put aside notions of legal rights and remedies and re-conceptualise their dispute as a problem that it would be best to resolve, assign to the past and move on from. Conversely, an evaluative mediator assumes that participants want and need the mediator to provide some direction about the appropriate grounds for settlement, based on law, industry practice or technology.[7] The mediator is qualified to give such direction because of his or her experience, training and objectivity.

The facilitative mediator assumes the parties are intelligent, able to work with their counterparts, and capable of understanding their own situations better than either their lawyers or the mediator; consequently, they may develop solutions that are better than any the mediator may create. For these reasons, the facilitative mediator assumes that his or her principal mission is to enhance and clarify communication between the parties to help them decide what to do, and that it is inappropriate to give

---

[6] See T Sourdin, 'Mediation in Australia: Impacts on Litigation' in N Alexander (ed), *Global Trends in Mediation* (2nd ed, The Hague, Kluwer Law International 2006) 42–43. As evaluation is likely to favour one side, it may give rise to claims of bias or mediator coercion, or result in the parties hardening their positions: see S Blake, J Browne and S Sime, *The Jackson ADR Handbook* (2nd ed, Oxford, Oxford University Press 2016) 171–72. Conversely, it has been suggested that if the mediator adopts a 'slavish' neutral approach, this can result in a suboptimal outcome for the parties: see K Gibson, L Thompson and M H Bazerman, 'Shortcomings of Neutrality in Mediation: Solutions Based on Rationality' (1996) 12(1) *Negotiation Journal* 69.

[7] An evaluative approach is sometimes called a 'directive' approach: see L Riskin, 'Retiring and Replacing the Grid of Mediator Orientations' (2003) 21(4) *Alternatives to the High Cost of Litigation* 69.

his or her opinion, as this could impair the appearance of impartiality and thereby interfere with the mediator's ability to function.[8] An evaluative mediator is viewed by some as similar to other types of evaluator such as judges, arbitrators and other third-party decision-makers. As the role of the mediator is fundamentally different, and requires the crucial task of facilitating evaluation, assessment and decision-making by the parties themselves, some believe a mediator cannot effectively facilitate when evaluating.[9]

The evaluative/facilitative distinction has been the subject of considerable debate. Evaluative mediation was characterised by some as an 'oxymoron',[10] while others believed that some level of evaluation is unavoidable.[11] For facilitative mediators, the evaluative/ facilitative debate defined an important distinction between what they did and what was commonly thought of as mediation (that is, evaluative mediation). This resulted in more mediation training courses in facilitative styles. It also led to less time spent in private caucus meetings with each party and more time spent in joint meetings with all parties during mediation sessions.[12]

---

[8] See Riskin (n 4) 24. Len Riskin introduced the concept of a grid that plotted mediators based on whether they were facilitative or evaluative, and whether they remained within a narrow problem definition or framed the process more broadly.

[9] L Love, 'The Top Ten Reasons Why Mediators Should Not Evaluate' (1997) 24(2) *Florida State University Law Review* 937, 938–40.

[10] ibid. Lela Love and Kimberlee Kovach believe that evaluative mediation is something of an oxymoron, and that an unfortunate consequence of 'Riskin's Grid' is that it appears to have encouraged mediators to play a more judgmental role. There should, in their view, be clarity of purpose in mediation, and no confusion of roles: see K K Kovach and L Love, 'Mapping Mediation: The Risks of Riskin's Grid' (1998) 3 *Harvard Negotiation Law Review* 71, 71–75. Cultural differences also appear to have given rise to variances in approach, even among common law countries. While comprehensive verifiable statistics about mediator style are not available, in the USA and Australia mediators often adopt an evaluative approach, while in the United Kingdom mediators tend to be more facilitative. For example, most mediators selected from the International Centre for Dispute Settlement adopt an evaluative style: see T Allen, *Mediation Law and Civil Practice* (2nd ed, London, Bloomsbury Professional 2019) 68; E Tuchmann and others, 'The International Centre for Dispute Resolution's Mediation Practice and Experience' in C Titi and K Fach Gómez (eds), *Mediation in International Commercial and Investment Disputes* (Oxford, Oxford University Press 2019) 119.

[11] Others became weary of the debate: see R Birke and L E Teitz, 'US Mediation in the Twenty-First Century: The Path that Brought America to Uniform Laws and Mediation Cyberspace' in N Alexander (ed), *Global Trends in Mediation* (The Hague, Kluwer Law International 2003) 380.

[12] ibid 380–81.

4.2.2   A Mixed Process

A purely facilitative approach to mediation is unlikely to exist in practice, and successful mediations often emanate from a 'mixed process'.[13] Mediators frequently evaluate on many levels and react to opportunities arising during the process, and the strategies and techniques used should be determined by the mediator's assessment of the participants and the substance of the dispute.[14] The adoption by the mediator of a line of query involves 'reality' from the mediator's experience. A transparent and direct approach is healthier for both the parties and the process. As the process is intended to be a true alternative method of communication, restricting mediators and parties is likely to be self-defeating, and regulations that intrude into the process may inhibit the parties' self-determination.

An effective mediator must fashion the process to suit the parties and the nature of the dispute, and marshal the necessary skills and personal qualities to help the parties find a resolution. Hence, a sensible approach would involve the mediator discussing with the parties his or her role, including what he or she is going to do, and why, so that the mediator can serve as the proverbial 'agent of reality' by meeting the parties' expectations and acting consistently with the core values of the process. Discussing the mediator's role and how the process will work, including joint sessions and separate caucuses, depending on what the parties feel most comfortable with and what is likely to advance the negotiations, should help elicit or enhance the parties' commitment to the process and their sense of ownership.[15]

---

[13] S Roberts and M Palmer, *Dispute Processes: ADR and the Primary Forms of Decision-Making* (revised ed, Cambridge, Cambridge University Press 2005) 186; Feehily (n 1) 378–79.

[14] The choice of approach in the process involves a degree of evaluation by the mediator, although this relates to process rather than substance: R A Creo, 'Business and Practice Issues of US Mediators' in C Newmark and A Monaghan (eds), *Butterworths Mediators on Mediation: Leading Mediator Perspectives on the Practice of Commercial Mediation* (Haywards Heath, Tottel Publishing 2005) 316. For a discussion on mediator techniques and interventions to handle parties' emotions and interests, overcoming impasse and moving parties towards settlement, see S B Goldberg and others, *Dispute Resolution: Negotiation, Mediation, Arbitration, and Other Processes* (7th ed, New York, Wolters Kluwer 2020) 114–51.

[15] Creo (n 14) 316–17. Experience suggests that the most effective approach can involve the parties meeting with the mediator face to face without their lawyers. While often initially resisted by the parties, this tends to be where most progress is made: see M Kallipetis and S Ruttle, 'Better Dispute Resolution: The Development and Practice of Mediation in the United Kingdom Between 1995 and 2005' in J C Goldsmith, A Ingen-Housz and G H Pointon (eds), *ADR in Business: Practice and Issues Across Countries and Cultures* (Alphen aan den Rijn, Kluwer Law International 2006) 246. For a discussion on the

Many mediators do not maintain a single orientation but adapt their approach to the conditions they encounter as the process moves forward. Some begin with a facilitative approach and then proceed to evaluate. Some mediators change their style several times, even within the same private caucus meeting. It seems that many successful mediators are not consistently either facilitative or evaluative. A mediator's approach can also be influenced by the bargaining approach and values of the parties and their lawyers, rather than a preferred style. Mediators should not use evaluation as a first resort, and are likely to begin with a facilitative style, adopting an evaluative approach where it is helpful and necessary. The key point is that the parties give informed consent to the approach and intervention adopted.[16] Apart from style, many mediators bring idiosyncratic qualities and consequently exert personal influence that can prove significant during the process in moving the parties towards settlement.[17]

4.3   The Mediation Process

4.3.1   Pre-mediation Practicalities

Ideally, a mediator will be appointed subject to the terms of a clearly drafted agreement to mediate.[18] Once appointed, the mediator will usually contact the parties or their lawyers and set up a pre-mediation

methodology for conducting caucus mediation, and what the mediator can seek to accomplish at each stage of the process, see R M Calkins and F Lane, *Lane & Calkins Mediation Practice Guide* (New York, Aspen Publishers 2006) 80–103. In the USA, many commercial mediators conduct the entire mediation process in caucus format, adopting the 'all caucus' model, with no face-to-face communication between the parties: see D Golann and J Folberg, *Mediation: The Roles of Advocate and Neutral* (3rd ed, New York, Wolters Kluwer 2016) 110. From a practical perspective, the critical point is that both the mediator and the style used help the parties to reach settlement: see C Chern, *International Commercial Mediation* (London, Informa 2008) 136–39.

[16] See K Mackie and others, *The ADR Practice Guide: Commercial Dispute Resolution* (3rd ed, Haywards Heath, Tottel Publishing 2007) 266–67; D N Frenkel and J H Stark, *The Practice of Mediation* (2nd ed, New York, Wolters Kluwer Law & Business 2012) 12–14. Provision for a change in style from facilitative to evaluative should be reflected in the agreement to mediate, or added by way of addendum if an evaluative approach is sought during the mediation process and not reflected in the agreement: see Blake, Browne and Sime (n 6) 171–72.

[17] See Golann and Folberg (n 15) 97, 172; Moore, *The Mediation Process* (n 1) 517. See also Riskin (n 7); D Bowling and D Hoffman, 'Bringing Peace into the Room: The Personal Qualities of the Mediator and their Impact on the Mediation' (2000) 16(1) *Negotiation Journal* 5–28.

[18] If the agreement to mediate is not signed before the pre-mediation meeting, it is important that it be signed by the conclusion of the meeting. See Chapter 3 at Section 3.6.

meeting to outline how the process will work, how they can best prepare for it and the mediator's role and the parties' roles in it. It is important that the parties are aware of the mediator's role and give their informed consent before the process begins. This includes consenting to the mediator's role in managing the process, including setting the agenda in consultation with the parties, acting as facilitator during the process and serving as an intermediary between the parties, and the use of joint and private caucus meetings.

The mediator will also discuss who will attend the mediation, and, where third parties are present, the importance of them signing confidentiality agreements as they will not be covered by the agreement to mediate. The parties who attend the mediation should have authority to settle; if they do not, it is important that the mediator is aware of any limits on their power and how consent to any proposed settlement can be given without delay. The mediator will also discuss time constraints that may affect the process and how these can be accommodated; the time frame in which position statements outlining each parties' case, and other relevant documents, should be exchanged; and, ultimately, the time frame for the mediation.

Where the parties source a mediator through a mediation service provider, the provider will usually deal with the pre-mediation practicalities including organising the venue and the timing of the mediation, completing a mediator conflict-of-interest check, ensuring the completion of the agreement to mediate, and responding to any queries the parties may have.[19]

4.3.2   Temporal Contours

It can be important to know when a mediation begins and ends. The confidentiality that attaches to the process is likely to only cover this period. The statutory limitation period and whether it will be suspended may also be relevant if the parties ultimately proceed to court. The mediation clause may require that the process be concluded within a particular time frame. It may also have implications for the mediation costs, and it may be important to know whether an offer was made during or after the end of the mediation process.[20]

---

[19] Blake, Browne and Sime (n 6) 152–55, 169–94. For a comprehensive discussion on laying the groundwork for effective mediation, see Moore (n 1) 181–297.

[20] This relates to the form of settlement and can be relevant, for example, if the agreement to mediate provides that any agreement reached must be reduced to writing and signed by

It can be difficult to pinpoint accurately the moment when mediation begins and ends. The moment of commencement can often only be ascertained by assessing the parties' intention from the facts and circumstances of the case, and this may not be easy to determine. It is therefore important to consider these issues, and to record the start and end of the process in the agreement to mediate, or at least in correspondence.[21]

4.3.3   Four Stages

Before the mediation meeting formally commences, the mediator should ensure that confidentiality agreements have been signed by those present who are not parties to the agreement to mediate. The mediator should also go through concerns or queries anyone may have about the process, or any new issues that may have arisen since he or she was last in touch with the parties or their lawyers.

From a practical perspective, a typical mediation goes through four key stages.[22] First is the opening stage, involving introductions and then an opening statement from the mediator followed by opening statements from each party. It normally takes place in a joint or plenary session. Second is the exploration or information stage. This can take place partly in joint meetings and partly in private caucus, or exclusively in either joint or private meetings, depending on the parties' preferences, the issues in the case and the mediator's view. This stage involves the

---

the parties. In *Brown* v. *Rice* [2007] EWHC 625 (Ch), an offer that remained open for acceptance after the mediation was held to still be an offer made in the mediation; consequently, an oral acceptance of it did not constitute a legally binding agreement as one party reneged before the agreement was reduced to writing and signed by the parties, as required in the agreement to mediate: see Blake, Browne and Sime (n 6) 195.

[21] It could, for example, start when the mediator is appointed, when the pre-mediation meeting takes place, when the agreement to mediate is signed or when the substantive mediation takes place: see Blake, Browne and Sime (n 6) 195–96. Article 5(1) of the Mediation Model Law, which deals with commencement of mediation proceedings, provides: 'Mediation proceedings in respect of a dispute that has arisen commence on the day on which the parties to that dispute agree to engage in mediation proceedings.' According to the Guide to Enactment, the exact determination of when and how the 'agreement to engage in mediation' is reached is left to be determined by laws outside the Mediation Model Law. Hence, there could be significant variance across jurisdictions: see P Binder, *International Commercial Arbitration and Mediation in UNCITRAL Model Law Jurisdictions* (4th ed, Alphen aan den Rijn, Kluwer Law International 2019) 586.

[22] The terms 'stages' and 'phases' are often used interchangeably when characterising the sequential development of the mediation process. For clarity, in this book the 'stages' represent the structural sequence that a mediation may progress through, while the 'phases' tend to be more fluid and may permeate the entire mediation process.

mediator using 'reality-testing' techniques, probing the underlying issues and helping the parties to devise options for settlement. Third is the negotiation or bargaining stage. This usually takes place in private caucus meetings, with the mediator acting as broker between the parties, often devising strategies to help parties work through deadlocks. Fourth is the settlement or closing stage. This usually takes place in joint meetings involving all the parties and/or the parties' lawyers who will be responsible for drafting the settlement agreement.

The stages may not progress in strict sequential order, and not all cases will go through each stage. Mediation is a flexible process which can be adapted to suit the needs of the parties and the particular case. Complex commercial disputes with multiple issues and parties may span days or weeks, and the parties may be at different stages in respect of different issues. For example, they may be in the bargaining stage in relation to one issue, the information stage with another, and the settlement phase with a third.[23]

4.3.4   Three Phases

The mediation process also has three broad phases, though there can be considerable overlap between them.[24] For example, while the issue of trust is discussed under the heading 'building bridges of understanding', in practice, efforts to develop and build trust should permeate the entire process and not be thought of simply as a phase in it. Culture can also play a significant role in the mediation process and certain phases of the process will be given greater emphasis in some cultures compared with others.[25]

[23] Multi-party disputes can also require a more bespoke process and a team of mediators. They can last several months, particularly where there are a large number of claimants and defendants or, as often occurs in construction disputes, where there are a limited number of parties to the main dispute, but a large number of parties that are added to the dispute as additional parties: see Blake, Browne and Sime (n 6) 196–213, 224–26. See also D Richbell, 'Mediating Multi-Party Disputes' in Newmark and Monaghan (eds) (n 14) and generally Moore (n 1) 555–70.

[24] See L Street, 'Commentary on Some Aspects of the Advent and Practice of Mediation in Australia' in Newmark and Monaghan (eds) (n 14) 362–65. For an overview of what happens at a typical commercial mediation, where resolution is often achieved within a day, see Mackie and others (n 16) 247–69. For a discussion on the varying approaches to the mediation process adopted across various jurisdictions, see K Hopt and F Steffek, 'Mediation: Comparison of Laws, Regulatory Models, Fundamental Issues' in K Hopt and F Steffek (eds), *Mediation: Principles and Regulation in Comparative Perspective* (Oxford, Oxford University Press 2013) 59–68.

[25] For example, the interest in relationship building has traditionally been perceived as more important for Asian negotiators compared with parties from the USA: see R J Lewicki, B Barry and D Saunders, *Essentials of Negotiation* (6th ed, New York, McGraw Hill 2016)

4.3.4.1   Opening Channels of Communication

When parties are in dispute, free-flowing communication becomes inhibited, if not non-existent, as commercial litigants are warned to communicate only through their lawyers so that direct rational dialogue between the parties is sterilised. A central and essential element of effective mediation is to open channels of communication between the parties.[26]

Mediators should help parties manage both the context and the process of their negotiations. A key contextual factor in this process is the creation of a free flow of information so that each party can understand the real needs and objectives of the other side; this helps in the search for a solution that meets the goals and objectives of both parties. Effective information exchange is critical to developing good integrative solutions. In order for the necessary channels of communication to develop to facilitate information exchange, the mediator should encourage the parties to reveal their true objectives and to listen to each other carefully, in this way creating the conditions for a free and open discussion of all related issues and concerns.[27]

As the parties have different values and preferences, the realisation by each party that the other's priorities are not the same as its own, can stimulate them to exchange more information, understand the nature of the negotiation better, and achieve better joint results. Similarly, integrative agreements are facilitated when parties exchange information about their priorities for, rather than their positions on, particular issues. Effective communication of relevant information, as assisted by a mediator, is critical to ensure that the exchange of such relevant information occurs. The communicative aspects of information flow and understanding, while critical to integrative negotiation, also require that issues such as trust and honesty (discussed in Section 4.3.4.2) are managed. To sustain a free flow of information and to understand each other's needs and objectives, parties may need a different outlook or frame of reference, possibly requiring, for example, that individual goals are redefined as being best achieved through collaborative efforts directed towards a collective goal. In addition, parties

---

242–69; D Lax and J Sabenius, *3-D Negotiation: Powerful Tools to Change the Game In Your Most Important Deals* (Boston, Harvard Business School Press 2006) 171–72. See also Chapter 2 at Section 2.3 on the role of culture in commercial mediation. For a comprehensive discussion on conducting productive mediation meetings, including the influence of cultural variations, see Moore (n 1) 301–485.

[26]   Street (n 24) 362.

[27]   See Lewicki, Barry and Saunders (n 25) 60–61.

may have varying abilities to distinguish needs and interests from positions, and the mediator may need to help less experienced parties to
discover their underlying needs and interests so they can be communicated
clearly to the other side.[28]
The success of integrative negotiation depends on the search for
solutions that meet the needs and objectives of both sides, and the parties
are likely to be firm about their primary interests and needs, but flexible
about how these needs and interests are met. Mediators must attempt to
probe the surface of each party's position to discover the party's underlying needs. Parties must also be willing to share information about
themselves – specifically, what they want and why they want it – in
specific, concrete and clearly understood terms. Each party must understand the meaning of what is being said by each side. While mutual
understanding is the responsibility of each party, the mediator can help
the communication process by encouraging the parties to engage in
active listening and by testing whether (and ensuring that) each side
has received the message that was intended.[29]
While open channels of communication for relevant information
exchange would be the ideal in every mediation, in practice, feelings may
be running so high that direct flows of communication are impossible, and
the channels may, initially at least, need to be indirect, being routed
through the mediator.[30] Similarly, in mediations where there are strong
negative feelings or where one or more of the parties is likely to dominate,
mediators, with the consent of the parties, may need to create formal,
structured procedures for communication, ensuring that such a procedure
gives everyone a chance to speak.[31]

---

[28] ibid 62; Moore (n 1) 122–30.
[29] See Lewicki, Barry and Saunders (n 25) 63, 85.
[30] When caucusing, mediators serve as buffers, filters and interpreters, reframing statements
as they shuttle between parties, with the intention that such efforts will make joint
sessions more productive and move the parties towards settlement. The concern is that
parties or their lawyers may try to manipulate the process by shaping the narrative during
such sessions, in the absence of corrections or context from the other party. Experienced
mediators will remain mindful of such efforts, and effectively use private sessions to glean
information from parties that will prove useful in facilitating settlement: see J J Coe,
'Concurrent Co-Mediation: Toward a More Collaborative Centre of Gravity in Investor–
State Dispute Resolution' in Titi and Fach Gómez (eds) (n 10) 490–98.
[31] Street (n 24) 362.

4.3.4.2   Building Bridges of Understanding

The central focus of mediation is to achieve a dispassionate, objective appraisal of the dispute. This is where the skills of the mediator are critical in helping each party enlarge its understanding of the other party's point of view, so that it can accurately assess a possible outcome. If the mediator can help each party to gain an understanding of where the other party is coming from, the parties can be far more effective in negotiating an outcome, and the mediator can then help each party assess the sort of consensus that can be achieved.[32]

A central element of building bridges of understanding is to create trust, though efforts should be made to develop trust at each stage of the mediation process as well. Trust in a mediation context operates on two levels: trust between the parties, and trust between the mediator and each party. For a mediator, trust is achieved as a by-product of other efforts, such as listening empathetically and respectfully, clarifying issues, carefully checking on the changing positions of the parties in caucus, and ensuring that any information shared in caucus remains confidential and is only shared when explicit consent is given.[33] In terms of trust between the parties, there are two dilemmas directly related to trust that all parties face, and that mediators should be conscious of. The first is the dilemma of honesty, which concerns how much of the truth a party should reveal to the other side. As discussed in Section 4.3.4.1, information exchange is critical to progress in a mediation as there needs to be an element of openness on both sides to move from opening positions. The second dilemma is the dilemma of trust itself, which relates to how much a party should believe of what another party is telling them. If there is not a sufficient degree of trust between parties in a mediation, and between the parties and the mediator, it is likely to prove difficult to reach an agreement.[34]

The search for an optimal solution through giving information and making concessions is assisted by trust and a belief that there is honesty and fairness in the process. Two elements in negotiations in particular help to create trust. One is based on perceptions of outcomes and can be influenced by managing how the proposed result is perceived by the recipient. The other is based on perceptions of the process and can be enhanced by

---

[32] ibid 363–65.

[33] See A T Trollip, *Alternative Dispute Resolution in a Contemporary South African Context* (Durban, Butterworths 1991) 51. See also Chapter 9 at Section 9.4 for a discussion on the different approaches to protecting mediation evidence.

[34] See Lewicki, Barry and Saunders (n 25) 14.

conveying signs of fairness and reciprocity in proposals and concessions. Satisfaction with negotiations is determined as much by the process through which the agreement is reached as it is by the outcome obtained; efforts to eliminate or reduce 'give and take' will short-circuit the process, and could destroy both the basis for trust and any possibility of achieving a mutually satisfactory result.[35]

While there is no guarantee that trust will lead to collaboration, experience leaves little doubt that mistrust inhibits it. Interdependent parties that do not trust each other will act tentatively or defensively. This is likely to elicit a hesitant, cautious and distrustful response from the other party, and in turn, undermine the process. Building trust, as part of the process of understanding, is complex and uncertain and depends in part on how the parties behave and on their personal characteristics. Parties that trust each other are more likely to share information and to communicate accurately their needs, positions and the facts of a situation. Conversely, parties that do not trust each other are more likely to engage in positional bargaining, use threats and remain tied to uncompromising positions. To develop trust effectively, each party must believe that they and the other party choose to behave in a co-operative manner and believe that this behaviour is a signal of the other's honesty, openness and mutual commitment to a joint solution.[36]

4.3.4.3 Facilitating Informed Negotiations

The interdependence of people's goals can determine whether it is a competitive 'zero-sum' or 'distributive' situation, where there can only be one winner, or a 'mutual-gains', 'non-zero-sum' or 'integrative' situation, where all the parties can achieve their goals. The structure of the interdependence can shape the strategies and tactics that parties use. In distributive situations, the parties are motivated to win, so they will use win-lose strategies and tactics. The distributive bargaining approach to negotiation considers that there can only be one winner in the particular situation and pursues a course of action to be that winner. The purpose of the negotiations is to 'claim value' by doing whatever is necessary to attain the prize.

The number of issues in a negotiation, together with the relationship between the parties, can also prove critical in the choice of strategy. For example, single-issue negotiations tend to be distributive negotiations as

[35] ibid 15.
[36] ibid 83–85.

the only real negotiation issue is the price or 'distribution' of that issue, while multiple-issue negotiations are more likely to be integrative as parties strive for agreements that are mutually beneficial.[37] In integrative situations, the parties use win-win strategies and tactics and attempt to find solutions that let both parties achieve their goals. The goals of the parties are not mutually exclusive; one party's gain does not have to be at the other party's expense, and both parties can achieve their objectives. The purpose of the negotiation is to 'create value', for example, by identifying more resources or finding unique ways to share and co-ordinate the use of existing resources.[38]

There are four key steps in the integrative negotiation process: (1) identify and define the problem; (2) understand the problem and bring interests and needs to the surface; (3) generate alternative solutions to the problem; and (4) evaluate those alternatives and select among them. The first three steps are important for 'creating value' while the last step involves 'claiming value'. It is important that processes to create value precede processes to claim value, as the former are only effective when engaged in collaboratively without a focus on who gets what, while the latter involves distributive bargaining processes that need to be introduced carefully into integrative negotiation or they could adversely affect the relationship and resolution progress.[39] While the situation in a mediation may initially appear to be 'win-lose', discussion and mutual exploration can often uncover alternatives where both parties can gain.

While this approach to negotiation contemplates the parties devising agreements by identifying underlying interests and exploring options in an atmosphere of mutual respect to achieve a 'win-win' result, it has elicited criticism. Critics have argued that it makes parties in negotiations vulnerable to exploitation and is 'naïve', even misleading, by neglecting

---

[37] See ibid 28–29, 97. See also W Fisher and R Ury, *Getting to Yes: Negotiating Agreement Without Giving In* (New York, Penguin, 1981) updated and most recently revised in 2012 (London, Business Books). This seminal book on negotiation urged commercial parties, lawyers and other decision-makers to find win-win resolutions that would better serve all disputing parties rather than divisive distributive outcomes. Fisher and Ury believed that integrative or interest-based negotiations had the potential to maximise joint gains for disputants and preserve relationships. While dealing primarily with negotiation, it provided a framework for mediating disputes that was adopted by commercial parties: see D R Hensler, 'Our Courts, Ourselves: How the Alternative Dispute Resolution Movement is Re-Shaping our Legal System' (2003) 108(1) *Penn State Law Review* 165, 182.

[38] Lewicki, Barry and Saunders (n 25) 16. See also M Moffitt, 'Disputes as Opportunities to Create Value' in Moffitt and Bordone (eds) (n 2) 173–88.

[39] See Lewicki, Barry and Saunders (n 25) 63–80. See also Lax and Sabenius (n 25) 16–18.

the inherent limits of problem-solving as a model of negotiation, over-emphasising the potential of integrative negotiation, and ignoring the fact that the most demanding element of almost all negotiations is the distributional one. It has also been suggested that an inherent danger is that individuals who are predisposed by their personality towards co-operative strategies might internalise only the positive, problem-solving element of such an approach to negotiation and become caught in a co-operative pathology of appeasement. While some of these criticisms may seem justified, others appear to be based on misperceptions. The underlying commitment to co-operative problem-solving and the attempt to combat conventional wisdom about how to 'win' in negotiations through deceptive and over-reaching behaviour may have resulted in a perceived over-emphasis of the co-operative element in negotiations.[40]

The approach is effectively to facilitate parties in a mediation to further their self-interest by developing choices that are better than the 'no agreement' alternatives. The mediator does this by encouraging the parties to look at the strengths and weaknesses of their own case as well as that of other parties, by reference to the BATNA (best alternative to a negotiated agreement) as well as the WATNA (worst alternative to a negotiated agreement), ensuring they have carried out a comprehensive risk assessment, including the costs, and irrecoverable costs, of proceeding to trial.[41] The mediator is essentially attempting to help the parties find a solution they can live with rather than litigating, arbitrating or allowing the dispute to continue. A 'win-win' in a mediation is not so much about both sides winning. It involves the distinction between the terms of the settlement, which are likely to involve some compromise,

---

[40] C Buhring-Uhle, L Kirchhoff and G Scherer, *Arbitration and Mediation in International Business* (2nd ed, Alphen aan den Rijn, Kluwer Law International 2006) 157–58. 'Negotiators' dilemma' reflects the choice between pursuing a co-operative or competitive strategy, between value creating and value claiming. The inherent tension in this dilemma – between co-operative moves necessary to create value jointly and the competitive moves to claim it individually – must be carefully and productively managed: see Lax and Sabenius (n 25) 131–34. For a discussion on the 'collaborative' element in negotiation, including some of the critiques that have emerged since the original publication of *Getting to Yes* in 1981 (n 37), see B Patton, 'Negotiation' in Moffitt and Bordone (eds) (n 2) 279–303.

[41] Buhring-Uhle, Kirchhoff and Scherer (n 40) 157. A rational party's alternative to agreement should also be their minimum acceptable settlement, i.e., their BATNA. The bargaining range or Zone of Possible Agreement (ZOPA) should therefore be between each of the parties' BATNA. The ZOPA reflects the set of possible agreements that is better for each side, given its interests, than its best no-deal option: see Golann and Folberg (n 15) 29; Lax and Sabenius (n 25) 88–90; Blake, Browne and Sime (n 6) 154.

and the fact of the settlement, which is effectively the 'win-win' factor for the parties as they realise that the dispute has been resolved and is relegated to the past. Uncertainty has been replaced by a workable resolution.[42]

For an integrative approach to succeed, the parties must be willing to collaborate rather than to compete and be committed to reaching a goal that benefits all, rather than pursuing only their own agenda. They must effectively be willing to make their own needs explicit, to identify similarities and to recognise and accept differences. This does not mean that, for successful integrative negotiations to occur, each party should be just as interested in the objectives and problems of the other party as they are in their own. Assuming responsibility for each other's needs and outcomes as well as for their own is more likely to be dysfunctional than successful, as parties that are deeply committed to each other and each other's welfare often do not achieve the best solution. However close the parties may feel to each other, it is unlikely that they will completely understand each other's needs, objectives and concerns. They can consequently fall into the trap of not meeting each other's objectives while believing that they are.

Disputing parties maximise their outcomes when they assume a healthy, active self-interest in achieving their own goals while also recognising that they are in a collaborative, problem-solving relationship.[43] When parties and the mediator are mindful of this fact, the prospect of an integrative solution is more likely to result from the mediation process.

4.4   Mediated Solutions

At the end of a trial or arbitral proceeding, one party will obtain a judgment or an award, an outcome that will facilitate the enforcement of established legal rights. However, as this outcome will be based on past events, there will be a limited range of options: in most cases this results in an award of damages as the remedy. In mediation, the only limits on the solutions possible are the limits of the parties' imagination and resourcefulness. In mediation, parties create an opportunity to empower themselves to resolve the dispute by not restricting themselves to debating it simply in terms of their legal rights and obligations. It is a context in

---

[42] Street (n 24) 366–67.
[43] Lewicki, Barry and Saunders (n 25) 82.

which the parties can essentially determine their future, through a process that offers them the opportunity to emerge from commercial conflict stronger – personally and contractually.[44]

A mediated solution can give the parties an outcome that reflects their needs and interests better than a win/lose outcome decreed by a judge or arbitrator would. The settlement is negotiated in 'the shadow of the law': case law acts as a frame of reference for the alternative for either party if a negotiated commercial settlement does not best serve their interests or proves impossible to achieve. While commercial settlements often emerge from concessions made by the parties, there can be a sense of 'equality of discomfort', made tolerable by the fact that they have mutually and positively put the dispute behind them and agreed an outcome through a process that addresses not only their legal and commercial terms, but their human and emotional concerns as well. In this context, parties may be willing to settle for more than they would have received if they lost, but less than they would have received if they won. Mediation can deliver a sense of equality about the outcome. There is a fundamental symbiosis between mediation and the civil justice system, which is essential to the effective resolution of contemporary commercial disputes. Mediation needs a robust civil justice system, and the more mediation becomes embedded as an alternative to judicial adjudication, one could contend that a modern, sophisticated civil justice system needs mediation.

Parties can be motivated to settle by a variety of reasons that are unconnected to their perceptions of success at trial. Issues such as reputation, publicity, limited means, risk and litigation aversion, loss of face, commercial realities and unconnected commercial considerations, such as a planned merger, can all be motivators to settle that are often not revealed during the mediation. Similarly, mediation is a process through which information and views previously undisclosed can be exchanged, risks re-appraised and strengths and weaknesses tested in a private, confidential way in a context where no one must settle against their will or against the advice they receive, and where a party's case is not endangered should they ultimately proceed to court or arbitration.[45]

Consider the situation of a manufacturer contracting with a technical expert to establish and maintain a new type of manufacturing plant. The

---

[44] See generally N Alexander and M LeBaron, 'The Alchemy of Mediation' in I Macduff (ed), *Essays on Mediation: Dealing with Disputes in the 21st Century* (Alphen aan den Rijn, Wolters Kluwer 2016) 265.

[45] See Allen (n 10) 336–38.

manufacturer signs a five-year contract with the technical expert to secure the expertise and establish the plant. As part of the arrangement, the technical expert undertakes to be bound by a restraint-of-trade clause effective throughout the European Union, for two years from the termination of the contract. Three years into the agreement, when the manufacturing plant is well established, there is a downturn in the economy. The manufacturer finds that it is no longer feasible to retain the technical expert whose expertise is now redundant. The manufacturer purports to cancel the contract and in response the technical expert sues for the remaining two years' remuneration under the contract, which the manufacturer cannot afford to pay.

The technical expert could enforce his or her legal rights and claim the payments, but his or her real interest lies in establishing a processing plant in a related but distinctly different field not in competition with the manufacturer. The manufacturer's real interest lies in preventing the technical expert from establishing a plant in competition with it, both within the European Union and further afield. A mediated solution could produce an agreement by which the restraint-of-trade arrangement was redrafted to permit the technical expert to work on his or her new project, while the restraint on his or her working in the same field as the manufacturer was renewed for the European Union and extended to certain other countries.[46] A judge or arbitrator could never make such a creative order and an adjudicated solution would never meet the parties' real interests in this way. Mediated settlements are also less likely to require legal enforcement, as the parties have created the agreement; compliance is generally forthcoming, while in normal circumstances the risk of appeals and reviews is also eliminated.[47]

---

[46] Given that transactional lawyers have more expertise and experience in helping to negotiate and draft commercial agreements than most litigators or dispute resolution lawyers, there is a strong argument for their involvement in the mediation process and drafting of the re-negotiated commercial agreement. They may well have been involved in the negotiation and drafting of the original commercial agreement, including how any disputes arising should be resolved. Transactional lawyers are also more likely to be required to advise on the implications of the re-negotiated commercial agreement reflecting the settlement: see Allen (n 10) 187.

[47] See M Antrobus and R Sutherland, 'Some ADR Techniques in Commercial Disputes: Prospects for Better Business' in P Pretorius (ed), *Dispute Resolution* (Cape Town, Juta 1993) 169–70. See also Hopt and Steffek (n 24) 45. There is empirical evidence from many jurisdictions that procedural satisfaction rates with mediation are notably high, while mediated settlements are fulfilled earlier and with less difficulty than court judgments; this implies the practical effectiveness of the mediation process from the parties' perspective in terms of reconciliation and securing justice: see Hopt and Steffek at 105–7.

4.5 Conflict Avoidance, Conflict Management and Conflict Resolution

The use of mediation in a commercial context need not be restricted to circumstances when a dispute arises. The mediation concept is broader and can include conflict *avoidance*, conflict *management* and conflict *resolution*, as three closely-related sequential approaches in the field of commercial interaction.[48] Mediation is used with success in commercial transactional settings that are non-contentious and complex, where it is known as 'transactional mediation', 'deal mediation' or 'assisted deal-making'. The mediator manages the process to help the parties create a mutually favourable contract, often at the start of their relationship, long before conflict arises. The process anticipates that differences will develop in the course of the contractual negotiations. It is effectively a form of preventative or pre-emptive dispute resolution.[49] 'Project mediation', sometimes referred to as 'strategic mediation', is often used effectively to resolve problems that arise during the performance of long-term contracts or contracts with many parties, such as contractors and subcontractors on large construction projects, to ensure the project is not delayed.[50]

4.6 Concluding Thoughts

Mediation is often used as the process to resolve disputes that span multiple jurisdictions and involve highly technical issues, complex laws

---

[48] See Street (n 24) 361. See also A Georgakopoulos, H Coleman and R Storrow, 'Organisational Conflict Management Systems, The Emergence of Mediators as Conflict Resolution Professionals' in A Georgakopoulos (ed), *The Mediation Handbook: Research, Theory, and Practice* (Abingdon, UK, Routledge 2017) 153–163; D Spencer and M Brogan, *Mediation Law and Practice* (Melbourne, Cambridge University Press 2007) 460–71.

[49] See R Pepper, 'Contract Formation in Imperfect Markets: Should We Use Mediators in Deals?' (2004) 19(2) *Ohio State Journal on Dispute Resolution* 283; S B Goldberg, 'Mediating the Deal: How to Maximise Value by Enlisting a Neutral's Help At and Around the Bargaining Table' (2006) 24(9) *Alternatives to the High Cost of Litigation* 147. For a practical example of deal mediation in the context of a construction project, see Chern (n 15) 141–44.

[50] A project mediation model was used in the construction of the Olympic Park for the London Olympics 2012: see Blake, Browne and Sime (n 6) 226; Mackie and others (n 16) 248. Parties have also used mediation in the re-negotiation of existing contracts: see H Wollgast and I de Castro, 'WIPO Mediation: Resolving International Intellectual Property and Technology Disputes Outside the Courts' in Titi and Fach Gómez (eds) (n 10) 268; A Fortún and A Iglesia, 'Mediation and Other ADR in International Construction Disputes' in Titi and Fach Gómez (eds) 282. See also Golann and Folberg (n 15) 276–82.

and sensitive information. For example, commercial disputes involving intellectual property can involve various commercial issues including patents, know-how and software licences; franchising and distribution agreements; trademarks; joint venture agreements; research and development contracts; technology transfer agreements; technology-sensitive employment contracts; mergers and acquisitions involving IP assets; sports marketing agreements; publishing; and music and film contracts. Mediation offers disputing parties the opportunity to transform complex cross-border litigious hostility into an agreement that best suits their commercial interests.[51]

The process is sufficiently flexible to be designed in a way that responds to the needs of the parties.[52] The mediator, in consultation with the parties, can use the most helpful techniques and interventions to help the parties reach a settlement. Mediation is ultimately about exploring the possibilities of settlement where the process belongs to the parties and only they determine its outcome. Even where mediation does not result in an immediate settlement, it can positively affect the dynamics of the existing personal or commercial relationship, narrow the issues, help the parties to better understand the conflict and their own and the other party's interests and, given enough time, ultimately lead to the resolution of the dispute.[53]

The capacity to reorient the parties toward each other, by helping them to achieve a new and shared perception of their relationship – a perception that will redirect their attitudes and dispositions toward one another – has

---

[51] For a number of World Intellectual Property Organization case examples of creative mediation settlements comprising contracts for future collaboration, see Wollgast and de Castro (n 50) 262, 274–77.

[52] In Pathfinder Mediation, for example, the mediator helps the parties design their own process for resolving their dispute; mediation can be used to address purely procedural questions, ignoring substantive ones, at least at the outset. It can be used where the parties want to address only their disagreement over the extent of document disclosure that should take place, and not the substantive claims and counterclaims. Rather than argue their respective cases at an interim hearing, they bring the matter to mediation. Once the mediation is under way, they then address the substantive issues as well and can settle the case overall: see Mackie and others (n 16) 248.

[53] See Hopt and Steffek (n 24) 47–48, 105. While experience suggests that most mediations settle on the day, some settle after the mediation itself due to the momentum created during the process. Hence, the absence of a settlement on the day should not be viewed as a failure. Experience suggests that it can be helpful to leave the final offers that parties exchanged at the mediation open for an additional twenty-eight days and possibly organise a further mediation day (including the exchange of additional information) within that time frame, where this would prove helpful: see Kallipetis and Ruttle (n 15) 247.

been characterised as the central quality of mediation.[54] Within the mixed process of commercial mediation there is scope for a transformative dimension; the process offers the potential to modify the parties' behaviour, such that their response to conflict – and how best to deal with it when it arises – is changed as a result of their mediation experience.[55]

---

[54] L Fuller, 'Mediation: Its Form and Functions' (1971) 44(2) *Southern California Law Review* 305, 325.

[55] See R A Baruch Bush and J Folger, *The Promise of Mediation: The Transformative Approach to Conflict* (San Francisco, Jossey-Bass 2005) 41–84. To do this effectively, it has been suggested that it requires an interdisciplinary orientation, human knowledge and understanding drawn from various fields; older ones like history, law, psychology, sociology, economics, political science and international relations, and newer ones, including decision sciences, game theory and urban planning: see C Menkel-Meadow, *Mediation and Its Application for Good Decision Making and Dispute Resolution* (Cambridge UK, Intersentia 2016) 11.

5

Mediators and Their Appointment

5.1 Introduction

It is important that the role of a commercial mediator within the process is clearly understood. Issues of education, training, accreditation and standards are increasingly important, and this is reflected in the considerable efforts that have been taken to develop quality, standards and accountability in mediation to enhance process safeguards for commercial parties and professionalise the service. While mediator standards leave some issues unresolved, experience from practice and mediator training should help to clarify statements in codes of conduct on issues of neutrality, impartiality, confidentiality and the use of mediator power. Greater precision should also come from some standards being judicially defined, which would give more certainty to their scope and extent for legal purposes.

The possibility that legal proceedings might be brought against mediators is a significant form of accountability. While limited instructive jurisprudence is available from which to glean an exhaustive list of precautions that should be taken by commercial mediators, there are a number of factors for mediators to consider in avoiding liability claims. A carefully drafted mediator liability exclusion clause in an agreement to mediate is important, despite the fact that the effectiveness of such clauses is unclear. As many commercial mediators come from the legal profession, it is important that there is a clear distinction between their role and the role of a lawyer, and that they have no role in legal advice or drafting. Where a judge mediates, private caucus mediation sessions should be avoided, and the mediation should be referred to a judge other than the trial judge or to a non-judicial court official to address procedural fairness and bias issues.

5.2 Qualities, Skills and Role of the Mediator

Honesty, integrity, impartiality, patience, communication and process skills are qualities and skills associated with an effective mediator. As mediation or 'to mediate' means 'to go between' or 'to be in the middle', the mediator's role is neither judge nor legal advisor, counsellor or therapist. The mediator's sole function is to bring the parties together to help them find a solution of their own making. This function requires the mediator to motivate without manipulating, persuade without coercing and use reality testing to encourage parties to open themselves to compromise. Ultimately an effective mediator must fashion the process to suit the parties and the nature of the dispute and ensure that they marshal the necessary skills and personal qualities to help the parties find a resolution of their dispute.[1] Rather than inducing the parties to accept formal rules to govern their future relationship, the mediator's role is to help the parties free themselves from the encumbrance of rules and instead accept a relationship of mutual respect, trust and understanding that will enable them to meet shared possibilities without the aid of formal prescriptions laid down in advance.[2]

5.3 Education

An increasing number of dispute resolution and conflict management courses are being offered to students. Advanced degrees and mediator training programmes for lawyers, judges and others have been developed, as have peer mediation education and training in elementary and secondary schools across the USA. There is a mediation programme on most US college campuses, run by students, for students, and the concept of mediation as an integral aspect of education has been promoted and integrated into the education systems at all levels.[3] Similarly, UK and

---

[1] See P Lovenheim and L Guerin, *Mediate, Don't Litigate: Strategies for Successful Mediation* (Berkeley, Nolo 2004) 1/5; R Feehily, 'The Role of the Commercial Mediator in the Mediation Process: A Critical Analysis of the Legal and Regulatory Issues' (2015) 132(2) *South African Law Journal* 373–74. There are also practical threshold requirements when selecting a mediator such as the mediator's availability, billing rates and language skills and nationality in international disputes. Nationality is unlikely to be as important as experience, credentials, accreditation and personal qualities such as rapport building: see C H Brower, 'Selection of Mediators' in C Titi and K Fach Gómez (eds), *Mediation in International Commercial and Investment Disputes* (Oxford, Oxford University Press 2019) 303–7.

[2] L Fuller, 'Mediation: Its Form and Functions' (1971) 44(2) *Southern California Law Review* 325–26.

[3] D N Frenkel and J H Stark, *The Practice of Mediation* (2nd ed, New York, Wolters Kluwer Law & Business 2012) 1–2. See also N H Katz 'Mediation and Dispute Resolution Services in Higher Education' in A Georgakopoulos (ed), *The Mediation Handbook: Research, Theory, and Practice* (Abingdon, UK, Routledge 2017) 170–78. Education on mediation

Australian tertiary institutions offer courses and qualifications in mediation and other dispute resolution disciplines in the faculties of law, humanities, social science and business. At the postgraduate level there is a wide range of dispute resolution topics, diplomas and master's degrees specialising in dispute resolution. Programmes both academic – dealing with theory, principles and developments in the literature – and practical – covering skills development and competency-based training – are now present in many jurisdictions.[4]

5.4   Efforts to Professionalise

It has been suggested that any occupation that wants to exercise authority must establish a technical basis for it, claim an exclusive jurisdiction, link both skill and jurisdiction to standards of training, and convince the

can take place long before tertiary level. Student studies pre-third level have revealed that students who receive conflict resolution education have improved attendance and academic achievement, fewer suspensions from high school, better peer relationships and a greater interest in learning: see D K Crawford and R J Bodine, 'Youths, Education and Dispute Resolution' in M Moffitt and R Bordone (eds), *The Handbook of Dispute Resolution* (San Francisco, Jossey-Bass 2005). See also V Ozoke, 'From Peers to Community, Transferring Peer Mediation Skills from School to Community' in A Georgakopoulos (ed), *The Mediation Handbook: Research, Theory, and Practice* (Abingdon, UK, Routledge 2017) 243–50.

[4] See R A Creo, 'Business and Practice Issues of US Mediators' in C Newmark and A Monaghan (eds), *Butterworths Mediators on Mediation: Leading Mediator Perspectives on the Practice of Commercial Mediation* (Haywards Heath, Tottel Publishing 2005) 312; L Boulle and R Field, *Mediation in Australia* (Chatswood, NSW, LexisNexis Butterworths 2018) 247–48; Feehily (n 1) 379–81; R Feehily, 'Problem Based Learning and International Commercial Dispute Resolution in the Indian Ocean' (2018) 52(1) *The Law Teacher* 17; R Feehily 'Learning to Think Like a Lawyer' (2018) 9(1) *Mauritius Institute of Education, Journal of Education* 23; R Feehily, 'An Alternative Approach to Postgraduate Legal Education' in R Feehily and S Seeparsad (eds), *Governance, Globalisation and Dispute Resolution* (New Delhi, Star Publications 2017) 46–64. Courses similar to those offered by US universities have been offered by tertiary institutions in numerous countries as diverse as China, Lebanon and Uganda: see C W Moore, *The Mediation Process: Practical Strategies for Resolving Conflict* (4th ed, San Francisco, Jossey-Bass 2014) 582–83. For a discussion on a number of proposals to incentivise the use of mediation based on comparative empirical evidence, including mandatory training within the university and education sector that ensures the characteristics and effect of the process are understandable, see F Steffek and others, 'Guide for Regulating Dispute Resolution (GRDR): Principles and Comments' in F Steffek and others (eds), *Regulating Dispute Resolution: ADR and Access to Justice at the Crossroads* (Oxford, Hart Publishing 2013) 31–32. See also K Fach Gómez, 'The Role of Mediation in International Commercial Disputes: Reflections on Some Technological, Ethical and Educational Challenges' in Titi and Fach Gómez (eds) (n 1) 15–19.

public that the services it offers are uniquely trustworthy and based on professional standards.[5] Professionalisation requires that high minimum transparent practice and ethical standards are created and observed internationally and perceived as working effectively by parties in mediation and the public.

Three regulatory approaches or models to the qualification and regulation of mediators can be found internationally. The first is the market approach, where the state refrains from regulating education and admission to the profession. Instead, mediators, their associations, the parties and academia develop professional training, accreditation and practice standards. This approach trusts in the disciplining effects of demand and supply, and the rational and self-regulating behaviour of market participants who offer and use mediation services. The second is the incentive approach, where the mediation market is open to everyone and the state refrains from authorising individuals as a prerequisite to act as a mediator. However, it creates incentivising quality rules for mediators and the parties to opt into. For example, it sets incentives to meet certain qualification criteria, which may lead to recognised certification. This certification carries with it favourable rules for the parties concerning the confidentiality and quality of the process that only apply if the appointed mediator is listed in a register. This incentivises the parties to appoint a registered mediator and that mediators become certified. The third is the authorisation or admission approach, where the state establishes admission procedures for access or admission to practise as a mediator.[6]

---

[5] H J Wilensky, 'The Professionalisation of Everyone' (1964) 70(2) *The American Journal of Sociology* 137, 138. See generally this seminal article on professionalisation. It has been suggested that a number of milestones indicate the development and formal establishment of a profession. These include: (1) codification and terminology that characterise the social practice; (2) an extensive body of written knowledge that presents theory, approaches, procedures and practices that are employed in the discipline; (3) formal training programmes to prepare practitioners to offer the service; (4) university departments offering courses including certificates and degrees in the discipline; (5) a significant number of private professional and independent practitioners, in addition to organisations that provide the service; (6) local, national or international associations of professional practitioners; (7) professional codes of conduct and ethics; (8) qualifications for specific areas of practice; and (9) initiatives by the profession or governments to regulate entry, practice and the performance of practitioners to assure the public of predictable and high quality services: see Moore (n 4) 573–92.

[6] The three regulatory models are gleaned from a comparative analysis of approaches across many jurisdictions. The admission approach can be found in Hungary, the incentive approach in Austria and the market approach in England: see F Steffek, 'Principled Regulation of Dispute Resolution: Taxonomy, Policy, Topics' in Steffek and others (eds) (n 4) 55; Hopt and Steffek, 'Mediation: Comparison of Laws, Regulatory Models,

In commercial mediation – where the parties control the decision to enter the process, the choice of mediator and the outcome – regulation of the mediator's neutrality and qualifications does not need to be intensive.[7] Consequently a market approach or an incentive approach is viewed as advisable in this context.[8] Mediator training, accreditation and standards are important elements in the professionalisation of commercial mediation, both in ensuring that mediation is offered by suitably qualified individuals and that appropriate standards are observed.

5.5 Training

Requirements for mediator training vary across jurisdictions, and many countries have no national system of accreditation. However, commercial mediation service providers will generally require the mediators on their panels to have adequate training and accreditation.

5.5.1   CEDR Mediator Skills Training

The Mediator Skills Training course run by the Centre for Effective Dispute Resolution (CEDR) is an example of a commercial mediation skills training course; it is offered in the United Kingdom and internationally.[9] The programme runs over five days and is taught by

Fundamental Issues' in K Hopt and F Steffek (eds), *Mediation: Principles and Regulation in Comparative Perspective* (Oxford, Oxford University Press 2013) 120; F Steffek, 'Mediation' in J Basedow and others (eds), *The Max Planck Encyclopedia of European Private Law*, vol 2 (Oxford, Oxford University Press 2012) 1164. While there is a lack of detailed governing regulation, the development of mediation practice in England is generally significantly ahead compared with the rest of Europe. While many countries issued laws and other regulations to encourage the use of the process, mediation in England was led by demand rather than supply and began with practice. What lawyers in civil law jurisdictions may view as a lack of certainty, those in common law jurisdictions tend to embrace as enabling the preservation of party autonomy and the flexibility and choice that accompanies it: see J Tirado and E Vincente Maravall, 'Codes of Conduct for Commercial and Investment Mediators' in Titi and Fach Gómez (eds) (n 1) 349–50.

[7] See Steffek and others (eds) (n 4) 25. It may suit a party to choose a mediator who has a pre-existing relationship with, or shares the same nationality as the other party, as having a mediator that the other party trusts may entice them to engage meaningfully in the process and ultimately encourage compromise and settlement in a context where leverage counts for more than neutrality or the appearance of neutrality in building momentum for settlement. See Brower (n 1) 306–7, 316.

[8] See Steffek, 'Principled Regulation of Dispute Resolution' (n 6) 55.

[9] The Centre for Effective Dispute Resolution (CEDR) is registered with the UK Civil Mediation Council (CMC) as a commercial and civil mediation provider and fulfils the Council's

experienced practising mediators. Participants are trained in the skills required for effective mediation of commercial disputes and assessed for CEDR Accreditation. Participants receive a Mediator Handbook, case studies and role-play instructions one month before attending the training course. While designed to give participants a broad perspective on conflict management, the programme focusses on the mediation process and skills, using demonstration and practice. Case studies based on actual mediations are used throughout the course and participants experience the roles of mediator, advisor and mediation party.[10]

The programme includes a 'practice day' of shared learning. Using a single detailed case study, participants practise the skills required at each stage of a mediation. Trainers coach small groups of participants through the case study and provide personal feedback. In between the mediation sessions are group discussions about key issues encountered by the mediator. Each participant mediates one simulated case, and a trainer observes each session and assesses performance against a set of competencies. Individual feedback, group learning and discussion continue alongside this assessment.

Each participant is required to complete three assignments. These are: a written settlement agreement based on the case study undertaken during the course; a written self-assessment of the participant's mediation skills, including the strengths they bring to mediation and the areas they feel they need to work on; and a brief action plan for how they hope to take mediation forward in their career.

One of the advantages of mediation training such as the CEDR course is the opportunity it offers to deal in context with some of the grey areas found in mediator standards and guidelines. For example, where a mediator is faced with an imminent settlement that seems wholly inequitable, there are a number of strategic interventions that can be explored to deal with it. Experience suggests that training and simulated experience offer a more practical way of appreciating the subtleties of

standards for training, continuing professional development and administration. The CMC is a private but state-funded organisation that controls and promotes mediation, ensures standardisation among providers of mediation services, issues guidance notes for mediators, maintains a list of accredited mediation institutions and runs a complaints resolution service: see <https://civilmediation.org> accessed 10 May 2022.

[10] See G Bond and C Wall, *International Commercial Mediation Training Role-Plays: Cases from the ICC International Commercial Mediation Competition* (Paris, International Chamber of Commerce 2015) for a useful resource of twenty-one role-play exercises that includes expert commentary from various commercial, legal and training perspectives.

process responses to ethical dilemmas than the sometimes abstract and woolly articulation of standards and codes of conduct.[11]

5.6   Accreditation

Although accreditation is not an absolute indication of competence – or, for those who become accredited, a guarantee of a career in mediation – it does ensure the observance of certain standards.[12] CEDR Accreditation is based on assessments during the Mediation Skills Training course, and as mentioned above, participants must also complete three assignments within two weeks of completing the programme. The Certificate of Accreditation is awarded to participants who demonstrate the required level of competence. CEDR and similar organisations also provide continuing professional development to ensure mediators keep abreast of developments in the commercial mediation field.

5.7   Standards

Standards or codes of conduct guide mediators towards a sense of their basic commitments and professional responsibilities. They establish the parties' basic expectations of the mediator, creating norms against which mediator conduct can be assessed for discipline and liability. There are three general types of standard: those that bind practitioners, where a deviation could amount to professional misconduct; those that provide guiding principles only; and hybrid systems that contain both binding and guiding provisions. Binding standards generally cover elements such as ethical obligations, where a breach could result in a mediated

---

[11] Boulle and Field (n 4) 244. Education and training are growing academic fields that offer possibilities for translating theory into practice and practice into theory: see R C Bordone, M L Moffitt and F E Sander, 'The Next Thirty Years: Directions and Challenges in Dispute Resolution' in Moffitt and Bordone (eds) (n 3) 516. See also G A Lopez, 'Conclusion: The Future of Mediation in a Changing World' in A Georgakopoulos (ed), *The Mediation Handbook: Research, Theory, and Practice* (Abingdon, UK, Routledge 2017) 388–89.

[12] L A Mistelis, 'ADR in England and Wales: A Successful Case of Public Private Partnership' in N Alexander (ed), *Global Trends in Mediation* (2nd ed, Alphen aan den Rijn, Kluwer Law International 2006) 173. Mediator accreditation standards can vary considerably within and across jurisdictions. Europe tends to lead in offering specialist accreditation including commercial and intercultural mediation accreditation, compared with the generalist accreditation offered in many parts of the world: see N Alexander, *International and Comparative Mediation: Legal Perspectives* (Austin, Wolters Kluwer 2009) 122–27. See also D Golann and J Folberg, *Mediation: The Roles of Advocate and Neutral* (3rd ed, New York, Wolters Kluwer 2016) 358–60.

settlement agreement being set aside and potential legal liability for the mediator and exclusion from a professional panel; non-binding standards reflect guidelines or more tentative standards of care.[13]

The US Model Standards of Conduct for Mediators explicitly state that the use of 'shall' in a particular standard indicates that a mediator must follow the practice described.[14] The use of 'should' indicates that the practice described in the standard is highly desirable; while not required, it is to be departed from only for very strong reasons and to do so requires careful use of judgement and discretion.[15]

5.7.1 The US Model Standards and the European Code of Conduct

The US Model Standards of Conduct for Mediators ('Model Standards') were drafted in 1994 and revised in 2005 by a joint committee of the American Arbitration Association, the American Bar Association and the Association for Conflict Resolution. The Model Standards state that the fact that they have been adopted by the respective sponsoring entities should alert mediators to the fact that they may be viewed as establishing a standard of care for mediators. They are the most widely adopted national standards of conduct for mediators in the USA.

The European Code of Conduct for Mediators ('European Code') was developed in 2004 by a working group of mediation service providers, members of the legal profession and industry specialists across the European Union, supported by the European Commission. The European Code contains a number of principles but lacks the length and detail of the Model Standards. The preamble envisages that service providers may want to develop more detailed codes for the type of services that they offer.[16]

---

[13] In Australia, for example, the National Mediator Accreditation Standards provide that a recognised mediator accreditation body may suspend accreditation where a mediator is 'significantly non-compliant' with the standards: Approval Standards, section 5.1 (2015). See also Boulle and Field (n 4) 250–52.

[14] Model Standards of Conduct for Mediators (2005) ('Model Standards'), Note on Construction.

[15] ibid.

[16] The European Commission publishes a list on its website of the organisations that have committed to requesting that mediators appointed through them respect the European Code of Conduct for Mediators ('European Code'). It is the only code of conduct for mediators that seeks to have Europe-wide effect. Essentially it reflects principles contained in codes already developed by alternative dispute resolution organisations, such as ADR Group and CEDR in the United Kingdom, and in the mediation procedures advocated by other organisations, such as the International Chamber of Commerce, the

The issues that are generally covered by mediation standards are discussed in the following sections, with particular reference to the European Code and the Model Standards.[17]

5.7.2   Party Self-determination

This standard generally underscores the voluntary nature of the mediation process. Self-determination results in an uncoerced decision in which each party makes free and informed choices about process and outcome. Self-determination applies at any stage of the mediation process, including mediator selection, process design, participation in or withdrawal from the process, and outcomes. However, the Model Standards acknowledge that a mediator may need to balance party self-determination with the duty to conduct a quality process in accordance with the other standards. Where there is doubt about a party's ability to make free and informed choices, a mediator should make the parties aware of the importance of consulting other professionals to help them make informed choices. In practice, in commercial mediations, many parties will have legal advisors present. Mediators must remain mindful of their powers of persuasion and should not undermine the mediation process for any reason, such as achieving higher settlement rates.[18]

International Centre for Dispute Resolution and the CPR International Institute for Conflict Prevention & Resolution. See also S Blake, J Browne and S Sime, *The Jackson ADR Handbook* (2nd ed, Oxford, Oxford University Press 2016) 156. Article 4 of the EU Mediation Directive requires Member States to encourage the development of, and adherence to, voluntary codes of conduct by mediators and organisations providing mediation services: Directive 2008/52/EC of the European Parliament and of the Council of 21 May 2008 on certain aspects of mediation in civil and commercial matters [2008] OJ L136/3 ('EU Mediation Directive').

[17] As the Model Standards (n 14) are more detailed and comprehensive than the European Code (n 16), much of the information relating to standards that follows is gleaned from them. There are organisations that develop standards with global reach. For example, the International Mediation Institute (IMI) is a global organisation, supported by national mediation organisations, that develops global, professional standards for mediators and advocates. While not a service provider itself, the IMI also convenes stakeholders, promotes understanding of mediation and disseminates skills: see <https://imimediation.org> accessed 10 May 2022. One of the IMI's goals is to harmonise mediator certification requirements in both private and public service provider organisations globally, effectively an industry-led harmonisation process: see N Alexander, 'Harmonisation and Diversity in the Private International Law of Mediation: The Rhythms of Regulatory Reform' in Hopt and Steffek (eds) (n 6) 164.

[18] Standard I of the Model Standards (n 14) covers self-determination. Where parties elect to not have advisors present, it has been suggested that the mediator should obtain

5.7.3 Neutrality and Impartiality

While the terms 'neutrality' and 'impartiality' are sometimes used inter-changeably to mean simply that a mediator should be free from bias, there are distinctions between the two terms. Neutrality refers to the mediator's prior knowledge or interest in the outcome of disputes, while impartiality, a defining feature of the process and an ethical obligation, relates to the way they conduct the process and deal with the parties in a fair, even-handed, objective and unbiased way. Neutrality is a less absolute requirement and may be qualified depending on the context and circumstances.[19] Unlike neutrality, impartiality is effectively the rule against bias and should not be qualified. Hence a mediator may not always be neutral, but must act impartially, and this distinction is reflected in some standards, while other standards use the terms inter-changeably. Given this important distinction it is useful to consider each one separately.[20]

5.7.3.1 Impartiality

The impartiality of a mediator should emanate from their openness to any enforceable outcome. This helps the mediator to recognise any dynamic between the parties and to assess the agendas, ethics and values of the participants and the arguments and positions advanced by their advisors; accurate processing of this information can facilitate the mediator to respond with a strategy that moves the parties closer to a resolution of their own making.[21] Predicated on the concept of procedural justice, objective standards of impartiality are clearly crucial to the development

---

a written waiver of representation from each unrepresented party: see C Chern, *International Commercial Mediation* (London, Informa 2008) 198.

[19] The challenge, it has been suggested, is to change the focus from conflict resolution to constructive conflict engagement, such that mediators become conflict engagement specialists rather than neutral conflict resolvers: see B Mayer, *Beyond Neutrality: Confronting the Crisis in Conflict Resolution* (San Francisco, Jossey-Bass 2004) 3. Mayer argues that while neutrality is a source of mediator strength and credibility, it is also a significant limitation in terms of mistrust and doubt, resulting in a failure to offer parties sufficient opportunities for voice, justice, vindication, validation or impact: at 28–29.

[20] See K K Kovach, 'Mediation' in Moffitt and Bordone (eds) (n 3) 311. See also L Boulle, *Mediation: Principles, Process, Practice* (3rd ed, Chatswood, NSW, LexisNexis 2011) 71–80, 474–79. These distinctions are relevant to ensuring fairness in the arbitral process as well: see R Feehily, 'Neutrality, Independence and Impartiality in International Commercial Arbitration: A Fine Balance in the Quest for Arbitral Justice' (2019) 7(1) *Penn State Journal of Law and International Affairs* 88.

[21] Creo (n 4) 322.

of trust in the mediator and confidence in the fairness of the process, with any display of partiality being considered a breach of basic ethics.

Standards covering this area generally provide that mediators must conduct the process in an impartial manner and avoid conduct that gives the appearance of partiality. The confidentiality of the process can make it difficult to assess compliance with the impartiality requirement in mediator standards as there may be little objective evidence on which to assess the alleged partiality of a mediator's conduct. Some standards can require the mediator to withdraw if there is a challenge to their impartiality.[22] Some standards are quite specific: for example, the Model Standards state that mediators should not accept gifts, favours, loans or other items of value that raise questions of impartiality. The Standards permit the acceptance of 'de minimis' gifts or incidental items or services that are provided to facilitate the mediation or respect cultural norms, as long as they do not raise questions about a mediator's actual or perceived impartiality. If at any time a mediator is unable to conduct a mediation in an impartial manner, the mediator must withdraw from the mediation.[23]

5.7.3.2   Neutrality and Conflicts of Interest

Mediators should avoid a conflict of interest or the appearance of a conflict of interest during and after a mediation. Most standards require mediators to disclose to the parties their prior professional or personal relationships with any of the parties, or any actual or potential conflicts of

[22] See, e.g., section 5.2 of 'The Law Society Guidelines for those Involved in Mediations' in Law Society of New South Wales, *Dispute Resolution Kit* (2012). See also Boulle and Field (n 4) 257–58.

[23] Standard II of the Model Standards (n 14) and Part 2.2 of the European Code (n 16) cover impartiality. Regional and international mediation instruments also cover this theme: see, e.g., EU Mediation Directive (n 16) article 3(b), which defines a mediator as someone who conducts mediation in an impartial manner; UNCITRAL Model Law on International Commercial Mediation and International Settlement Agreements Resulting from Mediation, 2018 (Mediation Model Law) article 7(3), which provides that 'in conducting the proceedings, the mediator shall seek to maintain fair treatment of the parties and, in so doing, shall take into account the circumstances of the case'. Section 9 of the Uniform Mediation Act covers the mediator's disclosure of conflicts of interest. Interestingly, under s 9(g) of the Act, impartiality is optional; thus, fully informed parties can accept mediators who may not observe a strict standard of impartiality. The drafters of the Uniform Mediation Act did not consider impartiality to be a universal characteristic in practice and included strict disclosure provisions to minimise risks. In family disputes, for example, the mediator may act in the best interests of the child. States of the USA that adopt the Uniform Mediation Act can enact higher impartiality standards: see Alexander (n 12) 221–23.

interest that the mediator should reasonably be aware of. The Model Standards place a duty on the mediator to make reasonable inquiries into whether there are any facts that a reasonable individual would consider likely to create a potential or actual conflict of interest. While the disclosure obligation is a continuing one,[24] the extent of disclosure is often not clear,[25] but it would be consistent with the approach in other areas of law and professional practice to take a broad approach.[26]

The European Code specifies circumstances where disclosure would be required. These include any personal or business relationship with one of the parties; any financial or other interest, direct or indirect, in the outcome of the mediation; and whether the mediator, or a member of his or her firm, have acted in any capacity other than as mediator for one of the parties. Once such a disclosure has been made, the consent of the parties should be sought, and the mediator must be certain that they can mediate the dispute effectively before the mediation proceeds. The Model Standards provide that if a mediator's conflict of interest might reasonably be viewed as undermining the integrity of the mediation, a mediator shall withdraw from or decline to proceed with the mediation regardless of the expressed desire or agreement of the parties to the contrary.[27]

---

[24] Standard III of the Model Standards (n 14) and Part 2.1 of the European Code (n 16) cover conflicts of interest and independence.

[25] For example, article 6(5) of the Mediation Model Law (n 23) requires disclosure by the mediator of circumstances that may give rise to 'justifiable doubts' about his or her impartiality or independence, which seems quite vague. If the Model Law is to act as a framework for a mediation statute in a relevant jurisdiction, it would be worth considering whether to omit this provision. Issues such as independence and impartiality are best dealt with by way of a code of conduct which can be adapted as the needs of the process, the parties and mediation practice evolve over time. See also P Sanders, 'UNCITRAL's Model Law on International Commercial Conciliation' (2007) 23(1) *Arbitration International* 105, 114.

[26] While a code of conduct can give some guidance in this area, experience from comparable areas such as arbitration has shown that the extent of the duty of disclosure is difficult to determine in practice: see International Bar Association, 'Guidelines on Conflicts of Interest in International Arbitration' (2014).

[27] See Standard III(E) of the Model Standards (n 14). Section 9(a)(1) of the Uniform Mediation Act provides that, before accepting a mediation, an individual who is requested to serve as a mediator shall 'make an inquiry that is reasonable under the circumstances to determine whether there are any known facts that a reasonable individual would consider likely to affect the impartiality of the mediator, including a financial or personal interest in the outcome of the mediation and an existing or past relationship with a mediation party or foreseeable participant in the mediation'. If there is a failure to disclose, s 9(d) provides that the mediator loses the right to assert the mediation privilege under s 4 of the Act. See Chapter 9 at Section 9.4.6.3. Some codes impose more stringent requirements, such as section 5.4 of 'The Law Society Guidelines for those Involved in

Disclosure requirements are designed to enhance self-determination, in order that parties can make fully informed choices regarding mediator selection, and to remove concerns about the fairness of the process.[28]

5.7.4   Competence

This standard generally provides that a mediator should only mediate where they have the necessary process competence to satisfy the reasonable expectations of the parties. Competence includes proper training, experience in mediation and continuous updating of the mediator's education and practise of mediation skills, having regard to relevant standards or accreditation schemes. The Model Standards also refer to cultural understanding and other qualities that may be necessary. In commercial mediation, competence may include subject matter expertise – particularly in complex international disputes – and commercial parties are likely to seek and expect both subject matter and process competence when appointing a mediator. The obligation to maintain competence is a continuing obligation. If a mediator discovers during the mediation that they are no longer competent, they should discuss this with the parties and where appropriate withdraw from the mediation.[29]

Mediations' (n 22), which prohibits lawyers in New South Wales from mediating where they have acted for, or were previously employed by, a firm retained by one of the parties. See also Boulle and Field (n 4) 255–57; R Kulms, 'Mediation in the USA: Alternative Dispute Resolution Between Legalism and Self-Determination' in Hopt and Steffek (eds) (n 6) 1298.

28   See Alexander (n 12) 217.
29   Standard IV of the Model Standards (n 14) and Parts 1.1 and 1.2 of the European Code (n 16) cover competence. Some codes go into much greater detail about the mediator's functions and skills: see Boulle and Field (n 4) 253–54. For example, the Law Council of Australia's guidelines provide: 'Choosing the right mediator will enhance the parties' settlement prospects in the mediation. When selecting a mediator [lawyers should] (a) first look to a mediator's skill and experience as a mediator, and then to any additional qualifications that may be helpful, such as accreditation or expertise in the subject matter of the dispute or law; and (b) consider the role of the mediator and whether a particular style of mediation may be better suited to the dispute': *Guidelines for Lawyers in Mediations* (2011) section 4. It has been suggested that the more evaluative the parties want the mediator to be, the more helpful it will be for the mediator to have legal experience, particularly where reality testing of legal arguments is required: see M Kallipetis and S Ruttle, 'Better Dispute Resolution: The Development and Practice of Mediation in the United Kingdom Between 1995 and 2005' in J C Goldsmith, A Ingen-Housz and G H Pointon (eds), *ADR in Business: Practice and Issues Across Countries and Cultures* (Alphen aan den Rijn, Kluwer Law International 2006) 238–39.

5.7.5   Confidentiality

Most standards, such as the Model Standards and the European Code, reflect the fact that mediators are under a duty to maintain confidentiality in the separate caucus meetings, and with regard to the overall process, but allow possible exceptions such as where the parties agree to the disclosure of information, or where legal or public policy reasons require disclosure. The maintenance of confidentiality is under pressure in some jurisdictions from the compulsion to report to courts in subsequent actions, coupled with the requirement that mediators make subjective judgments on events during the mediation; even so, a mediator's duty to maintain confidentiality remains salient.[30]

However, confidentiality protection in mediation standards must be balanced against other policy considerations, such as the court's right to compel mediation evidence in appropriate circumstances. The Model Standards provide that mediators should promote understanding among the parties of the extent to which the parties will maintain the confidentiality of information they obtain in a mediation, and allow for the parties to create their own confidentiality rules in appropriate circumstances.[31]

5.7.6   Quality of the Process

This standard generally requires a mediator to conduct the process so that it promotes diligence, timeliness, presence of the appropriate participants, party participation, procedural fairness, party competency and mutual respect. It can deal with a mediator's availability, cautioning the mixing of a mediator's role with other roles, such as the role of a lawyer. The standard can also deal with the steps a mediator should take: to avoid using the mediation process to further criminal conduct; where the process is no longer justified, including ending the process; or to address other issues that may negatively impact the quality of the mediation process.[32]

---

[30] See Boulle and Field (n 4) 258–60. See Chapter 9 at Section 9.4.1.5.

[31] Standard V of the Model Standards (n 14) and Part 4 of the European Code (n 16) cover confidentiality.

[32] Standard VI of the Model Standards (n 14) and Parts 3.1–3.3 of the European Code (n 16) cover the quality of the process.

5.7.7   Advertising and Solicitation, Fees and Other Charges

This standard generally states that mediators must be truthful and transparent in the way that they advertise and solicit work, and charge fees and mediation expenses.[33]

5.7.8   Advancement of Mediation Practice

This standard generally provides that mediators should act in a way that advances mediation practice. The Model Standards provide the example of assisting new mediators through training, mentoring and networking.[34]

5.7.9   Implications of Standardisation

In some EU countries, such as France and Finland, the state has developed a national code of conduct, while private codes have also been developed. In other EU countries such as Spain and Germany, there is no national code, and codes of conduct have developed at an institutional or organisational level. Each approach generally follows the European Code. Consequently, the European Code is viewed as effective in that it is either directly used by parties or has inspired the development of national or private codes of conduct.[35]

The preamble to the Model Standards states that they serve three primary goals: to guide the conduct of mediators, to inform mediating parties and to promote public confidence in mediation as a process for resolving disputes. While such aspirations are noble, standards contain an inherent tension in promoting confidentiality, as the enforcement of confidentiality restricts the scope to examine mediator conduct. Codes of conduct can reduce some of the uncertainty about standards of competence and the contours of ethical behaviour, although they will leave some issues unresolved. Mediator training can help to address the unresolved subjective ethical issues. Ultimately, mediation standards are likely to reflect practice experience and judicial definition when cases involving ethical standards come before the courts. Consequently, mediation standards should be viewed as organic instruments, evolving and

---

[33] Standards VII and VIII of the Model Standards (n 14) and Parts 1.3 and 3.4 of the European Code (n 16) cover advertising and solicitation, and fees and other charges.

[34] Standard IX of the Model Standards (n 14) covers advancement of mediation practice.

[35] Tirado and Vincente Maravall (n 6) 342–52.

responding to the changing nature and requirements of mediation practice.[36]

5.7.10 Mediator Standards and the Singapore Convention

Mediator standards may be sourced from ethical codes, codes of conduct or practice standards, agreements to mediate, legislation, case law and court practice directions. This regulatory diversity is acknowledged and reflected in the Singapore Convention[37] by the drafters' intention that each states' competent authority should determine the standards applicable.[38] The provisions discussed here gave professional mediator standards an international visibility that was previously absent.[39]

Mediator misconduct is one of the grounds on which a court can refuse to grant relief under the Singapore Convention where a party seeks to enforce or have a mediated settlement recognised. The Convention refers to two types of mediator misconduct: breach of standards and failure of impartiality.[40]

Article 5(1)(e) provides that relief may be refused where:

> [t]here was a serious breach by the mediator of standards applicable to the mediator or the mediation without which breach that party would not have entered into the settlement agreement.

The provision only appears to apply to the extent that there are applicable standards – that is, where 'standards applicable to the mediator or the mediation' can be identified. The provision requires a serious breach of the applicable standard. It also requires that a causal link be positively established between the alleged misconduct and the decision to enter into the mediated settlement agreement, by the party seeking to rely on this ground for refusal.[41]

---

[36] See Boulle and Field (n 4) 261–63. In view of the character of the mediation process, for issues that are subject to changing practice requirements, a flexible form of regulation is preferable. National rules will likely be required for issues such as mediation confidentiality, the impact of mediation on limitation periods and the enforcement of settlement agreements as the parties may not be able to create all legal effects by contract: see Hopt and Steffek (n 6) 114–15.

[37] United Nations Convention on International Settlement Agreements Resulting from Mediation.

[38] N Alexander and S Chong, *The Singapore Convention on Mediation: A Commentary* (Alphen aan den Rijn, Kluwer Law International 2019) 114.

[39] ibid 125.

[40] See Chapter 8 at Section 8.6.7.

[41] Analogies with areas of contract law such as misrepresentation could prove helpful in defining the meaning and scope of the causal link that must be established: see ibid 125–26; T Schnabel,

Article 5(1)(f) provides that relief may be refused where:

> [t]here was a failure by the mediator to disclose to the parties circum-
> stances that raise justifiable doubts as to the mediator's impartiality or
> independence and such failure to disclose had a material impact or undue
> influence on a party without which failure that party would not have
> entered into the settlement agreement.

Consequently there must be a breach of the mediator's duty of disclosure;
the failure to disclose must raise justifiable doubts about the mediator's
impartiality or independence; and a causal link must be positively established between the alleged misconduct and the decision to enter into the
mediated settlement agreement by the party seeking to rely on this
ground for refusal. Further, the mediator's failure to disclose must have
had 'a material impact or undue influence' on that party for the ground
for refusal to be available. Similar to article 5(1)(e), this provision sets
a high threshold. The test is intended to be an objective one, such that the
failure to disclose would have led a reasonable person not to consent to
the mediated settlement agreement. Unlike article 5(1)(e), this provision
is autonomous and can be relied upon regardless of whether 'applicable
standards' require disclosure.[42]

5.8   Legal Liability of Mediators

The relative dearth of legal proceedings against mediators may be
attributed to the confidential nature of the mediation process and the
facilitative style adopted, particularly in commercial mediations. It also
appears to reflect substantial compliance with mediator obligations and
that the process is a low-risk activity from a user perspective. It
would be difficult to find a causal link between a mediator's actions
and loss suffered where a mediator was neither an advisor nor

---

'The Singapore Convention on Mediation: A Framework for the Cross-Border Recognition
and Enforcement of Mediated Settlements' (2019) 19(1) *Pepperdine Dispute Resolution Law
Journal* 1, 51–52.

[42] For example, if a party was aware of the information that should have been disclosed, it
would be difficult to establish a causal link between the failure to disclose and the party's
decision to enter the mediated settlement. In *Lehrer* v. *Zwernemann* 14 SW 3d 775 (2000),
a number of claims, including a claim of misconduct against a mediator, were summarily
dismissed by a Texas court on the basis that the plaintiff had constructive knowledge of
the non-disclosed information about the mediator's relationship with the legal representatives of the other party, and no damage could be shown from the alleged misconduct.
'Material impact' would include misrepresentation or unconscionability by the mediator:
see Alexander and Chong (n 38) 117, 126; Schnabel (n 41) 52–54.

a decision-maker.[43] However, while there may be few occasions where legal proceedings have been brought against mediators, it is nevertheless still possible that proceedings will be taken against mediators by aggrieved disputants or third parties.[44] Proceedings are likely to arise on either of two grounds: a substantive basis, where a party feels they could have settled on substantially better terms; or could have achieved more had they not settled at all; and a procedural basis, where a party feels aggrieved about some aspect of the procedure, regardless of the outcome. In commercial mediation, it is notionally easier to base liability on procedural rather than substantive matters, particularly where there are legal advisors involved and a clear process/content distinction is drawn by the mediator. However, as discussed in the context of contract, tort and fiduciary obligations, it can prove difficult to develop a basis for mediator liability.[45]

5.8.1   Liability in Contract

Private commercial mediation is a creature of contract. Mediators in this context have no implied authority; their power is conferred by the parties and lasts as long as the parties are willing to confer it. Their responsibilities and obligations emanate from the agreement to mediate. Mediation service providers usually have standard form agreements to mediate that detail such matters as the fees and costs arrangements, meeting procedures, roles and responsibilities of participants and the mediator, methods of terminating the agreement, and confidentiality provisions; these agreements may incorporate by reference mediation standards or codes of

---

[43] See A Koo, 'Exploring Mediator Liability in Negligence' (2016) 45 *Common Law World Review* 165, for an analysis, based on English, US and Australasian case law, of the challenging nature of proving a breach due to a lack of clear standards against which to measure mediator performance and the difficulty of establishing causation.

[44] In research carried out in the USA between 2013 and 2017, mediator misconduct was rarely raised and never successful as a defence to enforcement of mediated settlement agreements: see J R Coben, 'Evaluating the Singapore Convention through a US-Centric Litigation Lens: Lessons Learned from Nearly Two Decades of Mediation Disputes in American Federal and State Courts' in Singapore Mediation Convention Reference Book (2019) 20(4) *Cardozo Journal of Conflict Resolution* 1063, 1084. See Chapter 8 at Section 8.2 for a discussion of cases where actions have been taken against mediators by aggrieved disputants.

[45] See L Boulle and M Nesic, *Mediation: Principles, Process, Practice* (London, Butterworths Law 2001) 512; Alexander (n 12) 215, 240–44; Blake, Browne and Sime (n 16) 167. It is the experience across numerous jurisdictions that issues of mediator liability tend not to arise in practice: see Hopt and Steffek (n 6) 77–79.

conduct. As the agreements are drafted by service providers, they are likely to contain provisions limiting mediator liability. Agreements to mediate may also be unwritten or implied. Regardless of the form the agreement takes, as mediators are a party to them, courts could potentially find mediators liable for breach of contract in appropriate circumstances.[46]

A term may be implied into an agreement to mediate if it is reasonable or necessary to give the agreement business efficacy, or is so obvious that it is understood or can be clearly expressed and does not contradict an express term. An example of an implied term is where the mediator has a duty to perform with reasonable care, skill and diligence, with 'reasonableness' determined by the standard of care expected of a reasonable person in that activity or industry. The standard of care for mediators is difficult to determine given the flexible nature of the process and the influence on it of an individual mediator's style. As mediators hold themselves out as possessing special skill in facilitating negotiations, they would be expected to do what ordinary skilled people with that expertise would have done, and evidence of industry practice – including mediator codes of conduct – will assist in identifying what is regarded as reasonable skill and care.[47]

A contractual breach could result if a mediator's performance was inconsistent with the applicable standard of care. The party concerned would need to prove actual loss or damage and establish that it was caused by the mediator's conduct. Provided the damage flowed from the breach and was not too remote, an award of damages could be attained. However, many hurdles would be encountered in claiming damages for a mediator's breach of contract – particularly where the claim related to an allegation of negligence regarding the mediator's competence in managing a fair process as it is difficult to define reasonable standards of mediator behaviour. As the parties, not the mediator, make the decisions, it would also be difficult to establish that the mediator's breach was the cause of the damage that occurred. Calculating damages would be largely theoretical when assessing what the outcome of the mediation would have been had the breach not occurred, given the uncertainty of the settlement terms or whether an

---

[46] See Boulle and Nesic (n 45) 513; T Allen, *Mediation Law and Civil Practice* (2nd ed, Haywards Heath, Bloomsbury Professional 2019) 53, 56.

[47] In England, for example, adherence to the codes of mediator practice recommended by the Law Society is likely to be considered evidence of good practice where complaints are made against solicitor mediators: see Boulle and Nesic (n 45) 509–10, 513.

agreement would have resulted. A mediator could also argue that the party did not mitigate their damages: for example, in not acting to reduce the losses resulting from failing to reach a commercial settlement. Immunity clauses that exclude mediators from liability in discharging their obligations could also be an impediment if the issue complained of is covered by the clause.[48]

5.8.2 Liability in Tort

An action in tort against a mediator could be based on the mediator's act or omission. In a commercial context, this would most likely take the form of a negligence action based on an act or omission regarding the special skills and knowledge expected of professionals, or on a negligent misstatement that resulted in economic loss.[49] A party could take a negligence action on the basis that they are dissatisfied with a settlement and claim that the mediator's negligence resulted in their loss. The basic elements of negligence would have to be established: a duty of care, breach of the duty, actual loss or damage, a causal connection (or proximate cause) between the breach and the loss, and an absence of contributory negligence or other vitiating conduct by the party. The courts would look for a relationship of proximity between the mediator and party on which to base a duty of care to avoid foreseeable injury.

'Reasonable in the circumstances' is the standard of care, and mediator standards and agreements to mediate would inform this. The reasonableness assessment will be influenced by the parties' circumstances. In commercial mediations, particularly high-value disputes, parties tend to be sophisticated, well advised and well represented. If the mediator is not viewed as having imparted advice (particularly on matters where the mediator has professional expertise), recommends that the parties seek independent advice where they have none and avoids involvement in drafting the settlement agreement, a relationship of proximity would be difficult to establish.[50]

---

[48] Boulle (n 20) 718–22; P Brooker, 'Mediator Immunity: Time for Evaluation in England and Wales?' (2016) 36(3) *Legal Studies* 464, 483–84. It would be easier to prove breach of confidence or conflict of interest.

[49] Other possible forms of tort liability include defamation, breach of confidence, misleading and deceptive conduct, undue influence, unconscionability, negligence or statutory torts in appropriate circumstances: see Boulle (n 20) 722; Alexander (n 12) 241–42.

[50] See Boulle (n 20) 722–24. See C Jarrosson, 'Legal Issues Raised by ADR' in Goldsmith, Ingen-Housz and Pointon (eds) (n 29) 128.

Proving that the mediator's conduct caused or materially contributed to actual damage that otherwise would not have occurred is difficult, as it is impossible to know what the party would have done, or failed to do, had the mediator acted differently than the way alleged. Parties are engaged participants in a mediation process where causation is highly complex. Even if it could be shown that one party settled on particular terms only because of the mediator's conduct, it would be very difficult to prove that the other party would have agreed to an alternative settlement had the mediator discharged their obligations. It would also be difficult to establish causative responsibility where parties are legally represented, or where the alleged damages are incurred after the mediator advised the parties to seek independent legal or other expert advice.[51]

As damages are awarded to put plaintiffs in the position they would have been in had the tort not occurred, the nature of the mediation process makes such an assessment highly theoretical. It would be difficult for a party to establish their actual loss by referring to what a court or arbitrator may have decided. The basis for a claim in damages is likely to be an alleged negligent misstatement that caused a party economic loss. A stricter basis of liability than that applied for other acts or omissions, it requires evidence that a party relied on the mediator, and that the mediator was aware (or should have been aware) that his or her words would cause the reliance. A mediator can guard against such allegations by expressly disclaiming responsibility for the accuracy of a particular statement and recommending that the parties seek independent advice.[52] The nature of the mediation process and the role of the mediator within it makes a successful action in negligence very difficult to achieve where a party is dissatisfied with a mediated settlement. For liability to arise, a mediator's role would need to be redefined as one with greater control over both the process and the outcome.[53]

---

[51] In the US case of *Lange* v. *Marshall* 622 SW 2d 237 Mo Ct App (1981), the appeal court dismissed a negligence action against the mediator on the basis that he failed to negotiate a more favourable settlement for the plaintiff, as a causative link between the settlement that was ultimately repudiated and the mediator's actions could not be established: see Boulle and Nesic (n 45) 516. However, where a mediator drafts a settlement agreement at the end of the mediation, he or she could be subject to the requirement that the draft accurately reflects what was agreed. In the Australian case *Tapoohi* v. *Lewenberg (No 2)* [2003] VSC 410, the mediator dictated the terms of the settlement agreement but omitted an important provision regarding tax advice: see the discussion in Section 5.8.5.

[52] In an extreme case, where a mediator knowingly makes a false statement with the intention that a party will act on it and a loss results because of the party's reliance, it would amount to fraudulent misrepresentation: see Boulle and Nesic (n 45) 517.

[53] See Boulle (n 20) 724–26; Hopt and Steffek (n 6) 77–79. See also Brooker (n 48) 485–86.

5.8.3   Fiduciary Obligations

A fiduciary relationship is a relationship of trust and reliance where the fiduciary (for example, an agent) should act in the best interest of the beneficiary (in this example, the principal). In a mediation, the question arises whether the mediator has fiduciary obligations towards the parties and could therefore be held liable for a breach. Fiduciary obligations do not require the existence of a predefined legal standard, as is the case with a tort; nor is a formal contract required, as they impose a strict liability. Trustworthiness, diligence and absence of bias are three general fiduciary-like obligations that mediators owe parties. They may be breached if a mediator fails to provide information that could have proved influential regarding a party's decision to agree to a settlement, creates an atmosphere of coercion that a party believes led to their acceptance of a settlement, communicates secretly with one party or is dishonest with the parties about his or her qualifications. However, a mediator cannot act for two beneficiaries in the same transaction as this would mean that they owe separate duties simultaneously to parties with conflicting rights and interests. A mediator is not appointed to act in the best interests of either or both parties in any direct sense, but to act as a neutral, and this is incompatible with the traditional status of a fiduciary.[54]

5.8.4   Other Forms of Liability and Accountability

Mediators could be held liable under fair trading and other consumer legislation for false advertising, misleading statements about their services and other unconscionable behaviour. Such laws are designed to supplement professional standards for service providers in various fields. They imply a warranty into services contracts, warranting that the services will be provided with due care and skill. The specific statutory definitions will determine the applicability of this legislation to mediators. Mediators could also potentially be held criminally liable where their conduct makes them a party to fraud or the commission of a statutory offence, or where they collude with the parties to commit

---

[54] While the courts are unlikely to find that a mediator has a fiduciary duty to parties in a mediation, the confidential nature of the mediator–client relationship would produce an equitable duty of confidence requiring that the mediator not use information given by one party in confidence without that party's consent: see Boulle (n 20) 726–28. For a discussion on mediator duties of care and loyalty gleaned from empirical research across several jurisdictions, see Hopt and Steffek (n 6) 73–77. See also Brooker (n 48) 482–83.

a crime such as tax evasion. In the absence of a statute, this liability would be determined according to general principles of criminal law.

There is potential mediator liability to third parties not involved in the mediation, where the mediator's actions or inactions cause injury. In the mediation of a construction dispute, for example, the interests of sub-contractors could be indirectly represented by the principal contractor, and if the mediator provides advice to the principal contractor that is reasonably relied on by the subcontractors (third parties) and that causes them loss, there is potential for liability. While demonstrating a duty of care and causation would be problematic for a potential litigant, this situation highlights the importance of mediators adopting a non-advisory, facilitative role.

When professionals such as lawyers act as mediators, they remain liable for breaches of their professional standards as lawyers. Similarly, mediators could be exposed to liability if during the mediation they stray into professional areas in which they are not qualified. In *Werle* v. *Rhode Island Bar Association*,[55] a mediator was successfully sued by the Rhode Island Bar Association on the basis that his mediation practice caused him to engage in the unauthorised practice of law.[56]

The mediation service provider may have its own disciplinary process for dealing with complaints. This may result in a mediator's accreditation being revoked and the mediator being removed from the provider's panel if the complaint is upheld. A final form of accountability is the market-place. Mediators are unlikely to attract work if they have a reputation for receiving complaints. Many law firms maintain databases of mediators and remove or blacklist those who fail to observe professional standards.[57]

5.8.5 *Mediator Behaviour and the Steps to Limit Exposure*

It is not the responsibility of the mediator to ensure a fair or just settlement. The mediator's obligation is to facilitate an agreement that the parties freely and willingly sign. The mediator does not have a role in looking to the reasons why parties agree on particular terms, provided the agreement is enforceable.[58] However, a number of points can be gleaned

---

[55] 755 F 2d 195 (1st Cir 1985).
[56] See also Boulle (n 20) 728–31.
[57] See Allen (n 46) 54; Brower (n 1) 314.
[58] See Feehily (n 1) 403. Perceptions of fairness are often inappropriately grounded in legal rights, while mediation is about settlement based on interests. See also Kovach (n 20) 311–12;

from potential liability under contract and tort to determine the legal contours of what mediators should or must do to insulate themselves from potential liability. Many commercial disputants will attend mediation with legal or relevant expert advisors. If a party does not, a mediator should suggest that they may wish to do so, in appropriate circumstances. As discussed in Section 5.8.2, provided the mediator is not viewed as having imparted advice (particularly on matters where the mediator has professional expertise), recommends that the parties seek independent advice where they have none and avoids involvement in drafting the settlement agreement, a relationship of proximity would be difficult to establish. A mediator can also guard against allegations of negligent misstatement by expressly disclaiming responsibility for the accuracy of a particular statement and recommending that the parties seek independent advice. The importance of mediators bearing these points in mind has been demonstrated in cases in a number of jurisdictions.

In *Sejane v. Commission for Conciliation Mediation and Arbitration*,[59] a settlement agreement was set aside by the South African Labour Court because one of the parties, who was illiterate, had not been legally represented. The role of a CCMA Commissioner, like that of a facilitative mediator, is to steer the parties towards a mutually agreed outcome.[60] It was held that the Commissioner had been 'derelict in her duties for not properly considering the interests of the applicant in respect of representation'.[61]

The significance of a mediator not advising parties about the likely outcome if the case were to be litigated or proceed to arbitration was demonstrated in a subsequent South African case. In *TH Kasipersad v. CCMA*,[62] an applicant withdrew his case based on a CCMA Commissioner's advice to him that he had a 50/50 chance of success, that it would take two to three days before the matter would be heard in court and that he might have to pay for legal representation and, if he lost,

European Code (n 16) Part 3.2 (a mediator may end a mediation if a settlement is being reached that appears unenforceable or illegal).

[59] [2001] ZALC 156. The South African Labour Court is a division of the High Court.
[60] See Commission for Conciliation Mediation and Arbitration (CCMA), 'Guidelines on Conciliation Proceedings', GN 896, GG 18936, June 1998. The CCMA is an independent dispute resolution body established under the South African Labour Relations Act 1995.
[61] *Sejane* (n 59) [13].
[62] [2002] ZALC 89, (2003) 24 ILJ 178 (LC). The Court also held that the rule precluding commissioners and parties to conciliation proceedings from giving evidence about them is unconstitutional: at [5], [6]. See also A Rycroft, 'Settlement and the Law' (2013) 130(1) *South African Law Journal* 187, 201.

additional costs. She did not advise him of the possible outcome if he succeeded. In setting aside the settlement agreement, the Court held that by sketching only four possible outcomes, the Commissioner manifested bias against the applicant. It held that if a commissioner is to engage in scenario sketching, there is an obligation to 'present fully and dispassionately all the consequences of proceeding with and withdrawing the dispute'.[63]

A mediator is an independent actor, not an agent of either party, and must be careful not to be construed as an agent. In the English case *Clay* v. *Lenkiewicz Foundation*,[64] it was revealed that during a mediation, the mediator brought to the claimant the defendants' offer which included an oil painting. The mediator stated that the painting had been professionally valued at £80,000, 'If sold at auction', producing a written valuation the defendants had obtained the previous day. The claimant accepted the offer 'in reliance on the mediator's representation that the valuation was a market valuation'. However, the valuation had been obtained for insurance purposes and covered the cost of purchasing a similar painting if it was lost or destroyed, which was higher than the market value of the painting. The claimant sought damages alleging that the material misrepresentation had induced the mediated settlement. The case settled, but the parties agreed to disclose what happened during the mediation. The claimant asserted that the mediator had actual or apparent authority as an agent to make representations for the defendants who should be bound by any error. The defendants denied authorising the mediator to represent that the valuation indicated its market value, though accepting that the mediator was given the valuation with other papers. The mediator declined to become involved in this case. A mediator can limit their exposure in such situations by ensuring that the disclosure of a document is authorised and making no assertions about its provenance. Any material fact or representation upon which either party relies should be recited in the settlement agreement, as the settlement agreement will be admissible in evidence for the court to enforce, avoiding the need to breach mediation confidentiality.[65]

---

[63] *Kasipersad* (n 62) [20]. While the issue was not raised for review, the Court also opined that a Commissioner should only give advice on procedure if the parties jointly ask the Commissioner for advice on a given matter. See also Labour Relations Act 1995, ss 115(2) (a), 135(3)(c).

[64] *Clay* v. *Lenkiewicz Foundation* (Plymouth County Court 9PL05124).

[65] See T Allen, 'Should Mediators (and Mediation) Be Trusted?' (2012) 162 *New Law Journal* 842.

Tapoohi v. *Lewenberg (No 2)*[66] is an Australian decision given in interlocutory proceedings where mediator liability was addressed. It involved two sisters who settled a dispute about their mother's estate through mediation. Under the agreement Tapoohi agreed to pay Lewenberg $1.4 million in exchange for properties. The mediator dictated the terms of the settlement agreement, with little involvement from the parties' lawyers, and the terms of settlement were not made subject to tax advice despite this having been raised on a number of occasions by the lawyers present.

Tapoohi subsequently realised that there was a capital gains tax liability that reduced considerably the value of her settlement. As part of a complex litigation, Tapoohi sued several parties, including her former solicitors on the grounds that they had been instructed to obtain tax advice about any settlement. The solicitors sought contribution from the mediator on the basis that Tapoohi suffered damage from the mediator's breach of contractual and tortious obligations towards her. Justice Habersberger held it 'not beyond argument'[67] that the mediator could be in breach of contractual and tortious duties by a trial court. On this basis the mediator's application for summary judgment was dismissed.

While the parties settled their claim and consequently, from a jurisprudential perspective, the issues were not addressed at a full hearing, this interlocutory decision reinforces the importance of a mediator informing parties that they should seek their own legal, tax or other relevant professional or expert advice. It would also be helpful in limiting mediator liability if agreements to mediate contained clauses exonerating mediators from liability and if settlement agreements provided that the parties have not relied on any legal or drafting advice from the mediator.[68] Parties could also consider including a cooling-off clause in appropriate circumstances, enabling agreements to provide for subsequent withdrawal from settlements within a stated period of time.[69]

---

[66] [2003] VSC 410.

[67] ibid [86].

[68] The Court in *Tapoohi* made it clear that the mediator is responsible for establishing that immunity exists: ibid [89].

[69] The case arose from an evaluative mediation where, unusually, no agreement to mediate was signed, which meant that contractual immunity was not a factor: see Boulle and Field (n 4) 357–62. See also M Moffitt, 'Ten Ways to Get Sued: A Guide for Mediators' (2003) 8 *Harvard Negotiation Law Review* 81. See also Chapter 8 at Section 8.3 on drafting settlement agreements.

5.8.6   Mediator Immunity

In the USA and Australia, mediator immunity tends to be linked to court-annexed mediation programmes, which facilitate mandatory referral to mediation, while in England, there is currently no immunity as mediation remains largely in the private arena.[70] There are several policy justifications for this immunity. These include the importance of mediators being protected against defamation; to ensure the finality of mediated settlements, particularly in a context where facilitative mediators are not accountable for the outcome; to protect the integrity of the process by ensuring confidentiality; to ensure that mediators do not become risk averse due to concerns about being sued, with the result that the process becomes prescriptive or even legalistic; and that if mediator immunity were not available it would be difficult to ensure a supply of mediators for the efficient running of mediation programmes.[71]

Unlike judges or arbitrators, mediators do not perform judicial or quasi-judicial functions or make binding decisions. They make procedural not substantive decisions and consequently do not generally benefit from immunity under the common law. The two possible sources of immunity are statute and contract. Statutory immunities are either 'unqualified', where they prohibit any civil proceedings, or 'qualified', where mediators must satisfy certain requirements, such as acting in good faith. In the USA and Australia, there are very few provisions at state or federal level providing either full or partial immunity for mediators who act in a private capacity.[72]

In practice, commercial mediators operating privately are unlikely to receive the benefit of statutory immunity in most jurisdictions. This accentuates the need for mediators to ensure that agreements to mediate include appropriately drafted immunity clauses.[73] Most service providers draft agreements to mediate and will include an exclusion clause covering

---

[70] The court schemes in England tend to be 'opt-in', where either party can object: see Brooker (n 48) 465. For simplicity the term 'England' is used throughout this book to describe the jurisdiction of England and Wales.

[71] A key justification for mediator immunity in the USA is a connection to the judicial process: see Brooker (n 48) 469–72.

[72] There have been major initiatives in the USA and Australia to move disputes into court-annexed mediation programmes, and this has also involved introducing statutory immunity to augment the process and elevate the status of mediators: see Boulle and Field (n 4) 362–64; Brooker (n 48) 472–78.

[73] This may take the form of a contractual indemnity: see Alexander (n 12) 118. In the US case *Morgan Phillips Inc* v. *JAMS/Endispute LLC* 44 Cal Rptr 3d 782 (Cal Ct App 2006), an arbitrator who withdrew from the role at an early stage to mediate the dispute lost the

both the mediator and the provider but it is unclear whether they are effective. The agreement may also include an indemnity to cover costs if an action is taken against the mediator. Courts will normally imply a term into the agreement that mediators will act with reasonable care and skill, and mediators who purport to possess particular expertise are likely to be held to a higher standard. Exclusion clauses will usually exonerate mediators from liability for negligence, breach of contract, defamation and other civil wrongs. They are likely to be ineffective if a mediator acts outside the scope of the agreement to mediate, if they conflict with statutory provisions or if they attempt to exclude liability for fraud or deliberate breach. Similar to other types of exclusion clauses, they must be clear and unambiguous; the mediator must show that the clause excludes the relevant liability when relying on it, and doubts or ambiguities would be construed against a mediator attempting to rely on it.[74]

In practice, immunity clauses tend to be clearly drafted in both scope and intent and present a significant impediment to liability actions against mediators. Few cases have featured to date and finding the appropriate balance between liability and immunity will ultimately require judicial direction. Whether mediator immunity emanates from statute or contract, it is likely to be subject to a good faith requirement and to the relevant code of conduct that reflects the appropriate professional standard of care required of commercial mediators. Immunity should fall away where it is demonstrated that a mediator breached ethical obligations through bias or coercion, or provided professional advice that proved defective.[75]

5.9 Mediation and the Practice of Law

As ethics codes and codes of professional responsibility emerged for lawyers in jurisdictions across the world, they did not explicitly cover

---

benefit of arbitral immunity as the Court could not find a sufficient nexus between the two roles: see Alexander at 243.

[74] See Boulle and Nesic (n 45) 520–23; Boulle (n 20) 737–46. See Chapter 9 for a discussion on the varying approaches adopted across jurisdictions with respect to testimony by mediators (at Section 9.4.1.5) and the mediator obligation to report allegations of fraud and criminality (at Section 9.4.5).

[75] Mediators may obtain professional indemnity insurance to limit the negative financial impact of liability exposure. Some law societies include this as part of their professional insurance as they view mediation as part of their members' practice. Such cover is often a requirement in mediator codes of conduct, such as the CEDR Code in the United Kingdom. As there is no recorded claim against mediators in the United Kingdom, premiums are low: see Boulle (n 20) 746–55; Allen (n 46) 56.

or provide guidance on mediation, and therefore failed to address issues such as confidentiality, conflicts of interest and unauthorised practice. If mediation is understood in its 'pure' form of facilitation, it does not involve the practice of law. The absence of a lawyer–client relationship has been used as the governing test, and jurisprudence from the USA has attempted to define the practice of law as applying legal principles to concrete facts. For example, a court defined the practice of law as skills that included the ability to evaluate the strengths and weaknesses of the client's case vis-à-vis that of an adversary.[76] While 'client representation' can be a central focus, reliance can also be instrumental, and where there is increased liability imposed on lawyers for reliance by third-party beneficiaries on legal opinions or advice given to others, the lawyer–client relationship may not be as decisive. When mediators engage in some prediction or application of legal standards to concrete facts, particularly when they draft settlement agreements, it is reasonable to conclude that it is the work of a lawyer, whether or not there is a lawyer–client relationship. Mediators are more likely to 'deserve' immunity when all parties in a mediation are receiving independent legal advice. A lawyer acting as a mediator must clearly differentiate his or her role as a lawyer from that of a mediator, and the optimal approach is to adopt a facilitative model of mediation, which does not permit advice giving and emphasises impartiality in how the mediator treats the parties and conducts the process.[77]

Many bar associations and law societies treat mediation as a specialised form of legal practice as opposed to a distinct profession, and consequently issue ethical and practice guidelines for their members who mediate rather than the more inclusive standards offered by service providers and

---

[76] *Dauphin County Bar Association* v. *Macaro* 456 Pa 545 (1976).

[77] These issues have been a concern for some time, particularly in North America: see C Menkel-Meadow, 'Is Mediation the Practice of Law?' (1996) 14(5) *Alternatives to the High Costs of Litigation* 57, 60–61; S Purnell, 'The Attorney as Mediator: Inherent Conflict of Interest?' (1985) 32(5) *UCLA Law Review* 986; A Pirie, 'The Lawyer as Mediator: Professional Responsibility Problems or Profession Problems?' (1985) 63(2) *Canadian Bar Review* 378. The Uniform Mediation Act sidesteps the issue with an impartiality provision that is optional and default, where informed parties can waive the requirement. This provides for an advisory model of mediation that could result in the unauthorised practice of law: see Alexander (n 12) 223. Article 7(4) of the Mediation Model Law (n 23) provides: 'The mediator may, at any stage of the mediation proceedings, make proposals for a settlement of the dispute.' Adopting states would need to be careful that this provision is not interpreted as giving mediators scope to offer advice within mediation.

standards bodies.[78] Lawyer-mediators could find that their legal professional duties of confidentiality, disclosure and reporting conflict with mediator codes of conduct.[79] As many commercial mediators come from the legal profession it is important that they distinguish their role as a mediator from that of a lawyer, and clarify for the parties from the outset of the process that they have no role in legal advice or drafting. The American Bar Association offers helpful guidance in this regard.

To clarify the issue, the American Bar Association adopted a resolution explicitly stating that mediation is not the practice of law. The resolution defines mediation as a process in which an impartial individual assists the parties in reaching a voluntary settlement, that such assistance does not constitute the practice of law and that the parties to a mediation are not represented by the mediator. If the mediator's discussions with the parties involve legal issues, the resolution confirms that this does not create an attorney–client relationship or constitute legal advice, whether or not the mediator is an attorney. The preparation of a memorandum of understanding or settlement agreement by a mediator, incorporating the terms of settlement specified by the parties, does not constitute the practice of law, either. If the mediator drafts an agreement that goes beyond the terms specified by the parties, he or she may be engaged in the practice of law. However, the resolution provides that the mediator will not have engaged in the practice of law if all parties are represented by counsel and the mediator discloses that any proposal that he or she makes with respect to the terms of settlement is informational as opposed to the practice of law, and that the parties should not view or rely on such proposals as advice of counsel, but merely consider them in consultation with their own attorneys. It also states that mediators have a responsibility to inform the parties in a mediation about the nature of the mediator's role in the process and the limits of that role, and that they should inform the parties that the mediator's role is not to provide them with legal representation, but to assist them in reaching a voluntary agreement, that a settlement agreement may affect the parties' legal rights, and that each of the parties has the right to seek the advice of independent legal

---

[78] See, e.g., in Australia, the Queensland Law Society, *Standards of Conduct for Solicitor Mediators* (1996) and in England and Wales, Law Society Code of Practice, Civil and Commercial Mediation Accreditation Scheme (2011). See also Alexander and Chong (n 38) 113.

[79] See Alexander and Chong (n 38) 121.

counsel throughout the mediation process and should seek such counsel before signing a settlement agreement.[80]

5.10   Judges as Mediators

Disputants may be referred to mediation by a court or tribunal under statute, civil procedure rules, practice directions, judicial precedent or informally by the court or tribunal depending on the jurisdiction. Referral may be voluntary, with the parties' consent,[81] or mandatory, without both parties' consent. There are two approaches to referral: the market approach, where disputants select the mediator, and the court's role is to manage but not conduct the process; and the justice approach, where the mediator is appointed by the court and is typically drawn from a pool of judges, registrars or court employees.[82]

There are four main judicial dispute resolution models in operation, all of which involve mediation to some degree. The first is judicial settlement, where the trial judge facilitates settlement, and will subsequently hear the case if no agreement is reached. Longer established in civil law than in common law jurisdictions, it is usually directive, legalistic and short in duration and does not usually involve private sessions with the parties and the judge. The second is judicial mediation, which tends to be based more on legal authority with a settlement approach and focus compared with non-judicial mediation, and unlike judicial settlement, the mediating judge cannot be the trial judge.[83] The settlement usually takes the form of a summary judgment or an order of the court, for finality and easier enforcement. The third is judicial moderation, which comprises a wider range of techniques than those used in judicial settlement and facilitative mediation. They include investigative, directive, advisory, managerial, settlement and facilitative interventions. Unrestricted by a particular process, judicial moderators can choose their intervention depending on their perceptions of the needs of the

---

[80] American Bar Association Section on Dispute Resolution, 'Resolution on Mediation and the Unauthorized Practice of Law' (adopted by the Section on 2 February 2002).

[81] The parties may sometimes feel they have little choice where a judge recommends mediation, in view of the prospect of a penalty such as costs sanctions where the refusal to mediate is deemed unreasonable by the court. Even so, compulsion to mediate is not compulsion to settle. See Chapter 7 at Section 7.5.

[82] See Alexander (n 12) 148–70 for a discussion on court referral to mediation including the referral criteria and how they are applied.

[83] This distinction is made in recital 12, article 3 of the EU Mediation Directive (n 16) and s 3(b)(3) of the Uniform Mediation Act.

parties. In some jurisdictions, the judicial moderator may go on to hear the case if it does not settle, unless a party objects. The fourth model is facilitative judging, also known as mediative adjudication. It involves the conscious integration of communication and facilitation skills into judicial tasks including decision-making and adjudication. As with judicial settlement there is no separation of judicial roles in facilitative judging.[84]

Judicial involvement in mediation appears to be a contradiction in terms, as judges are supposed to judge rather than mediate, apply the law rather than discuss interests, evaluate rather than facilitate, order rather than accommodate, and decide cases rather than settle them.[85] Courts were instituted not to mediate disputes but to decide them.[86]

Incompatibility concerns relate to constitutional and human rights principles, procedural fairness, independence and impartiality. It is generally accepted that judicial power should be exercised independently and impartially, consistent with procedural fairness and constitutional requirements. Public confidence in the judicial role may be eroded when judges move between delivering judgments and mediating cases. Judges have significant influence both within the court room and beyond, and the perception of judicial coercion is a legitimate concern for the credibility of the mediation process and the judiciary. Party autonomy, a fundamental element of the mediation process, can be severely weakened.[87] Rights, privileges and obligations of judicial mediators can be significantly different to non-judicial mediators; the latter carry greater risks. There is a concern about oversight of judicial behaviour in mediation, where judicial immunity can protect judicial mediators from allegations of duress and coercion.[88]

Judges have been characterised as fiduciary custodians of the justice system, effectively custodians of the sovereign power of dispute adjudication through the mechanism of due process and the application of the principles and rules of law. It is consequently inappropriate to second a judge from their primary role of court adjudication to the very different process of helping with the settlement of disputes. This would be a particular issue where each of the parties meets with the mediator

---

[84] See Alexander (n 12) 130–39.
[85] D Spencer and M Brogan, *Mediation Law and Practice* (Melbourne, Cambridge University Press 2007) 391.
[86] Fuller (n 2) 328.
[87] See generally J Resnik, 'Managerial Judges' (1982) 96(2) *Harvard Law Review* 374.
[88] ibid 380; L Street, 'Mediation and the Judicial Institution' (1997) 71(10) *Australian Law Journal* 794, 795–96.

privately in caucus to discuss the dispute without the other party present which would amount to a breach of natural justice principles. Privately discussing settlement options with the parties would be inconsistent with their judicial role and would undermine public confidence in the integrity and impartiality of the judicial institution. A mediator is not subject to appellate mechanisms when acting within a confidential process, and when judges mediate, public confidence in the integrity and impartiality of the judiciary is at risk.[89]

To address procedural fairness and bias issues, some judicial mediation models in Germany, Australia and the USA either avoid private mediation sessions or refer the mediation to a judge other than the trial judge or a non-judicial court official.[90] Public confidence is less likely to diminish where the role of judicial mediator is full time and separate from the role of trial judge.[91] Many jurisdictions prohibit a judicial mediator from subsequently acting as the judge in the case should it proceed to court.[92] For example, the EU Mediation Directive defines mediation and expressly excludes mediation involving the judge who attempts to settle the dispute within the course of judicial proceedings.[93] Similarly, the Uniform Mediation Act does not apply to mediation conducted by a judge who might make a ruling on the case.[94] Some jurisdictions expressly prohibit active judges from acting as mediators to clearly distinguish the judicial function from the mediator function,[95] and it is important that there clearly be a separation of the mediating and adjudicating roles to protect the integrity of both the judicial and mediation processes.[96]

While a segregation of the mediator and judicial roles is critical, in jurisdictions such as England and South Africa, senior judges have become

---

[89] See L Street, 'Note on the Detachment of Judges to Mediation' (2006) 17(4) *Australasian Dispute Resolution Journal* 188; Street, 'Mediation and the Judicial Institution' (n 88). See also O Fiss 'Out of Eden' (1985) 94(4) *Yale Law Journal* 1669–73, 1672–73.

[90] There are limits to the perception of bias. In the US case *Zhu* v. *Countrywide Realty Co Inc* 66 F App'x 840 (10th Cir 2003) the court refused to set aside a settlement where the judge that facilitated the settlement heard an application to enforce it. The court saw no impropriety in the judge's approach. Judicial mediation is employed in several targeted areas in England. For an overview of judicial mediation in England in the Technology and Construction Court, see Blake, Browne and Sime (n 16) 220–22.

[91] Resnik (n 87) 428.

[92] See Hopt and Steffek (n 6) 48–49.

[93] EU Mediation Directive (n 16) article 3(a).

[94] Uniform Mediation Act, s 3(b)(3).

[95] Poland is an example. See Hopt and Steffek (n 6) 88.

[96] See Alexander (n 12) 140–48; Street (n 88) 796.

commercial mediators following their retirement from the bench. When former judges receive professional training and accreditation as commercial mediators, and successfully make the role transition from adjudicator to mediator, this can prove successful.[97]

5.11   Concluding Thoughts

The development of a profession is accompanied by regulating standards of practice and controlling membership entry through training and accreditation requirements.[98] Diversity in mediation practice and a lack of consensus regarding regulation have traditionally been cited as reasons for the difficulty of a profession to emerge. This may in part have resulted from mediation being grounded more in process skills than in unique substantive knowledge. In the USA, as in many jurisdictions, there is no register of certified mediators; nor is there national common mediator accreditation.[99] However, as discussed in this chapter, education, training, accreditation, the development of standards and the growth of mediation membership organisations all indicate movement towards professionalisation of commercial mediation. Similarly, developments such as the EU Mediation Directive at an EU regional level and the Uniform Mediation Act at a US federal level which protect mediators against disclosure of mediation evidence, and the Mediation Model Law and Singapore Convention at a global level, provide evidence of mediation's legitimacy and social recognition.[100] It is important that efforts to professionalise or institutionalise mediation do not stifle the creativity and innovation that inspired its birth or initial attraction, and made the process the growing success that it is in the commercial field.[101]

---

[97] See G Lightman, 'In My Opinion … CEDR Mediation Training for a Judge' (CEDR Publications, 27 November 2007), where the English High Court judge remarked, following his completion of mediation training, that the discipline required of a mediator takes time and experience to adopt when accustomed to the adversarial tradition. Experience suggests that in practice many former judges who act as mediators tend to adopt an evaluative style: see Kallipetis and Ruttle (n 29) 199–200.

[98] See Brooker (n 48) 486.

[99] The lack of regulation has elicited criticism: see A Hinshaw, 'Regulating Mediators' (2016) 21(2) *Harvard Negotiation Law Review* 163.

[100] See N A Walsh, 'Institutionalisation and Professionalisation' in Moffitt and Bordone (eds) (n 3) 494–98. See also Blake, Browne and Sime (n 16) 10–12.

[101] See Bordone, Moffitt and Sander (n 11) 516.

The global trend regarding mediation standards is consistent with the EU experience, where national codes tend not to be as prominent as developments at an institutional or an organisational level. The significant variance in the content of codes of conduct across jurisdictions presents a challenge to the development of commercial mediation. The interdisciplinary character of the mediation field, the flexibility of the process and the diversity of mediation practice are often named as reasons why it is difficult to establish common standards. However, if countries could strive towards having one national code for commercial mediation, it would assist the task of professionalisation in each jurisdiction, and in turn enhance the task of ultimately developing a common international code of conduct for commercial mediators that would bring greater consistency and transparency to international mediation practice.[102]

The regulation of mediation and the professionalisation of mediation practice are directly linked to mediator immunity, as legal action against mediators will be based on accepted standards of practice. Statutory immunity is driven by policy that supports the expansion of mediation within the court system to provide settlement opportunities to disputing parties – relieving resourcing pressure on courts and offering advantages to parties. Statutory immunity is unlikely to be extended to private mediation, as policy tends to favour parties having a means of redress, albeit that cases seldom arise.[103]

The type of mediation required by the parties, whether facilitative or evaluative, the level of client participation and the use of caucuses will influence the role and choice of mediator.[104] While training and accreditation are important for promoting trust and confidence in the process, experience is likely to be a more important consideration when selecting a mediator. In international commercial disputes, substantive law, industry knowledge and subject matter expertise are increasingly important in addition to procedural and process competence.[105]

---

[102] See Tirado and Vincente Maravall (n 6) 352–59.

[103] However, where policy favours the introduction of compulsory or mandatory commercial mediation schemes, the appropriate benchmarks by which to evaluate mediator competencies and determine immunity should not be left to the vagaries of the common law: see Brooker (n 48) 488–90.

[104] See Brower (n 1) 311–13. Culture will also be a relevant factor in cross-cultural mediations: see Chapter 2 at Section 2.3.

[105] The way mediation tools and techniques may have to be adapted for particular subject matters has been termed 'Mediation 2.0': see C Menkel-Meadow, *Mediation and Its Application for Good Decision Making and Dispute Resolution* (Cambridge, UK,

However, personal qualities and people skills such as rapport building, patience, persistence and creativity are likely to be the most important qualities in creating the space and dynamic within which parties are likely to share information that mediators need to shape the discussions that may lead to settlement.[106]

Interscentia 2016) 20. It has been suggested that subject matter expertise is more important where the mediator adopts an evaluative style, and where the mediator will express opinions on the issues in dispute: see Brower (n 1) 307–9; Frenkel and Stark (n 3) 12. Even from a facilitative perspective, it may be difficult to assist the parties if the mediator does not have sufficient subject matter expertise in order to effectively reality test: see Blake, Browne and Sime (n 16) 174.

[106] See Brower (n 1) 311. The ability to overcome impasse is critically important in this context: see H I Abramson, *Mediation Representation* (2nd ed, Oxford, Oxford University Press 2011) 180–82.

6

Lawyers and Other Professional Mediation Supporters

6.1   Introduction

Many jurisdictions require lawyers to advise clients about mediation. As gatekeepers of the process, lawyers have duties to fulfil before the mediation starts, during the process and when it ends. There are ethical considerations that mediators must consider and potential legal liability to bear in mind. While it is important to distinguish between acting as a lawyer and as a mediator to ensure there is no conflict of roles, the two roles can also have a symbiotic relationship. The flexibility of the mediation process can facilitate expert involvement in a non-adversarial way. Mediation has been instrumental in the emergence of the 'new lawyer' – a professional who has a greater focus on the potential for interest-based bargaining and problem solving, and accepts the value of non-legal solutions to legal problems.

6.2   The Lawyer's Role Transition

When legal disputes arise in a contentious atmosphere, commercial parties may be inclined to employ those lawyers who are considered to be the most adversarial, to assert their legal rights. As time passes and the significant costs of the exercise are realised, attitudes may mellow. Costs in this context are not limited to legal fees, but include the emotional and commercial costs, including loss of valuable management time. Often unprepared, most parties settle, either before the court is about to hear the case or during the litigation process before judgment is given.

Lawyers can change their traditional roles from legal advocate and representative to legal advisor and counsellor, and counsel their clients about the possibility of reaching a voluntary settlement that addresses their needs and interests and defines their future behaviour, through participation in a process they can control to resolve their dispute in a confidential, collaborative, problem-solving atmosphere. Ideally this advice should be given at the contract drafting stage, and at each stage where mediation could effectively be used to resolve commercial conflict.[1] Once mediation is the agreed option, the lawyer's role is to help their client as much as required at each stage of the process, including with the preparatory steps, opening statements, plenary and caucus sessions and drafting of the settlement. The flexibility of the mediation process facilitates providing the level of involvement that a client requires.[2]

Unlike a judge or arbitrator, the third party is a facilitator rather than a decision-maker and may not be the primary audience. That is likely to be the party on the other side with whom any settlement that may result will need to be agreed. This requires a significantly different representational approach compared with the conventional advocacy approach adopted in court or arbitration; that approach is likely to prove ineffective and self-defeating in mediation. Lawyers must tailor their approach to take advantage of the opportunities mediation has to offer.[3]

---

[1] Law Council of Australia, *Guidelines for Lawyers in Mediations* (2011) section 3, comment (b): 'Mediation may be undertaken at any time and should be considered: (i) before proceedings are commenced; (ii) after pleadings have closed, but before the costs of discovery are incurred; (iii) before an action is set down for trial and trial costs are incurred; and (iv) after a trial and before judgment.'

[2] R Feehily, 'The Role of the Lawyer in the Mediation Process: A Critical Analysis of the Legal and Regulatory Issues' (2016) 133(2) *South African Law Journal* 352, 361–66. Experience suggests that some of the most effective contributions to a mediation are made when the legal advisor and client both address the other side's decision-maker: one from a legal and the other from a commercial and pragmatic perspective. The client can refer to previous business relationships, future business prospects and the polarising nature of litigation; show a willingness to actively listen and engage in an effort to reach a resolution; and, possibly, accept blame and even make an apology: see M Kallipetis and S Ruttle, 'Better Dispute Resolution: The Development and Practice of Mediation in the United Kingdom Between 1995 and 2005' in J C Goldsmith, A Ingen-Housz and G H Pointon (eds), *ADR in Business: Practice and Issues Across Countries and Cultures* (Alphen aan den Rijn, Kluwer Law International 2006) 245.

[3] H Abramson, 'Mediation Representation: Representing Clients Anywhere' in A Ingen-Housz (ed), *ADR in Business: Practice and Issues Across Countries and Cultures*, vol 2 (Alphen aan den Rijn, Kluwer Law International 2011) 294. For a discussion on the varying degrees of advisor involvement in different contexts and at different stages of the mediation process, and what mediators can do to influence the participation of advisors, see L Boulle and N Alexander, *Mediation: A How To Guide* (Chatswood, NSW, LexisNexis Butterworths 2015) 318–28. It has been suggested that mediation can make commercial parties think they can practise law and lawyers think that they can do business. It is important that participants are aware of their roles: see J F Guillemin, 'Reasons for Choosing Alternative Dispute Resolution' in Goldsmith, Ingen-Housz and Pointon (eds) (n 2) 50.

For many lawyers, the transition is not easy. The core values and methods of lawyers are more closely aligned with those of the courts. As the core values and methods of lawyers in mediation are different, this can lead to role conflict. The core values and methods of lawyers, and in turn judges and courts, involve linear thinking and linear systems such as rules, ethical codes, adversarial orientation, consistent predicable procedures and compartmentalisation of issues within the law; they are not aligned with the core values or methods of the mediation process. This mindset seems to be engendered through legal education, which focusses on the recognition of legal issues and a 'scientific' application of the law to the facts, disregarding elements such as culture, politics and values, and embedding at a fundamental level the idea that emotions have no place in the law. As a result, mediation practice can be fundamentally affected by the incongruity between the approach taken, and the approach required for the process to operate effectively. The education and training of lawyers, together with centuries of legal precedent and practice, emphasise the presence of rules and formal processes. The rules of evidence seem to work against providing a voice for the disputants, prescribing the lawyer to be the sole representative, articulating their client's legal rights. Traditionally, ethical codes to which lawyers subscribed were designed for a judicial dispute resolution system and contributed to the unhealthy tension created in the judicial process, as many lawyers ignored their role as advisor beyond that of legal advocate.[4]

6.3   The Lawyer's Duties

Many jurisdictions require lawyers to advise clients about dispute resolution options and the advantages of settlement. In Australia, the conduct rules for both barristers and solicitors oblige legal practitioners to inform clients about alternatives to contested adjudication, unless the clients

---

[4] See R A Creo, 'Business and Practice Issues of US Mediators' in C Newmark and A Monaghan (eds), *Butterworths Mediators on Mediation: Leading Mediator Perspectives on the Practice of Commercial Mediation* (Haywards Heath, Tottel Publishing 2005) 320–22; Feehily (n 2) 360–61. These issues have been a concern for some time, see D C Bok, 'A Flawed System of Law Practice and Training' (1983) 33(4) *Journal of Legal Education* 570–85. Empirical research from Australia indicates that lawyers are one of the factors that exacerbate conflict in franchise relationships, through miscommunication of information and expectations: see J Giddings and others, 'Understanding the Dynamics of Conflict Within Business Franchise Systems' (2009) 20(1) *Australasian Dispute Resolution Journal* 24, 30.

already understand these options.[5] In the UK, the Solicitors Regulation Authority Code of Conduct provides that solicitors should ensure 'clients are in a position to make informed decisions about the services they need, how their matter will be handled and the options available to them'.[6] More generally, the Civil Procedure Rules embody an overall framework for the conduct of litigation. Specific duties are laid on the court, which lawyers and parties must help the court discharge, including to use alternative dispute resolution (ADR) if appropriate and to facilitate its use.[7]

6.3.1   The Lawyer's Criteria to Consider

In *Halsey* v. *Milton Keynes NHS Trust*,[8] the English Court of Appeal gave the following non-exhaustive list of factors that it suggested were relevant to the issue of whether a party unreasonably refused to mediate: (1) the nature of the dispute and whether it was suitable for mediation; (2) the merits of the case and whether the pre-trial belief by the winning side that their case was watertight was reasonable; (3) the extent to which other settlement methods were attempted; (4) whether the costs involved in the mediation would have been disproportionately high; (5) whether any delay in the setting up of, and attendance at the mediation would have been prejudicial; and (6) whether the mediation had a reasonable prospect of success.[9]

The application of the *Halsey* factors has given rise to a significant body of case law in England.[10] The *Halsey* jurisprudence highlights the importance the court places on parties considering mediation while also providing lawyers in England with valuable clarification on the objective criteria that should be considered when analysing the suitability of the process in a particular context. However, legal advisors must remain mindful that if a refusal to mediate is decided on the wrong criteria, or

---

[5] Legal Profession Uniform Conduct (Barristers) Rules 2015, r 36; Legal Profession Uniform Law Australian Solicitors' Conduct Rules 2015, r 7.2.

[6] Solicitors Regulation Authority Code of Conduct 2011, r 1.12. See also S Blake, J Browne and S Sime, *The Jackson ADR Handbook* (2nd ed, Oxford, Oxford University Press 2016) 63–70.

[7] Civil Procedure Rules, r 1.4. See Chapter 7 at Section 7.2.

[8] [2004] EWCA Civ 576.

[9] ibid [17]–[23] (Dyson LJ). See also Chapter 7 at Section 7.4.1.1.

[10] For a detailed discussion on *Halsey* and subsequent cases, see Chapter 7 at Section 7.4. For simplicity the term 'England' is used throughout this book to describe the jurisdiction of England and Wales.

if the criteria are applied to a case but the court reaches a different conclusion, adverse cost consequences may follow.

Halsey and the jurisprudence that followed it have had the practical effect of making it unwise for a party to ignore, or for their lawyer to advise against accepting, a good faith invitation to mediate unless there are clear and demonstrable reasons to decline the invitation. If a lawyer believes that mediation is inappropriate, they should elucidate the reasons fully in writing, mindful of the fact that they are likely to be reviewed by a judge at a later date.[11] The *Halsey* jurisprudence has also underlined the important distinction for lawyers that unreasonableness demonstrated in declining to mediate can give rise to a sanction, but unreasonableness alleged to have occurred within a mediation is usually not admissible later due to confidentiality constraints.[12]

A court in South Africa adopted a robust approach to encourage legal advisors to consider mediation as an option with disputing parties. Brassey AJ in the High Court case of *Brownlee* v. *Brownlee*[13] imposed a costs sanction on the parties' lawyers as a direct consequence of their failure to advise their clients on the mediation option. The lawyers effectively agreed not to advise mediation in a case which the judge believed would have benefited from it. He consequently limited what the lawyers could charge their own clients and made no order between the parties. Brassey AJ said that the lawyers had 'positively rejected the use of the [mediation] process. For this they are to blame and they must, I believe shoulder the responsibility that comes from failing properly to serve the interests of their clients'.[14]

The approach adopted in such cases as *Halsey* and *Brownlee* presents a clear caution to the legal profession to encourage parties to settle

---

[11] It has been suggested that lawyers will be negligent to the same extent if they advise their clients to ignore a reasonable request to mediate where it is made in arbitration to the same extent as if it is made in litigation. This means that the number of mediations that will take place during arbitral references is likely to increase where costs sanctions are a possibility: see Kallipetis and Ruttle (n 2) 222.

[12] In the normal course, it is only in cases where both parties agree to disclose attitudes taken within a mediation that the court can have the right to adjudicate on such matters. See Chapter 9 at Section 9.4.1.1.

[13] High Court (Provisional Division), Brassey AJ, 25 August 2009.

[14] ibid [59]. Each party covered its own costs, as they were not 'blameless', but the lion's share of the Court's 'displeasure' was reserved for the lawyers; it deprived them of their attorney and client costs for failing to recommend mediation. The lawyers' costs were capped at inter-party rates (the equivalent of standard basis costs rather than indemnity costs). See the discussion on this case in Chapter 7 at Section 7.4.3.

disputes, given what judges might order if lawyers fail to advise their clients about mediation.

6.3.2 Preparing for Mediation

Lawyers should begin preparing their clients for mediation by explaining the nature of mediation, how the process will work and what the client's role will be. In addition to assessing the legal issues, lawyers should consider the practical and commercial aspects of the dispute in light of their client's business, personal and commercial needs to help in developing possible solutions. Lawyers should prepare clients for mediation by helping them identify their interests, developing a risk analysis, linking risks to their client's interests and developing strategies to achieve options for settlement.[15]

A pre-mediation meeting or conference with the mediator is a useful exercise to establish a relationship with the mediator and arrange any practical matters relating to the mediation. The first such meeting is usually between the lawyers and the mediator and covers practical details such as when and where the mediation will take place, fees, the individuals attending, the agreement to mediate and the documents to be exchanged or brought to the mediation. A second preliminary meeting may take place immediately before the mediation, giving the mediator an opportunity to meet with the parties individually. At this meeting, the mediator can begin to establish a relationship with the parties, explain the process, format and structure of the mediation and answer any questions the parties have before the mediation.[16]

An important issue to discuss and agree at the first preliminary meeting is confidentiality. This may commence from the first preliminary meeting and continue throughout the process. Unless the parties agree to disclose mediation evidence or disclosure is required by law, anything that is said or done in a mediation should be strictly confidential. Lawyers must also maintain the confidentiality required by any statute, the parties or any agreement to mediate. A lawyer must not reveal any information disclosed by the mediator during private sessions to the other parties or their legal representatives. All information and documents disclosed during the mediation, including any settlement or draft offers or counter-offers, are confidential and privileged between the

---

[15] See Law Council of Australia (n 1) section 5 and 5.1 and comment.
[16] See ibid section 5.2 and comment.

parties and their advisors. A lawyer should consider rules about confidentiality before attending a pre-mediation meeting so that they may be established by the parties and the mediator before the mediation.[17]

6.3.3   Legal Advisors at Mediation

Whether legal advisors are present at a mediation of a commercial dispute can depend on the size and nature of the dispute, and the resources of the parties. The larger the corporate party and the amount in dispute, the more likely it is that legal advisors will be present. As mediation is an informal meeting between parties in a non-legal context, parties should be free to exchange views about the issues and possible solutions, and legal advisors should be as involved in the process as their clients ask them to be. Where lawyers are unfamiliar with the process or unwilling to adapt their conventional advocate role to advisor, mediation is less likely to result in settlement. As noted in Section 6.2, lawyers in a mediation are not present as advocates: they are there as legal *advisors* rather than legal *representatives*, and lawyers who do not understand and appreciate this distinction can directly obstruct the mediation process.

The rationale for the involvement of legal advisors and their consequent duties when the process has commenced can be seen as threefold.[18] First, lawyers should advise and help their clients during the mediation, which includes giving advice on strategies, risk analysis and settlement options relative to possible court or tribunal outcomes. While this advice and help will begin during the preparations for the mediation, it will also continue throughout the process.

Second, lawyers should discuss with the mediator, with each other and with their respective clients the legal, evidentiary and practical matters that arise. A lawyer's role is to help clients to present their case in the best way, and assist them and the mediator by giving practical and legal advice and support. It is the parties rather than the lawyers or the mediator who must be convinced, and acknowledging the parties' concerns and being

---

[17] See ibid section 2.1 and comment. See also Chapter 9 generally on confidentiality. For a comprehensive framework for representing clients in mediation, from selecting the correct mediator to navigating the relevant legal issues when drafting the settlement, see H Abramson, *Mediation Representation* (2nd ed, Oxford, Oxford University Press 2011).

[18] L Street, 'Commentary on Some Aspects of the Advent and Practice of Mediation in Australia' in Newmark and Monaghan (eds) (n 4) 367; Feehily (n 2) 367. Where one party attends mediation with legal representation and the other party attends with none, this can give rise to a power imbalance, or be perceived as doing so. See Chapter 10 at Section 10.2.1.

persuasive rather than adversarial is more likely to contribute to a settlement. Language is important, and arguments should be presented in appropriate and convincing terms. Careful listening is helpful in creating an atmosphere for settlement, and simple techniques such as summarising the contribution of the other party can help to demonstrate understanding.[19]

Third, lawyers should prepare the mediated settlement agreement and ensure that it is enforceable. A central part of a lawyer's role is to help in formulating offers and assessing the practicality and reasonableness of offers made by other parties, and to assist in drafting the settlement agreement. It is important that lawyers or parties never mislead and are careful of hyperbole and exaggeration in case such statements are taken as fact and relied upon. Final offers or ultimatums should be carefully used as they can limit future options and damage credibility for future negotiations. Draft settlements should be easily accessible and if it seems that the mediation will not result in a comprehensive settlement, lawyers should explore whether a written settlement on as many issues as possible can be achieved. This could advance future negotiations or narrow the issues for a court or arbitral tribunal, and the parties will feel that the mediation has been a useful exercise. Where a partial settlement is agreed, it would also be helpful for future purposes to draft a list of issues on which agreement was not achieved as a possible roadmap for a future mediation.[20]

6.3.4 Legal Advisors Post-mediation

Post-mediation legal advice is likely to be sought if there is an error in the settlement agreement that requires rectification or if a party is in breach and enforcement action is required. If there is no settlement, or a partial settlement, the lawyer's role will normally revert to the traditional role of advocate or representative, to assess and advise on the next steps, including litigation or arbitration, to resolve the dispute or the part of the dispute that remains. Lawyers may also become involved if a party claims that a mediated settlement should be set aside due to fraud, undue influence, unconscionability, duress, lack of capacity or authority to contract, or illegality.[21]

---

[19] See Law Council of Australia (n 1) sections 6 and 6.1 and comments.
[20] See ibid sections 6.1 and 6.2 and comments. See also Chapter 8 at Section 8.3.
[21] See Chapter 8 at Section 8.2.

6.3.5   *Ethical Considerations*

Lawyers must observe professional ethical obligations that relate to their work generally, covering issues such as conflicts of interest and legal professional privilege. Mediation should not be engaged in for ulterior motives, such as information gathering, or to delay a hearing. Preservation of confidentiality and other fiduciary duties are often restated in lawyer codes of conduct. Competence is a central ethical requirement. As noted already, lawyers must advise and educate their clients, both during the mediation process and about possible settlement options and their implications. While lawyers normally have ostensible, and possibly implied, authority to bind their clients to a settlement, some (as discussed in Section 6.4) have been held liable for exceeding their client's express instructions in reaching a settlement. In addition to legal liability, if lawyers breach their ethical obligations, they are likely to be in breach of their professional standards or code of conduct, which may give rise to a professional sanction.[22]

The Law Council of Australia has developed guidelines to assist lawyers representing clients in the mediation of civil and commercial disputes. The guidelines provide for a general obligation of good faith, requiring that lawyers and clients should act, at all times, in good faith to attempt to achieve settlement of a dispute. Lawyers should also advise clients about what it means to act in good faith; and if a lawyer suspects the other parties to the mediation are acting in bad faith, this may be raised privately with the mediator.[23]

The American Bar Association (ABA) Model Rules of Professional Conduct (the 'Model Rules') prescribe baseline standards of legal ethics and professional responsibility for lawyers in the USA, and contain a number of provisions that have relevance in the mediation context. The Model Rules have formed the basis for many ethics codes and have been applied by courts, disciplinary bodies and ethics committees across the USA.[24] The Preamble to the Model Rules notes that a lawyer's functions include the duty as a negotiator to seek 'a result advantageous

---

[22] See L Boulle, *Mediation: Principles, Process, Practice* (3rd ed, Chatswood, NSW, LexisNexis 2011) 298–99; Blake, Browne and Sime (n 6) 41–42.

[23] Law Council of Australia (n 1) section 2.2 and comment. Confidentiality, covered at section 2.1 of the guidelines, is also an ethical issue.

[24] See Center for Professional Responsibility, *Annotated Model Rules of Professional Conduct* (9th ed, American Bar Association 2019).

to the client but consistent with requirements of honest dealings with others'.

Rule 1.2 of the Model Rules covers the scope of representation and the allocation of authority between a client and lawyer, reflecting the principle of party self-determination:

> (a) A lawyer shall abide by a client's decisions concerning the objectives of representation ... and shall consult with the client as to the means by which they are to be pursued. ... A lawyer shall abide by a client's decision whether to settle a matter.

Rule 1.4 of the Model Rules covers communications. It obliges a lawyer to explain a matter 'to the extent reasonably necessary to permit the client to make informed decisions.' Rule 2.1 covers the advisor, and requires that a lawyer deliver advice in a candid manner and in providing the advice, a lawyer may refer to considerations other than law, including moral, economic, social and political factors, that may be relevant to the client's situation.

Rule 4.1 of the Model Rules covers truthfulness in statements to others, and reflects an honesty requirement:

> In the course of representing a client a lawyer shall not knowingly: (a) make a false statement of material fact or law to a third person; or (b) fail to disclose a material fact to a third person when disclosure is necessary to avoid assisting a criminal or fraudulent act by a client.

This rule relates to statements of fact. Whether a statement should be regarded as fact depends on the circumstances, including whether the person to whom the statement is addressed would reasonably regard it as fact.[25] For example, hyperbolic statements such as 'puffs' should not be taken as statements of material fact.[26] Additional information may be required to gain the trust of the mediator or to provide critical information to the mediator about the client's goals or intentions so that the mediator can effectively help the parties to reach an agreement. While a failure to do so is unlikely to violate rule 4.1, in 'extreme cases' it

---

[25] American Bar Association (ABA) Standing Committee on Ethics and Professional Responsibility, Formal Opinion 06-439 'Lawyer's Obligation of Truthfulness When Representing a Client in Negotiation: Application to Caucused Mediation' (12 April 2006) fn 3.

[26] Puffs are hype or hyperbole consisting of exaggerated statements that no reasonable person would take seriously or believe: see R Feehily and R Tiong, *Commercial Law and the Legal System* (Wellington, Thomson Reuters 2020) 116.

may amount to a breach of a lawyer's duty to provide competent representation.[27]

6.4   Legal Liability of Lawyers in Mediation

6.4.1   An Obligation to Advise on the Mediation Option

It is conceivable that lawyers could be sued in negligence for failing to advise clients on the mediation option. Public policy is clearly changing in this area.[28] For example, the principle of 'reasonable prospects' prohibits solicitors in New South Wales from acting in litigation unless they believe, on reasonable grounds, that the claim or defence has 'reasonable prospects of success'.[29] In light of the increasing use of mediation to resolve commercial disputes, it is likely that a lawyer who fails to advise on the mediation option in the appropriate circumstances will be found professionally liable. This could occur where a lawyer fails to advise mediation in a case where it would have been in a client's interests, or where a failure to mediate causes loss in terms of a poorer outcome or irrecoverable costs or indeed a costs sanction.[30]

In England, a failure to advise or at least explore with clients the option to refer a dispute to mediation could amount to professional negligence. Following the introduction of the Civil Procedure Rules, the courts have made clear that '[a]ll members of the legal profession who conduct litigation should now routinely consider with their

---

[27] Rule 1.1 of the ABA Model Rules of Professional Conduct provides: 'A lawyer shall provide competent representation to a client. Competent representation requires the legal knowledge, skill, thoroughness and preparation reasonably necessary for the representation.' However, attorneys are not held to a higher standard when dealing with mediators compared to dealing with opponents in direct negotiation: see ABA Formal Opinion 06-439 (n 25). The Model Rules do not impose a higher duty on lawyers when acting as mediators. Rule 4.1 does not apply to lawyers as mediators and rule 8.4(c), which bars lawyers generally from engaging in dishonesty or misrepresentation, does not impose higher obligations on lawyers when acting as mediators than when they represent clients: ABA Formal Opinion 06-439, 6, fn 19. However, the ABA Section of Dispute Resolution has a Mediator Ethical Guidance Committee that issues opinions when requested. See also D Golann and J Folberg, *Mediation: The Roles of Advocate and Neutral* (3rd ed, New York, Wolters Kluwer 2016) 367.

[28] In the Australian case *Caboolture Park Shopping Centre Pty Ltd (in liq)* v. *White Industries (Qld) Pty Ltd* (1994) 45 FCR 224, the Full Court of the Federal Court said it could order a solicitors' firm to cover the other side's costs after advising their client to pursue litigation as a delaying tactic, aware of the fact that there was little prospect of success.

[29] Legal Profession Act 2004 (NSW) s 349.

[30] See Boulle (n 22) 291–92; Blake, Browne and Sime (n 6) 47–49.

clients whether their disputes are suitable for ADR',[31] and '[t]he profession can no longer with impunity shrug aside reasonable requests to mediate'.[32]

Numerous US states – including Colorado through its bar association, Arkansas by statute, and Ohio, New Jersey and Massachusetts through court rules – require lawyers to advise clients about the nature of ADR and the potential for using it in their dispute. Numerous federal and state courts have adopted similar rules.[33] Federal district courts in the USA expect attorneys to be knowledgeable about mediation in general and about the court's programmes in particular. The local rules of many courts now require attorneys to discuss mediation with their clients and opponents, to address in their case management plan the appropriateness of mediation for the case, and to be prepared to discuss mediation with the judge at the initial scheduling conference. These rules indicate the extent to which the courts expect attorneys to work with the judge to determine whether mediation should be used in a case.

The attorneys' and judge's responsibilities merge at the initial case management conference, which in many courts has become the critical event, or the first of several in determining how and when mediation will be used in the case.[34] Lawyers can best protect themselves from liability actions by keeping evidence of the clear advice on mediation and other ADR options and costs provided to the client, and the client's instructions based on that advice.[35]

---

[31] *Halsey* (n 8) [11] (Dyson LJ).

[32] *Burchell v. Bullard* [2005] EWCA Civ 358 [43] (Ward LJ). Cost orders have been employed to penalise parties where they unreasonably refuse to mediate. See Chapter 7.

[33] See Golann and Folberg (n 27) 366.

[34] This has been the position for some time: see E Plapinger and D Stienstra, *ADR and Settlement in the Federal District Courts: A Sourcebook for Judges and Lawyers* (Washington DC, Federal Judicial Center 1996) 8. The Alternative Dispute Resolution Act 1998, 28 USC 652(a) provides that a federal court may require the litigants in all civil cases to consider the use of ADR processes at an appropriate stage of the litigation: '[E]ach district court, shall by local rule adopted under section 2071 (a), require that litigants in all civil cases consider the use of an alternative dispute resolution process at an appropriate stage in the litigation. Each district court shall provide litigants in all civil cases with at least one alternative dispute resolution process, including, but not limited to, mediation, early evaluation, minitrial, and arbitration ... Any district court that elects to require the use of alternative dispute resolution in certain cases may do so only with respect to mediation, early neutral evaluation, and if the parties consent, arbitration.'

[35] See Blake, Browne and Sime (n 6) 47.

6.4.2   Negligence in a Settlement Context

Liability could arise from a failure to provide a client with sufficient advice on the merits of a case such that the client accepts a mediated outcome that is clearly less favourable than they should reasonably have received. Alternatively, it could arise from a failure to obtain reasonably clear instructions, or from acting beyond authority where the consequence is that the client receives a clearly less favourable outcome. Liability could also arise from providing inadequate advice on the appropriateness of proposed settlement terms or on enforcement issues.[36]

Australian courts have evaluated lawyer conduct in a settlement context. In *Secombs* v. *Sadler Design Pty Ltd*,[37] the defendants alleged that after they left the mediation, their lawyers executed settlement terms without their consent and neither communicated this nor explained the consequences of non-compliance. The solicitors were found to be negligent in not communicating with their clients on the day of the mediation, or the next business day, and in not performing to the appropriate professional standard.

In *Studer* v. *Boettcher*,[38] claims that mediation took place in an environment that was oppressive and coercive were not upheld. The Court stressed that advice to compromise would not amount to negligence simply because a more favourable outcome could have been attained through litigation, and referred to the negative toll that litigation involves, including its unpredictability and financial and personal costs.[39] The Australian jurisprudence demonstrates that decisions to settle are for clients to make, with lawyers ensuring that they are

---

[36] See ibid 47.

[37] [1999] VSC 79. The defendants were being sued for legal fees. See also *Abriel* v. *Australian Guarantee Corp* [1999] FCA 1198 where allegations that a lawyer convinced their client to settle without attaining the best mediated settlement were not substantiated.

[38] [2000] NSWSCA 263. Three courts commented on lawyer behaviour in the same mediation. See also *Studer* v. *Konig* (Supreme Court of New South Wales Equity Division, McLelland CJ, 4 June 1993); *Studer* v. *Boettcher* [1998] NSWSC 524. The original case involved claims and cross-claims over land dealings between the parties who ultimately settled at mediation. Konig then sought to compel Studer to comply with the settlement, and Studer unsuccessfully sought to have the agreement rescinded on the basis of undue influence, negligence and misleading conduct by his solicitor. The subsequent case and appeal were between Studer and his solicitor, Boettcher. Studer's additional claims that Boettcher was negligent and careless in mediation in inadequately assessing the strength of Studer's case were not upheld.

[39] [2000] NSWCA 263 [62]–[63] (FitzGerald JA).

informed decisions; lawyers may persuade but not coerce.[40] Lawyers should protect themselves by ensuring that any settlement terms that result are subject to client approval.[41]

6.4.3   Lawyering and Mediation: The Conflict and Confluence of Professions

In the USA, as in many other jurisdictions, more mediators come from the legal profession than any other profession, and a tension can exist when a mediator maintains an active bar licence. While they are two different professions, there can be a perceived overlap. This is seen in Texas, for example, where some mediators refer to themselves as 'attorney-mediators'. Having arisen as an issue of competition and credentials, this designation is confusing in both the legal and mediation realms and harms both professions.[42] The impact of disciplinary rules in the USA varied depending on whether the relevant bar considered a lawyer who was mediating to be practising law. If it was deemed to be the practice of law, rules about client confidences and duties to report could conflict with or alter local mediation rules and guidelines. Some states expressly stated that mediation is not the practice of law, while others had more nuanced tests to determine if an activity that was likely to occur in a mediation was considered to be the practice of law.[43] Where professional rules conflict, the specific legal regime that applies to mediators is likely to prevail over the provisions regulating other professions. Where a specific issue is not regulated by the professional law of mediation, the law governing legal professionals may apply.[44]

---

[40] See also *Louis* v. *Galbally & O'Bryan (legal practice)* [2008] VCAT 2186, where the Tribunal dismissed the claims against the lawyer, as it would have to be demonstrated that the lawyer's negligence caused the loss of opportunity to settle the case for a greater amount than the amount offered. Conversely, in the US case *Attorney Grievance Commission of Maryland* v. *Steinberg* 910 A 2d 429 (Md 2006), an attorney who failed to appear at a client meeting and arrived late and unprepared at the mediation was in breach of professional conduct rules: see Boulle (n 22) 299–301; N Alexander, *International and Comparative Mediation: Legal Perspectives* (Austin, Wolters Kluwer, 2009) 236–39.
[41] Blake, Browne and Sime (n 6) 140.
[42] Creo (n 4) 314.
[43] R Birke and L E Teitz, 'US Mediation in the Twenty-First Century: The Path That Brought America to Uniform Laws and Mediation Cyberspace' in N Alexander (ed), *Global Trends in Mediation* (The Hague, Kluwer Law International 2003) 377.
[44] K Hopt and F Steffek, 'Mediation: Comparison of Laws, Regulatory Models, Fundamental Issues' in K Hopt and F Steffek (eds), *Mediation: Principles and Regulation in*

While it is important to distinguish between the two professions, there is also much that each profession can learn from the other. Experience suggests that a symbiosis of knowledge can develop from practice in both fields. Observing the work of lawyers in mediation from a detached perspective is beneficial, as opportunities arise to see behaviours that are counter-productive as well as behaviours that encourage more constructive and less defensive responses. This in turn acquaints a lawyer with a variety of ways to respond to difficult behaviours by clients or opposing counsel that can help in meeting the parties' substantive needs.[45]

In some countries, such as the USA and Germany, there has been discussion of whether mediators should also be lawyers and whether non-lawyer mediators are engaging in the unauthorised practice of law. For example, in Germany, mediation advertising that highlighted the lack of lawyer involvement and consequent financial savings for parties was the subject of litigation. However, such debates have now largely subsided and mediation is principally recognised as a practice that is not reserved for any single professional group.[46]

6.5 Lawyers as Gatekeepers

Lawyers are gatekeepers of the mediation process. Participation in mediator skills training and experience of mediation have proved instrumental for many in their transition from sceptics to mediation proponents. This has caused a change in legal professional culture such that non-adversarial advice is now seen as central to a lawyer's role. However, one of the main challenges for the development of this field is the supply of sufficient numbers of competent lawyers who have a genuine understanding of, and willingness to participate in, the process. Education and training have helped in meeting this challenge. Law faculty curricula in many institutions offer a broader range of communication, negotiation and mediation skills, reflecting the fact that understanding the human and

---

Comparative Perspective (Oxford, Oxford University Press 2013) 92. The ABA adopted a resolution explicitly stating that mediation is not the practice of law in order to clarify the issue. See American Bar Association Section of Dispute Resolution, Resolution on Mediation and the Unauthorized Practice of Law (adopted by the Section on 2 February 2002). See also Chapter 5 at Section 5.9.

[45] M Berzon, 'Beyond Altruism: How I Learned to Be a Better Lawyer by Being a Pro Bono Neutral' (Summer 2004) *Dispute Resolution Magazine* 27.

[46] See N Alexander, 'Harmonisation and Diversity in the Private International Law of Mediation: The Rhythms of Regulatory Reform' in Hopt and Steffek (eds) (n 44) 134–35.

commercial dynamics behind disputes is as important as interpreting legal issues when seeking the most effective commercial solutions for clients. Lawyer training in many jurisdictions now includes the development of communication skills and periods working in non-contentious legal areas before moving on to conflict work. Another development is specialised training for lawyers and other professionals in performing roles before, during and after mediation conducted by universities, law societies, continuing professional development providers, law firms on an in-house basis and mediation service providers.[47] All these initiatives have been central to the cultural shift and changing nature of a lawyer's role in dispute resolution and have enhanced lawyers' gatekeeper roles.[48]

6.6   Other Professionals

In commercial litigation, the services of experts are employed by parties to provide an opinion, reflected in documentary or oral evidence, on technical concerns such as accounting, tax or engineering issues. Their role is usually partisan on behalf of a party, and as their views can differ fundamentally from one another, dual experts become 'duelling experts' and the judge or arbitrator must choose between the conflicting views in arriving at their decision. In mediation, expert reports may be shared by each party in advance, and the flexibility of the process facilitates expert involvement in a non-adversarial way, avoiding the duelling experts syndrome. For example, experts may meet with the mediator separately to discuss their differences or may be asked to produce a joint report

---

[47] For example, the International Mediation Institute (IMI) introduced a certification process for mediation advocates in 2013, which includes competency criteria reflecting general knowledge and practical skills requirements: see IMI, 'Certify' <https://imimedia tion.org/practitioners/certify> accessed 10 May 2022. The Centre for Effective Dispute Resolution (CEDR) in the United Kingdom also offers a Mediation Advocacy Skills Training Course and an Advanced Course: see CEDR, 'Mediation Training' <www .cedr.com/skills/individuals/mediationtraining/advocacy> accessed 10 May 2022.

[48] See E Carroll, 'The Future Belongs to Mediation and its Clients' in Newmark and Monaghan (eds) (n 4) 401–2; Feehily (n 2) 381–83. The International Chamber of Commerce (ICC) International Commercial Mediation Competition and the ABA Representation in Mediation Competition also facilitate students gaining a better understanding of the process by assessing their skills as advocates or party representatives. Lawyers must be trained and persuaded of the value of mediation for the process to develop and spread: see Hopt and Steffek (n 44) 111–12; A Leoveanu and A Erac, 'ICC Mediation: Paving the Way Forward' in C Titi and K Fach Gómez (eds), *Mediation in International Commercial and Investment Disputes* (Oxford, Oxford University Press 2019) 99–100.

outlining points of consensus and explanatory commentary on areas of disagreement. Independent or neutral experts can also be consulted on areas of disagreement, to help in finding party consensus.

Professional advisors other than lawyers may also be present at a mediation, with the parties' consent. They may help a party with elements outside the scope of legal advice, such as the tax implications of a settlement agreement, and will be subject to their own professional duties. In intercultural or international mediations, interpreters may be required, and it is important that their primary duty is to the process and not to one of the parties. As experts or advisors are not parties to the agreement to mediate, it is important that they sign confidentiality agreements before becoming involved in a mediation to ensure information shared is protected.[49]

6.7 Mediation and the Practitioner: The Umbilical Link to Justice

Aristotle believed that equity is the kind of justice that goes beyond the written law, comprising a correction of legal justice.[50] Courts of Chancery were originally developed to advance justice or 'equity' beyond the constraints of the common law courts. While it may seem radical to suggest that mediation is a modern analogue to these developments, there are clearly constraints on what the legal system can offer, and the outcome that it can provide in terms of justice or fairness from the perspective of commercial parties. Mediation is consequently used as a means of bridging the chasm between what the legal system can offer and what commercial parties may require, by providing a system that helps parties to exercise personal power and autonomy to settle their differences with the assistance of their lawyers through the facilitating skills of a mediator.[51]

---

[49] See Boulle (n 22) 303–4, 308–11; Boulle and Alexander (n 3) 315–18; N Alexander (n 40) 239–40; Blake, Browne and Sime (n 6) 183. It seems that, in practice, experts may not be necessary, and where their input is not required, debating the conflicting expert opinions can detract from the settlement process: see C Chern, *International Commercial Mediation* (London, Informa 2008) 56–57. For an overview of the various roles an expert can play in mediation, see C W Moore, *The Mediation Process: Practical Strategies for Resolving Conflict* (4th ed, San Francisco, Jossey-Bass 2014) 117–19.

[50] Equity has been characterised as 'applied justice, living justice, concrete justice – true justice': see A Comte-Sponville, *A Short Treatise on the Great Virtues: The Uses of Philosophy in Everyday Life* (London, Heinemann 2002) 84.

[51] See F Armstrong, 'Lost in Translation' (August/September 2004) *Law Society Gazette* 26, 30; J Nolan-Haley, 'Mediation Exceptionality' (2009) 78(3) *Fordham Law Review* 1247, 1250–51. See also T L Shaffer and A W McThenia 'For Reconciliation' (1985) 94(7) *Yale Law Journal* 1660–68, 1664–65. See generally T O Main, 'ADR: The New Equity' (2005) 74 *University of Cincinnati Law Review* 329.

Legal theorists and philosophers have debated for millennia the differences between law and justice.[52] In the mediation context, a related issue is the relationship between mediation and justice, specifically the mediated settlement that results from the process and its relationship to the justice concept. One approach to the justice concept that has particular relevance in this context is to favour 'equality, reciprocity or equivalence between individuals', where justice is the virtue of order and exchange – specifically, equitable order and honest exchange. For an exchange to be just, it follows that it must take place between equals, or there should at least be no difference between the parties in matters such as wealth, power or knowledge that might make them accept an exchange contrary to their interest, or contrary to their free and enlightened will as expressed in a situation of parity. The critical point is that the equality essential to justice is not so much about the *objects* exchanged, as it is about equality between the *subjects* involved in the exchange, which presupposes that they are equally informed and free, at least to the extent that their interests and the conditions of the exchange are concerned. Consequently, a transaction is just only if equals in power, knowledge and rights might have agreed to it.[53]

We get from this a 'golden rule of justice':

> In any contract and exchange, put yourself in the other's place, but knowing everything you know and supposing yourself to be as free from need as it is possible for someone to be and see if, in his place, you would approve this exchange or contract.[54]

This approach provides a helpful criterion for lawyers and parties to assess what is fair or just in a given context. Since the parties fashion the settlement that results from the process, it is more likely to align with their needs and interests and be viewed as a fair and just outcome by them. Experience suggests that the mediation process provides the

---

[52] See Comte-Sponville (n 50) 60–102.

[53] See ibid 67–70. Similarly, it can be argued that justice and efficiency need not be perceived as conflicting goals, where the aim of efficiency is to increase the range of realisable interests parties have, by using resources as efficiently as possible. Where justice is viewed as the primary objective of the law, what is just may be determined on the basis of the interests of the parties, and efficiency can be a principle that contributes to fulfilling these interests: see F Steffek, 'Principled Regulation of Dispute Resolution: Taxonomy, Policy, Topics' in F Steffek and others (eds), *Regulating Dispute Resolution: ADR and Access to Justice at the Crossroads* (Oxford, Hart Publishing 2013) 43–50.

[54] Emile-Auguste Chartier (Alain), Quatre-vingt-un chapitres sur l'ésprit et les passions [Eighty-One Chapters about the Spirit and Passions] (1917) VI, 4, 1230, quoted in Comte-Sponville (n 50) 70.

opportunity for practitioners to engage in the most satisfying of legal work, which involves examining a client's rights in a measured way with consideration of relevant authority, and discussing this and their client's interests in civil dialogue with opposing colleagues to help achieve a settlement.[55]

For some time, concerns have been expressed that a spiritual crisis has affected the legal profession. This is a result of what has been described as the collapse of the ideal of the 'lawyer-statesman' who expresses a set of values that gives precedence to good judgement over technical competence and encourages a public-spirited devotion to the law. While the aspirations of lawyers were originally shaped by their allegiance to a distinctive ideal of professional excellence, it seems that over the past fifty years, particularly in the USA, this ideal has failed, eroding the identity of lawyers as a group, and making it unclear to those in the profession what it means for them personally to have chosen a legal career. Many factors have contributed to this, including the prevalence in legal scholarship of a counter-ideal that denigrates the importance of wisdom and character as professional virtues. Institutional forces have also played their part, including the explosive growth of leading law firms and the bureaucratisation of the courts. All these factors have compromised the values from which the ideal of the lawyer-statesman draws strength and adversely affected the identity of lawyers.[56]

Changes to the nature of the profession have been driven in part by a belief that lawyers must be multi-disciplined to attain a rigorous understanding of the law.[57] The concern with this development is that if the lawyer is viewed as a jack-of-all-trades, with a dilettante's understanding of many fields but no expertise of his or her own, and serving only as an intermediary between other disciplines, then the lawyer's generalist or perhaps amateur position will be one marked by deference to the real experts in those areas. However, if the lawyer is an amateur in the fields of these other experts, they are amateurs in the lawyer's, and when it comes to the imaginative probing of specific cases, it is the

---

[55] It follows that as the costs of mediation are usually well below the usual costs of the litigation process, there is better scope to give the process the time it needs: see Armstrong (n 51) 26, 30.

[56] See A Kronman, *The Lost Lawyer: Failing Ideals of the Legal Profession* (Cambridge, MA, Harvard University Press 1995).

[57] This has been a pressure for some time: see, e.g., A A Leff, 'Law and . . .' (1978) 87(5) *Yale Law Journal* 989. See also rule 2.1 of the ABA Model Rules of Professional Conduct: 'In rendering advice, a lawyer may refer not only to law but to other considerations such as moral, economic, social and political factors, that may be relevant to the client's situation.'

lawyer who is best equipped by training and temperament to provide the required leadership. The ability to fashion cases and to empathetically explore both real and hypothetical ones can be seen as the lawyer's professional forte. If we view the justice ideal as central to a lawyer's unique contribution, mediation offers an opportunity for members of the profession to assert their unique professional role, and their sense of value in the work that they do.[58]

6.8 Professional Transcendence

While the basic principle of the rule of law is that we are all equal before the law, this principle has proven more a façade than a reality, and has led to supplementing the law with alternatives such as mediation to help make justice fair and accessible. This brings with it an added responsibility for lawyers, where a lawyer's role transcends the ascertainment and mechanical application of the law. Lawyers have what can be characterised as the 'beauty of responsible freedom' – a duty to contribute to making law and legal remedies reflect the parties' real needs and interests.[59] Mediation has contributed to the reformulation of court rules and practice directions and reshaped the contours of legal processes. Practitioners' experiences of the process have resulted in some lawyers becoming less legalistic and more client-centred, collaborative and self-reflective.[60]

As most cases settle, for some time, lawyers have been dispute-resolvers rather than litigators. The effect of settlement practices in the USA and Canada has been instrumental in shaping the 'new lawyer', partly influenced by global mediation movements in law characterised by factors including awareness of the central place of negotiation in legal procedures, recognition of the potential for interest-based bargaining and problem solving, and acceptance of the value of non-legal solutions to legal problems. The new lawyer builds on their traditional expertise as

---

[58] Kronman concludes that the ideal of the lawyer-statesman transcends the acquisition of purely intellectual skills, requiring the development of character traits such as practical wisdom, which presents a challenge to the whole person, and this is why it possesses such deep personal meaning for those who view their profession in this light and identify with it: see Kronman (n 56) 354–64. See also Armstrong (n 51) 28–29; D C Bok, 'A Flawed System of Law Practice and Training' (1983) 33(4) *Journal of Legal Education* 570–85, 584.

[59] M Cappelletti, 'Alternative Dispute Resolution Processes Within the Framework of the World Wide Access to Justice Movement' (1993) 56(3) *Modern Law Review* 282, 294–96. See also Chapter 10 at Section 10.1.

[60] Boulle (n 22) 186.

an advocate and legal technician, but modifies their existing skill set and develops new skills to engage in detailed mining of client needs and interests, and adapts their knowledge in view of a disputing culture that places renewed emphasis on settlement and consensus building. This has modified the lawyer's role from the zealous advocacy of the 'rights warrior' focussed on legal argument, narrow technical advice and arcane court procedures to dispute resolution advocacy with a broader scope of client goals that include a holistic, efficient and practical problem-solving approach. This requires that lawyers put themselves 'in the shoes' of the other side to strategise about what would encourage settlement on the best possible terms for their client, where the clients are active participants and decision-makers. Building on the role of the lawyer as a technical advisor, specialist legal knowledge is used in a nuanced way to explore all the opportunities to attain the best possible settlement for their client.[61]

6.9   Concluding Thoughts

Most lawyers are likely to encounter mediation as advisors rather than mediators.[62] While lawyers have a duty to advise clients on the use of mediation, there is not a positive obligation to persuade a client to use the process.[63] When advising parties, it is important that lawyers do not overpromise when 'selling' mediation, as this will decrease its legitimacy. Insisting on mediation when it is unsuitable in a particular context, or inappropriate for a particular dispute, does a disservice to this growing field. A complete understanding of dispute resolution requires an understanding of what processes work best in the context faced by the disputants, and lawyers must remain mindful of this when advising clients.[64]

Settlement is more likely where lawyers support the mediation process and engage constructively in it. Continuing education initiatives and training of lawyers in effective mediation representation will help ensure

---

[61] See J Macfarlane, *The New Lawyer: How Clients Are Transforming the Practice of Law* (2nd ed, University of British Columbia Press 2017).

[62] See generally, C Zelizer and C Chiochetti 'Mediation Career Trends Through Time, Exploring Opportunities and Challenges' in A Georgakopoulos (ed), *The Mediation Handbook: Research, Theory, and Practice* (Abingdon, UK, Routledge 2017) 9–19.

[63] See Blake, Browne and Sime (n 6) 41.

[64] R C Bordone, M L Moffitt and F E Sander, 'The Next Thirty Years: Directions and Challenges in Dispute Resolution' in M Moffitt and R Bordone (eds), *The Handbook of Dispute Resolution* (San Francisco, Jossey-Bass 2005) 510–11. See also Chapter 1 at Section 1.9.

that lawyer participation is productive for both lawyers and their clients. Education and training in commercial mediation are growing academic fields that facilitate possibilities of translating theory into practice and practice into theory.[65] This is important in a context where mediation continues to serve as an instrumental catalyst for the emergence of the 'new lawyer' from a profession that many believed had lost its way.

---

[65] See Bordone, Moffitt and Sander (n 64) 516.

7

Conduct and Costs

7.1 Introduction

The weight of litigation costs is often the primary reason that parties look to mediation to resolve their disputes in a cost-effective manner. Many jurisdictions, notably England[1] among them, have equipped courts with the powers and authority to use mediation as a device for containing costs. Attempting to assess a party's conduct to determine whether a costs sanction is appropriate has significant implications for mediation confidentiality. Objective criteria developed in seminal cases offer guidance to the courts in determining whether a party's refusal to mediate was reasonable, and guidance to advisors and parties when considering mediation. While there are potential human rights implications where sanctions are construed as a means of making mediation compulsory, costs sanctions have proved to be an effective form of targeted incentive setting where regulatory aims are integrated into the parties' decision-making process.

7.2 Commercial Mediation as a Costs Containment Device

The introduction of the Civil Procedure Rules in England[2] ushered in a cultural change in the way courts manage cases. The Rules followed the release of *Access to Justice*, a report completed by Lord Woolf, later the Lord Chief Justice of England and Wales. The final report, released in 1996, changed the culture and mindset of those who litigate civil cases in England. In his foreword to the Civil Procedure Rules, the Lord Chancellor Lord Irvine wrote 'we should see litigation as the last and

---

[1] For simplicity the term 'England' is used throughout this book to describe the jurisdiction of England and Wales.
[2] The Civil Procedure Rules 1998 provide a new code of civil procedure for the civil courts in England, replacing the Rules of the Supreme Court 1965 and the County Court Rules 1981 with effect from 26 April 1999.

not the first resort in the attempt to settle a dispute' and he confirmed the intention of the Rules by noting that 'the changes introduced in April 1999 are as much changes in culture as they are changes to the Rules themselves'.

By tradition, English courts have made the legal costs of conducting litigation subject to a court order in addition to an award or refusal of damages and any other court orders. The Civil Procedure Rules extended this costs jurisdiction. Judges can now make costs orders that reflect the court's view of any party's conduct during litigation, whether before or after the start of court proceedings. If a party behaves unreasonably then – however legally correct that party's case – a costs sanction or penalty might be applied. Thus, a party might win entirely on the law and the evidence but forfeit their costs – or even have to pay the unsuccessful party's costs – because of the unreasonable way they conducted the litigation. Pre-action conduct has for the first time been opened to judicial scrutiny, and a number of pre-action protocols, drafted in consultation with experienced practising lawyers, define how parties should clarify their claims, and exchange information and views in cases, before the claims are issued at court. A party's failure to follow these protocols could result in costs penalties.[3]

Part 1 of the Civil Procedure Rules defines the overriding objective of the civil justice system in England as 'enabling the court to deal with cases justly and at proportionate cost'. Dealing with a case in this way includes: (1) ensuring that the parties are on an equal footing; (2) saving expense; (3) dealing with it in a way that is proportionate to the amount involved,

---

[3] Since 1995, beginning in the Commercial Court, the English courts have made 'ADR orders' 'robustly recommending' that parties attempt settlement through mediation or some other alternative dispute resolution (ADR) process. Ignoring such an 'order' could lead to a costs sanction if a party unreasonably refuses to comply. While the courts can encourage it, they cannot require that mediation be used. For an overview of the English courts' approach to ADR orders, see T Allen, *Mediation Law and Civil Practice* (2nd ed, Haywards Heath, Bloomsbury Professional 2019) 97–129; S Blake, J Browne and S Sime, *The Jackson ADR Handbook* (2nd ed, Oxford, Oxford University Press 2016) 2–10, 99–100. The Civil Procedure Rules have been amended more than 100 times, most significantly through the Civil Procedure (Amendment) Rules 2013 which incorporated the reforms proposed in Lord Justice Jackson, 'Review of Civil Litigation Costs: Final Report' (Ministry of Justice, December 2009) ('Jackson Report'). For an overview of the Civil Procedure Rules and their amendments following the Jackson Report, see Allen at 71–95. See also Blake, Browne and Sime at 84–138. For an overview of mediation cost incentives and sanctions across various jurisdictions, see K Hopt and F Steffek, 'Mediation: Comparison of Laws, Regulatory Models, Fundamental Issues' in K Hopt and F Steffek (eds), *Mediation: Principles and Regulation in Comparative Perspective* (Oxford, Oxford University Press 2013) 32–34.

the importance of the case, the complexity of the issues and the financial position of each party; (4) ensuring it is dealt with expeditiously and fairly; (5) apportioning an appropriate share of the court's resources to it; and (6) enforcing compliance with rules, practice directions and orders.

The court must seek to give effect to the overriding objective when exercising any power under the Civil Procedure Rules or interpreting any of the rules, and the parties are required to help the court in doing this.[4] Specifically, the court is required to engage in active case management by identifying the issues, managing the court timetable and running cases efficiently. One significant requirement is 'encouraging the parties to use an alternative dispute resolution procedure if the court considers that appropriate[,] and facilitating the use of such procedure'.[5] A central feature of the Civil Procedure Rules is Part 36, which deals with offers to settle and payments into court. It is designed to encourage parties to make, and promptly to accept, realistic offers of settlement and to provide parties with a degree of protection against costs risk. Significant costs penalties can be imposed on parties who fail to improve on a Part 36 letter of offer to settle.[6]

7.3   Costs Variance

While the court has discretion, the general rule in England is that costs follow the event, which means the unsuccessful party will be ordered to pay the costs of the successful party.[7] This is in contrast to the position in the USA where the general rule is that each party to an action pays their own costs, regardless of the outcome.[8] As costs in an action can often

---

[4] CPR 1.2 and 1.3.

[5] CPR 1.4.

[6] CPR 36 introduced the right of claimants to make offers to settle. CPR 36.17, which deals with costs consequences following judgment, was amended in light of proposals in the Jackson Report (n 3). It now provides that where a defendant does not beat a claimant's part 36 offer, an additional penalty could be imposed of 10 per cent of the amount awarded, for an award of up to £500,000, and 5 per cent of any amount awarded above that, with a ceiling of £75,000. This applies to damages and costs in a monetary claim and on costs in a non-monetary claim. CPR 36.17 does not apply where a claimant does not beat a defendant's part 36 offer. See Jackson Report (n 3) 113.

[7] CPR 44.2.

[8] In the USA pre-trial discovery can result in substantial costs, and costs considerations are instrumental for parties in deciding whether to commence settlement negotiations during trial, notwithstanding that costs do not follow the event: see R Kulms, 'Privatising Civil Justice and the Day in Court' in Hopt and Steffek (eds) (n 3) 222. See also R Korobkin, 'The

dwarf the damages claimed, costs can feature as more significant than the substantive issues in a case.

The Civil Procedure Rules provide that a court may assess costs on either the indemnity basis or the standard basis. If costs are assessed on the indemnity basis, the benefit of any doubt as to whether the costs were reasonably incurred, or were reasonable in amount, will be given by the court in favour of the receiving party. If costs are assessed on the standard basis, the benefit of any such doubt will be given in favour of the paying party. Costs can also be disallowed on the standard basis if they are deemed by the court to be disproportionate to the matters in issue, while proportionality is disregarded if costs are assessed on an indemnity basis.[9]

While standard basis costs are the norm in practice, they will not cover the receiving party's liability to its lawyers for their costs, which means the party may be left with a liability of 20–30 per cent of its costs of the claim. Conversely, the indemnity basis for paying costs is close to 100 per cent of the receiving party's costs of the claim. The factors that the court will take into account when assessing costs include the conduct of the parties – before, as well as during, the proceedings – and any efforts made before and during the proceedings to try to resolve the dispute.[10]

Hence, a party's conduct in response to an invitation from a court or offer from a party to mediate can have significant implications when

Role of Law in Settlement' in M Moffitt and R Bordone (eds), *The Handbook of Dispute Resolution* (San Francisco, Jossey-Bass 2005) 267–69.

[9] CPR 44.3.

[10] CPR 44.4(3)(a). CPR 44.2(5) further provides that when the court exercises its discretion as to costs: 'The conduct of the parties includes (a) conduct before, as well as during, the proceedings and in particular the extent to which the parties followed the Practice Direction – Pre-Action Conduct or any relevant pre-action protocol.' For a discussion of mediation and litigation costs in England, see Allen (n 3) 283–301. See also Blake, Browne and Sime (n 3) 117–38. Many jurisdictions similarly take conduct into account when determining costs. For example the Singapore Rules of Court, O 59 r 5(1)(c) provides: 'The court in exercising its discretion as to costs shall, to such extent, if any, as may be appropriate in the circumstances, take into account ... the parties' conduct in relation to any attempt at resolving the cause or matter by mediation or any other means of dispute resolution.' See also Hong Kong Practice Direction 31, para 4: 'In exercising its discretion on costs, the Court takes into account all relevant circumstances. These would include any unreasonable failure of a party to engage in mediation where this can be established.' Hong Kong courts look closely at developing English jurisprudence in this area. For example, in *iRiver Hong Kong Ltd* v. *Thakral Corp (HK) Ltd* (Court of Appeal, Yeung JA, 3 August 2008), Yeung JA referred to several English judgments, including *Dunnett* v. *Railtrack plc* [2002] 2 All ER 850, *Burchell* v. *Bullard* [2005] EWCA Civ 358 and *Halsey* v. *Milton Keynes NHS Trust* [2004] EWCA Civ 576.

costs are determined. As the Court remarked in *Reid* v. *Buckinghamshire Healthcare NHS Trust*:

> If the party unwilling to mediate is the losing party, the normal sanction is an order to pay the winner's costs on the indemnity basis, and that means that they will have to pay their opponent's costs even if those costs are not proportionate to what was at stake. This penalty is imposed because a court wants to show its disapproval of their conduct. I do disapprove of this defendant's conduct . . . from the date they . . . received the . . . offer to mediate.[11]

It has been the tradition in England in commercial cases for the parties to share equally the mediation fees, those being the cost of the mediator and the mediation service provider, and to pay their own legal costs of preparing for and attending the mediation, regardless of the outcome of the process. This will normally be reflected in the agreement to mediate. In a commercial context, where equal bargaining power often exists between the parties, the confidentiality and outcome of the process are often the most important factors, outweighing other considerations. If parties would prefer that the mediation fee and both parties' legal costs of preparing for and attending the mediation should be treated as costs in the case, they should provide this in the agreement to mediate, to be ultimately determined by the court.[12]

7.4   Costs Jurisprudence

The English courts have developed a significant costs jurisprudence since the introduction of the Civil Procedure Rules. In *Dyson* v. *Leeds City Council*,[13] Ward LJ, when ordering a retrial due to a judicial error by the trial judge, recommended that the parties mediate in advance of the new

---

[11] [2015] EWHC B21 [12] (Master O'Hare). See also *Virani* v. *Manuel Revert y Cia SA* [2003] EWCA Civ 1651, where the Court of Appeal ordered an unsuccessful defendant who refused mediation before losing both the trial and the appeal despite encouragement and advice from the Lord Justice, to pay the successful claimant's costs on an indemnity basis.

[12] See Allen (n 3) 296, 299. There is considerable variance in how mediation costs are treated across jurisdictions: see Hopt and Steffek (n 3) 38–43. See also N Alexander, *International and Comparative Mediation: Legal Perspectives* (Austin, Wolters Kluwer 2009) 331–35. For a discussion on how the potential expense of mediation in England may be determined, with reference to other ADR processes, and how that expense may be funded, see Blake, Browne and Sime (n 3) 71–83. For an overview of costs and cost-shifting in ADR in England, see Blake, Browne and Sime at 105–16.

[13] [2000] CP Rep 42.

trial date and cautioned them on the possibility of a costs sanction for an unreasonable failure to do so. In *Cowl* v. *Plymouth City Council*,[14] Woolf LJ said that enough should be known about ADR to make the failure to adopt it indefensible, particularly when public money is involved.

Following *Dyson* and *Cowl*, the English courts continued to offer strong words of encouragement but did not impose a costs sanction until the following year, in the landmark case of *Dunnett* v. *Railtrack plc*.[15] In granting permission to appeal, Schiemann LJ strongly suggested that the parties should attempt to resolve the dispute by arbitration or mediation. Railtrack refused, even though the Court of Appeal then offered a free mediation scheme. In his costs judgment, Brooke LJ of the Court of Appeal said that skilled mediators could achieve results that went far beyond the Court's powers, and that lawyers who dismissed the opportunity for arbitration or mediation out of hand 'may have to face uncomfortable costs consequences',[16] despite being successful in the appeal.

Consequently, the Court declined to award costs against Dunnett, due to Railtrack's refusal to consider arbitration or mediation in the face of the Court's recommendation to do so. No order to mediate was made, nor did any protocol require that mediation be used as best practice. The Court dismissed Railtrack's rationale for refusing mediation, which was that they believed they would have had to offer more to Dunnett than they wanted to in a mediation. While Railtrack won the appeal, by not making a modest investment in mediation, they lost their costs of the appeal. Hence, *Dunnett* is particularly significant in being the first English decision where a successful litigant, who correctly assessed their legal risk, was sanctioned in costs by a court that viewed their refusal to mediate as unreasonable.[17]

---

[14] [2001] EWCA Civ 1935. Costs sanctions were not, in fact, threatened: just a warning given to parties that it was unacceptable to waste costs on proceedings.

[15] See *Dunnett* (n 10) [14], [15] (Brooke LJ).

[16] ibid [14]–[15].

[17] It did not, however, completely reverse the normal rule in England that costs follow the event. While Railtrack had to pay its own costs, Dunnett had to do likewise, even though her costs were likely to have been minimal given that she was originally represented by the Bar Pro Bono Unit and represented herself in the appeal. The 'shock' effect of the case led to a significant increase in the use of mediation as legal advisors, wary of costs consequences, encouraged their disputing clients to mediate their disputes in England. The Centre for Effective Dispute Resolution calculated that mediation usage increased by 25 per cent per annum in the two years following *Dunnett*. The costs sanction in *Dunnett* resulted from judicial encouragement to settle, thus it is not authority for a costs sanction in the context of an inter-party refusal to mediate. It appears, however, that for a number

7.4.1   Development of Costs Criteria

In *Hurst* v. *Leeming*,[18] the English courts clarified the circumstances in which costs sanctions would be justified. The case involved a dispute between Hurst and his former partners in a solicitors' practice. Having initially represented himself, Hurst eventually hired solicitors and through them instructed his barrister Mr Leeming QC. As Hurst's claims failed at first instance and in the Court of Appeal and the House of Lords, a costs order was made against him, and he was declared bankrupt. Having failed in his efforts to sue his solicitors for negligence, he finally pursued an action against Leeming.[19]

Hurst withdrew his claim following the intervention of Lightman J, the presiding judge, who convinced him that the claim was hopeless. Hurst then claimed that Leeming was not entitled to his costs as he had asked Leeming to proceed to mediation over their dispute and Leeming had refused, and that if Leeming had agreed to mediate, a mediator could have convinced Hurst to withdraw his claim and consequently avoid the costs of the court action.

When Hurst suggested mediation, Leeming had written a response citing a number of reasons for refusing mediation. Lightman J looked at each of these reasons which were based on the following:

> [F]irst, the legal costs already incurred in meeting the allegations and the threat of proceedings; secondly, the seriousness of the allegations of professional negligence; thirdly, the total lack of substance of the claims made; fourthly, the lack of any real prospect of a successful outcome to the mediation proceedings, [particularly in light of Hurst's objective] of obtaining a substantial financial payment from Mr Leeming when in fact there was no merit in the claim; and fifthly, the character of Mr Hurst as revealed by [his numerous prior claims and his actions, as] a man obsessed with the notion that [he was the victim of injustice].[20]

Justice Lightman did not agree that the first three arguments should cause any barrier to considering mediation: the critical factor was whether, when objectively viewed, a mediation had any real prospect of success; but he added that there was a high risk accompanying the refusal.

---

of months following the decision, it was used as authority by parties, on the advice of their lawyers, to engage in mediation based purely on an offer to mediate from another disputing party: see Allen (n 3) 134–37. See also Lord Phillips of Matravers, 'Alternative Dispute Resolution: An English Viewpoint (2008) 74(4) *Arbitration* 406, 412.

[18] [2002] EWHC 1051 (Ch).

[19] This was after the House of Lords decision in *Arthur JS Hall & Co* v. *Simons* [2000] UKHL 38, which removed the immunity from suit for negligence from counsel: see *Hurst* (n 18) [3] (Lightman J).

[20] *Hurst* (n 18) [11].

He commented that in making the objective assessment of the prospects of mediation, the starting point must be the fact that the mediation process can and often does succeed in bringing about a more sensible and more conciliatory attitude on the part of the parties than might otherwise be expected to prevail before the mediation. It follows that this may cause each party to recognise the strengths and weaknesses of their case and their opponent's case, and to develop a willingness to accept the compromise essential to a successful mediation. He remarked: 'What appears to be incapable of mediation before the mediation process begins often proves capable of satisfactory resolution later'.[21] Leeming's decision to refuse to mediate was, in his view, the correct one, as there was no real prospect of success in pursuing mediation; therefore, Leeming should not suffer any cost consequences.

A similar decision was reached in *Société Internationale de Télécommunications Aéronautiques SC* v. *Wyatt Co (UK) Ltd*,[22] where the Court declined to award a costs sanction against a third party who refused the defendant's offer to mediate due to the defendant's behaviour in effectively attempting to coerce the third party into the process. Justice Park believed the defendant would never have been convinced that their case had no merit. Similarly, a costs sanction was refused by the Court of Appeal in *Valentine* v. *Allen*.[23] The Court confirmed that if a party can show it has made real efforts to reach a compromise over the dispute – for example, by making reasonable and generous settlement offers that were rejected or by attempting other settlement methods – a refusal to mediate would not result in a costs sanction.[24] However, the English courts continued to deploy costs sanctions in appropriate circumstances, as in cases such as *Leicester Circuits Ltd* v. *Coates Bros plc*.[25] There, the Court of Appeal penalised a successful appellant in costs for withdrawing from

---

[21] ibid [15].

[22] [2002] EWHC 2401 (Ch). An almost equitable requirement of 'clean hands' for those seeking costs relief seems to emanate from these decisions: see Allen (n 3) 141.

[23] [2003] EWCA Civ 915.

[24] A similar decision was reached in *Corenso* v. *Burnden Group* [2003] EWHC 1805 (QB). See also *McCook* v. *Lobo* [2002] EWCA 2002, where the defendant ignored a letter from the claimant offering to mediate, but the failure to mediate was excused by the court as it believed mediation would have had no reasonable prospect of success. However, the court warned the defendants that they should have responded both 'as a matter of courtesy' and to avoid the risk of a '*Dunnett* type order': at [34] (Judge LJ).

[25] [2003] EWCA Civ 333. See also *Neal* v. *Jones* [2002] EWCA Civ 1730, where the Court reduced the successful respondent's costs because judicial advice to mediate was not accepted.

a mutually agreed mediation the day before it was to take place without any valid explanation.

7.4.1.1   The *Halsey* Factors

The decisions in cases where mediation was proposed by one party but ignored by others in the absence of judicial pressure have been the most controversial in terms of costs jurisprudence in England.[26] While almost all of these decisions were at first instance, this changed in 2004, when the issue was reviewed when *Halsey* v. *Milton Keynes NHS Trust*[27] came before the Court of Appeal. *Halsey* is the most significant case to be decided by the English courts relating to costs sanctions since *Dunnett*. In *Halsey*, the Court dismissed the two appeals against costs awarded in favour of successful claimants who had refused to mediate. Lord Justice Dyson held that in seeking a costs sanction, the unsuccessful party had to discharge the burden of demonstrating why there should be a departure from the general rule that costs should follow the event, and that such a departure was not justified unless it was shown that the successful litigant was unreasonable in refusing mediation.

The Court of Appeal gave the following non-exhaustive list of factors it suggested were relevant to the issue of whether a party unreasonably refused to mediate ('the *Halsey* factors'):

(1) the nature of the dispute and whether it was suitable for mediation;
(2) the merits of the case and whether the pre-trial belief by the winning side that their case was watertight was reasonable;
(3) the extent to which other settlement methods were attempted;
(4) whether the costs involved in the mediation would have been disproportionately high;
(5) whether any delay in the setting up of, and attendance at, the mediation would have been prejudicial; and
(6) whether the mediation had a reasonable prospect of success.[28]

---

[26] See Allen (n 3) 138.

[27] *Halsey* (n 10). The appeal in *Halsey* v. *Milton Keynes NHS Trust* was joined with *Steel* v. *Joy and Halliday*. The former involved a negligence action by a spouse against the hospital in which her husband died, while the latter was a dispute between two insurers about how to apportion liability for the damage caused by successive torts. For a critique and discussion of the conjoined appeal, see Allen (n 3) 141–54.

[28] *Halsey* (n 10) [17]–[23] (Dyson LJ). In *Halsey*, the claimant relied in particular on *Dunnett* (n 10) and *Hurst* (n 18), but the trial court declined a costs sanction for a refusal to mediate as it believed that the claimant would not have been prepared to walk away from a mediation without a monetary settlement.

The Court disagreed with Lightman J's test in *Hurst*, with Dyson LJ proposing a wider test:

> We do not ... accept ... it is appropriate for the court to confine itself to a consideration of whether, viewed objectively, a mediation would have had a reasonable prospect of success. That is an unduly narrow approach: it focuses on the nature of the dispute, and leaves out of account the parties' willingness to compromise and the reasonableness of their attitudes.[29]

The *Halsey* factors have been criticised. The assessment of the merits of the case is objective and is made by the court with the benefit of hindsight after judgment. As lower and higher courts often disagree on what the outcome of a case should be, notwithstanding legal advice, it would be difficult for a litigant centrally involved in the case to make an accurate, objective assessment. It is also unclear how much weight should be given to each factor when determining if a litigant's refusal was unreasonable.[30] The 'non-exhaustive' aspect of the list of factors has been criticised as potentially 'infinite' and consequently as unhelpful to the rule of law which demands clarity and consistency about what constitutes unreasonable refusal to mediate.[31] As can be seen from the jurisprudential analysis that follows, in practice some of the factors have featured more prominently than others.[32]

While *Halsey* did not explicitly overrule *Dunnett*, it was initially criticised for not going far enough in encouraging parties to mediate and that, consequently, courts in England would be reluctant to impose costs sanctions.[33] However, despite such concerns, the application of the *Halsey* factors has given rise to a significant body of case law in England

---

[29] *Halsey* (n 10) [26]. This was echoed by Briggs LJ in *PGF II SA v. OFMS Company* [2013] EWCA Civ 1288: 'When the question concerns the reasonableness or otherwise of a party's conduct, the party's own perceptions may play an important part in the analysis, as is apparent from the treatment of a party's reasonable belief in the strength of its case, in the *Halsey* case at paragraph 26, rejecting as too narrow the purely objective approach applied by Lightman J in *Hurst v Leeming*': at [36].

[30] The more robust the judicial encouragement, the more likely a party's refusal will be viewed as unreasonable: see *Halsey* (n 10) [29] (Dyson LJ). See also S Shipman, 'Waiver: Canute Against the Tide?' (2013) 32(4) *Civil Justice Quarterly* 470, 487–89.

[31] See A K C Koo, 'Unreasonable Refusal to Mediate: The Need for a Principled Approach: PGF II' (2014) 33(3) *Civil Justice Quarterly* 261, 264.

[32] For a discussion on the application of the *Halsey* factors in various English cases, see Allen (n 3) 155–85. See also Blake, Browne and Sime (n 3) 119–25.

[33] See, e.g., Sir Gavin Lightman, 'Mediation: An Approximation to Justice' (2007) 73(4) *Arbitration* 400, 401–2.

requiring the courts to engage in a delicate balancing act between the various criteria that may be in conflict.[34]

7.4.2   Costs Criteria Applied

The *Halsey*[35] approach was followed in *Reed Executive plc v. Reed Business Information Ltd*,[36] a case which involved an alleged trademark infringement and passing off over the use of the name 'Reed'. While Reed Executive plc ('RE') was successful at first instance, Reed Business Information Ltd ('RBI') appealed to the Court of Appeal and declined an offer by RE to use the Court of Appeal's mediation scheme. While RBI was largely successful in the appeal, RE argued for a departure from the normal rules as to costs[37] on the basis that RBI had rejected the offer to mediate, and that RE had discharged its burden of persuasion in accordance with the *Halsey* guidelines, in showing that RBI's conduct was unreasonable.

The Court of Appeal gave a number of reasons why it believed RBI's refusal was not unreasonable. RE would have been negotiating from a position of considerable strength when it suggested mediation, and it proposed mediation very late. RBI had a reasonable, and ultimately justified, belief in their prospects for a successful outcome and they had ongoing disputes in other jurisdictions to consider. The prospects for mediation did not look good given the wide disparity between the parties, and the case was full of novel points of law, including trademark concerns that would have made it more problematic to formulate a deal.[38]

In the later case *Re Midland Linen Service Ltd, Chaudhry v. Yap*,[39] the *Halsey* guidelines were also applied. The case involved a petition brought by the claimant, a former director and minority shareholder in Midland Linen

---

[34] For example, a small value building dispute may ordinarily be viewed as suitable for mediation in light of the monetary amount involved, but such a case could give rise to an arguable point of law leading to an important judicial precedent. The issue arises as to whether the other factors prevail over the desire or need to establish precedent: see L Mulcahy, 'The Collective Interest in Private Dispute Resolution' (2012) 33(1) *Oxford Journal of Legal Studies* 59, 70–71.

[35] *Halsey* (n 10).

[36] [2004] EWCA Civ 887. This was one of many proceedings between the parties over the use of the name 'Reed'.

[37] In accordance with CPR 44.3(2)(a), which provides: 'Where the amount of costs is to be assessed on the standard basis, the court will (a) only allow costs which are proportionate to the matters in issue. Costs which are disproportionate in amount may be disallowed or reduced even if they were reasonably or necessarily incurred.'

[38] *Reed* n (36) [45], [46].

[39] *Re Midland* [2004] EWHC 3380 (Ch).

Services Ltd ('MLS').[40] The claimant accepted a payment into court[41] less than twenty-one days before trial; subsequently, the parties applied to the Court for an order as to costs.[42] MLS contended that the claimant should receive a costs sanction for rejecting an alleged oral offer to settle and offers to mediate. The Court found that MLS had not engaged sufficiently in the process of mediation to justify a finding that the claimant should receive a costs sanction, and that MLS had failed to give sufficient evidence to support its argument that the claimant's refusal to engage in mediation had been unreasonable. The Court found that MLS's attitude to mediation was 'inconsistent and uncertain',[43] whereas, where a party is seeking a reversal of the normal costs rule for a refusal to mediate, its attitude to mediation should be unequivocal. The case is a good example of the approach of the English courts where the proposer of mediation lies about or exaggerates their willingness to mediate and ultimately loses their case. Such behaviour appears to be one of the primary reasons that courts decline to award a costs sanction against a party who refuses to mediate in England.[44]

Similar to *Halsey*,[45] the case of *Burchell*[46] only involved inter-party offers to mediate. This was a small building dispute involving a builder, Nicholas Burchell, and Mr and Mrs Bullard. Before commencing proceedings, Burchell's solicitor wrote to the Bullards suggesting that the dispute be referred to mediation. The Bullards' building surveyor replied, saying that the issues in dispute were technically complex and therefore mediation was not an appropriate means of resolving them. Burchell subsequently issued proceedings against the Bullards claiming £18,318.45, and the Bullards counterclaimed for £100,815.34. Burchell also commenced another claim against the roofing subcontractor who had completed some of the building works in dispute.[47] Burchell received £18,327.04 plus costs on his claim, and the Bullards received £14,373.15 plus costs on their counterclaim. The Bullards effectively had to pay Burchell the difference plus interest and VAT (the relevant tax), equalling £5,025.63. Burchell was

---

[40] The petition was brought under the Companies Act 1985, s 459.
[41] This was made under CPR 36, which deals with offers to settle and payments into court.
[42] This was in accordance with CPR 36.11.
[43] [2004] EWHC 3380 (Ch) [60] (Leslie Kosmin QC, Sitting as a Deputy Judge of the High Court).
[44] Allen (n 3) 157–58.
[45] *Halsey* (n 10).
[46] *Burchell* (n 10).
[47] The claim was brought under CPR 20 which deals with counterclaims and other additional claims. There were no payments made into court and no part 36 offers were made under the Civil Procedure Rules.

also awarded £79.50 on his counterclaim against the roofing subcontractor, but was ordered to pay the roofing subcontractor's costs as the roofing subcontractor only had £79.50 awarded against him and had made many offers to settle from an early stage.

Before appealing the costs award, the Bullards declined Burchell's offer to mediate the issue of costs under the Court of Appeal scheme. On the issue of costs, the Court of Appeal found that the trial judge's approach did not consider the available alternatives to the general rule that costs follow the event.[48] The Court of Appeal was influenced by Burchell's honest and unexaggerated claim, the conduct of Bullards' expert and their exaggerated 'kitchen sink' approach to the counterclaim,[49] and the unreasonable behaviour of the Bullards during the litigation. Most significant, however, was the Bullards' refusal to mediate.

Lord Justice Ward considered the Bullards' conduct in light of the *Halsey* guidelines. As to the nature of the dispute he observed: 'A small building dispute is *par excellence* the kind of dispute which . . . lends itself to ADR.'[50] Regarding the merits of the case he stated:

> The merits of the case favoured mediation. The defendants behaved unreasonably in believing, if they did, that their case was so watertight that they need not engage in attempts to settle . . . The stated reason for refusing mediation that the matter was too complex for mediation is plain nonsense.[51]

As to whether the costs of ADR would be disproportionately high, Ward LJ observed: 'The costs of ADR would have been a drop in the ocean compared with the fortune that has been spent on this litigation'.[52] And on whether ADR had a reasonable prospect of success:

> The way in which the claimant modestly presented his claim and readily admitted many of the defects, allied with the finding that he was

---

[48] See *Burchell* (n 10) [29], [30] (Ward LJ).

[49] Under CPR 44.3(5)(d) this is a relevant consideration when exercising discretion regarding costs.

[50] *Burchell* (n 10) [41] (Ward LJ). In *Couwenbergh* v. *Valkova* [2005] All ER (D) 98, the Court of Appeal held that a dispute relating to the validity of a will in addition to allegations of fraud was perfectly suited to mediation.

[51] *Burchell* (n 10) [41] (Ward LJ).

[52] ibid. See also the comments of the court in *Egan* v. *Motor Services (Bath) Ltd* [2007] EWCA Civ 1002, where the costs spent on a claim were in the region of £100,000, with the claim worth about £6,000; Ward LJ described the parties as '"completely cuckoo" to have engaged in such expensive litigation with so little at stake' and proceeded to say that it was a 'case that cries out for mediation': at [53].

transparently honest and more than ready to admit where he was wrong and to shoulder responsibility for it augured well for mediation. The claimant has satisfied me that mediation would have had a reasonable prospect of success. The defendants cannot rely on their own obstinacy to assert that mediation had no reasonable prospect of success.[53]

While Burchell discharged the burden of showing that the refusal to mediate was unreasonable, the offer to mediate was made before the decisions in Dunnett[54] and Halsey,[55] and the Court of Appeal therefore believed that the reasonableness of the Bullards' actions in refusing mediation had to be judged against the 'background of practice ... and [i]n the light of the knowledge of the times'.[56] While the Court of Appeal did not impose any additional sanction on the Bullards for their refusal to mediate, the appeal decision was still quite severe. Mr Burchell was awarded 60 per cent of the costs of the proceedings, claim and counterclaim and the Bullards were ordered to pay Burchell 60 per cent of the costs that Burchell was liable to pay to the roofing subcontractor. The cost of the litigation to the parties would ultimately be in the region of £185,000. This was described by the Court, in view of the fact that the original judgment was £5,025.63, as 'an horrific picture'.[57]

7.4.3   Costs Sanctions and the Duty to Advise

While Burchell and similar cases discussed illustrate the onus on parties to consider mediation, and the consequences that can follow where the court believes that their refusal is unreasonable, the Court of Appeal in Burchell also stressed that the legal profession in England must now take note of Halsey[58] and can no longer dismiss reasonable requests to mediate:

Halsey has made plain not only the high rate of a successful outcome being achieved by mediation but ... it is now the legal profession which must become fully aware of and acknowledge its value. The profession can no longer with impunity shrug aside reasonable requests to mediate. The parties

[53] Burchell (n 10) [41] (Ward LJ).
[54] Dunnett (n 10).
[55] Halsey (n 10).
[56] Burchell (n 10) [42] (Ward LJ).
[57] ibid [23] (Ward LJ).
[58] Halsey (n 10). See also Chapter 6 at Section 6.4 for a discussion on the legal liability of lawyers in mediation and their obligation to advise of the mediation option.

cannot ignore a proper request to mediate simply because it was made before
the claim was issued. With court fees escalating, it may be folly to do so . . . .
These defendants have escaped the imposition of a costs sanction in this case
but defendants in a like position in the future can expect little sympathy if
they blithely battle on regardless of the alternatives.[59]

This requirement has been put on a statutory footing in other jurisdictions.
In Ireland, for example, before issuing proceedings on behalf of a client,
practising solicitors[60] (and barristers, where a client is directly represented
by a barrister[61]) must advise clients to consider mediation as an alternative
to litigation. If the client elects to institute proceedings after being given
information on mediation services,[62] the solicitor must provide a statutory
declaration with the application confirming that the obligations to advise
on the mediation option to resolve the dispute have been discharged.

A court in South Africa has also adopted a robust approach to encourage legal advisors to consider mediation as an option with disputing
parties. In the High Court case of *Brownlee* v. *Brownlee*,[63] Brassey AJ
imposed a costs sanction on the parties' lawyers as a direct consequence
of their failure to advise on the mediation option. The lawyers effectively
agreed not to advise mediation in a case which the judge believed would
have benefited from it, and he consequently limited what the lawyers
could charge their own clients as a result and made no order between the
parties. The lawyers had 'positively rejected the use of the [mediation]
process. For this they are to blame and they must, I believe shoulder the

---

[59] *Burchell* (n 10) [43] (Ward LJ). The Court also stated that it 'is entitled to take an
unreasonable refusal into account, even when it occurs before the start of formal
proceedings; see rule 44.3(5)(a) of the Civil Procedure Rules 1998': at [50] (Rix LJ).
Rule 44.3(5) states that the conduct of the parties includes conduct before, as well as
during, the proceedings – in particular, the extent to which the parties followed any
relevant pre-action protocol. See also the subsequent case of *Rolf* v. *De Guerin* [2011]
EWCA Civ 78, that also involved a small-building dispute, where Rix LJ, in applying the
Halsey principles, underlined the need to mediate small-building disputes if negotiation
fails.

[60] Irish Mediation Act 2017, s 14. Section 21 of the Mediation Act 2017 provides that in
awarding costs, where the court has invited parties to consider mediation, it may have
regard to any unreasonable refusal or failure by a party to consider or attend mediation.

[61] Irish Mediation Act 2017, s 15. This would be quite rare in practice as most clients would
in the first instance be represented by a solicitor, who would then instruct a barrister on
their behalf.

[62] This includes details of mediators and information about the advantages and benefits of
mediation, confidentiality obligations and the enforceability of mediated settlements. On
the Irish Mediation Act generally, see P McRedmond, *Mediation Law* (Dublin,
Bloomsbury Professional 2018).

[63] High Court (Provisional Division), Brassey AJ, 25 August 2009.

responsibility that comes from failing properly to serve the interests of their clients'.[64] The approach adopted in such cases presents a clear caution to the legal profession to encourage parties to settle disputes, given what judges might do if lawyers fail to advise their clients about mediation.

7.4.4   Timing, Information and Justified Refusal

Any commercial dispute that can be resolved through negotiation is suitable for mediation, and the process can take place at any time up to trial and even where an appeal is pending. However, the later the mediation takes place in the litigation process, the lesser the costs savings that can result from the mediated settlement.[65] An unjustified delay in proceeding to mediation can give rise to a costs sanction in England. In *Costain Ltd* v. *Charles Haswell & Partners Ltd*,[66] a delay of seven months between the pre-action protocol meeting and the first mediation was determined by the Court to be 'considerably too long once it was clear that the process of mediation was the next step to take'.[67] The consequence was a reduction in Costain's costs award to reflect the amount of time wasted by the unjustified delay in organising the mediation. A cautious approach would need to be adopted by parties and their advisors when making this assessment, however, to avoid the consequences of being considered to have proceeded to mediation too early. In *Nigel Witham Ltd* v. *Smith*[68] and *Wethered Estate Ltd* v. *Davis*,[69] mediation was proposed early in the proceedings and the parties (in *Nigel Witham* the defendant and in *Wethered Estate* the claimant) were vindicated in declining the offer to mediate as they did not have sufficient

---

[64] ibid [59]. Each party covered their own costs, as they were not 'blameless', but the lion's share of the Court's 'displeasure' was reserved for the lawyers, as the Court deprived them of their attorney and client costs for failing to recommend mediation. The lawyers' costs were capped at inter-party rates (the equivalent of standard basis costs rather than indemnity costs: see Section 7.3).

[65] Blake, Browne and Sime (n 3) 148–49.

[66] [2009] EWHC B25 (TCC).

[67] ibid [285] (R Fernyhough QC, Sitting as Deputy High Court Judge). See also *Palfrey* v. *Wilson* [2007] EWCA Civ 94, where the claimant's offer to mediate at an advanced stage in the proceedings did not affect the costs award. However, there is not just one appropriate time to attempt mediation. Ideally, there should be a mediation strategy alongside the litigation strategy. For a discussion on timing the use of ADR in relation to the progress of a case, see Blake, Browne and Sime (n 3) 28–38.

[68] [2008] EWHC 12 (TCC).

[69] [2005] EWHC 1903 (Ch); [2006] BLR 86.

information from the other party to ensure that the process could be effective. In *Beattie PN* v. *Canham Consulting*[70] the defendant was justified in refusing mediation as the claimant, when proposing mediation, did not present a true case consistent with what it turned out to be at trial.[71] Hence, imposing a precondition such as access to relevant information to adequately assess the commercial and legal risk that a claim presents before mediation can be deemed reasonable behaviour by the English courts.

In *PGF II*,[72] the Court of Appeal dismissed the appeal of a costs sanction on the basis that the defendant's silence following 'two requests to mediate was itself unreasonable conduct of litigation sufficient to warrant a costs sanction'.[73] Lord Justice Ward believed that there were sound practical and policy reasons for what he called a 'modest extension' to the principles and guidelines elucidated in *Halsey*,[74] such that:

> [S]ilence in the face of an invitation to participate in ADR is, as a general rule, of itself unreasonable, regardless whether an outright refusal, or a refusal to engage in the type of ADR requested, or to do so at the time requested, might have been justified by the identification of reasonable grounds.[75]

While the Court acknowledged that there may be a valid reason that could justify refusal, the onus would be on the silent party to assert it at the relevant time or face the possibility of a costs sanction for an unreasonable refusal to mediate.[76]

PGF II[77] effectively extends *Halsey* by requiring that parties respond to an invitation to mediate and either accept or clearly justify their refusal (even where their refusal may ultimately be deemed reasonable) to avoid

---

[70] [2021] EWHC 1414 (TCC).

[71] ibid [32], Fraser J: 'I find that the refusal by Canham during 2020 to engage in mediation was not unreasonable in all the circumstances of the case. This refusal came at a time when the claimants were advancing, and continued to advance, a factually untruthful case.'

[72] *PGF II* (n 29).

[73] ibid [40] (Briggs LJ).

[74] *Halsey* (n 10).

[75] *PGF II* (n 29) [34] (Briggs LJ).

[76] In *ADS Aerospace Ltd* v. *EMS Global Tracking* [2012] EWHC 2904 TCC, Akenhead J applied the *Halsey* principles in declining to sanction a winning defendant for refusing to mediate, in part due to mediation being suggested too late, 'with less than 20 working days before the trial': at [8(d)].

[77] *PGF II* (n 29).

a sanction when the court deals with the issue of costs.[78] Where there is insufficient information to engage in the process effectively, it is critical that parties set this out and state clearly what they require before they can consider the invitation; they must provide cogent and clear reasons for any refusal, as required under *Halsey*. As Briggs LJ said, quoting the comments of the trial judge:

> It would seem to me consistent with the policy which encourages mediation by depriving the successful party of its costs in appropriate circumstances that it should also deprive such a party of costs where there are real obstacles to mediation which might reasonably be overcome but are not addressed because that party does not raise them at the time.[79]

In the subsequent case *Thakkar* v. *Patel*,[80] both parties were ostensibly prepared to consider settlement through mediation, but the defendant was 'slow to respond to letters and raised all sorts of difficulties',[81] effectively making progress impossible. Upholding a costs sanction against the defendant, Jackson LJ said:

> The message which this court sent out in *PGF II* was that to remain silent in the face of an offer to mediate is, absent exceptional circumstances, unreasonable conduct meriting a costs sanction, even in cases where mediation is unlikely to succeed. The message which the court sends out in this case is that in a case where bilateral negotiations fail but mediation is obviously appropriate, it behoves both parties to get on with it. If one party frustrates the process by delaying and dragging its feet for no good reason, that will merit a costs sanction.[82]

The case of *Garritt-Critchley* v. *Ronnan*[83] involved a claim relating to whether a binding agreement regarding the sale of shares had been reached, a claim which was heavily dependent on issues of fact pertaining

---

[78] In *McMillen Williams* v. *Range* [2004] EWCA Civ 294 the appellant won the appeal, but the parties ignored the Court's recommendation to mediate and no order was consequently made as to costs of the appeal due to the intransigence of the parties in their mutual failure to mediate. Lord Justice Ward declared 'a plague on both your houses' in concluding it was 'a case where we should condemn the posturing and jockeying for position taken by each side of this dispute and thus direct that each side pay its own costs': at [30].

[79] *PGF II* (n 29) [33].

[80] [2017] EWCA Civ 117.

[81] ibid [10].

[82] ibid [31] (Briggs LJ agreeing [32]).

[83] [2014] EWHC 1774 (Ch).

to both oral[84] and documentary-based evidence. The judge, believing
the case to be suitable for mediation, applied the *Halsey*[85] principles to
the witness statement provided by the defendant's solicitors and
rejected all of them, despite the burden of proof being on the claimant.
The judge would not accept the contention that the absence of middle
ground was a justification for not mediating, remarking 'parties don't
know whether in truth they are too far apart unless they sit down and
explore settlement'.[86] In view of the fact that the defendants had
accepted the claimant's Part 36 offer after trial, their assessment that
it was a case they were bound to win was questioned, as was their failure
not to seek a summary judgment.[87] The judge, citing *Hurst*,[88] as well as
Halsey,[89] remarked that a party's belief in the watertight nature of their
case is not sufficient to justify refusal. Acrimony among the parties was
rejected as a sufficient reason to refuse to mediate as, in the Court's
view, mediators are experienced in working in such a context. The
defendants' attempt to use *PGF II* as a defence by stating that they
had responded promptly to the offers to mediate, while refusing them,
was unsuccessful. The difficulty, according to the judge, is that their
reasons were misguided.

In *Northrop Grumman Mission Systems Europe Ltd* v. *BAE Systems (Al
Dariyah C41) Ltd*,[90] Ramsey J went through the *Halsey* factors one by
one, but the primary issue that occupied the Court was BAE's belief in the
strength of their case. Justice Ramsey believed mediation had the potential
to succeed, despite the parties being far apart – for Northrop Grumman
£3 million plus costs against, for BAE no payment plus costs. He remarked
that, given the significant commercial concerns and overlapping interests
of the parties, a skilled mediator could have helped them find some mutual
benefit in coming to an agreement. Justice Ramsey found that BAE had

---

[84] In *MWB Business Exchange Centres* v. *Rock Advertising* [2018] UKSC 24, the UK Supreme
Court ruled, overturning a decision of the Court of Appeal, that full force and effect will
be given to a 'No Oral Modification Clause'. Hence, the decision confirms that parties can
bind themselves to an agreed type of formality for any variation to be binding.

[85] *Halsey* (n 10).

[86] [2014] EWHC 1774 (Ch) [22] (Waksman HHJ). This may be contrasted with the earlier
decision not to award a costs sanction for a refusal to mediate on the basis that '[a]t all
stages the parties in reality were a hundred miles apart' in *Swain Mason* v. *Mills & Reeve*
[2012] EWCA Civ 498 [75] (Davis LJ). See also *Patel* v. *Barlows* [2020] EWHC 2795 (Ch).

[87] This is dealt with under CPR 24.

[88] *Hurst* (n 18).

[89] *Halsey* (n 10).

[90] [2014] EWHC 3148 (TCC).

a reasonable belief in the strength of their case, but he concluded that the belief, while reasonable, was not sufficient to excuse their refusal to mediate.[91]

7.4.5   The Civil Procedure Rules Journey

The English courts have travelled a long journey since the introduction of the Civil Procedure Rules and the subsequent seminal decision in *Dunnett*,[92] which imposed a costs sanction for a refusal to mediate when recommended by the court. *Dunnett* was the first time that judicial encouragement turned to 'quasi compulsion', when the English courts made it clear that a successful party could be sanctioned in costs due to a refusal to mediate.[93] *Halsey*,[94] which followed, was significant in part for establishing authority that a costs sanction would be imposed as a result of an inter-party refusal to mediate, reflecting the importance of parties and their advisors seriously considering mediation in appropriate cases. As discussed in Section 7.4.1.1, the case also elucidated a non-exhaustive list of factors the court should consider in deciding whether a sanction is appropriate. The post-*Halsey* jurisprudence discussed above clearly indicates that the most significant of these include factors that involve the merits of the case and whether the pre-trial belief by the winning side that their case was watertight was reasonable, and whether the mediation had a reasonable prospect of success.

The English courts' reliance on the sixth *Halsey* factor (whether the mediation had a reasonable prospect of success) has been criticised on the basis that it is not clear what success means to a court; success may comprise resolution of all or some pending issues, depending on the circumstances.[95] However, it would seem reasonable to conclude that 'a reasonable prospect of success' effectively means a reasonable prospect of 'achieving settlement', and that if it did not, this was due to the

---

[91] The *Halsey* test is in fact whether the party reasonably believed that their case was 'watertight', which is not a test that Ramsey J applied. However, BAE had made a without-prejudice-save-as-to-costs offer, which the claimant did not improve at trial; as a result, the normal rule applied and costs followed the event, with BAE not being sanctioned in costs. Nevertheless, it has been suggested that the case weakens the force of *Halsey* (n 10): see Allen (n 3) 182–84.

[92] *Dunnett* (n 10).

[93] See J M Nolan-Haley, 'Mediation Exceptionality' (2009) 78(3) *Fordham Law Review* 1247, 1258.

[94] *Halsey* (n 10).

[95] See Nolan-Haley (n 93) 1263.

intransigence of the party who won at trial, rather than the intransigence of the losing side.[96]

7.5   Conduct, Costs and Compulsion

Consent in the context of mediation has two aspects: 'front-end, participation consent', which should occur at the beginning of the process and continue throughout it; and 'back-end, outcome consent', which should be present when the parties reach a mediated settlement agreement. While front-end consent may be dispensed with in the appropriate circumstances, back-end outcome consent is always required.[97] However, there are varying views on whether front-end consent can be dispensed with, on the basis that mediation must be a voluntary process based on party self-determination at each stage, including entry into the process, during the process and in the event that a settlement is reached. While non-consensual mediation may be useful for case management or clearing the court backlog, it has been suggested that meaningful mediation requires consent.[98] Ten years after the *Halsey* judgment, Lord Dyson remarked, 'it is one thing to compel parties to consider mediation; it is another to frog march them to the mediation table and deny them access to the courtroom if they refuse to participate in the mediation'.[99]

A recurring theme in some of the costs jurisprudence in England is concern that the more vigilant the judiciary becomes in encouraging mediation through the use of costs sanctions, the more it appears that mediation is becoming compulsory. In jurisdictions where sanctions for a refusal to mediate have been deployed, the courts when determining

---

[96] See also Allen (n 3) 144.

[97] Consent should also be fully informed. This means parties should be aware of the mediator's style, and whether it is, for example, settlement, facilitative, transformative or evaluative as this can directly impact on the outcome of the process. See Chapter 4 at Section 4.2. Mediation litigation in the USA has tended to relate to back-end consent, while litigation in England has tended to focus on front-end consent. There appear to be far fewer cases in the USA that relate to front-end consent. See Chapter 8 at Section 8.2. In contrast with the position in the USA, very few post-*Halsey* cases involve challenges to the enforceability of mediated settlement agreements, and this is likely to result from the fact that parties who agree to participate in mediation are more likely to honour the agreement that results from the process: see Nolan-Haley (n 93) 1263–1264.

[98] See, e.g., J M Nolan-Haley, 'Mediation: The Best and Worst of Times' (2015) 16(3) *Cardozo Journal of Conflict Resolution* 731, 737–39.

[99] Lord Dyson, 'Halsey 10 Years On: The Decision Revisited' in *Justice, Continuity and Change* (Oxford, Hart Publishing 2018) 381–83.

costs have had to decide, when reviewing the parties' behaviour, whether they are willing to look inside the process and consequently infringe upon mediation confidentiality to assess conduct.[100] The concern is that the further that sanctions extend, the greater the likelihood that mediation confidentiality will be eroded.

Compulsory forms of mediation, if used in jurisdictions where costs sanctions are applied by the courts to parties who unreasonably refuse to mediate, are likely to run into allegations that they violate the rights guaranteed by article 6 of the European Convention on Human Rights[101] ('ECHR') or other equivalent constitutions or declarations.[102] Lord Justice Dyson, in delivering the *Halsey* judgment, remarked:

> [T]o oblige truly unwilling parties to refer their disputes to mediation would be to impose an unacceptable obstruction on their right of access to the courts ... and, therefore, a violation of article 6 [of the ECHR].[103]

---

[100] See *Malmesbury* v. *Strutt & Parker* [2008] EWHC 424 (QB), [2008] 5 Costs LR 736, where both parties, unusually, waived confidentiality and the successful claimant's costs award was reduced due to his unreasonable conduct in the mediation process. The financial quantum awarded was significantly less than his claim and final offer during the mediation. Article 7 of the EU Mediation Directive requires EU Member States (except Denmark, which opted out of the Mediation Directive) to ensure that mediators and others involved in a mediation process, in the absence of agreement, are not compelled to give evidence in civil, commercial or arbitration proceedings regarding information arising out of the mediation process except where necessary for overriding reasons of public policy or where necessary to enforce a mediated settlement agreement: Directive 2008/52/EC of the European Parliament and of the Council of 21 May 2008 on certain aspects of mediation in civil and commercial matters [2008] OJ L136/3 ('EU Mediation Directive').

[101] Article 6(1) of the ECHR provides: 'In the determination of his civil rights and obligations or of any criminal charge against him, everyone is entitled to a fair and public hearing within a reasonable time by an independent and impartial tribunal established by law. Judgment shall be pronounced publicly.'

[102] See, e.g., the American Convention on Human Rights, article 6, which provides: 'Every person has the right to a hearing, with due guarantees and within a reasonable time, by a competent, independent, and impartial tribunal, previously established by law, in the substantiation of any accusation of a criminal nature made against him or for the determination of his rights and obligations of a civil, labor, fiscal, or any other nature'; African Charter on Human and Peoples' Rights, article 7(1), which provides: 'Every individual shall have the right to have his cause heard. This comprises: (1) The right to an appeal to competent national organs against acts of violating his fundamental rights as recognized and guaranteed by conventions, laws, regulations and customs in force.' See also R Feehily, 'Creeping Compulsion to Mediate: The Constitution and the Convention' (2018) 69(2) *Northern Ireland Legal Quarterly* 127 for a comprehensive discussion of this issue in the context of Ireland.

[103] *Halsey* (n 10) [9].

He later refined his remarks on the issue of compulsion, conceding that 'in and of itself compulsory mediation does not breach article 6',[104] based on the judgment of the European Court of Justice in *Alassini* v. *Telecom Italia SpA*.[105] The Court in *Alassini* decided that a provision in Italian law which required parties to submit to an out-of-court settlement procedure, otherwise they lost their right to bring judicial proceedings, did not breach article 6 of the ECHR.[106]

---

[104] See Lord Dyson, 'A Word on Halsey v Milton Keynes' (2011) 77(3) *Arbitration* 337, 338–39 (3rd Annual Mediation Symposium of the Chartered Institute of Arbitration, London, October 2010). See also Lord Dyson (n 99). See also the views of Professor Dame Hazel Genn QC, who questions the motivation for the English judiciary to publicise the de facto retraction of this aspect of the *Halsey* judgment, or in her words, there appears to have been a 'campaign, launched at the highest judicial level, to undermine the authority of Lord Justice Dyson's decision in *Halsey*': H Genn, *Judging Civil Justice* (Cambridge, Cambridge University Press, 2010) 101–2. Professor Genn is one of the chief sceptics of civil justice reforms in England to encourage parties to use mediation. For example, she has stated: 'The outcome of mediation is not about *just* settlement, it is *just about settlement*': see Genn at 117. Such comments have elicited counter arguments: see, e.g., Allen (n 3) 120–21. In *Lomax* v. *Lomax* [2019] EWCA Civ 1467, the English Court of Appeal confirmed that the ordering of early neutral evaluation by a judge, permitted by CPR 3.1(2)(m), even where a party objects, is not in breach of article 6 of the ECHR. Similar to mediation, early neutral evaluation does not prohibit the parties from proceeding to trial if they fail to reach agreement. For an overview of the process in England, see Blake, Browne and Sime (n 3) 265–69.

[105] Joined Cases C-317–320/08 *Alassini* [2010] 3 CMLR 17.

[106] The case involved the referral of four Italian cases to the European Court of Justice for a preliminary ruling. The Court had to determine if the Italian legislation breached article 6 of the ECHR. The legislation required parties to attempt settlement through an out-of-court procedure during a thirty-day period for disputes about electronic communications services, where a precondition to commencing court proceedings was an alleged breach of contract involving consumers by telecoms providers. The Court held that the legislation did not breach article 6 because: the settlement procedure was not binding and did not prohibit court proceedings subsequently being brought; the thirty-day limit did not amount to a substantial delay and the limitation period was suspended during the required process; and no significant costs were involved in using the procedure. Provided such schemes are in the general interest and proportionate, the principle of effective judicial protection does not preclude them. However, *Alassini* is limited in scope as far as it relates to mediation, since it does not deal with mediation per se but with another type of compulsory ADR process. As noted by Lord Dyson: 'The judgment of the ECJ in *Rosalba Alassini* does not rule that compulsory mediation will never breach article 6': see Lord Dyson (n 104) 340. See also Allen (n 3) 122–23; Feehily (n 102) 133. Other leading English jurists, such as Lightman J, Lord Phillips CJ and Lord Justice Clarke MR, have also commented that the basis for an order for mediation does not interfere with the right to trial, as it does not propose mediation in lieu of a trial, but merely imposes a delay. See Chapter 3 at Section 3.3.4. The UK Civil Justice Council that advises the Lord Chancellor, the Judiciary and the Civil Procedure Rule Committee on civil matters, has also concluded that compulsory mediation is compatible with article 6 of the ECHR and is, therefore, lawful. See UK Civil Justice Council, *Compulsory ADR* (June 2021) 29.

However, the official position in England is that compulsory mediation is not part of the civil justice landscape.[107] This was reflected by Dyson LJ, when he made it clear that his support for mediation and the use of costs sanctions to support it is not unqualified: '[T]he court should not exercise that power if it is satisfied that the parties are truly unwilling to embark upon a mediation'.[108] He argued that mandatory mediation could constitute a denial of access to justice in certain circumstances – for example, where it is coupled with high mediation costs – and that it is not the role of a court of law to force compromise upon unwilling disputants who do not want it.[109] With regard to the first contention, the chance that such situations would materialise in practice is highly unlikely in light of the seemingly low cost of mediation when compared with the high cost of going to trial. With regard to the second contention, a degree of compulsion to enter into a process from which settlement may result, a process that parties may exit at any time, is markedly different from a legal compulsion to settle. A settlement will usually be arrived at only when it is reduced to writing and signed by both parties, and in a commercial context, drafted and reviewed by the party's respective legal teams.[110]

The European Parliament commissioned a study to investigate the limited use of mediation five and a half years after the adoption of the EU Mediation Directive. The report proposed a 'mitigated' form of mandatory mediation as a way of ensuring that the process is adopted in appropriate cases.[111] Specifically, this would require compulsory

---

[107] See Jackson Report (n 3) xxiii. See also Chapter 3 at Section 3.3.4.

[108] Lord Dyson (n 104) 339. See also Lord Dyson (n 99).

[109] See Lord Dyson (n 104) 339–40; Lord Dyson (n 99) 21–22. However, policy in this area may change. In *Wright* v. *Michael Wright (Supplies) Ltd* [2013] EWCA Civ 234, the parties remained intransigently opposed to mediation despite strong encouragement from the courts. Sir Alan Ward said: 'Perhaps ... it is time to review the rule in *Halsey* ... "that to oblige truly unwilling parties to refer their disputes to mediation would be to impose an unacceptable obstruction on their right of access to the court".' at [3]. See also Blake, Browne and Sime (n 3) 95–97.

[110] See A K C Koo, 'Ten Years after Halsey' (2015) 34(1) *Civil Justice Quarterly* 77, 79–80.

[111] G De Palo and others, '"Rebooting" the Mediation Directive: Assessing the Limited Impact of its Implementation and Proposing Measures to Increase the Number of Mediations in the EU' (Luxembourg, European Parliament 2014). The study involved a comparative analysis of the legal frameworks in the twenty-eight Member States of the European Union, and an assessment of the impact of the EU Mediation Directive (n 100). The study solicited the views of up to 816 experts from all over Europe, and the proposal with regard to mandatory mediation reflected the majority view of the experts. Guiseppe De Palo and Romina Canessa were among those selected by the European Parliament to be the authors of the study. For an examination of the European Union's continued initiatives to foster the use of cross-border mediation, including its review of the EU Mediation

attendance at information sessions coupled with mandatory mediation with the ability to opt out if litigants do not intend to continue with the process. The logic is that these two measures combined would force litigants to consider mediation seriously and together.[112] The basis for this recommendation was the experience in Italy, where the model of mandatory mediation with opt-out was adopted and resulted in a high number of mediations.[113]

Directive, an analysis of insights provided by in-house counsel, together with recommendations on how cross-border commercial mediation can be promoted, see A Howard, *EU Cross-Border Commercial Mediation: Listening to Disputants – Changing the Frame; Framing the Changes* (Alphen aan den Rijn, Kluwer Law International 2021).

[112] Similar to the experience in Italy (discussed at n 113), it is suggested that such reforms could initially be introduced on a trial basis for a specified period such as four years. At selected intervals during and at the end of the required trial period, the reforms could be reviewed and assessed to determine if they have proved effective: see De Palo and others (n 111) 9–10, 163–64. The 'mitigated' form of mandatory mediation proposed in the study is essentially mandatory consideration of mediation: see G De Palo and R Canessa, 'Sleeping? Comatose? Only Mandatory Consideration of Mediation Can Awake Sleeping Beauty in the European Union' (2014) 16(3) *Cardozo Journal of Conflict Resolution* 713, 725. For a discussion on some criticisms of the study, and the authors' responses to those criticisms, see De Palo and Canessa at 724–27.

[113] The mandatory mediation rules were introduced by the Italian Government and put on a legislative footing in article 5, 1-bis, Legislative Decree 28, initially for a trial period of four years that ended in September 2017. Under article 5, the following cases are subject to mandatory mediation: tenancy, land rights, partition of property, hereditary succession, leases, loans, rental companies, medical and sanitary malpractice, defamation by the press of other means of advertising, contracts, insurance and banking and finance. The legislation also introduced rules for mediation, and a non-mandatory procedure that applies to any civil and commercial litigation outside those under article 5: see De Palo and others (n 111) 40. If a party withdraws from the mediation, a mediator has the authority to propose a solution to the dispute; if this is rejected by a party and the case subsequently goes to trial, the judge may shift all mediation and litigation costs onto the party who rejected the proposed solution, if the judgment is consistent with the mediator's proposed solution: see De Palo and others at 41. The evidence from the Italian experience suggests that elements of mandatory mediation can have a positive effect on the uptake of voluntary mediation as well. In Italy, until 2011, there were fewer than 2,000 mediations annually. When mandatory mediation was introduced (making mediation a condition precedent to litigation in certain cases) between March 2011 and October 2012, the number of voluntary mediations increased to almost 45,000, out of over 220,000 proceedings overall. When mediation was no longer mandatory, between October 2012 and September 2013 (due to a ruling in the Italian Constitutional Court that a parliamentary statute was required, not a government decree, to require litigants to attempt mediation before going to court) the number of voluntary mediations fell to almost zero. Following the introduction of the 'mitigated' form of mandatory mediation in September 2013, both mandatory and voluntary mediations occurred at a rate of tens of thousands per month: see De Palo and others at 7. See also De Palo and Canessa (n 112) 722. The other main proposal in the study was that the European Union should affirm the theory of the Balanced

In the USA, schemes of compulsory mediation have emerged in a number of states with federal district courts empowered to compel parties to mediate disputes under the Alternative Dispute Resolution Act 1998.[114] Signatories to the ECHR, such as Belgium and Greece, have adopted compulsory mediation schemes without any successful article 6 ECHR challenges. Similarly in Germany, federal states can introduce legislation to compel parties to engage in either court-based or court-approved mediation before litigation commences.[115] The European Commission has stated that the European Union actively promotes and encourages the use of mediation to help dispute resolution and avoid the worry, time and cost associated with litigation.[116] This is reflected in article 5(2) of the EU Mediation Directive which provides that the encouragement it offers to mediate is made 'without prejudice to national legislation making the use of mediation compulsory ... provided that such legislation does not interfere with the right of access to justice'. Such experiences reveal that schemes of compulsory mediation do not in and of themselves give rise to a violation of article 6, provided mediation is presented as a condition precedent to litigation or arbitration and is not

Relationship Target Number (BRTN), where each Member State, using a pro-mediation policy of its choice, determines a clear target minimum percentage of mediations to take place annually. The study suggests that in view of the policies that have proved to generate mediations in the European Union, it is likely that EU Member States will naturally converge in adopting similar policies: see De Palo and others (n 111) at 163–64. The push for a BRTN is motivated by article 1 of the EU Mediation Directive (n 100), which states: 'The objective of this Directive is to facilitate access to alternative dispute resolution and to promote the amicable settlement of disputes by encouraging the use of mediation and by ensuring a balanced relationship between mediation and judicial proceedings.' The BRTN, it is suggested, is the only quantifiable way of ascertaining if the balanced relationship called for by the Mediation Directive has been achieved: see De Palo and Canessa (n 112) 714.

[114] Alternative Dispute Resolution Act 1998, 28 USC 652. See also Nolan-Haley (n 93) 1247. Australia and New Zealand have proceeded much further towards mandatory mediation: see M Hanks, 'Perspectives on Mandatory Mediation' (2012) 35(3) *University of New South Wales Law Journal* 929.

[115] See N Alexander, W Gottwald and T Trenczec, 'Mediation in Germany: The Long and Winding Road' in N Alexander (ed), *Global Trends in Mediation* (2nd ed, The Hague, Kluwer Law International 2006) 233. The experience in Ontario, Canada suggests that an enhanced voluntary mediation scheme is a better solution and less financially burdensome on the state than a compulsory one: see Ministry of Justice, *Solving Disputes in the County Courts: Creating a Simpler, Quicker and More Proportionate System – A Consultation on Reforming Civil Justice in England and Wales – The Government Response* (Cm 8274, February 2012) 172.

[116] European Commission, 'EU Rules on Mediation' (17 November 2021) <https://e-justice .europa.eu/content_eu_overview_on_mediation-63-en.do> accessed 10 May 2022.

the only means of resolution.[117] It is therefore difficult to see how costs sanctions could be characterised as breaching article 6 of the ECHR, or an equivalent constitution or declaration, where they simply require parties to consider mediation in advance of trial. If parties refuse an offer of mediation in such a context, they may be excused if the court believes that their refusal to mediate was reasonable in the circumstances.[118] Where parties attempt mediation that proves unsuccessful in reaching a settlement, they may proceed to trial.

7.5.1   Breaches Arising from the Pressure to Mediate

As discussed in the previous section, various jurisdictions have adopted compulsory mediation schemes without any successful challenges under article 6 of the ECHR. However, there are potentially at least three situations where an applicant may seek to claim that their article 6(1) rights have been infringed in the context of the pressure to undertake mediation.[119] The first is where a party has reached a mediated settlement agreement and consequently cannot pursue an action in court. As the agreement that results from a successful mediation is likely to reflect the interests of the parties rather than their legal rights, it is less likely to reflect the legal merits involved in a potential claim; parties may settle for less than they would achieve through a court judgment and will often discharge their own costs. However, the courts have proved reluctant to review mediated settlement agreements as they are binding contracts.[120]

---

[117] Courts in the USA have developed a tradition of ordering mediation in the face of resistance from the parties. In *Re Atlantic Pipe Corp* [2002] 304 F 3d 135, the Court of Appeals for the First Circuit said that a federal trial court has the inherent authority to order compulsory mediation where appropriate. It remarked that in some cases a court may be warranted in believing that compulsory mediation could yield significant benefits even if one or more parties object, believing that while the parties may fail to reach agreement, the benefit of settlement can be worth the risk. Conversely, state courts have arrived at different outcomes. For example, in *Jeld-Wen* v. *Superior Court* 146 Cal App 4th 536 (2007) an appellate court found that while Californian courts have the statutory power to order smaller civil cases to mediation where the cost is covered by the state, they could not order parties to attend and fund private mediation.

[118] Indeed if costs sanctions did breach article 6 of the ECHR, the Civil Procedure Rules in England and similar initiatives elsewhere would be jeopardised: see Allen (n 3) 261.

[119] See R Smith, *Textbook on International Human Rights* (5th ed, Oxford, Oxford University Press 2012) 106–7. See also P Leach, *Taking a Case to the European Court of Human Rights* (3rd ed, Oxford, Oxford University Press 2012) 26–76; Shipman (n 30) 475–76.

[120] The court would only look to set aside the mediated settlement agreement if there were, for example, evidence of duress or coercion. See Chapter 8 at Section 8.2 for further discussion of this issue.

The second possible challenge arises where funds are expended on an unsuccessful mediation that could have been used as litigation costs. However, in the context of commercial mediation, mediating disputes is likely to cost significantly less than litigation, and this challenge would have greater relevance to low value, non-commercial claims.

The third possible basis for a challenge could occur where a party is successful in their court action but, due to their unreasonable refusal to mediate the dispute, they receive an adverse costs award and consequently contend that this constitutes a denial of their right of access to court: that the right is 'theoretical and illusory'.[121] While there may be a degree of compulsion at the initial stage, continued participation in mediation and agreement on settlement is voluntary. If either party does not like the way the mediation is progressing, they can choose to exit the process and pursue their claim in court. There is no requirement to reach a settlement or indeed remain in the process. As consideration of mediation is a step in the process where parties may ultimately proceed to court, it would be difficult to contend that access to court in this context is 'theoretical and illusory'.

The first and second bases of challenge could also be defeated if it were shown that the party waived their right by going to mediation, provided the type of dispute falls within the European Court of Human Rights (ECtHR) autonomous definition of 'civil rights and obligations' and is consequently covered by article 6(1). The right of access to court is not absolute, and the ECtHR has confirmed on many occasions that article 6 does not prevent a party from waiving the 'entitlement of the guarantees of a fair trial' of their own free will, either expressly or tacitly.[122]

7.5.2 Conditions to Effectively Waive Article 6(1) Rights

In determining whether a right under article 6(1) of the ECHR has been effectively waived, the ECtHR has reviewed whether four criteria have been satisfied.[123] First, the waiver must be unequivocal, but this can be

---

[121] In England this challenge could only arise where the refusal to mediate was deemed unreasonable by the courts. If the refusing party could justify their refusal by reference to the *Halsey* criteria, adverse costs consequences would not arise.

[122] See *Sejdovic* v. *Italy* (2006) 42 EHRR 17; Shipman (n 30) 476; R Stone, *Textbook on Civil Liberties and Human Rights* (10th ed, Oxford, Oxford University Press 2013) 184. Arbitration clauses provide an example of an effective waiver of the right of access to court that does not conflict with the ECHR. This was acknowledged in *Deweer* v. *Belgium* [1980] 2 EHRR 429.

[123] For a detailed discussion of each criterion, see Shipman (n 30) 476–91.

implied. For example, an arbitration agreement can amount to a voluntary waiver of court proceedings and a tacit, unequivocal waiver of certain article 6(1) guarantees.[124] This principle could be extended to mediation, where a party who voluntarily acquiesces in a mediation that results in a settlement could be perceived as tacitly but unequivocally waiving their article 6(1) rights.[125] Second, the waiver must be made in a context where there are sufficient minimum safeguards appropriate to the significance of the right waived.[126] A waiver of the right of access to court must be accompanied by appropriately high safeguards in light of the importance the ECtHR places on the right of access to court.[127] While it is unclear what safeguards are sufficient, appropriate representation would appear to constitute a sufficient safeguard in appropriate circumstances,[128] such that a person who had the benefit of legal counsel before and during the mediation process could be deemed to have waived their right of access to court when they agreed to a mediated settlement agreement.[129] The third condition is that the right waived must not run counter to any important public interests.[130] Provided that parties to a commercial mediation are legally represented and are made aware that the settlement agreement when reduced to writing is final, it is unlikely that a waiver in such circumstances could be considered counter to important public interests.

The final condition is that the waiver must not be tainted by constraint. In *Deweer* v. *Belgium*,[131] a butcher faced the stark choice between a fine or the closure of his business until a hearing could take place to determine whether he was guilty of over-pricing meat. In light of the economic

---

[124] In *Suovaniemi* v. *Finland* App no 31737/96 (ECtHR, 23 February 1999) a 'voluntary waiver of court proceedings in favour of arbitration' could amount to a tacit, unequivocal waiver of certain article 6(1) procedural guarantees.

[125] See Shipman (n 30) 477–79; C Jarrosson, 'Legal Issues Raised by ADR' in A Ingen-Housz (ed), *ADR in Business: Practice and Issues Across Countries and Cultures*, vol 2 (Alphen aan den Rijn, Kluwer Law International 2011) 114–15.

[126] *Poitrimol* v. *France* (1994) 18 EHRR 130.

[127] *Golder* v. *United Kingdom* (1975) 1 EHRR 524; *Tsirlis* v. *Greece* (1996) 21 EHRR CD 30; *Giorgiadis* v. *Greece* [1997] ECHR 28.

[128] See *Suovaniemi* (n 124); *Zu Leiningen* v. *Germany* App no 59624/00 (ECtHR, 17 November 2005).

[129] See Shipman (n 30) 479–81.

[130] *Hakansson* v. *Sweden* (1991) 13 EHRR 1. See Leach (n 119) 172–73. The substantive legal matter at stake must be of such public importance that a waiver cannot be accepted, such as racial discrimination or fundamental human rights claims: see Shipman (n 30) 481–82.

[131] *Deweer* (n 122).

pressures of closure and uncertainty about the timing and length of the trial, he opted to pay the fine, despite having an arguable defence that could have vindicated him. The threat of closure of his business within forty-eight hours, the loss of income, continuing salary costs and the loss of customers over a period of months, constituted constraint according to the ECtHR. The fact that the settlement fine was modest, compared to a potential fine of up to 3,000 times more if found guilty in court, contributed to the pressure of the closure.[132]

It has been suggested that the principles established in this case could be applied in a context where a party waives their right of access to court by engaging in mediation that results in a mediated settlement agreement. The Court in *Deweer* concluded that where the possibility of a trial caused fear – for example, where refusing a settlement resulted in a trial and the possibility of a more severe sanction – this pressure on its own would not be inconsistent with the right of access to court.[133] However, in determining whether to refuse to mediate a dispute, when proposed by either a judge or another party, a disputant encounters the additional pressures of authoritative encouragement from their legal advisors and the courts, and potential adverse costs. While the former in isolation would not constitute constraint, the threat of a costs sanction will no doubt put pressure on parties to mediate rather than litigate, and it has been suggested that it is arguable in the appropriate circumstances that this constitutes constraint, with the effect that a disputant's waiver of their article 6(1) rights could be considered tainted.[134]

Since the *Deweer* case, the ECtHR has introduced the concept of the margin of appreciation when dealing with article 6(1) cases. In further developing the doctrine of waiver, the ECtHR could recognise that the threat of adverse costs sanctions amounts to pressure with the effect that any waiver of the right of access to court is tainted by constraint. This would need to be balanced against contentions by state parties that the constraint may be justifiable in appropriate cases – for example, where the measure restricting access pursues a legitimate aim, does not impair the essence of the right, and finds a proportionate balance between the public interest and the fundamental right of the individual in the particular circumstances of the case.[135] Legitimate aims that the ECtHR has accepted include measures to enable the general or efficient functioning

---

[132] ibid [51(b)].
[133] ibid.
[134] See also Shipman (n 30) 482–90.
[135] *Ashingdane* v. *United Kingdom* (1985) 7 EHRR 528.

of the civil justice system, such as ensuring the efficient use of court resources, or in a context where the concern is the protection of the interests of others.[136] Financial constraints that prevent disputing parties from taking or defending claims in court have been a particular concern for the ECtHR. While not a direct financial constraint, the threat of adverse costs may, as discussed, be used to encourage recalcitrant parties to engage in mediation. In practice, however, the ECtHR does not usually find that a restrictive measure does not pursue a legitimate aim, and it will depend on the issue of proportionality – that is, whether the restricting measure, being the threat of adverse costs compounded by robust authoritative encouragement to mediate, has a disproportionate impact on the individual.[137]

Provided that compulsion is restricted to the initial stage, with continued participation in mediation and agreement on settlement remaining voluntary and with legal counsel advising commercial parties on the legal implications of settlement, it is difficult to see how article 6(1) of the ECHR would be breached.

7.6   Conduct, Costs and Confidentiality

Formal attempts to encourage parties to settle, such as the relevant provisions of the Civil Procedure Rules in England, raise the issue of the extent to which the courts should examine the conduct of parties at a mediation. The issue arises of whether only superficial behaviour should be considered, or whether the courts should set aside mediation confidentiality to decide whether a party behaved reasonably. The concern that can emerge in the mediation context is that some parties may participate in the process solely because they fear a costs sanction. The extent to which such a recalcitrant party may be held accountable in contract for the wasted costs depends on the privileged and confidential status of the mediation. Confidentiality clearly creates a conundrum for a litigant who believes that an opposing party is only willing to mediate to avoid a costs sanction at the end of the case. The opposing party's obstructive behaviour is concealed by the cloak of privilege, and even if the agreement to mediate includes an express term that the parties agree to negotiate in good faith, the question remains: who is to decide whether

---

[136] See S Shipman, 'Compulsory Mediation: The Elephant in the Room' (2011) 30(2) *Civil Justice Quarterly* 163, 181–82.

[137] See also Shipman (n 30) 490–91.

or not the term has been breached, and how is such a determination to be made?[138] Courts in different jurisdictions have taken varying approaches.

In Australia, for example, courts in different states have taken markedly different approaches. Even where a confidentiality clause in an agreement to mediate requires settlement proposals made during the process to be privileged and prohibited from being tendered as evidence in any proceeding relevant to the dispute, courts in Australia have admitted such evidence when determining the issue of costs. The applicants in *Silver Fox Co Pty Ltd (as trustee for the Baker Family Trust)* v. *Lenard's Pty Ltd (No 3)*[139] attempted to rely on an affidavit from their solicitor that referred to the final proposals put forward by both parties at the stage when the mediation broke down. Justice Mansfield confirmed that the public interest often requires adherence to the principle that evidence of a communication made when attempting to negotiate a settlement of a dispute will not be used.[140] This is in order for negotiations to be conducted 'genuinely and realistically' and without the 'risk of such negotiations influencing the outcome on those primary issues'.[141] However, Mansfield J concluded that no such public interest exists to prevent a communication being admitted when only costs issues are being determined. He noted that the affidavit would not represent improperly or illegally obtained evidence to justify exclusion,[142] so the affidavit referring to the mediation information was admitted into evidence.[143] Similarly, the disclosure of the terms of the mediation agreement would not be unfairly prejudicial to the respondents.[144] However, Mansfield J confirmed that circumstances could

---

[138] See also T Jones, 'Using Costs to Encourage Mediation: Cautionary Tales on the Limits of Good Intentions', IBA Legal Practice Division Mediation Committee Newsletter (September 2006) 35. For a detailed discussion on confidentiality in mediation, including an analysis of the challenge a court faces in finding the balance between the two competing public policies of encouraging settlement and accessing evidence in appropriate cases, see Chapter 9.

[139] [2004] FCA 1570. See also O Shub, 'Evidence Act Trumps Confidentiality Clause of Mediation Agreement', IBA Legal Practice Division Mediation Committee Newsletter (April 2005) 8.

[140] Section 131(1) of the Evidence Act 1995 (Cth) ingrained the longstanding principle, confirmed in *Field* v. *Commissioner for Railways for New South Wales* [1957] 99 CLR 285, 291–92, that evidence of a communication made in connection with an attempt to negotiate a settlement of a dispute will not be admitted.

[141] *Silver Fox Co* (n 139) [36].

[142] Evidence Act 1995 (Cth) s 138.

[143] Section 131(2)(h) of the Evidence Act 1995 (Cth) applied to the mediation agreement, removing the prohibition in s 131(1) so far as to allow offers made during mediation to be admitted where they are relevant to determining liability for costs.

[144] Evidence Act 1995 (Cth) s 135.

arise where the exposure of mediation communications could be unfairly prejudicial to a party.[145]

In *Western Areas Exploration Pty Ltd* v. *Streeter (No) 2*,[146] the court-ordered mediation was unsuccessful, leading to a number of affidavits being produced by the parties that made claims about what transpired at the mediation to inform the court's determination of the issue of costs. The Western Australia Appeal Court decided that the affidavits could not be presented to the Court as this would breach mediation confidentiality. The underlying legislation considered by the Court provided that a mediator can only reveal what happened in a mediation to a court in relation to the costs issue in the form of a formal report about a party's failure to cooperate.

In another Australian case, *Tracy* v. *Bifield*,[147] the plaintiff alleged that the defendant offered a settlement figure at a pre-trial mediation conference that could have had implications for the costs order. In costs proceedings, the Court did not allow the disclosure that an offer had been made during the mediation, despite a statute[148] providing that a mediator could admit a report to be used in deciding the costs issue, so that confidentiality was upheld despite legislative policy to the contrary.[149]

The English courts have shown that they will not breach mediation confidentiality to determine whether a party's conduct was reasonable when deciding the issue of costs. In *Reed*,[150] the Court of Appeal refused

---

[145] See Shub (n 139) 8. This decision followed the seminal decision of *AWA Ltd* v. *Daniels (t/a Deloitte Haskins & Sells)* (1992) 7 ACSR 463, where the New South Wales Supreme Court ordered the disclosure of a deed of indemnity that had been produced at a mediation between the parties on the basis that it was a disclosable document, and that it should not be possible to prevent a document from being disclosed merely because it had been furnished within the context of a privileged mediation setting. However, in *Lukies* v. *Ripley (No 2)* (1994) 35 NSWLR 283, the Court held that privilege will apply where there are genuine attempts at settlement such as efforts to narrow issues, even where there is no expectation of overall settlement.

[146] [2009] WASCA 15.

[147] Supreme Court of Western Australia, Templeman J, 19 May 1998.

[148] Western Australian Rules of the Supreme Court, O 29 r 3(2).

[149] See L Boulle, *Mediation: Principles, Process, Practice* (3rd ed, Chatswood, NSW, LexisNexis 2011) 698. In *Union Carbide Canada Inc* v. *Bombardier Inc* [2014] 1 SCR 800, the Canadian Supreme Court decided that parties could contract a level of confidentiality enforceable by the courts through which they can exclude the exceptions to without prejudice privilege, but only on very clearly drafted terms. It was academic in this case as the terms of the agreement were not clear enough. See Chapter 9 at Section 9.4.2.1.

[150] *Reed* (n 36). See Chapter 9 at Section 9.4.1.1 for a discussion on a number of English cases where judges have received evidence about what happened at a mediation, with the parties' consent, to determine the issue of costs.

to consider, for the purpose of assessing the question of costs, 'without prejudice' negotiations that the claimant contended would have revealed that the defendant's refusal to mediate was unreasonable.[151] The Court held that there was an established principle that disclosure of without prejudice negotiations could only take place with the consent of the parties, and it refused to draw an adverse inference from the fact that one party had refused to allow disclosure of without prejudice communications. The Court acknowledged that this meant it would not always be possible to decide whether a party had unreasonably refused to mediate. If the parties wanted to admit such evidence, the Court said they could have made a 'without prejudice except as to costs' offer that could be admitted.

The English court was similarly unequivocal in *Halsey*:

> We make it clear at the outset that it was common ground before us (and we accept) that parties are entitled in an ADR to adopt whatever position they wish, and if as a result the dispute is not settled, that is not a matter for the court. As is submitted by the Law Society, if the integrity and confidentiality of the process is to be respected, the court should not know, and therefore should not investigate, why the process did not result in agreement.[152]

The subsequent English case of *Cumbria Waste Management Ltd v. Baines Wilson*[153] confirms this position. The Court declined to order disclosure of mediation documentation against one party's wishes, and saw this as an exception to the general rule that confidentiality is not a bar to disclosure of material to a court.[154]

---

[151] In the earlier case of *Rush & Tompkins Ltd* v. *Greater London Council* [1988] 3 All ER 737, the House of Lords clarified that all genuine oral or written negotiations to settle a dispute are protected in subsequent proceedings, regardless of whether the label 'without prejudice' is attached to them. Hence, in England, if discussions occur before an agreement to mediate is signed, or if no agreement is signed at all, the discussions are protected by the without prejudice rule, subject to the normal exceptions and limitations of the rule. It is unclear if such privilege would extend to information passed through a mediator, but it is likely that it would on public policy grounds: see Allen (n 3) 207–8. See also Chapter 9 at Section 9.4.1.1.

[152] *Halsey* (n 10) [14] (Dyson LJ). This sentiment was subsequently echoed in *Reed* (n 36) and *PGF II* (n 29).

[153] [2008] EWHC 786 (QB).

[154] The position on mediation confidentiality remains uncertain in England, as the cases dealing with the issue, such as *Cumbria Waste Management* (n 153), have been largely first instance decisions, and consequently difficult to rely on. See Chapter 9 at Section 9.4.1.1.

7.6.1 *Rules Defining Good Faith*

Where costs sanctions are employed, courts must wrestle with the conundrum of how far to look inside a mediation to assess a party's conduct.
While there is no commonly accepted definition of what constitutes
'good faith' conduct in a mediation, various rules have been proposed,
and can be characterised as either narrow or broad. Narrow rules involve
basic requirements from parties such as attending the mediation, attending for a fixed period, submitting a position paper in advance, making an
offer to settle and having sufficient authority to settle. Experience in the
USA suggests that the common feature of such rules is that it is easy for
the court to establish non-compliance, as the mediator simply hands
a checklist to the court without comment. Courts in the USA have
applied narrow rules in diverse ways. For example, some have emphasised the requirement that the parties present at the mediation have
settlement authority[155] while others have only required that authorised
individuals are available by phone.[156] Experience from the USA suggests
that, similar to the approach of costs sanctions for a refusal to mediate
under the Civil Procedure Rules, the most effective approach is to design
a narrow rule and provide that parties can decline to abide by it where it is
reasonable. Apart from varying approaches by courts, compliance with
narrow rules can be quite easy but may not be effective. For example,
a requirement to attend does not mean that good faith efforts to mediate
will follow, and parties can take advantage of such a rule by exploiting the
length of time requirement to satisfy attendance but not participate in the
mediation process. However, there is still significant support for narrow
rules, largely because they have helped make mediation a central
mechanism of the US justice system. However, the US experience
suggests that only the narrowest of requirements, such as compulsory
attendance, proves workable in practice.[157]

   Due to the limitations of narrow rules, 'broad' rules have also been used.
These focus on a party's general conduct beyond superficial behaviour,
where the court attempts to determine motivation. Examples include

---

[155] *Nick v. Morgan's Foods of Missouri Inc* 270 F 3d 590 (8th Cir 2001).
[156] *Re United States* 149 F 3d 332 (5th Cir, 1998).
[157] Jones (n 138) 35–38. For example, in Australia under s 331(2)–(3) of the Queensland
    Uniform Civil Procedure Rules 1999, the mediator can report that a party failed to attend
    but not how they performed during the mediation. In the USA under s 7(b)(1) of the
    Uniform Mediation Act, outside the exceptions to privilege and other policy exceptions,
    a mediator is restricted to disclosing to a court or arbitral tribunal whether the mediation
    occurred or was terminated, whether a settlement was reached, and attendance.

insisting that parties prepare adequately, engage meaningfully, evaluate their case rationally, do not delay proceedings unnecessarily and generally act in good faith. However, there are numerous problems with such broad rules, many of them resulting from the difficulty in gleaning evidence of bad faith from a confidential process. It is primarily in an effort to protect mediation confidentiality that broad rules are no longer favoured by US courts. In a policy statement, the American Bar Association said that sanctions should only be used to enforce narrow rules, and that broad rules were too difficult to define.[158]

7.7   Concluding Thoughts

In light of the evidential limits of what can be considered in many jurisdictions, there is an obvious difficulty in trying to assess retrospectively whether a refusal to attend mediation was reasonable. The US experience shows that only the narrowest of rules, such as compulsory attendance, proves workable in practice. However, where a party is reluctant to engage in the process due to fears of unreasonable behaviour by another party, experience from England suggests that few inherently unreasonable parties restrain their unreasonableness to circumstances where mediation confidentiality restricts judicial access to what transpired at the mediation.[159] This approach also means that the courts do

---

[158] ABA Section of Dispute Resolution, Resolution on Good Faith Requirements for Mediators and Mediation Advocated in Court Mandated Mediation Programs, 7 August 2004. See also Jones (n 138) 36–37. See also the discussion on *Rojas* v. *Superior Court* 33 Cal 4th 407 (2004), and similar cases in Chapter 9 at Section 9.4.6.3, that reflects the strict application of mediation confidentiality by some courts. Good faith has created definitional difficulties in many jurisdictions as most statutes that require it avoid defining the term: see Alexander (n 12) 230. Some also contend that a good faith bargaining requirement arguably conflicts with self-determination, a key value of the process: see D Golann and J Folberg, *Mediation: The Roles of Advocate and Neutral* (3rd ed, New York, Wolters Kluwer 2016) 350–54; R Kulms, 'Mediation in the USA: Alternative Dispute Resolution Between Legalism and Self-Determination' in Hopt and Steffek (eds) (n 3). However, maintenance of good faith in a mediation need not be inconsistent with having regard to self-interest. See Chapter 3 at Section 3.3.7.

[159] See Allen (n 3) 300. The *excluder* theory of good faith suggests that good faith is more easily described and applied by reference to the various forms of bad faith that it excludes, as examples of bad faith are tangible and thus easier to grasp compared with good faith. Hence, positive requirements of good faith can be given meaning in practice, by reference to the negative attributes that preclude it. This theory has been applied by the courts in England, Australia and the USA: see R Summers, 'Good Faith in General Contract Law and Sales Provisions of the Uniform Commercial Code' (1968) 54(2)

not have to explore the subjective intentions of the parties during the process. The court also has the power to excuse a reasonable refusal to mediate, such as where a party needs a legal point determined or where unreasonable behaviour by another party can be shown.

The success of mediation does not depend on whether the process is subject to comprehensive regulation, or selective regulation. As a form of targeted incentive setting, costs sanctions can achieve the same procedural effects as mandatory rules,[160] and may be viewed as a compromise between the conflicting goals of voluntariness, regulation and access to justice, where regulatory aims are integrated into the parties' decision-making process. There is a clear link between the deployment of costs sanctions for unreasonable refusal to mediate and the increased use of mediation by commercial parties. Where there is a significant risk of onerous costs being imposed on recalcitrant parties, a substantial increase in the number of disputes being mediated is the likely outcome. This has been the reason for the growth of commercial mediation in many jurisdictions.[161] Adverse costs orders remain the most common sanction for unreasonably failing to use mediation to resolve disputes in England.[162] However, in recent years there have been fewer reported decisions on costs sanctions emanating from the English courts. This may indicate that the policy works in encouraging more parties to accept invitations to mediate.

Virginia Law Review 195, 196 and the table of contract law examples ('Forms of Bad Faith Conduct: Meaning of Good Faith'), with supporting case law given at 203. See also Alexander (n 12) 230–33, where a table of examples of 'Good Faith Participation as Absence of Bad Faith Conduct' in mediation is provided, along with relevant case examples. *Dunnett* (n 10) is an illustrative example, where the meaning of good faith would have been a reasonable and proportionate approach to using dispute resolution options, while a form of bad faith conduct was unreasonable refusal to consider or engage in mediation.

[160] This is reflected in a comparative analysis of mediation laws and empirical data on mediation across a number of jurisdictions. For example, mediation has established itself as firmly in countries with little regulation such as England compared with countries with advanced regulation such as Japan: see Hopt and Steffek (n 3) 110.

[161] See generally R Feehily, 'Costs Sanctions: The Critical Instrument in the Development of Commercial Mediation in South Africa' (2009) 126(2) *South African Law Journal* 291; R Feehily, 'Commercial Mediation and the Costs Conundrum' (2019) 23(1) *Vindobona Journal of International Commercial Law and Arbitration* 1.

[162] Blake, Browne and Sime (n 3) 117. See *Wales* v. *CBRE and Aviva* [2020] EWHC 1050 (Comm); *DBE* v. *Biogas* [2020] EWHC 1285 (TCC).

8

Mediated Settlement Agreements

8.1 Introduction

A mediated settlement agreement must be enforceable for its obligations to be binding. Several elements can result in mediated settlements being set aside: the absence of contractual certainty to bind the disputing parties, rescission on account of an unjust factor, undue influence, duress and coercion, unconscionability, incompetence or incapacity, lack of authority, fraud and mistake. The jurisprudence resulting from attempts to evade mediated settlement agreements provides guidance on the practical steps that can be taken to avoid problems with their enforcement. Where compliance may be an issue, the settlement can be converted into an arbitral award or a court judgment, or enforced under the Singapore Convention which elevates international mediated settlement agreements to a new status that can be recognised and enforced within the framework of private international law.

8.2 Review of Mediated Settlement Agreements and Grounds for Evading Them

The contractual requirement that mediated settlements are only binding if reduced to writing and signed by the parties is designed to avoid confusion over the content of the agreement. While settlement agreements are subject to normal contractual principles, the agreement must be drafted to ensure that it accurately reflects the mediated settlement. A complex fact-finding exercise is undertaken by a court or tribunal if a matter comes before it and it is unclear what was agreed in the mediation. While courts will usually only 'look behind' mediated settlement agreements between willing parties in exceptional circumstances, there have been circumstances, notably in Australia, where this has occurred. An eight-day hearing was required in one case to resolve the question whether a final settlement was reached in a mediation.[1]

There have also been situations where courts were asked to construe mediated settlement terms to assess the intention of the parties or whether there had been compliance with an agreement, or to determine whether a valid mediation agreement existed between the parties, and if so, what were its terms, whether a mediated settlement was represented in a particular document, whether settlement terms had sufficient certainty, and whether performance was consistent with the terms of a mediated settlement agreement. Courts can be required to interpret clauses in complex mediated settlements – for example, on the effect of statutory obligations on a mediated settlement.[2]

Comprising fifty state jurisdictions and the federal jurisdiction, the USA has no single body of law governing all mediations or the enforcement of all mediated settlement agreements. Some states have enacted legislation that requires a signed written agreement, that the agreement contain a specific confirmation of understanding of the significance of the agreement, a provision for a 'cooling off' period during which consent to an agreement can be withdrawn, a provision for greater confidentiality, and a provision for less confidentiality protection for the mediation process. While summary procedures are emerging in some US states for the enforcement of mediated settlement agreements, courts generally view them as contracts and apply traditional contract law principles to disputes arising from efforts to enforce them. Some courts apply contract law with little regard to the special nature of negotiations in the mediation process. Although they repeatedly state that they favour the enforcement of agreements that settle disputes, where contract law claims and defences are raised regarding a settlement agreement, the courts will usually consider evidence to determine whether a binding contract was entered into, and will normally review any defences raised as if it were any other contractual dispute.[3]

---

[1] *Barry* v. *City West Water Ltd* [2002] FCA 1214 [8]. See L Boulle, *Mediation: Principles, Process, Practice* (3rd ed, Chatswood, NSW, LexisNexis Butterworths 2011) 649–52.

[2] For an overview of the associated case law, see Boulle (n 1) 652–53.

[3] See E Sussman, 'A Brief Survey of US Case Law on Enforcing Mediation Settlement Agreements over Objections to the Existence or Validity of Such Agreements and Implications for Mediation Confidentiality and Mediator Testimony', IBA Legal Practice Division Mediation Committee Newsletter (April 2006) 32.

8.2.1   Without Prejudice Bar

While the mediation proceeds on a 'without prejudice' basis, once an agreement is reached, it will no longer be protected. The courts in Australia have held that a settlement agreement reached at mediation may be regarded as a document that comes into existence after, not in the course of or pursuant to, a mediation; if it were otherwise, the parties could reach an agreement at mediation and subsequently refuse to comply with it on the basis that it is inadmissible.[4]

In England, communications during the mediation process have been admitted as evidence to establish whether there was a settlement, notwithstanding the presence of a clause in the agreement to mediate requiring that any settlement reached be reduced to writing and signed by the parties.[5] In *Dow* v. *Bombardier*,[6] the Supreme Court of Canada also clarified that a confidentiality clause in an agreement to mediate will not restrict a party from producing evidence of communications made during a mediation in order to prove the terms of the settlement, unless that is clearly detailed in the agreement. Hence, a communication that has led to a settlement will cease to be privileged, if disclosing it is necessary to prove the existence or scope of the settlement. While parties in Canada may contract out of common law rules, including the exception to settlement privilege, in this case there was no evidence that the

---

[4] See *State Bank of New South Wales* v. *Freeman* (New South Wales Supreme Court, Badgery-Parker J, 31 January 1996); *Commonwealth Bank of Australia* v. *McConnell* (New South Wales Supreme Court, Rolfe J, 24 July 1997). See also L Boulle and M Nesic, *Mediation: Principles, Process, Practice* (London, Butterworths Law 2001) 507. Article 10 of the Mediation Model Law (discussed in Section 8.5 of this chapter) provides: 'Unless otherwise agreed by the parties, all information relating to the mediation proceedings shall be kept confidential, except where disclosure is required under the law or for the purposes of implementation or enforcement of a settlement agreement.' Some US states prohibit the introduction of mediated settlement agreements as evidence unless they meet specified conditions. For example, under California Evidence Code, s 1123(b), a mediated settlement agreement will be admissible if the agreement is signed by the parties and satisfies any of the following: '(a) The agreement provides that it is admissible or subject to disclosure, or words to that effect. (b) The agreement provides that it is enforceable or binding or words to that effect. (c) All parties to the agreement expressly agree in writing, or orally . . . to its disclosure. (d) The agreement is used to show fraud, duress, or illegality that is relevant to an issue in dispute.' Section 4(a) and 6(a) of the US Uniform Mediation Act prevents participants testifying about mediated settlement agreements, but permits the admission into evidence of signed written settlement agreements or settlements that are electronically recorded.

[5] *Brown* v. *Rice* [2007] EWHC 625 (Ch). See also Chapter 9 at Section 9.4.1.1 for a discussion of this case.

[6] [2014] SCC 35 Canada. See also Chapter 9 at Section 9.4.2.1 for a discussion of this case.

parties thought they were deviating from the settlement privilege that usually applies to mediation when they signed the agreement.[7]

8.2.2   Binding Contract

Agreements to mediate commercial disputes usually contain a provision that any agreement reached in the mediation will only be binding when reduced to writing and signed by the parties.[8] This approach avoids uncertainty and reflects best practice. A mediated settlement agreement must be enforceable for its obligations to be binding, and it will be reviewed to ensure that it complies with the criteria for a valid contract including the intention to create legal relations, certainty of terms and any specific formalities required.[9] In jurisdictions such as England,[10] the parties' intentions are assessed objectively from the circumstances. Consequently where parties act as if the original dispute still exists, evidence can be provided that no binding agreement was intended, while conversely, commencement of performance provides evidence to the contrary.[11] With regard to certainty of the terms, if a term is reasonable or necessary to give the contract business efficacy or is so obvious that it is understood or can be clearly expressed and does not contradict an express term, it may be implied into the contract.[12] In *Frost* v. *Wake*

---

[7] See also *Unilever plc* v. *The Proctor & Gamble Company* [1999] EWCA Civ 3027 [23], where Walker LJ remarked that in England there seems to be no reason in principle why parties to 'without prejudice' negotiations should not expressly or impliedly agree to vary the public policy rule, either by extending or limiting its reach.

[8] See Chapter 3 at Section 3.6.

[9] The required formalities and necessary steps to ensure the enforceability of mediated settlement agreements vary considerably across jurisdictions: see K Hopt and F Steffek, 'Mediation: Comparison of Laws, Regulatory Models, Fundamental Issues' in K Hopt and F Steffek (eds), *Mediation: Principles and Regulation in Comparative Perspective* (Oxford, Oxford University Press 2013) 43–47. The Singapore Convention, discussed in Section 8.6 of this chapter, was developed to address this issue.

[10] For simplicity the term 'England' is used throughout this book to describe the jurisdiction of England and Wales.

[11] For example, in the US case *Cook* v. *Hughston Clinic PC* No 3:14-CV-296-WKW [WO], 2015 WL 6082397 (MD Ala Oct 15, 2015), the Court held that the words and actions of both parties were inconsistent with the continued existence of the settlement agreement, and it applied the doctrine of rescission to find an otherwise valid and binding agreement to be no longer enforceable: see J R Coben, 'Evaluating the Singapore Convention through a US-Centric Litigation Lens: Lessons Learned from Nearly Two Decades of Mediation Disputes in American Federal and State Courts' in Singapore Mediation Convention Reference Book (2019) 20(4) *Cardozo Journal of Conflict Resolution* 1083.

[12] See Boulle and Nesic (n 4) 509–10.

Smith & Tofields Solicitors,[13] the English Court of Appeal confirmed that a working document that required further work (such as the definition of critical terms, the description of properties relevant to settlement and the treatment of tax consequences) lacked sufficient certainty to constitute a legally enforceable agreement.[14]

A lack of certainty was also critical in the Canadian case *Gutter Filter Company LLC* v. *Gutter Filter Canada Inc.*[15] During the course of litigation, the parties attended a mediation session at the conclusion of which they came to a mutual understanding that was confirmed in writing and signed 'Minutes of Settlement'. The Federal Court of Canada ruled that, to be enforceable, the terms of a settlement agreement must be certain. It found that the parties had intended to further negotiate and sign 'comprehensive Minutes of Settlement', as reflected in the agreement signed by the parties, to settle all of their disputes. The Court held that a further document was therefore needed to formalise the agreement reached at mediation.

The absence of a binding contract has been the most successful basis in defeating efforts to enforce mediated settlement agreements in the USA and in an international dispute context, where the parties are generally sophisticated, legally represented and, consequently, less likely to establish other possible issues that could be raised such as duress, lack of competence and lack of authority. However, US courts have recognised the difficulty in completing a final settlement agreement in complex cases at the mediation meeting, and have enforced settlement agreements where all the material terms had been the subject of mutual consent, and the fact that a subsequent complete document was contemplated has not reversed this. The wording of the agreement can be critical. For example, a settlement that was 'subject to' a formal agreement, rather than to 'be followed' by a formal agreement implementing the agreed

---

[13] [2013] EWCA Civ 772.

[14] ibid. In the case, a solicitor was not deemed to be negligent as it was not in his power at the time to deal with finality of these matters, including the issue of tax liability. For a commentary on this case, see J S del Ceno, 'Case Comment: Mediated Settlements and Enforceable Settlements: *Frost v Wake Smith*' (2013) 79(4) *Arbitration* 467. See also *Tapoohi* v. *Lewenberg (No 2)* [2003] VSC 410, an Australia decision given in interlocutory proceedings, where the mediator dictated the terms of settlement with little involvement from the parties' lawyers and failed to make the settlement subject to independent tax advice, with serious financial consequences for one of the parties. While the case ultimately settled, the Court remarked that a mediator could, in such circumstances, be held to be in breach of contractual and tortious duties by a trial court.

[15] [2011] FC 234.

terms, was held to not be enforceable. While insufficiently definite material terms in an agreement will not be a basis for finding an enforceable agreement, the fact that a few ancillary issues remain to be resolved will not defeat enforcement of a mediated settlement agreement. Even if there was no written agreement, the courts, in applying general contract principles, have not allowed second thoughts to affect the enforceability of a mediated settlement agreement. Provisions in mediated settlement agreements stating that a release will be provided have caused problems where the exact nature of the release is unknown. For example, where the release was to be mutually agreeable, the courts have held that there was no enforceable agreement as there was no meeting of the minds on a material term. Rather than nullify the entire agreement, the courts have made agreements enforceable by deleting terms, such as expanded release language, that were included in the final agreement but had not been expressly included in an original draft of the written settlement.[16]

8.2.3   Oral Agreements

In accordance with the standard contract law principle that recognises the validity of oral contracts, excepting the Statute of Frauds requirements, courts in the USA have enforced a mediated settlement agreement in the absence of an executed written agreement where they were persuaded that there was a meeting of the minds regarding all material terms and that it was the intention of the parties to be bound. However, where it was the intention of the parties not to be bound until there was an executed written document, an oral settlement agreement will not be enforced. Similarly, the enforcement of oral mediated settlement agreements will be affected where the governing law or applicable court rules require that settlements be in writing, and both federal and state courts have enforced such requirements.[17] The exclusion of evidence of oral agreements is also consistent with the Uniform Mediation Act. This is in keeping with the international trend of exempting written, as opposed to oral, settlements from the privilege that protects mediation communications. The Uniform Mediation Act exempts written settlement agreements from the privilege that protects mediation communications,

---

[16] For a discussion of the relevant US case law in respect of these issues, see Sussman (n 3) 32–33.

[17] For a discussion of the relevant case law, see Sussman (n 3) 33–34. See also D Golann and J Folberg, *Mediation: The Roles of Advocate and Neutral* (3rd ed, New York, Wolters Kluwer 2016) 355–56.

but does not make oral settlement agreements exempt, so that the latter are inadmissible in court.[18]

8.2.4 Rescission on Account of an 'Unjust Factor'

In an attempt to have the mediated settlement agreement set aside, a party may claim factors such as fraud, undue influence, unconscionability, duress, lack of capacity or authority to contract, or illegality. The remedy is equitable and consequently is at the court's discretion.[19]

8.2.5 Undue Influence

In the Australian case *Studer* v. *Konig*[20] all the parties agreed to participate in a mediation to be conducted by an experienced commercial mediator following claims and cross-claims between the applicant and respondent about land dealings. The mediation resulted in a signed settlement agreement that was handed up in court and included terms covering the settlement figure, mortgage security pending payment of it, interim occupation of the land, interest and other ancillary matters. Following further proceedings by Konig, Studer initially took steps to fulfil the terms of the settlement but subsequently sought an order to rescind the agreement on the grounds of undue influence, negligence and misleading conduct by his solicitor during the mediation. While the Court dismissed the application on procedural grounds, McLelland CJ suggested that Studer would have encountered two major impediments in making his claim: the lack of evidence that Konig was aware of the allegations against Studer's solicitor; and the fact that Studer executed the mortgage and consequently endorsed the terms of settlement.

---

[18] See US Uniform Mediation Act, s 6. See Chapter 2 at Section 2.4.8 for an overview of the Act. However, in the English case of *Brown* (n 5), the judge held that communications during the mediation process could be admitted as evidence to establish whether there was a settlement, reasoning that parties may vary, waive or even be estopped from asserting the writing requirement in the agreement to mediate. See Chapter 9 at Section 9.4.1.1.

[19] See Boulle and Nesic (n 4) 510–11. A court could also decline to enforce a settlement where there is an alternative equitable reason to not enforce it, or where it can be argued that the terms have been frustrated. It could also be argued by a party that they are not bound by it as the other side repudiated it, as with any contract: see S Blake, J Browne and S Sime, *The Jackson ADR Handbook* (2nd ed, Oxford, Oxford University Press 2016) 255.

[20] Supreme Court of New South Wales Equity Division, McLelland CJ, 4 June 1993. See also *Rojanasaroj* v. *Rachan* [2010] WASC 63 which resulted in a similar outcome. See also Boulle (n 1) 657–58 for a discussion of these cases.

It is important that parties give informed consent to mediated settlements. There are a number of interventions that mediators can make, including informing parties about the importance of having their own professional advisors to help and advise them throughout the process, and to draft and review the settlement agreement.[21] A cooling off clause could also be considered in appropriate circumstances.

8.2.6   Duress and Coercion

In the Australian case *Abriel* v. *Westpac Banking Corp*[22] the Court declined an application to strike out a claim where a party to a mediated settlement agreement claimed duress on the basis that the other side took unfair advantage when its lawyers withdrew from the mediation, believing that, while the claim was novel, it could not be concluded that it would fail. In such circumstances, it seems that consideration must be given to whether the party protested at the time, had an alternative course of action open, and received independent advice. Commercial pressure to settle is not likely to amount to duress.[23]

In the USA, the courts have adopted the basic contract principle that an agreement obtained through duress or coercion is unenforceable. However, it is only in rare cases that the courts accept the claims as persuasive in establishing duress or coercion to defeat enforcement of a settlement agreement. For example, courts have enforced a mediated settlement agreement where one of the parties testified that he was not permitted to leave the room during a lengthy mediation, or exercise free will, and where a party claimed that he was threatened with an insolvency prosecution. An example of the restrictive approach the court takes was reflected in *Olam* v. *Congress Mortgage Co*,[24] where a sixty-five-year-old woman claimed duress at a mediation, which started at 10 a.m. and concluded at 1 a.m. the next morning. At the time, she claimed that she suffered from high blood pressure, intestinal pain and headaches, and was told by both the mediator and her lawyer that if she went to trial, she would lose her house. Olam sought to have the mediated settlement agreement set aside, claiming that due to her physical, intellectual and emotional state during the mediation, she was incapable of giving

---

[21] See Chapter 5 at Section 5.8.5.
[22] [1999] FCA 50.
[23] See *Atlas Express Ltd* v. *Kafco* [1989] QB 833. See also Boulle and Nesic (n 4) 511.
[24] 68 F Supp 2d 1110 (ND Cal 1999) (discussed in Chapter 9 at Section 9.4.6.3). See also Sussman (n 3) 34.

consent. Both parties requested that the mediator be compelled to testify as the mediator's evidence was necessary to determine the credibility of Olam's testimony. Olam's testimony that she did not participate in negotiations or discussions and that she did not understand the agreement was contradicted by the mediator's testimony and the settlement agreement was enforced. Similarly, in *Vela* v. *Hope Lumber & Supply Co*,[25] the plaintiff alleged that she was under economic duress as the mediator warned her about liability for insurance fraud. The Court of Appeal concurred with the lower court that there was no basis for the allegations and that she had freely signed the settlement agreement with an understanding of its implications.

As outlined by the court in *Olam*, factors in the USA that have been illustrative of excessive pressure include settlement discussions at an unusual or inappropriate time; completion of the agreement in an unusual place; incessant demands that the agreement be completed promptly; emphatic emphasis on the adverse consequences of delay; use of many influences by a dominant party against a servient party; absence of third-party advisors to a servient party; and statements that there is no time to consult professional advisors.[26]

Where a party was legally represented at the mediation and had an opportunity to reflect on the mediated settlement agreement, an attack based on duress and coercion in the USA is unlikely to succeed. An increasing number of cases have arisen from allegations that the mediator was the cause of duress and coercion, including allegations of bullying and financial pressure to settle, but the courts have largely rejected such attempts to defeat settlement agreements. However, if sufficient facts are presented to raise a question of fact on duress or coercion, such as allegations that an extreme time pressure was imposed by the mediator, the courts will require an evidentiary hearing.[27] However, in the vast majority of cases where duress and coercion are used to rescind a settlement, the courts have been unsympathetic, observing that what the client labels 'coercion' is 'merely the garden variety exercise in bargaining power'.[28]

---

[25] 966 P 2d 1196 (Okla Civ App 1998).
[26] *Olam* (n 24).
[27] For a discussion of relevant US case law, see Sussman (n 3) 34.
[28] See R Korobkin, 'The Role of Law in Settlement' in M Moffitt and R Bordone (eds), *The Handbook of Dispute Resolution* (San Francisco, Jossey-Bass, 2005) 264.

8.2.7   Unconscionability

In the Australian case *Pittornio v. Meynert (as Executrix of the Wills of Guiseppe Pittornio (dec) and Guiseppina Pittornio (dec))*,[29] the applicant argued that the mediator attempted to influence her, that the mediation was excessively lengthy, that she had ruptured a cyst and that she was ignored when she asked to have the mediation adjourned. The Court found that there was no acceptable evidence that the defendants had knowledge of the difficulties faced by the plaintiff and rejected the allegations of unconscionability.

8.2.8   Incompetence or Incapacity

In light of the presumption of mental competence, the burden of proof in establishing that an adult is incompetent rests on the person claiming it, and claims of incompetence, even based on ostensibly exceptional facts, have not proved successful in court in defeating the enforcement of mediated settlement agreements in the USA. For example, the courts have rejected claims that a party was incompetent due to the side-effects of medication such as severe depression, physical pain and memory loss.[30] Such issues turn on the evidence that is presented to support the allegations that individual parties are incapable or incompetent. It is primarily for a party's lawyer to advise a party against proceeding if there is evidence that their client may not be competent or capable of concluding a settlement agreement. In the absence of legal advisors, a vigilant competent mediator should propose a break from the process to the parties and should ensure that the process resumes only when both parties are competent and capable of proceeding.

8.2.9   Lack of Authority

In the USA, a party's attorney is presumed to have authority to consent when present at a mediation that is intended to settle a case, with affirmative proof to the contrary required to overturn that presumption. Consequently, claims by a party that it had not signed the settlement

---

[29] [2002] WASC 76. See Boulle (n 1) 658 for a discussion of this case.
[30] See Sussman (n 3) 34. In *Domangue v. Domangue* No 12-04-00029-CV (Tex App Aug 3, 2005), a Texas court found that a party was competent to enter into a mediated settlement agreement, notwithstanding illness from Hepatitis C and the effects of medication that it was claimed caused memory loss and depression.

agreement and that the signature by its attorney was unauthorised have not been viewed favourably. A settlement agreement signed by an attorney can also be upheld on the basis that apparent authority existed where the attorney advising the party on the other side had no reason to doubt that authority.[31] In England, solicitors attending settlement discussions on behalf of parties were found to at least have ostensible authority to bind their clients to a settlement.[32] The approach of the English and US courts in holding that the legal representative has ostensible authority to bind their client is consistent with the contract law principle generally that a legal advisor has the power to bind their client, and this principle would apply in the mediation context.

8.2.10 Fraud

While the courts in England have not had extensive exposure to cases where mediated settlement agreements have been challenged, *Crystal Decisions (UK) Ltd* v. *Vedatech Corp*[33] is a case where it did arise. The claimants were seeking a declaration from the court that the mediated settlement agreement was valid and enforceable, as the defendant was relying on the effectiveness of notices of rescission previously served as the basis for refusing to recognise the enforceability of the agreement, but declined to commence proceedings of their own based on the allegations contained in those notices.[34] The Court held that there was nothing in the

---

[31] In *Georgos* v. *Jackson* 790 NE 2d 448 (Ind 2003), where the governing state statute required a party's signature, the Court upheld a settlement agreement despite the absence of the required signature, where the party's absence from the mediation was unexcused: see Sussman (n 3) 35.

[32] *Waugh* v. *HB Clifford & Sons Ltd* [1982] Ch 374; *Von Schulz* v. *Morriello* [1998] QCA 236. See also Boulle and Nesic (n 4) 510.

[33] [2007] EWHC 1062 (Ch).

[34] In light of this the Court remarked: 'The purpose of these proceedings has been to establish the enforceability of the Settlement Agreement and in so doing to determine the challenges by the Defendants to its enforceability both on grounds of misrepresentation and also on the basis of alleged repudiation by the Claimants ... an application for judgement in default does limit the Court to granting only the relief to which the Claimants are clearly entitled on the basis of their own unchallenged statement of case. It was essentially for this reason that I indicated ... that I was not prepared to grant declarations pronouncing on issues such as the alleged misrepresentations or duress during the course of the mediation which required a consideration of evidence from those present at the time. On the other hand where an issue raised in the Particulars of Claim turns simply on the construction of a document referred to in the pleadings, then the court can in my judgement look at the material and decide the point': *Crystal Decisions* ibid [49] (Patten J).

agreement itself on which to base a challenge to its enforceability, and that rescission based on innocent or negligent misrepresentation was not sufficient as a basis for setting aside the mediated settlement agreement. The Court held that the claimants were entitled to a permanent injunction to enforce the mediated settlement agreement.

In the Australian case *Gillford Pty Ltd* v. *Burdon Pty Ltd*,[35] the Court declined to grant relief, finding that a claim was not sufficiently established where a claimant sought to have a mediated settlement agreement set aside on the basis that fraudulent misrepresentations were made by a party in the mediation about its assets and liabilities.

Despite the negotiating framework and relationship context of the mediation process, the courts in the USA have applied contract rules quite strictly, requiring a knowing and material misrepresentation with the intention of causing reliance on which a party justifiably relied.[36] In the absence of a duty to disclose, a mere failure to disclose a fact that could be material to the other party is not a basis for defeating a settlement agreement. For example, where a plaintiff believed the defendant's insurance limit was US$100,000 rather than US$1.1 million, the Court held that the defendant was in an adversarial position rather than a position of special trust or confidence that would create a duty to disclose to the plaintiff.[37] In those US states that have strict rules on the confidentiality of mediation communications, the courts have refused to accept any evidence of fraud claims based on what transpired at the mediation session, holding that such evidence is inadmissible in light of the confidential nature of the process. The Delaware Chancery Court has suggested a possible solution in view of the confidentiality conundrum, remarking that if parties in mediation know that their decision to settle is based on a factual representation, they must reflect that representation in a way that is not confidential, such as a representation in the settlement agreement.[38]

The defendant alleged that inaccurate financial information was furnished by the claimant as the basis for the agreed settlement, which amounted to fraudulent misrepresentation, and that consent was given to the settlement agreement on this basis.

[35] Federal Court of Australia, NSW Registry, General Division, No AG79 of 1994 FED No 169/95, Lockhart J, 20 April 1995. See also Boulle and Nesic (n 4) 511.

[36] *JMJ Inc* v. *Whitmore's BBQ Restaurant* 2005 Ohio 3841 (Ohio Ct App 2005).

[37] The Court did, however, require an evidentiary hearing to assess whether the defendant had made an affirmative misrepresentation that could be a basis for defeating the settlement agreement: see *Brinkerhoff* v. *Campbell* 994 P 2d 911 (2000). See also Sussman (n 3) 35.

[38] *Princeton Insurance Co* v. *Vergano* 883 A 2d 44 (Del Ch 2005). See also Sussman (n 3) 35.

8.2.11   Mistake

While often raised as a defence to enforcement, mistake is another ground that courts rarely accept to defeat a settlement agreement. Courts in the USA have rejected claims of mutual mistake, along with the more arduous claim of unilateral mistake, where a party claimed that the amount to be paid was to be offset by an amount already paid,[39] and where a plaintiff had not read the agreement to understand its terms.[40] Similarly, the courts have held that a party's misunderstanding of the law is not a valid basis to have a contractual obligation set aside.[41]

8.3   Providing Certainty to Enhance Enforcement

Several elements can help in limiting difficulties arising during the mediation process and the consequent likelihood that parties would want to rescind mediated settlement agreements. These include effective training and accreditation of mediators, the observance of mediation standards and the presence at mediation of legal advisors educated about the mediation process.[42] In light of the jurisprudence discussed in Section 8.2, the mediator and legal advisors to the parties can take steps to avoid subsequent enforcement difficulties. While each commercial dispute is unique and may demand specific requirements for its own form of settlement agreement, the following steps have been gleaned from jurisprudence covering many types of disputes.[43]

8.3.1   Writing and Signature

Ensuring that the agreement in is writing and signed by the parties or authorised signatories may seem an obvious step, but many mediations end with an oral agreement and a commitment by one of the parties to prepare the necessary documents. This can give rise to enforcement difficulties if a completed signed written settlement does not materialise.

---

[39] *Feldman* v. *Kritch* 824 So 2d 274 (Fla Dist Ct App 2002).
[40] *Stewart* v. *Preston Pipeline Inc* 36 Cal Rptr 3d 901 (2005). See also Sussman (n 3) 35. However, a claim of mutual mistake that led to a clerical error of US$600,000 was upheld in *Brandsmart USA* v. *DR Lakes Inc* 901 So 2d 1004 (Fla Dist Ct App 2005). This appears to have largely turned on DR Lakes' 'clear and convincing' evidence, which included a document in addition to the settlement agreement to support the claim: at 1005.
[41] *Edney* v. *Edney* 64 VI 661 (2016). See Coben (n 11) 1083.
[42] See Chapters 5 and 6.
[43] See Sussman (n 3) 38–39.

The settlement agreement should be signed by the parties or authorised representatives and provide that it is admissible in evidence in any proceeding to enforce its terms, and the parties should consider incorporating a provision that mediation confidentiality is waived if any issue arises regarding enforcement of the settlement.[44]

8.3.2   Material Terms and Clear and Certain Language

The settlement should incorporate all of the material terms; use language that is certain enough to be understood and to require performance; and confirm, where it is agreed, that the parties intend the agreement to be binding and enforceable. Careful language should be used for follow-up documents that implement the settlement terms. For example, the agreement should not be made 'subject to' follow-up documents or 'effective only upon' the execution of further documents, unless it is agreed and required. It is important that, if the document is stated to be a 'full and final settlement', it resolves all outstanding issues and that the dispute settled is clearly defined in the agreement. If a party wants to preserve their right to sue on other causes of action, they should expressly reserve that right in the settlement agreement.[45]

Clear and certain language is also important where a party may need to seek relief to enforce a mediated settlement in a foreign court where English is not the first language of the judiciary. If the parties are using different languages and the mediated settlement agreement is required in more than one language, a certified translation should be provided for the parties to sign, to avoid inconsistency in meaning.

8.3.3   Material Representations and Ancillary Documents

If settlement is predicated on material representations, they should be incorporated into the settlement agreement, and the agreement should unequivocally state that they reflect all the representations on which the

---

[44] It is a good practice to keep a record of what has been agreed during the course of the mediation, and then verify this again when completing the settlement agreement: see Blake, Browne and Sime (n 19) 241. Some mediators ask the parties to provide a sample settlement agreement, when preparing for the mediation, that can be modified in the course of the mediation as issues are agreed; this enhances the goal of ensuring that no one leaves the mediation until the settlement terms are reduced to writing and signed by the parties: see C Chern, *International Commercial Mediation* (London, Informa 2008) 177.

[45] See Blake, Browne and Sime (n 19) 240–41.

parties relied. This should make it unnecessary to breach the confidentiality of the mediation process to obtain such evidence if the settlement agreement is challenged. Material ancillary documents, such as an apology[46] or release, should also be agreed to and the detail finalised during the mediation process, to prevent later disputes over such documents.

8.3.4 Competence and Independent Judgement

As many commercial disputes involve sophisticated parties and legal representation, confirming the parties' competence and independent judgement may seem excessive or superfluous. However, for the avoidance of doubt, it may prove helpful to provide in the settlement agreement that the parties agree to the terms and understand them; they understand that the terms are binding and can be judicially enforced; they agree that all material representations made to them during the mediation were incorporated into the settlement agreement; they understand that neither the mediator nor the opposing party or the opposing party's advisors were under any positive obligation to furnish them with information; they were not suffering from any physical impairment that adversely affected their ability to exercise their judgement in approving the settlement; there were opportunities to consult their lawyers regarding the settlement terms; they acted voluntarily and exercised independent judgement throughout the process, including the decision to settle; and they have authority to legally bind the party that they represented in the mediation.

8.3.5 Litigation Considerations and Related Matters

The settlement should clearly state whether the agreement or fulfilment of the agreement settles the dispute that is the subject of litigation. In most cases it will be the former, such that rights will be based on the

---

[46] Experience from the USA suggests that when an apology occurs in a commercial mediation that is perceived as sincere, it can have a major impact: see Golann and Folberg (n 17) 150. Hong Kong enacted the Apology Ordinance (cap 631) in 2017, to encourage mediated settlements. It covers all apologies made at any stage between parties in dispute and provides that an apology does not constitute an admission of fault or liability, and an apology must not be taken into account in determining fault or liability or any issue in connection with the matter to the prejudice of the person, unless in exceptional circumstances it would be just and equitable to do so.

settlement agreement, not on underlying causes of action. It should also clearly state the dispute that is being settled. Where proceedings have issued, this can be done by reference to the 'disputes the subject-matter of the proceedings' between the parties. This can be widened to include claims and causes of action, present or future, that relate in some way to the dispute in the proceedings. It can also be widened to include any other disputes between the parties that they wish to resolve. Claims and counter-claims in the relevant proceedings will have to be withdrawn and costs must be reflected in the settlement. Some jurisdictions do not automatically assume that costs are included. Settlement agreements will often provide that the claims are withdrawn with the parties covering their own costs. Where monetary compensation is involved, the agreement must reflect how much is being paid and by whom to settle the claims. An interest provision may be appropriate for late payments. Confidentiality, and the basis upon which it can be waived, should be reflected in the agreement. The governing law and jurisdiction of the agreement should also be included. Other terms may need to reflect an ongoing business relationship, where intellectual or other rights must be considered, or where goods or securities must be delivered or returned.[47]

8.3.6   Converting the Agreement

If the dispute is being litigated, the terms of the settlement could be incorporated into the final judgment, or the settlement could provide for the court to retain jurisdiction over the matter for enforcement purposes. If the matter is not being litigated, it may be possible to request that the mediator act as an arbitrator to effectively make an arbitral award reflecting the mediated settlement agreement. However, not all jurisdictions permit a mediator to step into the role of arbitrator.[48] Some jurisdictions expressly provide for such a procedure,[49] while in a number

---

[47] See M Kallipetis and S Ruttle, 'Better Dispute Resolution: The Development and Practice of Mediation in the United Kingdom Between 1995 and 2005' in J C Goldsmith, A Ingen-Housz and G H Pointon (eds), *ADR in Business: Practice and Issues Across Countries and Cultures* (Alphen aan den Rijn, Kluwer Law International 2006) 246–47. For a discussion on practical considerations when drafting a mediated settlement, see Chern (n 44) 177–84.

[48] For example, in the US case *Minkowitz v. Israeli* 77 A 3d 1189 (2013), the New Jersey Appellate Division held that an individual retained to serve as an arbitrator cannot act as a mediator and then return to the role of arbitrator.

[49] From the perspective of a commercial relationship and amicable dispute resolution, a mediated settlement can be viewed as the ideal outcome of any arbitration. Indeed,

of jurisdictions the settlement agreement may also be deemed to have the same force and effect as an arbitral award.[50] This matter is discussed further in Section 8.4, as is the possible recognition of such an award under the New York Convention. The advent of the Singapore Convention, discussed in Section 8.6, should also have a significant impact in this area.

8.4 Making the Mediated Settlement Agreement a Judgment or Award

Traditionally, as discussed, the primary method for enforcing a mediated settlement agreement is to treat it as a contract. This is unsatisfactory since that enforcement mechanism leaves the party in an unenviable position – exactly where it started, in most cases, with a contract it was trying to enforce. In the international context, such agreements are subject to the private international law rules of the enforcing jurisdiction, and this can prove costly as further legal advice may be required.[51] Mediated settlement agreements can be entered as a judgment in some jurisdictions. Where the case has been filed before the mediation begins, many jurisdictions permit the court to enter the settlement agreement as a consent order or decree and incorporate it into the dismissal order.[52] The court may also retain jurisdiction over the court decree. Where there is no court proceeding, courts in some jurisdictions are available to enter a judgment on the mediated settlement agreement, possibly through an

---

the use of mediation during arbitral proceedings is steadily increasing: see P Binder, *International Commercial Arbitration and Mediation in UNCITRAL Model Law Jurisdictions* (4th ed, Alphen aan den Rijn, Kluwer Law International 2019) 412, 416.

[50] Sussman (n 3) 39.

[51] S Chong and F Steffek, 'Enforcement of International Settlement Agreements Resulting from Mediation under the Singapore Convention: Private International Law Issues in Perspective' (2019) 31 *Singapore Academy of Law Journal* 448, 452. Enforcement of mediated settlements could also yield different results depending on the enforcing jurisdiction: see N Alexander and S Chong, *The Singapore Convention on Mediation: A Commentary* (Alphen aan den Rijn, Kluwer Law International 2019) 70. See also Chapter 2 at Section 2.6.

[52] Even where litigation is already underway and consent orders have been made regarding the outcome of a mediation, the enforcement of a mediated settlement agreement can be time-consuming and difficult where there is opposition from one of the parties. In the English case *Crystal Decisions (UK) Ltd* v. *Vedatech Corp* [2007] EWHC 1062 (Ch), for example, the final judgment of the court upholding the terms of a mediated settlement agreement was issued almost five years after the agreement was executed. For an overview of methods of recording settlements during court proceedings in England, see Blake, Browne and Sime (n 19) 245–56.

expedited procedure; others have a system of deposition or registration at the court to make the settlement enforceable. Acts by a notary are required to ensure a mediated settlement agreement is enforceable in other jurisdictions. However, as court judgments and decrees do not have the same enforcement status as an arbitral award, due to the New York Convention, cross-border enforcement can be problematic. Consequently, even if a judgment can be obtained, the challenges of enforcing a foreign judgment are often significant. Indeed, it seems paradoxical that a settlement agreement resulting from the consensual process of mediation has traditionally been more difficult to enforce internationally than an award from the adjudicative process of arbitration.[53]

As an alternative to a court judgment, an approach adopted to address the cross-border enforcement problem is to convert the settlement agreement into an arbitral award. Where arbitral proceedings have already commenced but are suspended in order to mediate the dispute, the parties can request that the proceedings be reactivated in order to incorporate the result of the mediation into the award; this effectively converts the mediated settlement agreement into an internationally enforceable arbitral award. If the mediation concludes successfully resulting in a settlement, and no arbitration or judicial proceedings had commenced before the dispute was successfully mediated, the possibility of converting the agreement into an arbitral award or a judgment depends on the jurisdiction where (or the rules of the organisation under which) the mediation took place. Whether an award or a judgment is sought, some organisations or judicial systems will refuse to open formal judicial or arbitral proceedings for the sole purpose of incorporating a mediated settlement into an arbitral award or a judgment, as there is no longer any dispute to be resolved.[54] They may also object in

---

[53] See Note by the UNCITRAL Secretariat, *Settlement of Commercial Disputes: Enforceability of Settlement Agreements Resulting from International Commercial Conciliation/Mediation*, 8, A/CN.9/WG.II/WP.187 (27 November 2014) 4–6 and Note by the UNCITRAL Secretariat, *Settlement of Commercial Disputes: Enforcement of Settlement Agreements Resulting from International Commercial Conciliation/ Mediation: Compilation of Comments by Governments*, A/CN.9/846 (27 March 2015), reflecting the varied enforcement mechanisms employed across jurisdictions. See also the EU report reflecting a similar situation: G De Palo and others, '"Rebooting" the Mediation Directive: Assessing the Limited Impact of its Implementation and Proposing Measures to Increase the Number of Mediations in the EU' (Luxembourg, European Parliament 2014). See also E Sussman, 'A Path Forward: A Convention for the Enforcement of Mediated Settlement Agreements' (2015) 6 *Transnational Dispute Management* 1, 5–6.

[54] However, the arbitration rules of many institutions expressly provide that an agreement reached in mediation can be entered as an arbitral award. Article 14 of the Rules of the Mediation Institute of the Stockholm Chamber of Commerce (2014) provides that when

principle on the basis that their role is to resolve actual conflicts, not as a forum to convert private mediated settlement agreements into more easily enforceable international instruments.[55]

8.4.1 Enforcement Under the New York Convention

The Convention on the Recognition and Enforcement of Foreign Arbitral Awards (the 'New York Convention')[56] was adopted by a UN diplomatic conference in New York in 1958 and became effective the following year. Under the New York Convention, courts of contracting states must enforce private agreements to arbitrate and recognise and enforce arbitral awards from other contracting states. The Convention is the principal legislative instrument that regulates international commercial arbitration and has accomplished its drafters' aspirations, serving as a universal constitutional charter focussed on enforcement and

the parties reach an agreement, the mediator can act as an arbitrator and confirm the settlement in an arbitral award. Some jurisdictions in the USA expressly provide for the entry of an arbitration award to record an agreement reached in mediation: see, e.g., Title 9.3, s 1297.401 of the California Code of Civil Procedure (providing such a provision with respect to international mediations). See also Sussman (n 53) 7.

[55] The European Union recognised this issue and it is reflected in article 6 of Directive 2008/52/EC of the European Parliament and of the Council of 21 May 2008 on certain aspects of mediation in civil and commercial matters [2008] OJ L136/3 ('EU Mediation Directive'). Article 6 of the Directive provides that national law in each Member State of the European Union (except Denmark, which opted out of the Mediation Directive) must ensure that it is possible for the parties to request that the content of a written agreement resulting from mediation be made enforceable. The content must be made enforceable unless either the agreement is contrary to the law of the Member State, or the law does not provide for its enforceability. The agreement may be made enforceable by a court or other competent authority in the Member State where the request is made. These exceptions are quite broad, and it has been suggested that diversity in the regulation of the enforceability of mediated settlements is likely to continue within the European Union. If enforcement is or becomes a serious concern for the parties, within the European Union or elsewhere, legal advisors should check this point before the mediation concludes, so that, if necessary, the mediation can be finalised in a 'mediation friendly' legal environment – that is, one that will support the conversion of the mediated settlement agreement into an arbitral award or a judgment. See N Alexander, 'Harmonisation and Diversity in the Private International Law of Mediation: The Rhythms of Regulatory Reform' in Hopt and Steffek (eds) (n 9) 179; E W Fiechter, 'Mediation: Confidentiality and Enforcement Issues and Solutions', IBA Legal Practice Division Mediation Committee Newsletter (April 2005) 46–47. See also Chapter 2 at Section 2.4.7 for an overview of the EU Mediation Directive.

[56] The Convention on the Recognition and Enforcement of Foreign Arbitral Awards ('New York Convention'). See also Chapter 2 at Section 2.4.1.

recognition.[57] There is currently no international instrument concerning litigation that challenges the New York Convention's predominance in the area of recognition and enforcement of the outcome of a dispute.[58]

If arbitration laws or institutional rules provide for mediation to take place during the course of the arbitral process, and that any settlement reached can be made the subject of an arbitral award,[59] the issue arises as to whether such 'consent' awards[60] are enforceable under the New York Convention. The Convention applies to the recognition and enforcement of 'arbitral' awards;[61] thus, it could be interpreted that an arbitral tribunal must reach a decision on the issues in dispute. Arbitration begins under an agreement that convenes a tribunal and the result is binding on the parties. The tribunal may not conduct private communications with the parties, as due process requires that parties are present during the presentation of evidence in order to respond, and the tribunal has a strict mandate over the components of a dispute that are submitted to it. Due process standards, rules of evidence, natural justice and a legally based decision from a qualified expert all justify the limited basis for appeal, expedited enforcement and restrictive grounds for non-enforcement or the setting aside of an award under the Convention.

Mediation, as a fundamentally different process to arbitration, results in agreement from the decision of the parties to settle their conflict in

---

[57] See Y Rampall and R Feehily, 'The Sanctity of Party Autonomy and the Powers of Arbitrators to Determine the Applicable Law: The Quest for an Arbitral Equilibrium' (2018) 23(2) *Harvard Negotiation Law Review* 345, 356–57.

[58] International commercial arbitration's superior legal enforcement infrastructure is a primary reason for its success: see S I Strong, 'Applying the Lessons of International Commercial Arbitration to International Commercial Mediation: A Dispute System Design Analysis' in C Titi and K Fach Gómez (eds), *Mediation in International Commercial and Investment Disputes* (Oxford, Oxford University Press 2019) 45–46, 48–49.

[59] Many jurisdictions expressly empower the arbitrator to attempt mediation first and to enter a consent award: see, e.g., Article 30 of the Indian Arbitration and Conciliation Act of 1996 and Article 51 of the Arbitration Law of the People's Republic of China. Some jurisdictions, such as Brazil, go even further. Articles 21(4) and 28 of the Brazilian Arbitration Law provide that the arbitrator 'shall' attempt conciliation at the beginning of the procedure; if a settlement results, it can be converted into an arbitral award: see E Sussman, 'The New York Convention through a Mediation Prism' (2009) 15(4) *Dispute Resolution Magazine* 10, 12.

[60] Also known as 'awards on consent' or 'awards on agreed terms': see Alexander (n 55) 184–87.

[61] New York Convention (n 56) article 1 provides: 'This Convention shall apply to the recognition and enforcement of arbitral awards made in the territory of a State other than the State where the recognition and enforcement of such awards are sought.'

a context where due process standards are distinctly different; the mediator does not possess binding decision-making authority, and the outcome is generally not subject to substantive scrutiny from independent experts.[62] Converting a mediated settlement into an arbitral award means that it will not be subject to traditional contract law defences where there are efforts to set it aside. Consequently, applying arbitration standards to mediation may be viewed as an imperfect fit, and that, as a result, a consent award lacks the required adjudicative character for Convention purposes.[63]

Notwithstanding such concerns, a consent award would fall within the meaning of an award under the New York Convention, as parties are entitled to settle their claims in arbitration, and the resulting award would be binding and enforceable. This is also confirmed by the text of most national arbitration statutes and institutional rules.[64] For example, article 30 of the Arbitration Model Law provides:

> [I]f, during arbitral proceedings, the parties settle the dispute, the arbitral tribunal shall terminate the proceedings and, if requested by the parties and not objected to by the arbitral tribunal, record the settlement in the form of an arbitral award on agreed terms.[65]

Article 30(2) provides that 'such an award has the same status and effect as any award on the merits of the case'. Consequently, while the New York Convention does not expressly address the issue of awards on agreed terms, the predominant view appears to endorse the application of the Convention to consent awards.[66]

---

[62] However, as discussed in Section 8.4.2, there is the possibility in some jurisdictions for the arbitral tribunal to review a consent award.

[63] B L Steele, 'Enforcing International Commercial Mediation Agreements as Arbitral Awards Under the New York Convention' (2007) 54(5) *UCLA Law Review* 1385, 1398–99. See Alexander (n 55) 186.

[64] A number of national court decisions have reached comparable results despite the absence of statutory provisions: see G B Born, *International Commercial Arbitration* (3rd ed, Alphen aan den Rijn, Kluwer Law International 2020) 3275.

[65] UNCITRAL Model Law on International Commercial Arbitration ('Arbitration Model Law') article 30. Many rules and laws contain similar provisions, such as article 36 of the UNCITRAL Arbitration Rules and s 51 of the English Arbitration Act: see R Feehily, 'The Certainty of Settlement' (2016) 27(1) *Stellenbosch Law Review* 25, 53–54. Neither the New York Convention nor the Arbitration Model Law defines the term 'award'. Article 1.2 of the New York Convention (n 56) provides: 'The term "arbitral awards" shall include not only awards made by arbitrators appointed for each case but also those made by permanent arbitral bodies to which the parties have submitted.'

[66] This has been the position for some time: see T Wiwen-Nilsson, 'Conciliation: Enforcement of Settlements', *Modern Law for Global Commerce: Proceedings of the*

An issue that arises is the status of an arbitral award based on a mediated settlement that is agreed before the arbitral process begins. This is an area where national or domestic laws can prove instrumental. For example, the English Arbitration Act 1996 defines an arbitration agreement in s 6(1) as 'an agreement to submit to arbitration present or future disputes'. Similarly, New York state law provides that an 'agreement to submit any controversy thereafter arising or any existing controversy to arbitration' is enforceable.[67] As there is no 'present or future dispute' or 'controversy thereafter arising or . . . existing' once a mediated settlement agreement results, such provisions indicate that it is not possible to have an arbitrator appointed to record the mediated settlement as an arbitral award. It follows that any arbitral award issued by an arbitrator appointed after the mediated settlement agreement was concluded would be unenforceable under the laws of such jurisdictions, as the arbitrator appointed had no authority to make the award. Even if this difficulty could be resolved by providing that the mediated settlement agreement be governed by the law of a state where such an arbitrator appointment is effective, the issue of enforcement of such an award under the New York Convention remains.[68]

Article 1.1 of the New York Convention applies to the recognition and enforcement of awards 'arising out of differences between persons'. This is quite different language compared with the definition of an arbitration agreement in the English and New York laws just discussed, which require a 'present or future' dispute or a 'controversy thereafter arising or . . . existing'. Article 1.1 does not specify when the 'differences between persons' had to exist relative to when the arbitrator was appointed. It could be interpreted that the Convention language does not expressly prohibit the recognition of an award delivered by an arbitrator appointed after the dispute is resolved. If the law of the state where enforcement is sought would not permit the entry of an award by an arbitrator appointed after the dispute was resolved, such a legal difference may not conflict with the public policy of a state such that it would prohibit enforcement of such an award under the public policy exception in the Convention.

UNCITRAL Congress, Vienna, 9–12 July 2007, 411; G Lorcher, 'Enforceability of Agreed Awards in Foreign Jurisdictions' (2001) 17(3) *Arbitration International* 275, 277 fn 19 (listing many commentators who affirm this view). See also Born (n 64) 3274–75.

[67] New York Civil Practice Law and Rules, s 7501.

[68] See Sussman (n 53) 7; Born (n 64) 3274. See also E E Deason, 'Procedural Rules for Complementary Systems of Litigation and Mediation – Worldwide' (2005) 80(2) *Notre Dame Law Review* 553, 588–91.

However, views differ on the public policy implications of the ostensibly ambiguous Convention.[69]

Recognition and enforcement may be refused under article 5.2 of the New York Convention on the basis of public policy objections if the competent authority in the relevant country finds that '(a) The subject matter of the difference is not capable of settlement by arbitration under the law of that country; or (b) The recognition or enforcement of the award would be contrary to the public policy of that country'.[70] While the purpose of the provision concerns 'the subject matter of the difference', it is implicit that a 'difference' exists, and as a settlement agreement is not a 'difference' it is at least arguably 'not capable of settlement by arbitration'.[71]

8.4.2   Consent Award Considerations

Under the New York Convention, a party applying for recognition and enforcement of an award must produce both the award and the original arbitration agreement,[72] and recognition and enforcement may be refused where the agreement is invalid under the law to which the parties have subjected it.[73] While some commentators have adopted a broad interpretation of the New York Convention concerning the enforcement of consent awards where arbitrators are appointed after settlement is reached,[74] it is clear that procedures such as those in article 30 of the Arbitration Model Law can only be used when mediation follows the commencement of arbitral proceedings. The reverse is legally problematic as a mediated settlement agreement reached where an arbitration is

---

[69] It has been suggested that an interpretation of the New York Convention, involving a thorough review by UNCITRAL, Working Group II, which is assigned Arbitration and Conciliation, might resolve this issue: see Sussman (n 59) 12–13. However, the advent of the Singapore Convention (discussed in Section 8.6) and the revised Mediation Model Law (discussed in Section 8.5), completed by UNCITRAL, Working Group II, may in time make the calls for such clarification moot.

[70] Potential challenges to a mediated settlement agreement where enforcement is sought as an arbitral award under the New York Convention fall into two broad groups: procedural challenges and public policy challenges. For a discussion on such challenges and potential solutions to some of the dilemmas that may arise, see Steele (n 63) 1399–412.

[71] See C Newmark and R Hill, 'Can a Mediated Settlement Agreement Become an Enforceable Arbitration Award?' (2008) 16(1) *Arbitration International* 81, 84.

[72] New York Convention (n 56) article 4.1(b).

[73] New York Convention (n 56) article 5.

[74] See H I Abramson, 'Mining Mediation Rules for Representation Opportunities and Obstacles' (2004) 15(1) *American Review of International Arbitration* 103, 108.

not pending means there is no 'dispute' to be submitted to an arbitral tribunal for resolution.[75]

The appointment of an arbitrator where a settlement agreement has already been reached may be characterised as akin to requesting that a judge give a judgment by consent where proceedings have not been issued, or issuing proceedings after compromising a dispute; this would be an abuse of process as there would be no cause of action.[76] This issue could be resolved by parties entering into an arbitration agreement or by including an arbitration clause in their contract. The arbitration agreement or clause would have to be drafted to ensure that future disputes that may be resolvable through mediation would benefit from the enforcement mechanisms of the New York Convention where a settlement agreement was the result.[77] If parties want an arbitral award to reflect the agreement they reached through mediation, the arbitrator should be appointed before the mediation process begins. The optimal approach to ensure that a mediated settlement agreement is incorporated into an enforceable arbitral award under the New York Convention is to provide for an arbitrator to be appointed, and for the mediation to then take place. If the mediation is successful, the arbitrator can reflect the mediated settlement agreement in a consent award. If the mediation does not result in a settlement, the arbitrator can then proceed to make an award.[78]

---

[75] Born (n 64) 3274–75; Binder (n 49) 415, 626.

[76] Newmark and Hill (n 71) 85.

[77] See Steele (n 63) 1400. However, parties must be willing to proceed to arbitration if mediation fails to resolve the dispute, as either party could enforce an agreement to arbitrate where mediation is unsuccessful, and this may not be ideal for a party who only wants to mediate their disputes: see Deason (n 68) 588.

[78] This is effectively an arb-co-med-arb arrangement. Where parties will proceed to arbitration if mediation fails to resolve the dispute, they should confirm their consent to the individual who acted as mediator then acting as arbitrator. Alternatively, they should consider providing in their agreement that different individuals act in each role, to avoid concerns that article 5(2)(b) of the New York Convention (n 56) is breached, on the basis that it is construed that the mediator has made a binding decision and this could be viewed as a breach of natural justice and consequently public policy. While costs considerations may persuade parties to use the same person for both roles, the added advantage of using different individuals is as an effective 'health check' on the agreement, where the arbitrator must consent to making the settlement into an award: see Newmark and Hill (n 71) 85–87. The arbitrator should verify whether the award has any element that could deceive third parties (such as tax authorities) or if there are other public policy reasons justifying a refusal. In *Société Viva Chemical (Europe) NV v. APTD* Cour d'appel de Paris [Paris Court of Appeal], 07/17769, 9 April 2009, the Court found that a settlement agreement was part of a fraudulent scheme to reduce the assets of the

While arbitral awards will usually contain reasons, consent awards instead contain a description of the settlement.[79] Where the mediated settlement only disposes of some of the claims being arbitrated, this is akin to a situation where a partial award disposing of some of the claims in the arbitration is made. The remaining issues will then proceed to arbitration. It is also important to ensure that there is agreement consistency between the issues covered in the arbitration agreement and the mediated settlement. Where the mediated settlement deals with issues or a subject matter not covered by the arbitration or submission agreement, it is unlikely that the arbitral tribunal would have jurisdiction to render the award. This could be because such matters fall outside the arbitration agreement or because they have not been submitted for determination to the arbitral tribunal. If this occurs, it is important that the parties and the arbitrator agree to extend the terms of the arbitration or submission agreement.[80] If the mediated settlement includes matters that are being dealt with in a different forum, there could be an issue with regard to *lis pendens* (pending legal action).[81]

There may be circumstances where a mediated settlement obliges or gives rights to a party that is not a party to the arbitration. An example is where one or both of the parties belongs to a group of companies and the agreed performance should be made, or rights exercised, by a subsidiary,

respondent before an impending bankruptcy declaration. As the enforcement of such a consent award would violate international public policy, the ordinance rendered by the lower court was annulled. An arbitrator who issues an award that forms part of an unlawful scheme can be criminally liable: see G Marchisio, 'A Comparative Analysis of Consent Awards: Accepting Their Reality' (2016) 32(2) *Arbitration International* 331, 337, 342.

[79] Dispensing with the requirement for reasons in consent awards is provided for in many laws and instruments: see, e.g., article 31(2) of the Arbitration Model Law (n 65), and 52(4) of the English Arbitration Act. However, statutes usually require that other formalities be observed. Article 30 of the Arbitration Model Law requires that the arbitral tribunal record the settlement in an instrument satisfying the formal requirements of an award. It is the tribunal's award – not the parties' settlement agreement – that is an award under both the Model Law and the New York Convention (n 61). Some Model Law courts have held that only a settlement agreement recorded in the form of an award satisfying the formal requirements of article 30(2) and stating it is an award on its face will be recognised; a mere record of the settlement is insufficient: see Born (n 64) 3272–73.

[80] However, where the consent award has already issued, it may be possible to sever that part dealing with the subject matter that falls outside the terms of the arbitration or submission agreement from the remainder of the validly issued award, and seek enforcement of the severed part under the Singapore Convention, provided it conforms with the requirements of the latter: see New York Convention (n 56) article 5(1)(c). See also Alexander and Chong (n 51) 42–43.

[81] See Wiwen-Nilsson (n 66) 411–13; Lorcher (n 66) 282.

parent or sister company. This is problematic, as an award on agreed terms cannot bind or give rights to third parties.[82] Mediated settlements may also enter into force when certain events have occurred or certain conditions have been met, such as performance in the future by one of the parties. Similarly, they may be revocable if certain events do not occur, or certain conditions are not met. The enforcement of awards based on such settlements may be questioned on the basis that they are not final. Settlement agreements often contain a dispute resolution mechanism to resolve disputes arising out of the settlement agreement such as mediation or arbitration. Such provisions appear to be inconsistent with the concept of a final and binding enforceable award.[83]

Awards can be challenged on numerous grounds such as excess of mandate, errors in the procedure, invalid arbitration agreement, subject matter incapable of resolution by arbitration and violation of public policy.[84] An issue that arises is to what extent such grounds for setting aside an award are applicable to consent awards. Having settled their differences, agreed terms and requested that the settlement be converted into an arbitral award, the parties may be considered to have waived their right to challenge an award that relies on any of these grounds.[85] It has been suggested that the basis for parties' challenge to the award should be limited to grave defects, as they have, through their settlement agreement, confirmed the correctness of the arbitral procedure that could otherwise be challenged.[86]

Another issue that arises is what should happen if an arbitral tribunal considers that a consent award would improperly affect the rights of third parties, or breach public policy, and the extent to which they are obligated to convert settlements into arbitral awards. While arbitral tribunals rarely decline to make consent awards, they cannot be forced to sign an award that they object to, and they ultimately have the option of making an order terminating the arbitration without an award.[87] Regardless of the

---

[82] See Wiwen-Nilsson (n 66) 413. See also Born (n 64) 3273.

[83] However, it seems that in practice many consent awards do not contain dispute resolution clauses due to such provisions being inconsistent with the concept of a final and binding award: Alexander (n 55) 186.

[84] See, e.g., Arbitration Model Law (n 65) article 34.

[85] Alexander (n 55) 186.

[86] Binder (n 49) 415. However, just as consent awards are subject to recognition, confirmation and enforcement in the same manner as other arbitral awards, a consent award should also in principle be subject to annulment: see Born (n 64) 3275.

[87] For example, Arbitration Model Law (n 65) article 32(2)(c) provides: 'The arbitral tribunal shall issue an order for the termination of the arbitral proceedings when the

parties' contentions, they cannot require that an arbitral tribunal exercise its own authority to approve their settlement in an award. Further, matters that are not arbitrable or are contrary to public policy in the relevant jurisdiction are not waivable. As they cannot be arbitrated, they should not be insulated from review by the tribunal simply because they are made the subject of a mediated settlement that the parties want converted into an arbitral award.[88]

Article 30 of the Arbitration Model Law provides that the arbitral tribunal can refuse ('object') to record a settlement in the form of an award. The same approach has been adopted by the arbitration law in many countries,[89] effectively giving the arbitral tribunal the power to examine the settlement. While the extent of such scrutiny can vary from country to country, it is important that an arbitral tribunal bears the above issues in mind when requested to make a mediated settlement a consent award, and ensures that the consent award it is rendering is enforceable.[90]

8.5   Enforcement Under the UNCITRAL Mediation Model Law

Article 15 of the Mediation Model Law[91] provides: 'If the parties conclude an agreement settling a dispute, that settlement agreement is

---

arbitral tribunal finds that the continuation of the proceedings has for any other reason become unnecessary or impossible.'

[88] See Wiwen-Nilsson (n 66) 413–14; Binder (n 49) 414. In practice, the arbitral tribunal is likely to refuse to issue a consent award where there are well-founded reasons for doing so such as evidence of fraud, corruption or violation of applicable mandatory law, such as exchange controls, anti-money laundering regulations and competition laws: see Born (n 64) 3273–74.

[89] See, e.g., English Arbitration Act 1996, s 51(2); Swedish Arbitration Act 1999, s 27. Arbitration rules can provide for this also: see UNCITRAL Arbitration Rules, article 36(1); International Chamber of Commerce (ICC) Arbitration Rules, article 33; London Court of International Arbitration (LCIA) Arbitration Rules, article 26.9.

[90] In some jurisdictions, where parties to an arbitration agreement settle their dispute, the settlement agreement has the status and effect of an award on agreed terms for domestic enforcement purposes: see, e.g., Bermuda International Conciliation and Arbitration Act 1993, s 20; Hong Kong Arbitration Ordinance (cap 609) s 66(2). Without scrutiny by an arbitral tribunal, there is a substantial risk that the settlement agreement will not meet the minimum requirements for enforcement. There needs to be a correcting mechanism similar to that performed by the arbitral tribunal in the case of awards on agreed terms: see Wiwen-Nilsson (n 66) 410, 415.

[91] UNCITRAL Model Law on International Commercial Mediation and International Settlement Agreements Resulting from Mediation ('Mediation Model Law'). See Chapter 2 at Section 2.4.5.

binding and enforceable'. Until the Mediation Model Law was revised in 2018, this provision invited adopting states to insert their own enforcement regimes for settlement agreements. States that adopted the 2002 version of the Model Law would have adopted this approach.[92] States no longer need to insert their own enforcement regimes following the 2018 revision, which introduced section 3 (comprising articles 16–20). The new section covers international mediated settlement agreements and mirrors articles 1–6 of the Singapore Convention.[93] Article 16 of the Mediation Model Law covers the scope of application of the section and definitions,[94] article 17 covers general principles,[95] article 18 covers

---

[92] For a critique of the earlier provision on enforcement (article 14 of the 2002 Model Law), and how it represented the lowest acceptable common denominator of UNCITRAL negotiating participants, see Feehily (n 65) 55–57.

[93] United Nations Convention on International Settlement Agreements Resulting from Mediation ('Singapore Convention'). The Singapore Convention is discussed in Section 8.6 of this chapter.

[94] Article 16 of the Mediation Model Law (n 91), which mirrors articles 1 and 2 of the Singapore Convention (n 93), provides: '1. This section applies to international agreements resulting from mediation and concluded in writing by parties to resolve a commercial dispute ("settlement agreements"). 2. This section does not apply to settlement agreements: (a) Concluded to resolve a dispute arising from transactions engaged in by one of the parties (a consumer) for personal, family or household purposes; (b) Relating to family, inheritance or employment law. 3. This section does not apply to: (a) Settlement agreements: (i) That have been approved by a court or concluded in the course of proceedings before a court; and (ii) That are enforceable as a judgment in the State of that court; (b) Settlement agreements that have been recorded and are enforceable as an arbitral award. 4. A settlement agreement is "international" if, at the time of the conclusion of the settlement agreement: (a) At least two parties to the settlement agreement have their places of business in different States; or (b) The State in which the parties to the settlement agreement have their places of business is different from either: (i) The State in which a substantial part of the obligations under the settlement agreement is to be performed; or (ii) The State with which the subject matter of the settlement agreement is most closely connected. 5. For the purposes of paragraph 4: (a) If a party has more than one place of business, the relevant place of business is that which has the closest relationship to the dispute resolved by the settlement agreement, having regard to the circumstances known to, or contemplated by, the parties at the time of the conclusion of the settlement agreement; (b) If a party does not have a place of business, reference is to be made to the party's habitual residence. 6. A settlement agreement is "in writing" if its content is recorded in any form. The requirement that a settlement agreement be in writing is met by an electronic communication if the information contained therein is accessible so as to be useable for subsequent reference.'

[95] Article 17 of the Mediation Model Law (n 91), which mirrors article 3 of the Singapore Convention (n 93), provides: '1. A settlement agreement shall be enforced in accordance with the rules of procedure of this State, and under the conditions laid down in this section. 2. If a dispute arises concerning a matter that a party claims was already resolved by a settlement agreement, the party may invoke the settlement agreement in accordance

requirements for reliance on settlement agreements,[96] article 19 covers grounds for refusing to grant relief[97] and article 20 covers parallel applications or claims.[98]

with the rules of procedure of this State, and under the conditions laid down in this section, in order to prove that the matter has already been resolved.'

[96] Article 18 of the Mediation Model Law (n 91), which mirrors article 4 of the Singapore Convention (n 93), provides: '1. A party relying on a settlement agreement under this section shall supply to the competent authority of this State: (a) The settlement agreement signed by the parties; (b) Evidence that the settlement agreement resulted from mediation, such as: (i) The mediator's signature on the settlement agreement; (ii) A document signed by the mediator indicating that the mediation was carried out; (iii) An attestation by the institution that administered the mediation; or (iv) In the absence of (i), (ii) or (iii), any other evidence acceptable to the competent authority. 2. The requirement that a settlement agreement shall be signed by the parties or, where applicable, the mediator, is met in relation to an electronic communication if: (a) A method is used to identify the parties or the mediator and to indicate the parties' or mediator's intention in respect of the information contained in the electronic communication; and (b) The method used is either: (i) As reliable as appropriate for the purpose for which the electronic communication was generated or communicated, in the light of all the circumstances, including any relevant agreement; or (ii) Proven in fact to have fulfilled the functions described in subparagraph (a) above, by itself or together with further evidence. 3. If the settlement agreement is not in an official language of this State, the competent authority may request a translation thereof into such language. 4. The competent authority may require any necessary document in order to verify that the requirements of this section have been complied with. 5. When considering the request for relief, the competent authority shall act expeditiously.'

[97] Article 19 of the Mediation Model Law (n 91), which mirrors article 5 of the Singapore Convention (n 93), provides: '1. The competent authority of this State may refuse to grant relief at the request of the party against whom the relief is sought only if that party furnishes to the competent authority proof that: (a) A party to the settlement agreement was under some incapacity; (b) The settlement agreement sought to be relied upon: (i) Is null and void, inoperative or incapable of being performed under the law to which the parties have validly subjected it or, failing any indication thereon, under the law deemed applicable by the competent authority; (ii) Is not binding, or is not final, according to its terms; or (iii) Has been subsequently modified; (c) The obligations in the settlement agreement: (i) Have been performed; or (ii) Are not clear or comprehensible; (d) Granting relief would be contrary to the terms of the settlement agreement; (e) There was a serious breach by the mediator of standards applicable to the mediator or the mediation without which breach that party would not have entered into the settlement agreement; or (f) There was a failure by the mediator to disclose to the parties circumstances that raise justifiable doubts as to the mediator's impartiality or independence and such failure to disclose had a material impact or undue influence on a party without which failure that party would not have entered into the settlement agreement. 2. The competent authority of this State may also refuse to grant relief if it finds that: (a) Granting relief would be contrary to the public policy of this State; or (b) The subject matter of the dispute is not capable of settlement by mediation under the law of this State.'

[98] Article 20 of the Mediation Model Law (n 91), which mirrors article 6 of the Singapore Convention (n 93), provides: 'If an application or a claim relating to a settlement agreement has been made to a court, an arbitral tribunal or any other competent authority

Section 3 is more technical, rigid and detailed than the remainder of the Mediation Model Law to ensure that the procedures for the enforcement of settlement agreements have largely the same standards and function within the domestic laws of the adopting states. Adopting states should consequently not be too creative in their enacting process and only make the changes that are essential to make the procedure work effectively within their legal systems.[99]

Unlike the Singapore Convention, which focusses purely on mediated settlement agreements, the Mediation Model Law covers the enforcement of all settlement agreements, regardless of whether they resulted from mediation.[100] The Mediation Model Law provides the legal framework and procedures to implement the Singapore Convention. Apart from ensuring consistency in standards on cross-border enforcement of international mediated settlement agreements, the UNCITRAL Working Group II, in preparing both instruments concurrently, believed that the revised Model Law would be an alternative option for states that may not be ready to ratify the Singapore Convention due to varied levels of experience with mediation.[101]

8.6   The Singapore Convention

From a policy perspective, parties who elect to mediate their disputes should not have to use an additional form of alternative dispute resolution solely to receive the same legal enforcement status as an arbitral award. It may also be indelicate, for business relations, for one party to raise the issue of enhanced enforcement protection with another party with whom they hope to reach an amicable settlement. In mediation, the parties have given up contractual rights in settling, and agreed to both the process and the outcome; this justifies the settlement having a more privileged status than a 'mere' contract. Indeed, it seems ironic that mediated settlements have had a lower legal enforcement status than awards from arbitration – where parties agreed to the process but not the

---

which may affect the relief being sought under article 18, the competent authority of this State where such relief is sought may, if it considers it proper, adjourn the decision and may also, on the request of a party, order the other party to give suitable security.'

[99] While states are encouraged to adopt the Mediation Model Law (n 91) as a whole, it is theoretically possible to adopt it but exclude section 3, and choose their own enforcement regime: see Binder (n 49) 622–23, 632.

[100] See Chapter 2 at Section 2.4.5.

[101] H Abramson, 'New Singapore Convention on Cross-Border Mediated Settlements: Key Choices' in Titi and Fach Gómez (eds) (n 58) 369.

outcome.[102] Putting mediation on an equal footing with arbitration will help to reshape perceptions of the process and support a cultural shift; business also will likely be more willing to invest time and resources in the process where there is an international framework for enforcement.

To address the challenges of cross-border enforcement of mediated settlement agreements, the United Nations Convention on International Settlement Agreements Resulting from Mediation ('Singapore Convention') was adopted by the UN General Assembly on 20 December 2018 after almost three years of deliberations.[103] It was subsequently signed by forty-six states on 7 August 2019 at a ceremony in Singapore. This was the largest number of countries to sign a new convention, and included notably the world's two largest economies, China and the USA. States confirm their consent to be bound by the Convention when they ratify it.[104] The Singapore Convention came into force on 12 September 2020 following ratification by three states.[105] As the product of multilateral consensus, it responds to diverse legal traditions and commercial realities by embodying simplified and streamlined requirements that accommodate the flexible nature of the mediation process.[106] Mediated settlement agreements that qualify for enforcement under the Singapore Convention will be autonomously enforceable internationally, without dependence on domestic contract law or the need to be converted into an arbitral consent award.

---

[102] See T Schnabel, 'The Singapore Convention on Mediation: A Framework for the Cross-Border Recognition and Enforcement of Mediated Settlements' (2019) 19(1) *Pepperdine Dispute Resolution Law Journal* 1, 10–11.

[103] For a discussion on the empirical evidence on the need for the Singapore Convention, see S I Strong, 'Realizing Rationality: An Empirical Assessment of International Commercial Mediation' (2016) 73(4) *Washington and Lee Law Review* 1973.

[104] Singapore Convention (n 93) article 11 refers to 'ratification, acceptance or approval by the signatories' or 'accession by all States that are not signatories'. The latter group refers to states not involved in the negotiations that did not sign the Convention but later acceded. The practical effect of each method is the same. The article also provides: 'Instruments of ratification, acceptance, approval or accession are to be deposited with the depositary.' Article 10 confirms that the Secretary-General of the United Nations is designated depositary of the Convention. Article 15 covers the procedure for proposed amendments, while article 16 covers denunciations by those states wishing to withdraw, which will ordinarily apply twelve months after notice is received.

[105] Singapore Convention (n 93) article 14. The Convention applies to states six months after it is ratified, accepted, approved or acceded to.

[106] N Y Morris-Sharma, 'The Singapore Convention is Live, and Multilateralism, Alive!' in Singapore Mediation Convention Reference Book (2019) 20(4) *Cardozo Journal of Conflict Resolution* 1009, 1011.

The Singapore Convention provides a uniform and efficient framework for the recognition and enforcement of international mediated settlement agreements reached to resolve international commercial disputes. Inspired by the success of the New York Convention, six decades on, the Singapore Convention is expected to be to mediated settlement agreements what the New York Convention is to arbitral awards. It is designed to facilitate international trade and to promote mediation as an effective method of resolving commercial disputes. The lack of a cross-border mechanism to legally enforce mediated settlement agreements was viewed as a significant barrier to the more widespread adoption of the process by the commercial world. Significant time, effort and resources are often required to reach an agreement; if there was a failure to comply, the party requiring compliance would have to invest further time, effort and resources in litigation or arbitration. For many disputes arising out of breach of contract, mediation could prove unenticing if the success of the process resulted in another contract that would require enforcement through normal contract litigation. The Singapore Convention is designed to be a framework that is more efficient than litigation for contract enforcement. It effectively creates a new international legal instrument, elevating an otherwise mere contract to a sui generis status akin to an arbitral award or a judgment, within a legally binding international framework. With the primary objective of incentivising parties to mediate where mediation may not otherwise be attempted, the success of the Singapore Convention will be demonstrated through rarely being invoked, as parties will have complied with the settlements they concluded.[107]

8.6.1 Background

Five key compromises were essential to the Singapore Convention being concluded, and they explain why the Convention is framed the way it is. First, there were divergent views about the use of the term 'recognition' in view of its different meaning in different jurisdictions; a functional description was consequently used instead of the term. Second, there were varied views on the extent to which international mediated settlement agreements that are enforceable as court judgments or consent awards should be included; they were ultimately excluded as these instruments already benefit from expedited enforcement under other conventions. Third, discussions on the extent to which parties to an international

---

[107] See Schnabel (n 102) 1–4, 9–11.

mediated settlement agreement would have to consent for the Singapore Convention to apply resulted in opt-in and opt-out approaches being accommodated. Fourth, views differed on whether certain mediator misconduct defences should be included in the grounds for refusal of relief; they ultimately were included, although framed narrowly and with a high burden of proof. Fifth, there was debate on the form of instrument that would facilitate the enforcement of international commercial mediated settlement agreements – whether a convention or model law was most desirable; a convention and a revised model law that work in confluence emerged from the negotiations.[108]

8.6.2   Application

The Singapore Convention applies to international commercial settlement agreements resulting from mediation.[109] The settlement must have been international when it was concluded, and this will depend on the

---

[108] See K McCormick and S S M Ong, 'Through the Looking Glass: An Insider's Perspective into the Making of the Singapore Convention on Mediation' (2019) 31 *Singapore Academy of Law Journal* 520, 532–46.

[109] Singapore Convention (n 93) article 1 is titled 'Scope of Application' and provides: '1. This Convention applies to an agreement resulting from mediation and concluded in writing by parties to resolve a commercial dispute ("settlement agreement") which, at the time of its conclusion, is international in that: (a) At least two parties to the settlement agreement have their places of business in different States; or (b) The State in which the parties to the settlement agreement have their places of business is different from either: (i) The State in which a substantial part of the obligations under the settlement agreement is performed; or (ii) The State with which the subject matter of the settlement agreement is most closely connected. 2. This Convention does not apply to settlement agreements: (a) Concluded to resolve a dispute arising from transactions engaged in by one of the parties (a consumer) for personal, family or household purposes; (b) Relating to family, inheritance or employment law. 3. This Convention does not apply to: (a) Settlement agreements: (i) That have been approved by a court or concluded in the course of proceedings before a court; and (ii) That are enforceable as a judgment in the State of that court; (b) Settlement agreements that have been recorded and are enforceable as an arbitral award.'
     The Scope of Application includes the exclusions discussed in Section 8.6.3 of this chapter. The definition of 'international' is adapted from article 3.2 of the Mediation Model Law (n 91). While the Model Law permits parties to agree that their mediation is international, under the Singapore Convention the parties must meet the requirements in article 1.1. UNCITRAL does not commission official commentaries or explanatory reports for the treaties it provides, but Schnabel (n 102) gives a comprehensive discussion of the key provisions of the Singapore Convention, based on the negotiation records of the head of the US delegation and the initial proposer and a drafter of the Convention. For an article-by-article discussion of the Convention, including helpful case illustrations, see Alexander and Chong (n 51) 21–190. For an overview of the Convention from

identity of the disputing parties, the requirement being satisfied in most cases by the parties having their places of business in different states. If the place of business of the parties is in the same state, the international requirement can still be satisfied, if that state is different from the state where the obligations of the settlement are to be performed or where the subject matter of the mediated settlement is most closely connected. If a party has more than one place of business, the one most closely connected to the dispute is the relevant one. If a party does not have a place of business, reference should be made to the party's habitual residence. A party's habitual residence may be used where a party has entered into a commercial mediated settlement in a personal capacity.[110]

The focus on international settlements means that states can join the Singapore Convention without having to make significant changes to their existing laws that cover only domestic settlements (although they can choose to extend Convention standards to cover domestic settlements). As many jurisdictions may be involved in an international mediation, especially where a settlement is developed via email, the Singapore Convention does not attempt to incorporate a mediation 'seat' or mediated settlement state of origin. This means that the process and the resulting settlement do not have to comply with domestic legal requirements of any particular state of origin to be protected by the Convention, such as the requirement that particular mediation rules be used. The only domestic requirements that may apply are those that the Convention permits when relief is sought. Similarly, no state has the capacity to set aside the settlement in a way that would be binding on others. The international mediated settlement is effectively a stateless instrument.[111]

---

the perspectives of the various contributors and drafters, see Singapore Mediation Convention Reference Book (2019) 20(4) *Cardozo Journal of Conflict Resolution*.

[110] Singapore Convention (n 93) article 2.1 provides: 'For the purposes of article 1, paragraph 1: (a) If a party has more than one place of business, the relevant place of business is that which has the closest relationship to the dispute resolved by the settlement agreement, having regard to the circumstances known to, or contemplated by, the parties at the time of the conclusion of the settlement agreement; (b) If a party does not have a place of business, reference is to be made to the party's habitual residence.'

[111] This design element was based on the wish to avoid relying on the 'artificial' concept of the place ('seat') of the mediation and its consequences with regard to applicable law. Hence the Convention uses the term 'international' mediated settlement rather than 'foreign'. Without a 'seat' there is no reciprocity from the enforcing court's perspective: see Schnabel (n 102) 20–22. See also Chong and Steffek (n 51) 456. For a discussion on the implementation of the Singapore Convention in the USA, in particular that the fastest and most appropriate approach is to treat it as a self-executing treaty, see

8.6.3 Exclusions

The Singapore Convention excludes settlement agreements relating to consumer transactions or to family, inheritance or employment law. Apart from the Convention's focus on 'commercial disputes', which should be read in a broad manner, the rationale for the exclusion is partly the perception that in these contexts there is more likely to be unequal bargaining power between the parties,[112] and that including protections for such parties would overly complicate the Convention.[113] Unlike the Mediation Model Law, the Singapore Convention does not cover agreements to mediate, recognising that such agreements are not exclusive in nature – unlike arbitration agreements – and that they may not always form the basis for the mediation. If an agreement to mediate does exist, the scope of the agreement is irrelevant for the application of the Convention, and the settlement agreement that results may cover issues outside the scope of the agreement to mediate.[114]

To avoid overlaps, such as parties having two avenues of relief from one settlement agreement, and gaps between this Convention and those that apply to arbitral awards and judgments, the Singapore Convention does not apply to international settlement agreements approved by a court or concluded before a court in the course of proceedings and enforceable as a judgment.[115] Nor does it apply to settlement agreements made enforceable and recorded as an arbitral award. As discussed in Section 8.4, different jurisdictions adopt different approaches to whether a consent award is enforceable under the New York Convention where

---

T Schnabel, 'Implementation of the Singapore Convention: Federalism, Self-Execution, and Private Law Treaties' (2019) 30(2) *American Review of International Arbitration* 265.

[112] See Schnabel (n 102) 24.

[113] E E Deason, 'What's in a Name? The Terms "Commercial" and "Mediation" in the Singapore Convention on Mediation', Singapore Mediation Convention Reference Book (2019) 20(4) *Cardozo Journal of Conflict Resolution* 1149, 1154. This approach also avoids potential conflicts with domestic laws covering the excluded areas.

[114] Excluding agreements to mediate also made it easier to reach consensus on the Singapore Convention. See Schnabel (n 102) 14. Courts routinely enforce mediation clauses, and experience from the USA shows that disputes about contractual obligations to mediate represent a small proportion of mediation-related litigation cases and are declining: see Coben (n 11) 1089–90.

[115] This exclusion was designed to avoid overlap with the two Hague Conference treaties: the 2005 Convention on Choice of Court Agreements and the 2019 Convention on the Recognition and Enforcement of Foreign Judgements in Civil or Commercial Matters.

the mediated settlement is reached before the arbitration begins. Hence, in order to avoid not only an overlap but also a gap between the Singapore and New York Conventions, a mediated settlement converted into an arbitral award must be analysed from the perspective of where enforcement is being sought. Such an award may be excluded from the scope of the Singapore Convention in the jurisdiction where it is converted into an arbitral award, but not be treated as an arbitral award in the state where enforcement is sought.[116]

8.6.4   A Broad Process

Mediation is defined broadly in the Singapore Convention to reflect the flexible nature of the process and only requires that the disputing parties attempt to reach an amicable resolution with the assistance of a third party who lacks the authority to impose a solution.[117] The use of a single term with a broad definition can accommodate variations in processes and the way they are described in various jurisdictions. Hence the intention was not to define any process specifically, but to identify a group of processes and differentiate them from arbitration and negotiation.[118] The last element in the definition does not exclude med-arb, where the mediator subsequently acts as arbitrator, provided they did not have authority to issue an award when acting as a mediator. Conversely, a judge may not act as a mediator if they are charged with ultimately deciding the case, to protect parties from concern that they may be pressured into a settlement. There is no requirement that the mediator be involved for a particular period; the parties could resolve their issues after the involvement of the mediator and their settlement would still qualify as a mediated settlement under the Singapore Convention.[119]

---

[116] This is in contrast to the exclusion of mediated settlements as judgments, where there is some risk of a gap if the settlement agreement is enforceable as a judgment in the state of origin but not in the receiving state: see article 1.3(a); Schnabel (n 102) 25–27.

[117] Singapore Convention (n 93) article 2.3 provides: '"Mediation" means a process, irrespective of the expression used or the basis upon which the process is carried out, whereby parties attempt to reach an amicable settlement of their dispute with the assistance of a third person or persons ("the mediator") lacking the authority to impose a solution upon the parties to the dispute.'

[118] Deason (n 113) 1168–69. Due to this nuanced phrasing, parties do not have to refer to mediation in their agreement to resolve the dispute or their settlement agreement for the Singapore Convention to apply. The definition is focussed on the outcome, not how parties entered the process: see Alexander and Chong (n 51) 57–61.

[119] See Schnabel (n 102) 17.

8.6.5   Enforcement and Recognition

Article 3 of the Singapore Convention, covering enforcement and recognition, is the only provision that imposes positive obligations on states that join the Convention. As 'recognition' means different things in different legal systems and involves different consequences, the drafters avoided using the term; instead they adopted a functional approach, describing aspects of recognition that are required.[120] When asked to do so by a party to a mediated settlement agreement covered by the Singapore Convention, a state that is a party to it must enforce the agreement, which includes affirmatively compelling compliance where a party is in breach. As enforcement mechanisms for mediated settlement agreements vary across jurisdictions, this obligation does not require the use of particular procedures; it simply requires that enforcement takes place, and states may take different approaches in light of their existing procedures.[121] This provision effectively facilitates the direct enforcement of a settlement agreement without the need for prior contractual litigation on the merits or prior transformation of the settlement agreement into a judgment, a notarial act or an arbitral award. In terms of recognition, a settlement agreement covered by the Singapore Convention provides a complete defence to claims based on the underlying dispute.[122]

---

[120] Singapore Convention (n 93) article 3.1 covers enforcement: 'Each Party to the Convention shall enforce a settlement agreement in accordance with its rules of procedure and under the conditions laid down in this Convention.' Article 3.2 covers recognition, but gives a functional description of it without using the term itself: 'If a dispute arises concerning a matter that a party claims was already resolved by a settlement agreement, a Party to the Convention shall allow the party to invoke the settlement agreement in accordance with its rules of procedure and under the conditions laid down in this Convention, in order to prove that the matter has already been resolved.' Article 3.1 can be referred to as the 'sword', where the party seeks enforcement of the settlement agreement, and article 3.2 as the 'shield', where the settlement agreement comprises the defence against a claim related to the settled dispute. As the word 'recognition' was not used in this article, the word 'relief' is used instead to reflect recognition and enforcement in other articles in the Singapore Convention.

[121] Circumventing the fact that enforcement mechanisms for mediated settlement agreements vary across jurisdictions was critical to finalising the Convention as this issue hindered earlier efforts to achieve an enforcement mechanism for cross-border mediated settlement agreements: see E Sussman, 'The Singapore Convention: Promoting the Recognition and Enforcement of International Mediated Settlement Agreements' (2018) 3 *ICC Dispute Resolution Bulletin (Paris)* 42, 51.

[122] See Schnabel (n 102) 37–40. For a comprehensive discussion of this instrumental provision, and the discussions and compromises that led to its inelegant drafting, see T Schnabel, 'Recognition by any Other Name: Article 3 of the Singapore Convention on

8.6.6   Form Requirements

The exhaustive list of three form requirements for a settlement agreement are the threshold requirements to seek enforcement under the Singapore Convention. The agreement must be in writing[123] and signed by the disputing parties, and electronic communications such as an exchange of emails can meet this requirement. There must be evidence that the agreement resulted from mediation, and various forms are acceptable such as an attestation from the institution that administered the mediation.[124] This evidence requirement responds to concern that the Convention could be used for illegitimate or fraudulent purposes, such as illegal schemes like money laundering.[125] Meeting the minimal requirements should also make it easier for parties to obtain relief.

Mediation' in Singapore Mediation Convention Reference Book (2019) 20(4) *Cardozo Journal of Conflict Resolution* 1181.

[123] Singapore Convention (n 93) article 1.1 (reproduced at n 109).

[124] Singapore Convention (n 93) article 4 provides: '1. A party relying on a settlement agreement under this Convention shall supply to the competent authority of the Party to the Convention where relief is sought: (a) The settlement agreement signed by the parties; (b) Evidence that the settlement agreement resulted from mediation, such as: (i) The mediator's signature on the settlement agreement; (ii) A document signed by the mediator indicating that the mediation was carried out; (iii) An attestation by the institution that administered the mediation; or (iv) In the absence of (i), (ii) or (iii), any other evidence acceptable to the competent authority. 2. The requirement that a settlement agreement shall be signed by the parties or, where applicable, the mediator is met in relation to an electronic communication if: (a) A method is used to identify the parties or the mediator and to indicate the parties' or mediator's intention in respect of the information contained in the electronic communication; and (b) The method used is either: (i) As reliable as appropriate for the purpose for which the electronic communication was generated or communicated, in the light of all the circumstances, including any relevant agreement; or (ii) Proven in fact to have fulfilled the functions described in subparagraph (a) above, by itself or together with further evidence. 3. If the settlement agreement is not in an official language of the Party to the Convention where relief is sought, the competent authority may request a translation thereof into such language. 4. The competent authority may require any necessary document in order to verify that the requirements of the Convention have been complied with. 5. When considering the request for relief, the competent authority shall act expeditiously.'

While the list of formalities is exhaustive and cannot be extended, a mediated settlement cannot circumvent domestic law requirements regarding real property transfers or the registration of security interests, where the functioning of public registers must be complied with: see Schnabel (n 102) 33.

[125] Abramson (n 101) 371. Singapore Convention (n 93) article 2.2 further provides: 'A settlement agreement is "in writing" if its content is recorded in any form. The requirement that a settlement agreement be in writing is met by an electronic communication if the information contained therein is accessible so as to be useable for subsequent reference.' Given that the writing requirement in the Singapore Convention covers electronic communications, it can apply to online dispute resolution in cross-border

8.6.7 Refusal of Relief

The Singapore Convention contains an exhaustive list of nine defences or grounds for a competent authority, such as a court, to refuse the recognition and enforcement of a mediated settlement agreement.[126] Some of these grounds echo the New York Convention – namely, incapacity of a party; a settlement agreement that is null and void, inoperative or incapable of being performed; public policy grounds; and the subject matter of the dispute being incapable of settlement by mediation. Concern has been expressed about two of the defences under the Singapore Convention: one that an agreement is 'null and void, inoperative or incapable of being performed under the law to which the parties have validly subjected it';[127] the other that the obligations in the agreement are 'not clear or comprehensible'.[128] The concern is that the defendants may be able to use the defences to transform the new, expedited process under the

---

mediation; this can prove relatively affordable and consequently has the potential to expand access to commercial justice for small to medium businesses in cross-border disputes: see Alexander and Chong (n 51) 48–50, 81–84.

[126] Singapore Convention (n 93) article 5 provides: '1. The competent authority of the Party to the Convention where relief is sought under article 4 may refuse to grant relief at the request of the party against whom the relief is sought only if that party furnishes to the competent authority proof that: (a) A party to the settlement agreement was under some incapacity; (b) The settlement agreement sought to be relied upon: (i) Is null and void, inoperative or incapable of being performed under the law to which the parties have validly subjected it or, failing any indication thereon, under the law deemed applicable by the competent authority of the Party to the Convention where relief is sought under article 4; (ii) Is not binding, or is not final, according to its terms; or (iii) Has been subsequently modified; (c) The obligations in the settlement agreement: (i) Have been performed; or (ii) Are not clear or comprehensible; (d) Granting relief would be contrary to the terms of the settlement agreement; (e) There was a serious breach by the mediator of standards applicable to the mediator or the mediation without which breach that party would not have entered into the settlement agreement; or (f) There was a failure by the mediator to disclose to the parties circumstances that raise justifiable doubts as to the mediator's impartiality or independence and such failure to disclose had a material impact or undue influence on a party without which failure that party would not have entered into the settlement agreement. 2. The competent authority of the Party to the Convention where relief is sought under article 4 may also refuse to grant relief if it finds that: (a) Granting relief would be contrary to the public policy of that Party; or (b) The subject matter of the dispute is not capable of settlement by mediation under the law of that Party.'

[127] Singapore Convention (n 93) article 5.1(b)(i) (reproduced at n 126). This provision reflects the common grounds that render a contract void or voidable. These include duress, unconscionability, undue influence, misrepresentation, mistake, deceit, and fraud, which could have a material effect on consent and, in turn, the mediated settlement agreement.

[128] Singapore Convention (n 93) article 5.1(c)(ii) (reproduced at n 126).

Singapore Convention into a more protracted and expensive process, as previously existed.[129] It is to be hoped that courts will narrowly construe these and other defences, and experience from the USA offers encouraging evidence that litigation about enforcement of mediated settlement agreements is declining.[130]

It is likely that state courts will be guided by existing arbitral jurisprudence in determining whether the public policy grounds should apply or if the subject matter of the dispute was incapable of settlement by mediation,[131] and most courts have adopted a narrow interpretation.[132] The prevailing view is that courts have adopted a narrow interpretation of international or transnational public policy as distinct from domestic public policy in order to recognise and enforce arbitral awards.[133] It is likely that courts or other competent authorities would only refuse to enforce international mediated settlement agreements for public policy reasons under the Singapore Convention in exceptional circumstances, and similarly would refuse relief where the subject matter of the dispute

---

[129] Abramson (n 101) 371–72.

[130] From the available empirical evidence, disputes about enforcement of mediated settlements constituted 47 per cent of cases involving disputed mediation issues between 1999 and 2003 and 39 per cent between 2013 and 2017. Between 2013 and 2017, the overall average enforcement rate was 69 per cent, while alleging mediator misconduct as a defence to enforcement failed 100 per cent of the time, unconscionability claims were rejected in 93 per cent of cases, duress defences were rejected in 88 per cent of cases, incapacity claims were rejected in 87 per cent of cases and fraud defences were marginally different with an enforcement rate of 86 per cent: see Coben (n 11) 1073–74, 1083–84.

[131] The subject matter of the dispute may be incapable of settlement by mediation where the relevant law requires that the underlying dispute be subject to mandatory adjudicatory processes.

[132] The standard for the defences should be comparable to those in the New York Convention (n 56) and the Arbitration Model Law (n 65): see UNCITRAL, 'Report of Working Group II (Arbitration and Conciliation) on the Work of its Sixty-Seventh Session' (Vienna, 2–6 October 2017), A/CN.9/929, (11 October 2017) para 100.

[133] H Kronke, 'Introduction: The New York Convention Fifty Years On: Overview and Assessment' in H Kronke and others (eds), *Recognition and Enforcement of Foreign Arbitral Awards: A Global Commentary on the New York Convention* (Alphen aan den Rijn, Kluwer Law International 2010) 17–18; D Otto and O Elwana, 'Article V(2)' in Kronke and others (eds) at 365–67. In France, for example, foreign or international consent awards are enforceable, but domestic consent awards are not. Domestic consent awards are viewed as mere declaratory measures, and the act of recording a settlement without the arbitrator giving reasons does not constitute an adjudicative act: see MYS c Société BC, Cour de cassation [French Court of Cassation], 14 November 2012, 138 (a decision that has been characterised as the 'death sentence' for domestic consent awards in France): Marchisio (n 78) 342–43.

was incapable of settlement by mediation where statutory provisions clearly forbid it.[134]

There are two grounds for refusal specific to mediator misconduct. One is a serious breach by the mediator of applicable standards without which the party would not have agreed to the settlement.[135] The other is a failure to disclose circumstances that raise justifiable doubts about the mediator's impartiality or independence, and this failure of disclosure had a material impact or undue influence on a party that led them to enter into the settlement agreement.[136] If the US experience is indicative, these two grounds are largely symbolic as the prospect of a successful action seems quite remote, particularly in the context of commercial disputes where the parties are likely to be legally represented.[137]

Other grounds for refusal are: the settlement agreement is not binding or not final according to its terms; the settlement agreement has been subsequently modified; obligations in the agreement have been performed or are unclear or incomprehensible; or granting relief would be contrary to the terms of the settlement agreement.[138] Where

---

[134] See Schnabel (n 102) 54–55.
[135] Singapore Convention (n 93) article 5.1(e) (reproduced at n 126).
[136] Singapore Convention (n 93) article 5.1(f) (reproduced at n 126).
[137] See also Coben (n 11) 1099, see also n 130. See also Chapter 5 at Section 5.7.10.
[138] Singapore Convention (n 93) article 5.1(b)(ii)–(d) (reproduced at n 126). A court can raise the public policy defence or that the subject matter of the dispute was incapable of settlement by mediation of its own motion. For all of the other grounds, the burden is on the party opposing recognition and enforcement to prove the relevant defence. By placing the burden on the party opposing recognition and enforcement, the Singapore Convention reverses the pre-existing position where a party seeking enforcement would have to prove they had an enforceable settlement agreement. Due to the varying approaches to privilege and confidentiality, the ability to prove claims under article 5 will vary across jurisdictions: see M Kallipetis, 'Singapore Convention Defences Based on Mediator's Misconduct: Articles 5.1(e) and (f)', Singapore Mediation Convention Reference Book (2019) 20(4) *Cardozo Journal of Conflict Resolution* 1197. There is a degree of overlap between different grounds for refusing relief under article 5, and this concern was discussed by delegates in the negotiations that led to the Singapore Convention. Various attempts at regrouping the grounds in article 5 had been unsuccessful. A suggestion was made to add a new paragraph in article 5 aimed at providing guidance to competent authorities when considering the different grounds, which read: 'The competent authority, in interpreting and applying the various grounds for refusing requested relief under paragraph 5(1), may take into account that the grounds for such refusal identified under paragraph 5(1)(b) may overlap with other grounds for refusal in paragraph 5(1).' While the proposal was not accepted, it is included in the reported discussions and can offer guidance to courts and be taken into account when interpreting the various grounds: see UNCITRAL, 'Report of Working Group II (Dispute Settlement) on the Work of its Sixty-Eighth Session (New York, 5–9 February 2018)', A/CN.9/934 (19 February 2018) paras 61–65.

a mediated settlement is not final or binding according to its terms, a court cannot look outside the settlement agreement itself to determine whether it may not be final or binding. The prohibition on relief for an agreement that is subsequently modified simply ensures that it is the final version of the agreement that is enforceable. The requirement that the obligations have not been performed ensures that a court does not order duplicate relief. Where the obligations are unclear or incomprehensible, the court will not know how to apply them. Prohibiting relief where it would be contrary to the terms of the settlement agreement preserves the autonomy of the parties.

If parties make a choice of law that is valid under the law of the state where relief is sought, the choice will be effective; otherwise, that state's private international law rules will apply to determine the applicable law.[139] Limiting the grounds for refusal is intended to bar the use of defences based on domestic legal requirements such as requirements that mediators must be licensed in a particular jurisdiction, or that mediation must be subject to certain institutional rules, or that settlements must be notarised or meet other formal requirements outside Singapore Convention requirements.[140] This is a prudent approach, as technical formalities and procedural hoops are a growth area in the USA for mediation-related litigation.[141] The grounds for refusal are permissive, not mandatory: a court can elect to provide relief even if an exception might apply.[142] If the Singapore Convention is implemented through legislation in a particular state, the state is not obliged to permit courts to use all the grounds for refusal.[143]

---

[139] See Chong and Steffek (n 111) 478–84 for a discussion on the choice of law issues that arise when courts are asked to consider article 5 grounds for refusal.

[140] See Schnabel (n 102) 44–45.

[141] See Coben (n 11) 1097.

[142] Experience from arbitration suggests that such discretion will be exercised within narrow circumstances. For a discussion on the discretion that jurists exercise in the context of the grounds for refusal of recognition and enforcement of arbitral awards under article 5 of the New York Convention (n 56), gleaned from an analysis of cases reported in English (in particular English decisions) and leading academic commentary, see J Hill, 'The Exercise of Judicial Discretion in Relation to Applications to Enforce Arbitral Awards under the New York Convention 1958' (2016) 36(2) *Oxford Journal of Legal Studies* 304.

[143] See Schnabel (n 102) 42. There are two other areas where the application of the Singapore Convention can be affected. Article 12.1–12.3 establishes how a regional economic integration organisation (REIO), such as the European Union, may become a party to the Convention. Under article 12.4, the internal rules applied by the REIO take precedence over the Convention in limited situations. If relief under the Singapore

Apart from the nine defences or grounds for a court or other competent authority to refuse to recognise and enforce a mediated settlement agreement, discussed above, domestic courts have a discretion to adjourn a decision and to order security where the decision of another court or arbitral tribunal may affect the relief sought. This discretion applies both when enforcement is sought and when a settlement agreement is invoked as a defence.[144] This relates to a situation where parties apply for enforcement or recognition of a mediated settlement to courts in two or more states in parallel proceedings. Where there is a challenge in the first court, the second (or any additional) court may adjourn the recognition or enforcement proceedings and may also – on the request of a party – order the other party to the settlement to furnish suitable security. It has been suggested that this provision creates an implied ground for refusal of enforcement where a judgment refusing enforcement of a mediated settlement in the state of the first court (due, for example, to incapacity of the parties or misconduct by the mediator) is recognised in the courts of adjourning states.[145]

The Singapore Convention does not affect the right of any party to avail itself of a settlement agreement under the laws or treaties of the state where the settlement agreement is being relied upon. It effectively preserves the parties' right to enforce their mediated settlement agreement under a different enforcement regime, such as national law or an alternative treaty. The parties may elect to do this where it would provide a more favourable outcome.[146]

Convention is sought, and a REIO state grants a judgment, other states in that REIO must recognise the judgment rather than simply apply the Convention. Under article 13.1, a state that has two or more territorial units in which different legal systems apply can declare that the Singapore Convention extends to one or more of them, but such an exclusion will only affect the courts in that unit applying the Convention when relief is sought. The Singapore Convention will still apply to parties who have their place of business in that unit, as long as the settlement qualifies as international: see Schnabel (n 102) 58–59.

[144] Singapore Convention (n 93) article 6 provides: 'If an application or a claim relating to a settlement agreement has been made to a court, an arbitral tribunal or any other competent authority which may affect the relief being sought under article 4, the competent authority of the Party to the Convention where such relief is sought may, if it considers it proper, adjourn the decision and may also, on the request of a party, order the other party to give suitable security.'

[145] See Chong and Steffek (n 111) 477.

[146] Singapore Convention (n 93) article 7 provides: 'This Convention shall not deprive any interested party of any right it may have to avail itself of a settlement agreement in the manner and to the extent allowed by the law or the treaties of the Party to the Convention where such settlement agreement is sought to be relied upon.'

8.6.8 Reservations

While the Singapore Convention in the normal course will automatically apply once it has ratified, a state party can opt out of its automatic application by making a reservation, effectively defining the extent to which the Convention will be applied by its courts. Consequently, a state party can provide that the Singapore Convention will not apply to settlement agreements to which it – or any government, governmental agency or any person acting on behalf of a government agency – is a party. Similarly, a state can make a reservation to the effect that the Singapore Convention will only apply to private parties if they elect to opt in to the Convention's application.[147] The latter reservation if used would have significant implications as it would require commercial parties to opt in for the Singapore Convention to apply, which may not occur in practice.

No other reservations are permitted. Reservations have no reciprocal effect and apply only to the courts in the state that required them. Reservations may be lodged or withdrawn by a state at any time, but if either takes place after a state joins the Singapore Convention, there is a six-month delay before it takes effect. This provides certainty in the use

---

[147] Singapore Convention (n 93) article 8 provides: '1. A Party to the Convention may declare that: (a) It shall not apply this Convention to settlement agreements to which it is a party, or to which any governmental agencies or any person acting on behalf of a governmental agency is a party, to the extent specified in the declaration; (b) It shall apply this Convention only to the extent that the parties to the settlement agreement have agreed to the application of the Convention. 2. No reservations are permitted except those expressly authorized in this article. 3. Reservations may be made by a Party to the Convention at any time. Reservations made at the time of signature shall be subject to confirmation upon ratification, acceptance or approval. Such reservations shall take effect simultaneously with the entry into force of this Convention in respect of the Party to the Convention concerned. Reservations made at the time of ratification, acceptance or approval of this Convention or accession thereto, or at the time of making a declaration under article 13 shall take effect simultaneously with the entry into force of this Convention in respect of the Party to the Convention concerned. Reservations deposited after the entry into force of the Convention for that Party to the Convention shall take effect six months after the date of the deposit. 4. Reservations and their confirmations shall be deposited with the depositary. 5. Any Party to the Convention that makes a reservation under this Convention may withdraw it at any time. Such withdrawals are to be deposited with the depositary, and shall take effect six months after deposit.'
Singapore Convention (n 93) article 9 provides: 'The Convention and any reservation or withdrawal thereof shall apply only to settlement agreements concluded after the date when the Convention, reservation or withdrawal thereof enters into force for the Party to the Convention concerned.'

of the mechanism and avoids the potential for 'strategic' use or abuse of the Singapore Convention by states to avoid the obligation to enforce a settlement agreement where they are a party.[148]

The decision not to adopt an opt-in approach, coupled with the minimal form requirements outlined above, effectively reflects a default approach that assumes parties want their agreements to be enforceable. This should prove helpful in reducing post-mediation litigation, in light of the recent US litigation experience indicating that procedural and jurisdiction defences are becoming more common.[149]

8.6.9   Future of the Singapore Convention

The Singapore Convention facilitates parties who have concluded an international mediated settlement agreement that complies with the requirements discussed in this section[150] to seek relief in the court of a state where enforcement is sought to either directly enforce the agreement or use it as a complete defence to litigation or arbitration commencing where issues already resolved and contained within the agreement are contested.[151] As there is no 'seat', there is no need for a review in the country where the settlement was concluded. A court review will only take place in the state where enforcement is sought.

Careful and comprehensive drafting of settlement agreements incorporating all the intended commercial terms will be critical to ensure that

---

[148] See I Apter and C H Muchnik, 'Reservations in the Singapore Convention: Helping to Make the New York Dream Come True', Singapore Mediation Convention Reference Book (2019) 20(4) *Cardozo Journal of Conflict Resolution* 1267, 1279–80. There are concerns about states being a party to a mediated settlement, including transparency and the public interest, that would need to be addressed: see C Titi, 'Mediation and the Settlement of International Investment Disputes: Between Utopia and Realism' in Titi and Fach Gómez (eds) (n 58) 35–38.

[149] From the available empirical evidence, the lowest enforcement rate is where parties raised procedural or jurisdictional arguments in cases involving disputed mediation issues. Between 2013 and 2017, procedural/jurisdictional arguments were the most successful basis for attacking mediated settlements, with an enforcement rate of just 53 per cent, well below the 69 per cent average rate discussed at n 130: see Coben (n 11) 1066, 1084, 1090.

[150] The mediated settlement agreement must fall within the Singapore Convention (n 93) article 1 and article 2 scope and definition requirements, not be barred by the article 1.2 and 1.3 exclusions, satisfy the article 4 procedural requirements, not come within the article 5 grounds for refusal of relief and not be adversely affected by any article 8 reservations lodged by the enforcing state.

[151] Relief may be sought in the form of enforcement under Singapore Convention (n 93) article 3.1 and recognition under article 3.2.

settlement agreements receive the benefit of enforcement in any Singapore Convention state. As noted previously, enforcement of settlement agreements is not a significant issue in international commercial dispute resolution.[152] Consequently, the greatest impact of the Singapore Convention may be to give international acceptability, legitimacy and credibility to mediation as a process to resolve commercial disputes, alongside litigation and arbitration, particularly in respect of the enforcement of the outcome of the process. In view of this, the Convention may also have a secondary effect of influencing, or encouraging, the enactment of domestic mediation legislation and soft legal instruments, and the development of institutional capacity within states to serve as an international hub for the mediation of commercial disputes.

The fact that the Singapore Convention began with forty-six signatories augurs well for its future. The New York Convention, which has been in force for over 60 years, has over 160 contracting states and continues to attract new signatories, but it began with just 10 signatories. The Singapore Convention will give the international commercial mediation process regulatory robustness, credibility and visibility. It has broken new ground by elevating international mediated settlement agreements to a new status that can be recognised and enforced within the framework of private international law. However, experience with international commercial arbitration suggests that it will take some time for the cultural shift that will make the process a primary player in the international dispute resolution arena. Much may depend on whether state parties use the opt-in reservation[153] and whether courts, when requested to apply the instrument, adopt a robust interpretive approach similar to that generally applied in the arbitral context.[154]

8.7   Concluding Thoughts

Careful and comprehensive drafting incorporating all the intended commercial terms is critical to ensure that mediated settlement agreements are complete and enforceable. There are many steps the mediator and

---

[152] See generally R Feehily, 'The Legal Status and Enforceability of Mediated Settlement Agreements' (2013) 12(1) *Hibernian Law Journal* 1; Feehily (n 65). Some have questioned whether there is a need for the Singapore Convention: see, e.g., B Clark and T Sourdin, 'The Singapore Convention: A Solution in Search of a Problem?' (2020) 71(3) *Northern Ireland Legal Quarterly* 481.
[153] Article 8.1(b) (reproduced at n 147).
[154] See Alexander and Chong (n 51) 18–19, 74; Strong (n 103) 55.

legal advisors to the parties can take to provide certainty and support enforcement. However, it is important to bear in mind that the enforcement of settlement agreements is not a significant issue in international commercial dispute resolution. Where compliance may be an issue, the Singapore Convention offers an alternative enforcement option to converting the settlement into an arbitral award or court judgment, effectively elevating international mediated settlement agreements to a new status that can be recognised and enforced within the framework of private international law. Time will tell whether the Singapore Convention becomes to mediated settlement agreements what the New York Convention is to arbitral awards. In the interim it will serve to raise the international profile of the mediation process, giving it increased credibility and visibility and the promise of greater regulatory robustness.

9

Confidentiality

9.1 Introduction

Mediation confidentiality is often characterised as the cornerstone of the mediation process. The legal protection of mediation evidence can emanate from common law privilege, contract and statute. If comprehensive statutory protection is available, parties may not have to protect from disclosure mediation evidence in their contract or rely on common law privilege with its various exceptions. While a balance is required between supporting mediation and not freezing litigation or upholding illegality, this balance is not easy to achieve. The approach of making mediation confidentiality 'absolute' appears to create straightforward rules for an informal process, but it can prove to be either overreaching or inappropriate. While uniform laws offer consistency, experience indicates that they fail to gain sufficient traction or acceptability to have widespread impact. While mediation confidentiality must be protected, it is important that courts retain the power to admit mediation evidence in appropriate circumstances.

9.2 Confidentiality in Commercial Mediation

Confidentiality is often characterised as the cornerstone of mediation.[1] Confidentiality makes the mediation process attractive to potential users as it insulates them from negative publicity, protects them from disclosures subsequently being used against them and encourages settlement by providing the parties with a safe space to share their needs and interests and ultimately solve problems collaboratively. The integrity and reputation of mediation and mediators are also protected, and the impartiality of mediators is reinforced as confidentiality reduces

---

[1] See, e.g., R Kulms, 'Privatising Civil Justice and the Day in Court' in K Hopt and F Steffek (eds), *Mediation: Principles and Regulation in Comparative Perspective* (Oxford, Oxford University Press 2013) 228.

the pressure on them to make post-mediation disclosures. Confidentiality in the context of mediation operates on a number of levels. It can cover the information shared in the private caucus sessions between the mediator and each party, where parties are encouraged to be open and honest in a safe environment where only the mediator is constrained, and the relevant party can waive their rights to confidentiality. It can also cover the entire mediation process, preventing public disclosures and excluding the admissibility of mediation evidence in legal or arbitral proceedings. Confidentiality imposes obligations on both the mediator and the parties. One of the most important issues affecting the confidentiality of the mediation process is the extent to which mediation evidence can be used in a simultaneous or later arbitral, judicial or administrative proceeding. In practice, mediation is not always as confidential as it is often claimed to be.[2]

Parties are often unaware of the scope of the confidentiality protection they are entitled to in a mediation. In international disputes, parties frequently overlook the impact of the procedural rules that will govern proceedings if the mediation fails. If these procedural rules permit limited discovery in subsequent proceedings, maintaining strict confidentiality of information shared during mediation will be particularly important.[3]

In determining whether a mediated settlement agreement should be enforced, the courts in the USA have investigated what happens during the mediation process.[4] While the courts will not need to look to evidence outside the contract for interpretive purposes where there is no ambiguity, an investigation of the mediation process is likely to be required to

---

[2] L Boulle, *Mediation: Principles, Process, Practice* (3rd ed, Chatswood, NSW, LexisNexis 2011) 671–74; N Alexander, *International and Comparative Mediation: Legal Perspectives* (Austin, Wolters Kluwer 2009) 245–51. Confidentiality issues may be determined *in camera* (in the judge's private chamber) to ensure that the information is not compromised by being heard in open court. This is provided for in the USA in s 6 of the Uniform Mediation Act, and in England in the Civil Procedure Rules part 39.2(3)(c) and (g) where deemed necessary in the interests of justice: see Alexander at 256, 281.

[3] E Fiechter, 'Mediation: Confidentiality and Enforcement Issues and Solutions', IBA Legal Practice Division Mediation Committee Newsletter, April 2005, 45, 46. In England and in some US states, for example, evidence will be discovered well before trial during disclosure of documents and opinion evidence, and this evidence consequently will not require the same degree of protection as other types of shared information such as offers and counter-offers made during the mediation process reflecting the parties' willingness to compromise: see T Allen, *Mediation Law and Civil Practice* (2nd ed, Haywards Heath, Bloomsbury Professional 2019) 244.

[4] See Chapter 8 at Section 8.2.

determine whether an oral contract exists where there is no written agreement, and to review situations where ambiguities are claimed to clarify their meaning. The various contract law defences to enforcement of mediated settlement agreements, such as duress, lack of capacity, lack of authority, mistake and fraud, are all largely determined by what happened at the mediation. Both courts and policy makers have struggled to strike the appropriate balance between assessing what took place during a mediation to understand claims that parties have made, and protecting mediation confidentiality. Identifying the relevant circumstances and the types of evidence permitted, including the extent of mediator testimony, have all been central causes of concern.[5]

Laws in the USA preclude broad categories of post-mediation enforcement disputes, limit the scope of other disputes, and help mediators and participants develop practices that also reduce areas of potential enforcement conflict. The disputes that remain require the courts to strike a careful balance between the need for evidence to assess the claims made and the need for mediation confidentiality.[6] While an appreciation of the importance of mediation confidentiality would appear to be universal, court decisions in the USA cover the entire spectrum of attitudes. For example, courts have allowed limited disclosure of mediation communications based on a requirement for the evidence, found waivers of confidentiality because of the nature of the claims made, barred all evidence relating to mediation communications, ignored mediation confidentiality, and dealt with the issue as if it were any other contract with relevant evidence gleaned from all available sources, despite statutory protection of mediation confidentiality in some cases.[7]

9.3   Two Competing Public Policies

Determining the extent of confidentiality in mediation involves balancing two competing public policy interests. One is the interest in promoting and encouraging the settlement of disputes outside the court system and in

---

[5] Regarding the US experience, see E Sussman, 'A Brief Survey of US Case Law on Enforcing Mediation Settlement Agreements over Objections to the Existence or Validity of Such Agreements and Implications for Mediation Confidentiality and Mediator Testimony', IBA Legal Practice Division Mediation Committee Newsletter, April 2006, 35.
[6] See Sussman (n 5) 38. This is also the approach in other countries: see K Hopt and F Steffek, 'Mediation: Comparison of Laws, Regulatory Models, Fundamental Issues' in Hopt and Steffek (eds) (n 1) 50–51.
[7] See Sussman (n 5) 35.

protecting processes such as mediation that facilitate and support this policy. This was summed up by the High Court of Australia in *Field v. Commissioner of Railways (NSW)*, where the majority of the Court stated:

> The law relating to communications without prejudice is of course familiar. As a matter of policy the law has long excluded from evidence admissions by words or conduct made by parties in the course of negotiations to settle litigation. The purpose is to enable parties engaged in an attempt to compromise litigation to communicate with one another freely and without the embarrassment which the liability of their communications to be put in evidence subsequently might impose upon them.[8]

The other public policy interest is the interest in courts and tribunals having access to evidence regardless of what has transpired in mediation. This was referred to by Rogers CJ in *AWA Ltd v. Daniels (t/a Deloitte Haskins & Sells)*, who stated:

> [A]s a matter of principle it would be entirely too easy to sterilise other admissible, objective, evidence simply by saying something about it in the course of Mediation ... That of course is not to be contemplated.[9]

While the principle of freedom to contract supports the maintenance of confidentiality as prescribed by the parties, if it is too wide it will sterilise too much evidence and seriously undermine the litigation or arbitral process. If mediation confidentiality is too narrow, it will discourage parties from entering mediation and from using their best endeavours to settle through the process. A balance is required between supporting mediation and not freezing or frustrating litigation or upholding illegality, and the courts are required to weigh up the two competing public policies in deciding whether to allow or prevent disclosure of mediation evidence.[10]

9.4 Approaches to Protecting Mediation Evidence

9.4.1 Common Law Privileges

The most obvious way the law may attempt to protect mediation information is by creating a privilege.

---

[8] [1957] 99 CLR 285, 291.
[9] (1992) 7 ACSR 463, 468.
[10] See Boulle (n 2) 714; Alexander (n 2) 280–85. See also R Feehily, 'Confidentiality in Commercial Mediation: A Fine Balance (Part 1)' (2015) 3 *Journal of South African Law/ Tydskrif vir die Suid-Afrikaanse Reg* 516–36; R Feehily, 'Confidentiality in Commercial Mediation: A Fine Balance (Part 2)' (2015) 4 *Journal of South African Law/Tydskrif vir die Suid-Afrikaanse Reg* 719–37.

9.4.1.1 'Without Prejudice' Privilege

Where settlement is not reached, evidence of oral or written offers or admissions made in good faith to reach a settlement are inadmissible in subsequent litigation relating to the dispute. This rule is predicated on the policy that the law should encourage disputing parties to negotiate freely and based on the parties' implied intentions.[11] The 'without prejudice' privilege applies regardless of whether litigation has commenced or if the parties expressly provided that their negotiations are without prejudice.[12] It can be expressly or impliedly waived by the parties, and the mediator has no common law right to veto disclosure. Disclosure of privileged information to a mediator is not a waiver as it would be to a court or tribunal during a hearing. A court can order disclosure in appropriate circumstances, where a statutory or common law exception requires it, such as for reasons of public policy, reasons of criminality or because disclosure is outside the scope of dispute. For example, information that can be independently evidenced before a court or tribunal, such as an unqualified admission concerning objective facts, will not be excluded simply because it was disclosed in a mediation. Australian courts have confirmed that the 'without prejudice' privilege applies to mediation,[13] even where the process is employed to reduce the scope of litigation and only for resolving part of a dispute.[14] Where 'without prejudice' negotiations result in a settlement, evidence of agreements and statements made are subsequently admissible in arbitral or judicial proceedings.[15] Consequently, at common law, consistent with the policy favouring the enforcement of settlement agreements, a settlement reached following 'without prejudice' negotiations can be pleaded and proved for enforcement purposes.[16]

---

[11] See also B Thanki (ed), *The Law of Privilege* (3rd ed, Oxford, Oxford University Press 2018) 312–24. The rationale for the privilege was elucidated by Oliver LJ in *Cutts* v. *Head* [1984] Ch 290, 306: 'It is that parties should be encouraged so far as possible to settle their disputes without resort to litigation and should not be discouraged by the knowledge that anything that is said in the course of such negotiations (and that includes, of course, as much the failure to reply to an offer as an actual reply) may be used to their prejudice in the course of proceedings.'

[12] See, e.g., *Rush & Tompkins Ltd* v. *Greater London Council* [1989] 1 AC 1280.

[13] *AWA* (n 9).

[14] *Lukies* v. *Ripley (No 2)* (1994) 35 NSWLR 283.

[15] *Biala Pty Ltd* v. *Mallina Holdings Ltd* [1989] 15 ACLR 208.

[16] See Boulle (n 2) 674–78; L Boulle and M Nesic, *Mediation: Principles, Process, Practice* (London, Butterworths Law 2001) 491–95. Similarly, agreements to mediate would not normally be covered, subject to agreement to the contrary: see Alexander (n 2) 248.

In the normal course, it is only where all the parties to a mediation agree to waive the privilege that a court can access the information.[17] However, there are numerous exceptions to the 'without prejudice' privilege, where the court will admit evidence despite opposition from a party.[18] For example, the court may admit 'without prejudice' communications to determine whether they led to an agreement.[19] Allegations of misrepresentation, fraud, undue influence and duress can result in the court admitting such evidence.[20] A party may be able to call evidence to establish that they relied on a 'without prejudice' statement to their detriment, and enforce their right to what they relied upon, on the basis of an estoppel.[21] An act or statement amounting to 'unambiguous impropriety', such as threats that induce settlement, can result in the privilege being lost, and the courts take a restrictive approach when applying this exception focussing in particular on whether the privilege was abused.[22] The court may also wish to admit evidence to investigate delay where a failure to engage is claimed: for example, to prove the fact that communications have not ceased.

As noted above, evidence will be admitted where a waiver of 'without prejudice' privilege is asserted. The privilege may also be set aside to determine the costs order that should be made where 'without prejudice except as to costs' was used by the parties. Where there was no existing dispute for the privilege to protect communications, it will not apply. Admission of statements as evidence that they were made may also be a basis for setting aside the privilege, but again a restrictive approach is

---

[17] See *Malmesbury* v. *Strutt & Parker* [2008] EWHC 424 (QB) [24] (Jack J): 'I record here that it has been agreed that privilege shall be waived in respect of all "without prejudice" matters.'

[18] In the English case *Unilever plc* v. *The Proctor & Gamble Company* [1999] EWCA Civ 3027, Walker LJ at [23] summarised seven exceptions, to which three further exceptions have been added: see Allen (n 3) 214–21. See also Thanki (ed) (n 11) 324–30; S Blake, J Browne and S Sime, *The Jackson ADR Handbook* (2nd ed, Oxford, Oxford University Press 2016) 54–58, 163–66.

[19] See *Brown* v. *Rice* [2007] EWHC 625 (Ch) (discussed in text at n 33).

[20] See, in Australia, Evidence Act 1995 (Cth) s 131(2). Australian courts have found exceptions for misrepresentation, in *Williams* v. *Commonwealth Bank* [1999] NSWCA 345, and for unconscionability, in *Abriel v Australian Guarantee Corp Ltd* [2000] FCA 1198: see Alexander (n 2) 270.

[21] The privilege must also not be abused for the purpose of misleading the court: see the Australian case *McFadden* v. *Snow* (1952) 69 WN (NSW) 8. See also Alexander (n 2) 268.

[22] In *Unilever* (n 18), a threat to enforce a patent right was deemed reasonably justifiable, while in *Ferster* v. *Ferster* [2016] EWCA Civ 717, an email that the Court characterised as blackmail was admitted into evidence.

likely.[23] Facts that are identified during a negotiation that led to a settlement may also be admitted into evidence where they may assist in understanding the true meaning of the negotiated settlement.[24]

In general, the courts in England[25] are reluctant to investigate what happens during the mediation process. As Dyson LJ remarked in the leading English case of *Halsey* v. *Milton Keynes NHS Trust*:

> We make it clear at the outset that it was common ground before us (and we accept) that parties are entitled in an ADR to adopt whatever position they wish, and if as a result the dispute is not settled, that is not a matter for the court. As is submitted by the Law Society, if the integrity and confidentiality of the process is to be respected, the court should not know, and therefore should not investigate, why the process did not result in agreement.[26]

---

[23] The evidence is merely that certain statements were made and does not go to proof of admission against interest: see *Ofulue* v. *Bossert* [2009] UKHL 16 where Lord Hope held at [26] that the 'without prejudice' rule cannot extend 'to cover a statement of fact that, far from being an issue in the litigation, is common to the pleaded cases of both parties. Whether or not such a statement can sensibly be regarded as an 'admission', it cannot be described as an admission against interest'. This exception is helpful to third parties to mediation such as subcontractors who were not party to the original dispute but want to access information from a mediation to justify their own settlement proposals. Lord Neuberger also noted at [98] that a restrictive approach should be adopted with regard to the 'without prejudice' rule to avoid 'hampering the freedom parties should feel when entering into settlement negotiations'. See Alexander (n 2) 268; Blake, Browne and Sime (n 18) 51.

[24] The UK Supreme Court confirmed in *Oceanbulk Shipping & Trading SA* v. *TMT Asia Ltd* [2010] UKSC 44 that 'without prejudice' negotiations can be used to establish relevant background facts that assist in the interpretive exercise. The main difficulty with this approach lies in determining whether evidence of pre-contractual negotiations is being elicited to prove a fact which is objectively known to the parties, or to establish the meaning of the contract. Only the former is admissible as part of the relevant background used in the interpretive exercise. The courts have acknowledged that the line between what is admissible and inadmissible regarding pre-contractual negotiations is 'so fine it almost vanishes': see *Excelsior Group Productions Ltd* v. *Yorkshire Television Ltd* [2009] EWHC 1751 (Comm) [25]. The practical consequence is that the relationship between interpretation and rectification is growing even closer, and the relationship between the two doctrines requires greater clarification from the courts: see P S Davies, 'Negotiating the Boundaries of Admissibility' (2011) 70(1) *Cambridge Law Journal* 24. In addition to enforcing a settlement, this exception could be used where a party seeks to set aside a settlement agreement, as in the Australian case *Quad Consulting Pty Ltd* v. *David R Bleakley & Associates Pty Ltd* (1990) 98 ALR 659 on the basis of misleading conduct: see Alexander (n 2) 268–70.

[25] For simplicity the term 'England' is used throughout this book to describe the jurisdiction of England and Wales.

[26] [2004] EWCA Civ 576 [14] (Dyson LJ). See also *Swampillai* v. *Joseph* [2015] EWCA Civ 261, where Briggs LJ upheld the decision of the trial judge not to admit a 'mediator's note' because nothing at the mediation should be referred to in court.

The English courts will admit evidence of a failure to mediate and not treat the pre-mediation period as privileged, unless communications during this period are specifically made 'without prejudice'.[27] There are a number of cases where judges have received evidence about what happened at a mediation with the parties' consent to determine the issue of costs.[28] In *Chantrey Vellacott* v. *The Convergence Group plc,*[29] the defendants had lost at trial, and the claimants sought an order for their costs of an unsuccessful mediation attempted three years earlier. In making his decision, the judge received evidence regarding offers exchanged at the mediation and awarded the claimants their mediation costs due to the defendants' intransigence and unrealistic position both during the mediation and trial. Similarly, in *Malmesbury* v. *Strutt & Parker,*[30] the judge held that the claimant had adopted an unreasonable and unrealistic position during the mediation and reflected this in the costs order. The Court remarked that unreasonable behaviour during a mediation is similar to an unreasonable refusal to mediate. In *SITA* v. *Watson Wyatt; Maxwell Batley (Pt 20 defendant),*[31] the judge heard evidence of what a mediator had allegedly said during a mediation in determining that Maxwell Batley's refusal to mediate was not unreasonable. The evidence in these three cases was available to the Court only because the parties waived privilege; they illustrate that the confidentiality of the process belongs to the parties and not to the mediator or the process.

In *Aird* v. *Prime Meridian Ltd,*[32] proceedings were stayed so that the parties could attempt mediation, and an order was made for the parties' experts to produce a joint statement. The mediation failed. During the subsequent litigation, the defendant sought to rely on the joint statement,

---

[27] In *ARP Capita London Market Services Ltd* v. *Ross & Co* [2004] EWHC 1181, negotiations about whether to mediate did not attract 'without prejudice' protection, while in *Reed Executive plc* v. *Reed Business Information Ltd* [2004] EWCA Civ 887, the Court refused to admit correspondence relating to whether the parties would mediate where it was marked 'without prejudice'. See also Allen (n 3) 212–13. This may be contrasted with the statutory privilege available in Australia under s 30(1) of the Civil Procedure Act 2005 (NSW) which defines a mediation session for privilege purposes as including 'any steps taken in the course of making arrangements for the session or in the course of the follow-up of a session'.

[28] See Chapter 7 for a further discussion on conduct and costs.

[29] [2007] EWHC 1774 (Ch). See also *Leicester Circuits Ltd* v. *Coates Brothers plc* [2003] EWCA Civ 333, discussed in Chapter 7 at Section 7.4.1.

[30] *Malmesbury* (n 17).

[31] [2002] EWHC 2025 (Ch).

[32] [2006] EWCA Civ 1866.

claiming it was not privileged as it had been prepared in accordance with a court order for the purposes of litigation. The English Court of Appeal agreed, deciding that the joint statement produced by the expert witnesses in accordance with a court order was not privileged, despite the fact it was made with a contemplated mediation in mind. The order did not state that the joint statement would be privileged.

In the later case of *Brown* v. *Rice*,[33] the claimant had made a series of assertions that a binding agreement had been reached during a mediation. The agreement to mediate at clause 1.4 provided that a mediated settlement would not be binding unless it was reduced to writing and signed by the parties. The judge held that communications during the mediation process could be admitted as evidence to establish whether there was a settlement, over objections from the defendant and the mediation service provider, demonstrating the limits of privilege and confidentiality. The Court held:

> [I]t is possible in any given case that the parties may have expressly or impliedly agreed to vary or waive those provisions or that a party may be estopped from relying on them or that a collateral contract has arisen which is not subject to clause 1.4, with the consequence that a concluded settlement was or must be treated as having been made. These are matters which a court is entitled to investigate and determine by way of exception to the without prejudice rule.[34]

The judge effectively reasoned that parties may vary, waive or even be estopped from asserting the writing requirement in the agreement to mediate. Ultimately, the issue was whether a settlement had been reached and not the reason why it had not been reached, and, on the facts, no settlement had been concluded. This case illustrated to mediators at the time that the protection given to the mediation process may not be as comprehensive as mediators had informed parties it was. Confidentiality attached to the mediation process only to the extent it attached to 'without prejudice' negotiations, such that the limits of the 'without prejudice' principle applied with equal force to mediation.

In *Cumbria Waste Management Ltd* v. *Baines Wilson*,[35] the Court had to decide whether disclosure of mediation documentation could be

---

[33] *Brown* (n 19). See also *Cattley* v. *Pollard* [2006] EWHC 3130, [2007] Ch 353 where the Court permitted a third party access to position papers prepared for the purposes of mediation to assess whether there had been double-counting in a claim settled by claimants against her in the mediation with her husband's professional indemnity insurers.

[34] *Brown* (n 19) [25] (Mr Stuart Isaacs QC serving as Deputy High Court Judge).

[35] [2008] EWHC 786 (QB).

ordered against one party's wishes because of an exception to the 'without prejudice' privilege and whether the confidentiality provisions of the agreement to mediate precluded disclosure where one of the parties did not consent. The Court found that on the basis of the 'without prejudice' privilege and the contracted confidentiality between the parties, it would be wrong to order the disclosure of the mediation documents. Hence, the parties had a joint, but not several, right to waive 'without prejudice' privilege. In particular, the Court wanted mediators to be free to conduct mediations without fear that their notes might be disclosed to others, and saw this as an exception to the general rule that confidentiality is not a bar to disclosure of material to a court. The Court said:

> [W]hether on the basis of the without prejudice rule or as an exception to the general rule that confidentiality is not a bar to disclosure, the court should support the mediation process by refusing, in normal circumstances, to order disclosure of documents and communications within a mediation.[36]

This decision suggests that the courts in England may be willing to find that there is a special mediation privilege. However, as *Cumbria Waste Management* is a first instance decision, a court of appeal decision, or statutory intervention, would be required for mediators, lawyers and parties to know the precise contours of mediation confidentiality in England.

9.4.1.2 Other Participants and Interested Parties

Anyone who was present at a mediation is compellable as a witness once the parties have waived privilege. As witnesses, experts and other third parties who may be present during the mediation process are not usually parties to the agreement to mediate, or to confidentiality provisions in the settlement agreement, such parties should sign confidentiality agreements before participating in the process. The confidentiality clause of an agreement to mediate can (but does not always) bind legal advisors. While the 'without prejudice' privilege can only be asserted by participants in a mediation, parties who settled have been successful in using it defensively against other interested parties in appropriate circumstances.

In *Rush & Tompkins Ltd* v. *Greater London Council*,[37] the main contractor in a construction dispute reached a mediated settlement

---

[36] ibid [30] (Kirkham J).
[37] *Rush & Tompkins* (n 12). See also *Cumbria Waste Management* (n 35) (discussed in text to n 35); *David Instance* v. *Denny Bros Printing Ltd* [2000] FSR 869 (discussed in text to

with the owner. The subcontractors, who were not involved in the mediation, wanted to gain information about the weight their claims carried in the mediation, to pursue their claims against the contractor. Although a settlement had been reached, the Court held that the public interest required the extension of the privilege protection to cover the situation of the contractor, owner and subcontractors. The decision provides an exception to the established principle that the protection provided by the privilege ends when settlement occurs, and reveals the degree to which the courts are willing to adapt common law privileges in the mediation context.

An Australian court subsequently extended the principle to prevent disclosure of documents provided in a mediation to a party who did not participate in the process.[38] While such decisions are encouraging in terms of protecting mediation evidence, each case is likely to turn on its own facts and focus on who is seeking the information, from whom it is being sought and the purposes for which it is sought.[39]

9.4.1.3   Legal Professional Privilege and Lawyer–Client Protection

Legal professional privilege is a common law protection that covers documents, data and other communications that arise from legal proceedings, or from giving or obtaining legal advice, where the dominant purpose is legal advice. A strong suggestion of any other equal or more dominant purpose will destroy a claim of privilege. It enables clients and their lawyers to communicate openly, confidently and without fear of being forced to disclose their confidential communications. It is subject to exceptions. For example, it does not apply where communications are made to pursue any illegal purpose. Nor does it apply to any fact that reveals to a lawyer that a crime or fraud has been committed since the

---

n 71). However, see *Muller* v. *Linsley & Mortimer* [1996] PNLR 74 and *Cattley* (n 33), where a narrower approach to the privilege was adopted and evidence was not subsequently excluded.

[38] *Mercantile Mutual Custodians Pty Ltd* v. *Village/Nine Network Restaurants & Bars* [1999] QCA 276.

[39] Boulle (n 2) 709–10. See also, on the need for confidentiality to cover all relevant persons, different types of information carriers and transmission, within appropriate legal limits, F Steffek and others, 'Guide for Regulating Dispute Resolution (GRDR): Principles and Comments' in F Steffek and others, *Regulating Dispute Resolution: ADR and Access to Justice at the Crossroads* (Oxford, Hart Publishing 2013) 24. Some civil law jurisdictions, such as Slovakia, have introduced laws that extend confidentiality requirements to third parties: see Alexander (n 2) 260.

lawyer became involved. As it is intended to protect clients, a lawyer can disclose the communication with a client's express consent. The privilege can also be waived by a client making an intended or unintended disclosure, or if a client takes an action against their lawyer regarding the lawyer's advice. While the privilege is traditionally applied in judicial, administrative and tribunal proceedings where people can otherwise be compelled to furnish information, communications created for the purpose of giving or obtaining legal advice would cover work prepared by lawyers for clients going into mediation.[40]

Although the privilege can be waived by a party voluntarily disclosing communications to a party on the other side, disclosure to a mediator of documents such as legal opinions, that would otherwise be privileged, should not amount to a waiver as such disclosures are for the limited purpose of helping the parties reach a settlement. Otherwise a party on the other side could demand production of the documents if the matter ultimately went to trial. This would be particularly problematic where an agreement to mediate provided that the mediator can request documents from the parties. This is consistent with the approach taken in *Farm Assist Ltd (in liq)* v. *Secretary of State for the Environment, Food and Rural Affairs (No 2)*.[41] In this case Ramsey J clarified that, in England, a communication remains privileged even where the client shares it with the mediator on a confidential basis.[42] Consequently, the client can restrain the mediator from unauthorised use of the information.[43]

In the USA, lawyer–client communications are protected by attorney–client privilege and the related work product doctrine under rule 502 of the Federal Rules of Evidence. The work product doctrine protects materials prepared in anticipation of litigation from discovery by opposing counsel and is broader than attorney–client privilege. It may be overcome by a showing of necessity. Civil law counterparts of lawyer–client privilege include the 'professional secret' in France and the 'duty of silence' in Germany and Austria which are positive duties that extend to courts, tribunals and other bodies.[44]

---

[40] See Boulle (n 2) 678–80; Boulle and Nesic (n 16) 495–96; Blake, Browne and Sime (n 18) 53–54. In Australia, it is referred to as 'client legal privilege': see Evidence Act 1995 (Cth) ss 117–119.

[41] [2009] EWHC 1102 (TCC).

[42] ibid [44]: 'If another privilege attaches to documents which are produced by a party and shown to a mediator, that party retains that privilege and it is not waived by disclosure to the mediator or by waiver of the without prejudice privilege.'

[43] See A K C Koo, 'Confidentiality of Mediation Communications' (2011) 30(2) *Civil Justice Quarterly* 192, 200.

[44] See Alexander (n 2) 271–73.

9.4.1.4   A Privilege for Mediation or Mediators

'Without prejudice' privilege covers only the parties in a mediation; the mediator or the process will only be covered over and above the other common law privileges if this is provided for by statute. No specific privilege for mediators exists at common law; nor is there any authority extending the 'without prejudice' privilege to mediators. As mediators have not been viewed traditionally as possessing sufficient interest to warrant this protection, where there is no statutory or enforceable contractual protection, mediators are compellable witnesses. However, existing categories of privilege could be extended to mediators by applying the policies underlying other privileges to them. This would also avoid credibility conflicts between parties and mediators. If a privilege were extended to mediators, the consent of both the mediator and the parties would be required to waive it.

A related issue is the possibility of a privilege covering the whole mediation process, which would encourage a candid flow of information in a mediation. The English courts have indicated that a distinct mediation privilege may be developed.[45]

9.4.1.5   Testimony by the Mediator

From the court's perspective, the mediator is often best placed to give the court an independent perspective of what transpired at the mediation, including the parties' intention to be bound by the settlement, whether there was a misrepresentation, whether coercive behaviour occurred or whether a party was unwell to the extent that they lacked sufficient competence to settle. While some US courts have refused to admit mediator testimony,[46] many others have admitted such evidence, relied greatly on mediator

---

[45] In the English case *Brown* (n 19) [20], the sitting Deputy High Court Judge, Mr Stuart Isaacs QC, acknowledged that, while the case could be decided on the existing 'without prejudice' rule, 'it may be in the future that the existence of a distinct mediation privilege will require to be considered by either the legislature or the courts'. See also the text at n 35 about the English case of *Cumbria Waste Management* (n 35), in particular the suggestion that the English courts may be willing to find a special mediation privilege worthy of judicial protection. It remains to be seen whether a court will create an autonomous mediation privilege, separate from the 'without prejudice' privilege with its exceptions.

[46] See, e.g., *Princeton Insurance Co v. Vergano* 883 A 2d 44 (Del Ch 2005) 66, where the Court said that it would be a challenge to find a 'more poisonous means to weaken the promise of [mediation] confidentiality . . . than authorising the use of a mediator as an opinion witness against a mediating party'.

testimony[47] and used the mediator to determine the credibility of conflicting party testimonies.[48]

Evidence provided by a mediator has proved crucial in Australia. Where a party in a mediation rejected allegations of misleading and deceptive conduct and unconscionability by another, the Court placed 'considerable weight' on the mediator's evidence.[49] An Australian court also granted disclosure of mediation evidence, even though the mediator had specified to the parties when the mediation started that his notes would not be made available to them.[50] While the Court acknowledged that disclosure would fundamentally affect the mediation process, it believed it was essential in this case as the evidence was required to explain the parties' intention regarding the settlement.[51]

9.4.1.6 Mediator Secrets Privilege

A 'mediator secrets privilege' is a proposed option that would enable the parties to separately share information with the mediator, and facilitate the mediator to assist them in a protected environment.[52] Once the

---

[47] See, e.g., *White* v. *Fleet Bank of Maine* 875 A 2d 680 (Me 2005), where the Court relied, among other things, on the mediator's testimony that the parties reached a binding agreement during the mediation. See also *Bernabei* v. *St Paul Fire & Marine Insurance Co* Ohio App 5 Dist, WL 351754 (2005), where the Court relied, among other things, on the mediator's testimony that a settlement agreement had not been reached.

[48] See, e.g., *Standard Steel LLC* v. *Buckeye Energy Inc* Civil Action No. 04-538 (WD Pa Sep 29, 2005), where the Court held that the parties had reached a settlement at mediation, and credited 'in particular ... the testimony of the neutral mediator presiding over the mediation that day'. See also Sussman (n 5) 36.

[49] *National Australia Bank* v. *Freeman* [2000] QSC 295 (Ambrose J). See also the English case *AB* v. *CD* [2013] EWHC 1376 (TCC), where a mediator gave evidence in a professional negligence action that he had attempted to mediate, although the Court placed significant limits on the scope of his evidence. See Allen (n 3) 63–65, who discusses the lack of debate in this case (being the first known English case where a mediator has given evidence) on whether the confidentiality provision in the agreement to mediate permitted mediator testimony, and the lack of any reference to the issues raised in *Farm Assist (No 2)* (n 41) and subsequently much discussed. See also Blake, Browne and Sime (n 18) 166–67.

[50] *Knight* v. *Truss-Michaelis* (District Court of Queensland, Pratt DCJ, 14 April 1993).

[51] Boulle (n 2) 705–6. To limit the likelihood of such difficulties, the agreement to mediate should provide that there is no settlement until it is reduced to writing and signed by the parties. In *Rock Advertising Limited* v. *MWB Business Exchange Centres Limited* [2018] UKSC 24, the UK Supreme Court held that parties can contract to exclude oral variation by insisting that modifications be written and signed to be effective. See also Chapter 3 at Section 3.6.

[52] This was proposed in England by Mr Justice Briggs: see Sir Michael Briggs, 'Mediation Privilege?' (2009) 7364 *New Law Journal* 550. See also M Bartlet, 'Mediation Secrets "In the Shadow of the Law"' (2015) 34(1) *Civil Justice Quarterly* 112.

information was shared, either directly between the parties or as an authorised disclosure through the mediator, it would stop being a secret and lose the mediator secrets privilege, attracting only the 'without prejudice' privilege that applies to all information shared between the parties, with its exceptions.

The proposed privilege would be justified due to the unique role of the mediator in receiving information from one party and not sharing it with others, and to help the mediator use the knowledge gained to guide the parties towards a mutually agreeable settlement.[53] Analogous to communications under legal professional privilege, mediation secrets would be protected unless there was mediator misconduct. This would appear to be supported by public policy in the same way that legal professional privilege is. The privilege would not cover everything mediators learn in mediation but would be strictly limited to the information shared by a party with the mediator in the private caucus sessions. Consequently, it should not interfere with the recognised exceptions to the 'without prejudice' principle[54] that provide the courts with windows into the mediation process to assess and then determine disputes of that nature. It is difficult to imagine how the determination of any of those disputes would be assisted by the disclosure of mediator secrets, with the rare exception of mediator misconduct.[55] Mediators would have to be open about the circumstances that indicate illegality, either civil or criminal, such as fraud, money laundering or tax evasion, where 'mediator secrets' may have to be revealed. Apart from legal and policy requirements, this openness will most likely be required by the code of conduct under which the mediator, and the process, would operate.[56]

Ideally, this privilege would be established and develop as part of the common law in relevant jurisdictions, as a recognition that the public interest in the maintenance of confidentiality in relation to particular forms of communication in a mediation outweighs the competing public interest in the court gleaning all information that it feels may be required to determine a dispute.[57]

---

[53] See Koo (n 43) 202.

[54] See *Brown* (n 19) (discussed in Section 9.4.1.1). See also *Cattley* (n 33). If this privilege existed, the judge in *SITA* v. *Watson Wyatt; Maxwell Batley (Pt 20 defendant)* (n 31 and accompanying text) would have refused to hear what the mediator said.

[55] Briggs (n 52) 550.

[56] See Allen (n 3) 246.

[57] While in civil law jurisdictions it would require codification, in common law jurisdictions legislation is often less than ideal when dealing with emerging legal principles in a new field, hence development of this privilege through the common law and refined through

9.4.2 Contract

'Without prejudice' privilege (discussed in Section 9.4.1.1) is a rule of evidence; it does not make information that it protects confidential, but simply prevents it from being used in evidence at a subsequent trial. Hence, confidentiality, in the absence of a statute, must be contracted to ensure that information shared within the mediation process is protected.[58] This is the oldest way of attempting to protect mediation information. It involves the parties and the mediator, together with any other participants, entering into a confidentiality agreement in which each party agrees to keep information disclosed in the mediation confidential, and not to testify in subsequent arbitral or judicial proceedings.[59] While these provisions have not been extensively considered by courts in jurisdictions such as Australia, the traditional view is that public policy favours the enforcement of confidentiality clauses in agreements, but there are limitations on the types of remedy available for breaching such provisions.[60]

While confidentiality agreements are persuasive as to the parties' intentions, they often include the exception that a party may reveal mediation evidence where a law or court requires it. Even without this exception, a contractual duty to keep mediation information confidential can prove to be unenforceable due to the public policy that courts are entitled to every person's evidence; even where such a provision is deemed enforceable in subsequent proceedings between the parties, it may not be enforceable in proceedings involving third parties.[61]

Nonetheless, in the absence of a statute, an agreement may be the only way that the parties can attempt to protect mediation confidentiality. In Ontario, for example, there was no statute or rule of practice to protect mediation confidentiality when the issue came before the Ontario Superior Court of Justice in *Rudd v. Trossacs Investments Inc.*[62] The

---

judicial decisions would be preferable: see Briggs (n 52) 550. Some civil law jurisdictions either prohibit testimony by the mediator or provide a right of refusal to testify. In Austria, for example, accredited mediators are prohibited from being called as witnesses to share mediation evidence in civil proceedings, subject to limited exceptions, offering a high level of confidentiality protection: see Alexander (n 2) 263–66.

[58] See Thanki (ed) (n 11) 312.

[59] Van Ginkel, 'Mediation Under National Law: United States of America', IBA Legal Practice Division Mediation Committee Newsletter, August 2005, 48.

[60] See Boulle (n 2) 684. In civil law jurisdictions such as Austria and France, a breach of confidence can give rise to civil or criminal liability in appropriate circumstances: see Alexander (n 2) 279–80.

[61] Van Ginkel (n 59) 48.

[62] (2004) 72 OR (3d) 62 (OSCJ).

plaintiffs were seeking an interim order requiring the mediator to give evidence of events at a mediation, including the terms of settlement. The plaintiffs claimed that the record of the settlement, which was handwritten by the mediator with the assistance of counsel and executed at the mediation, inadvertently excluded Morris Kaiser ('Kaiser') as a party to the settlement. The defendants denied that Kaiser was a party to the settlement agreement. The Court referred to the mediation agreement which contained the following confidentiality provision:

> The parties agree that all communications and documents shared, which are not otherwise discoverable, shall be without prejudice and shall be kept confidential as against the outside world, and shall not be used in discovery, cross-examination, at trial, in this or any other proceeding, or in any other way.
>
> The mediator's notes and recollections cannot be soepoenaed [sic] in this or any other proceeding.[63]

Justice Lederman went on to address the balance that the court seeks to achieve when weighing competing interests:

> [S]ince privilege and confidentiality are critical to the success of the mediation process, they should not be lightly disturbed. Some evidence must be adduced on the motion to demonstrate that the mediator's evidence is likely to be probative to the issue and that the benefit gained by the disclosure for the correct disposal of the litigation will be greater than any injury to the mediation process by the disclosure of discussions that took place.[64]

On balance, Lederman J believed the mediator could provide important information about the executed settlement and whether it was inconsistent with any prior or oral agreement between the parties. He ordered that the mediator be examined as a witness, but limited questions to any knowledge and understanding he had of whether Kaiser was a party to the mediated settlement agreement.

Leave to appeal the decision was granted and the Ontario Bar Association was granted leave to intervene in view of the importance of the case for mediation confidentiality. As Howden J in the Divisional Court remarked: 'It is desirable that leave be granted because any added exceptions to the confidentiality principle in mediation will arise again, and as compelling testimony by order is per se an interlocutory matter there is no other way for the issue to

[63] ibid [16] (Lederman J).
[64] ibid [20].

be determined.'[65] He doubted whether the earlier decision was correct 'because it requires a mediator to in effect cast a tie-breaking vote in a case where he wrote the agreement during the latter stages of the mediation session with input from counsel'.[66] He added:

> The public importance of this (as the first decision re: exception to mediation confidentiality known to counsel who appeared before me) issue in respect of the expectation and significance of confidentiality in . . . mediation is, I think, self evident.[67]

Justice Howden effectively recognised that mediator testimony would conflict with the core mediation value of neutrality.[68]

The appeal was allowed and the earlier decision set aside. Subject to issues such as fraud or other criminal situations, the Court emphasised that confidentiality is required in order for the mediation process to be successful. As Swinton J stated: 'In this case, there is an important public interest in maintaining the confidentiality of the mediation process that, in all the circumstances of this case, outweighs the interest in compelling the evidence of the mediator.'[69] The case illustrates the disparate approaches courts in the same jurisdiction can take with regard to a clear and comprehensive clause that the parties have agreed on to protect mediation confidentiality. The earlier decision did not consider mediation confidentiality to be as important as the public interest in accessing mediation evidence, while the court on appeal disagreed. When a jurisdiction has no statute or rule protecting mediation confidentiality, clear case law is critically important.[70]

The English courts have gone even further in protecting confidentiality clauses in contracts. In *David Instance v. Denny Bros Printing Ltd*,[71] the agreement to mediate contained an express confidentiality provision. The parties attempted to mediate their dispute but were unsuccessful. A confidential letter written by the claimant before but in connection

---

[65] *Rudd v. Trossacs Investments Inc* 2005 CarswellOnt 887 [2005] OJ No 2024 (OSCJDC) [3] (Howden J). The Divisional Court is comprised of three Superior Court of Justice judges and is effectively a court of appeal.

[66] ibid [4].

[67] ibid [5].

[68] For a discussion of the case, and the decision to give leave to appeal, see P Jacobs, 'Confidentiality in Mediation: Right or Risk', IBA Legal Practice Division Mediation Committee Newsletter, September 2006, 15–17.

[69] *Rudd v. Trossacs Investments Inc* (2006) 79 OR (3d) 687 (OSCJDC) [42] (Swinton J).

[70] For a discussion of the decision to allow the appeal in the Divisional Court, see Jacobs (n 68) 12–17.

[71] *David Instance* (n 37).

with the mediation was subsequently attached as an exhibit to an affidavit in proceedings between the parties. The claimant sought an injunction to restrain the use of that letter and of other material produced in connection with the mediation. Justice Lloyd granted the injunction, remarking that the confidentiality provision in the agreement was wide enough to cover not only material written after the agreement to mediate had been made, but also material relating to the mediation which had been created before the agreement to mediate was formally made.

Another English decision has created some cause for concern. In *Farm Assist (No 2)*,[72] the mediator could not exempt herself from the duty to comply with a witness summons by arguing she had an express obligation in the mediation agreement not to divulge information or an implied duty of confidentiality arising from the nature of mediation. Mediation confidentiality yielded to the interests of justice in receiving her testimonial evidence for the purpose of assessing whether economic duress invalidated the agreement between the parties. The 'interests of justice' test employed by the judge appears to have been satisfied by looking at the issues solely through the prism of the parties' private rights.[73] While Ramsey J found that the mediator has a right to confidentiality which the parties themselves cannot unilaterally override, it seems that such a right was not solely

---

[72] *Farm Assist (No 2)* (n 41). In the first case, Farm Assist brought an action against the UK Department of Environment Food and Rural Affairs (DEFRA) which was successfully mediated. Farm Assist subsequently went into liquidation and the liquidator sold the right of action to Ruttle Plant Hire, which sought to have the agreement set aside on the grounds that it was entered into under economic duress. While Ruttle ultimately abandoned its attempt to pursue the action, a second action was taken by the liquidator. In this second action, DEFRA obtained a witness summons requiring the mediator to give evidence. Shortly after the decision, a settlement was reached and consequently the mediator did not have to give evidence.

[73] This contrasts sharply with the 'overriding considerations of public policy' test – the higher standard required by the EU Mediation Directive (n 112): see Allen (n 3) 61. Nor did the court in *Farm Assist (No 2)* (n 41) give any clear guidance on the meaning of 'interests of justice' or the issues involved in balancing the varied or conflicting public policies, other than to refer to the position between the parties as a matter of private law. While the Court recognised the basis for arguing for a separate 'mediation privilege', it did not provide a helpful examination of that possibility and made no decision on it. There was no finding that a court could compel, in the absence of agreement between the parties, a mediator to give evidence about private meetings. For further discussion of these issues, see D Cornes, 'Mediator Fails to Have Witness Summons Set Aside: *Farm Assist Ltd v Secretary of State for the Environment Food and Rural Affairs (No 2)*' (2009) 75 (4) *Arbitration* 582, 587–88.

dependent on the terms of the mediation agreement but also founded on general principles.[74]

Consequently, confidentiality protection under contract law may be no wider in England than it is under the 'without prejudice' rule. However, it may be the basis for the court to rule against production of mediation documents where exceptions to the 'without prejudice' rule do not apply or to grant an interim injunction restraining a threatened confidentiality breach of that mediation evidence. Hence, contractual confidentiality in England is enforceable by the mediator and the disputing parties, and it can exclude evidence from a subsequent trial unless the judge decides to admit it in the 'interests of justice', which is quite a vague term. As *Farm Assist (No 2)* is a first instance decision, it would be helpful if there were a definitive appeal court decision on the extent of contractual confidentiality. Alternatively, the legislature in England could follow the approach adopted in the USA and Australia by putting 'mediation privilege' on a statutory footing.[75]

In the absence of adequate statutory protection, it is critical that the terms of an agreement to mediate between the mediator and the parties, or confidentiality agreements with other participants and interested parties who may be present at the mediation, clearly express the intentions of the parties regarding confidentiality. In particular, they should specify the elements of the process that the confidentiality obligation covers,

---

[74] For a discussion on this issue, see J Tumbridge, 'Mediators: Confidentiality and Compulsion to Give Evidence' (2010) 21(4) *International Company and Commercial Law Review* 144. See also C Tapper, *Cross and Tapper on Evidence* (13th ed, Oxford, Oxford University Press 2018) 513–14.

[75] Koo (n 43) 199–200. In *Farm Assist (No 2)* (n 41) the language of the agreement referred only to litigation or arbitration in relation to the dispute. The judge held that this wording was not wide enough to cover a different dispute – the dispute as to whether duress had been deployed by one of the parties during the mediation. As the judge found that the clause which inhibited parties from calling the mediator to give evidence about the dispute did not prevent the mediator from being required to give evidence about the mediation, agreements to mediate are now usually drawn up to cover both situations: see Allen (n 3) 234. See also the UK Civil Mediation Council, Guidance Note No 1 'Mediation Confidentiality' (8 July 2009), released following *Farm Assist (No 2)*, which states that agreements to mediate should continue to specify that the mediation proceedings are conducted on a 'without prejudice' basis, continue to make it clear that what is said during mediation will be confidential, and not restrict the circumstances in which a mediator cannot be compelled to give evidence in court. It also suggests that mediators may wish to include a provision indemnifying them, if they are called to give evidence, for any costs they incur in dealing with the application, and possibly provide for mediators to be paid at their hourly rate for the time spent dealing with such applications or giving evidence.

the type of information that the confidentiality provision covers, the individuals that can claim confidentiality and the individuals against whom confidentiality can be claimed, the exceptions (if any) to confidentiality, and the mediator's obligations during and after the mediation regarding information received in confidence during the process.[76]

9.4.2.1   Contracting to Exclude Judicial Access to Mediation Evidence

The issue arises as to whether parties can agree to exclude judicial access to what transpired at a mediation, effectively excluding the exceptions to the 'without prejudice' privilege. While this may seem counterintuitive as it would mean that parties could not claim undue influence, for example, some parties may value confidentiality to the extent that they are willing to sacrifice such protection. In *Unilever plc* v. *The Proctor & Gamble Company*, Walker LJ remarked: 'there seems to be no reason in principle why parties to without prejudice negotiations should not expressly or impliedly agree to vary the public policy rule in other respects, either by extending or limiting its reach.'[77] However, there does not appear to be clear authority in England on this point.

In *Union Carbide Canada Inc* v. *Bombardier*,[78] a global purchaser/ supplier dispute was mediated. The agreement contained confidentiality provisions but no signed writing clause. Later one of the parties claimed that the settlement covered only the Canadian part of the claim, not the global dispute, and sought to elicit evidence of what transpired during the mediation to support this. The Canadian Supreme Court held that the exceptions to the 'without prejudice' privilege could be set aside by contractual confidentiality, but only on clearly drafted terms. As Wagner J remarked: 'In principle, there is relatively little that can displace the intent of the parties once it is clearly established.'[79] The terms of the agreement were not sufficiently clear in this case, as there was no signed writing clause, and the evidence of what transpired at the mediation was consequently admitted. Had a signed writing clause been included, it could have excluded the exception that 'without prejudice' evidence could be admitted to confirm whether agreement had been reached.[80]

---

[76] Boulle and Nesic (n 16) 500–1; Boulle (n 2) 684.
[77] *Unilever* (n 18) [23].
[78] [2014] 1 SCR 800.
[79] ibid [44] (Wagner J).
[80] See Allen (n 3) 222–23.

9.4.2.2   Mediation Rules and Guidelines

The duty of confidentiality can also result from the rules or guidelines established by the organisation under which the mediation takes place, incorporated by reference into the mediation clause or agreement to mediate between the parties. If a mediator breaches such rules, this could result in expulsion from the organisation; this can have a significant deterrent effect. Rules and guidelines are organic instruments and can be changed with relative frequency by the relevant organisation to reflect the changing nature of the process and the legal framework in which it operates. For example, in light of a Supreme Court of New South Wales decision, the New South Wales Law Society altered its guidelines for lawyer mediators. The Court held that where facts, information about which is revealed in the course of mediation, are discoverable in the normal course, evidence of these facts will be admissible in proceedings.[81] The Law Society now adopts a cautious approach:

> The mediator shall inform the parties that, in general, communications between them, and between them and the mediator, during the preliminary conference and the mediation, are agreed to be confidential. In general, these communications cannot be used as evidence if the matter does not settle at the mediation and goes to a court hearing. The mediator shall also inform the parties that they should consult their legal practitioners if they want a more detailed statement or if they have any specific questions in relation to confidentiality.[82]

While institutions often have slightly different approaches, the approach adopted under most rules with regard to the general duty of confidentiality is to impose on the parties and the mediator an obligation not to disclose any information about mediation proceedings in the absence of the parties' agreement to the contrary and/or subject to applicable law.[83] This duty tends to cover the settlement agreement, subject to any

---

[81] *AWA* (n 9).

[82] 'The Law Society Guidelines for those Involved in Mediations' in the Law Society of New South Wales, *Dispute Resolution Kit* (2012) section 6.6. See also L Boulle and R Field, *Mediation in Australia* (Chatswood, NSW, LexisNexis 2018) 340.

[83] See London Court of International Arbitration (LCIA) Mediation Rules, article 12.3; International Centre for Dispute Resolution (ICDR) Mediation Rules, rule 12(1), (3); Singapore International Mediation Centre (SIMC) Mediation Rules, rule 9.1(a); Rules of the Mediation Institute of the Stockholm Chamber of Commerce, article 3(1) (except where parties have agreed to the contrary); Australian Centre for International Commercial Arbitration (ACICA) Mediation Rules, rule 15.2 (except where parties have given prior written consent).

disclosure required for its implementation or enforcement.[84] In terms of
the admissibility of mediation communications as evidence in subsequent judicial, arbitral or similar proceedings, the common approach is
to provide a list of prohibited disclosures that will only be produced as
evidence when agreed to by the parties or required by applicable law.[85]
The possibility of the mediator acting as a witness in future proceedings
tends not to feature as frequently in institutional rules.[86] Similarly, the
flow of information within the mediation tends not to be covered, as most
rules leave this to the parties and the mediator to agree.[87] Where rules
regulate this form of confidentiality, they tend to reflect the 'open communication' approach rather than the more widely accepted
'in-confidence' approach. This is contrary to the more widely accepted
international approach of only sharing information outside of caucus
where explicit consent is given.[88] If the 'open communication' approach
is reflected in the institutional rules that are to govern a mediation, it is
important that parties are aware of the importance of providing in their
agreement to mediate that this rule is disapplied, and incorporate the
more internationally prominent 'in-confidence' approach to caucus
communications in their agreement if this is their preference.

9.4.3   Equitable Remedy for Breach of Confidence

Where individuals who receive information in confidence make
unauthorised use of it and contract law does not provide an effective
remedy, equity may be exercised by a court in granting relief against an

---

[84] See International Chamber of Commerce (ICC) Mediation Rules, article 9(1)(b);
UNCITRAL Mediation Rules, article 14; ACICA Mediation Rules (n 83) rule 15.2;
SIMC Rules (n 83) rule 9.1(b). Article 9(1)(a) of the ICC Mediation Rules further permits
disclosure of the fact that the mediation proceedings existed. Conversely, article 14 of the
UNCITRAL Mediation Rules does not provide for any exceptions to the general duty of
confidentiality, except with regard to the settlement agreement.

[85] See ICC Mediation Rules (n 84) article 9(2); ICDR Mediation Rules (n 83) rule 12(3);
LCIA Mediation Rules (n 83) article 12.4, 12.6; UNCITRAL Mediation Rules (n 84) article
20; ACICA Mediation Rules (n 83) rule 20; SIMC Mediation Rules (n 83) rule 9.2.

[86] See ICDR Mediation Rules (n 83) rule 12(2); LCIA Mediation Rules (n 83) article 14.2;
ACICA Mediation Rules (n 83) rule 20; SIMC Mediation Rules (n 83) rule 9.3.

[87] See LCIA Mediation Rules (n 83) article 6.3; UNCITRAL Mediation Rules (n 84) article
10; ACICA Mediation Rules (n 83) rule 11.

[88] It has been suggested that such rules should be amended to bring them into line with
current thinking: see C Brown and P Winch, 'The Confidentiality and Transparency
Debate in Commercial and Investment Mediation' in C Titi and K Fach Gómez (eds),
Mediation in International Commercial and Investment Disputes (Oxford, Oxford
University Press 2019) 332–33; Alexander (n 2) 348.

actual or a threatened abuse of confidential information. The information to be protected must have the required quality of confidence about it, which in a commercial context could, for example, be a trade secret; it must have been communicated in a context requiring an obligation of confidence and there must be unauthorised use of it.[89] As a result of the relationship that exists between a mediator and disputing parties, in a context where the mediator's role is to assist parties with their negotiations, a court of equity could protect confidential communications that are disclosed by a mediator without authorisation. The disclosures would include admissions, views or suggestions made by either party about a possible settlement; any proposal put forward by the mediator where an evaluative style is adopted; and any indications of a willingness on the part of either party to accept such proposals.[90] Where there is a breach, the affected party could seek an injunction,[91] and if the mediator's use of the information was for their own benefit, restitution of any profits acquired could be ordered, with damages also being ordered in appropriate circumstances. A mediator could raise a public interest defence where the information disclosed relates to a party's complicity in fraud or criminal activity. However, where there are alternative remedies available, equity is not likely to be a prominent means of protecting mediation confidentiality.[92]

9.4.4 Confidentiality and Conflicts of Interest

Circumstances can provide opportunities for communications that can undermine mediation confidentiality.[93] The concern can also arise that lawyers acting for one party in a mediation could acquire information that could be used against the other party in subsequent proceedings. In

---

[89] *Coco v. A N Clark (Engineers) Ltd* [1969] RPC 41; *A-G v Guardian Newspapers Ltd (No 2)* [1988] UKHL 6.

[90] This protection is covered in many rules: see UNCITRAL Mediation Rules (n 84) article 20; ICC Mediation Rules (n 84) article 9(2); ICDR Mediation Rules, rule 12(3); ACICA Mediation Rules (n 83) rule 21.

[91] See *David Instance* (n 37, discussed in text to n 71).

[92] Allen (n 3) 227–28; Boulle (n 2) 684–86; Boulle and Nesic (n 16) 501–2; Alexander (n 2) 259.

[93] See *Ruffles v. Chilman* (1997) 17 WAR 1, where a unanimous bench of the Supreme Court of Western Australia overturned the decision of a judge who had refused to disqualify himself from hearing a case that he had referred to mediation. The court-appointed deputy registrar communicated during a mediation that he believed that having been in contact with the judge, the judge had adopted an adverse view of the plaintiff's evidence.

England, a solicitor can act against a former client, even where the solicitor's firm holds confidential information relating to the client, where the client consents, or, if the client does not consent, where the solicitor can act consistently with their confidentiality obligations or other fiduciary duties owed to the client.[94] In making this determination, the possibility of increased risk of disclosure or misuse of a former client's confidential information must be considered. While the risk does not have to be substantial, it should be real, rather than theoretical. With regard to mediators, agreements to mediate usually prohibit a mediator from acting for or against a party in relation to a dispute where the mediator received confidential information in the course of the mediation. Codes of conduct can include similar requirements.[95]

9.4.5   Allegations of Fraud and Criminality

Allegations of fraud or other criminal conduct taking place during a mediation can be a basis for setting confidentiality aside in order to admit the relevant evidence. However, jurisdictions deal with this issue in different ways. Within Australia, for example, in New South Wales it is an offence simply to conceal a serious crime,[96] while in Victoria it is only an offence if the person receives a benefit from the non-disclosure.[97] While these laws may exonerate lawyers if they receive such information when practising their profession, this does not apply to mediators.[98]

In England it is an offence for a person to become concerned in an arrangement they know or suspect will facilitate the acquisition or control of criminal property by another person, unless they make an authorised disclosure.[99] However, if a mediator makes a disclosure that is not required under the Proceeds of Crime Act 2002 (UK), they may be sued for breach of confidence. The UK Civil Mediation Council has issued guidance indicating that it may be necessary for a mediator,

---

[94] *Prince Jefri Bolkiah* v. *KPMG* [1999] 2 AC 222.

[95] See Boulle (n 2) 706–9. See also Boulle and Nesic (n 16) 503–5.

[96] Crimes Act 1900 (NSW) s 316.

[97] Crimes Act 1958 (Vic) s 326.

[98] See, e.g., Crimes Act 1900 (NSW) s 316(4). See also Boulle (n 2) 695–96; Alexander (n 2) 284.

[99] Proceeds of Crime Act 2002 (UK) s 328. A disclosure may be made under s 338. Conviction can result in imprisonment for 14 years, or a fine, or both.

whether a legal professional or not, to either withdraw from a mediation or make a report under the Act.[100]

9.4.6 Statute

There are two primary reasons for statutory rules on confidentiality or privilege. First, state regulation is required where the parties cannot create their desired confidentiality by contract. For example, procedural law rules, such as the rules on the admissibility of evidence, are not open to contracting. Second, statutory confidentiality rules may be required where the parties waive confidentiality ex ante (before the event) only rarely, as with the confidentiality duty of the mediator.[101] If statutes were to provide comprehensive confidentiality protection, there would be no need for contractual protection as interpreted by the courts.

Privilege and secrecy provisions are often used in statutes dealing with mediation to protect the confidentiality of the process and reinforce the common law position, and sometimes extend it by providing increased protection for parties and broader obligations for mediators. While there is no internationally recognisable consensus on the appropriate extent of confidentiality, some statutes provide that the process is confidential and that evidence of what is said or admitted in a mediation is inadmissible in any proceedings before any court, and that documents prepared for the purposes of or in the course of a mediation are inadmissible.[102] The

---

[100] See the UK Civil Mediation Council's Guidance Note No 2, 'The Obligations of Mediators under the Proceeds of Crime Act 2002'. The guidance was issued following *Bowman* v. *Fels* [2005] EWCA Civ 226, where the English Court of Appeal reversed the approach adopted by the High Court in *P* v. *P* [2003] EWHC 2260, declaring that s 328 was not intended to apply to the ordinary conduct of litigation by legal professionals, including settlement, and in any event it did not override legal professional privilege. It is unclear whether this extends to mediators. Consequently, following the introduction of the Proceeds of Crime Act 2002 (UK), agreements to mediate in the United Kingdom often included a provision advising parties of the mediator's obligation to report under the Act: see H Brown and A Marriott, *ADR: Principles and Practice* (London, Sweet & Maxwell 2018) 325–6; M Kallipetis and S Ruttle, 'Better Dispute Resolution: The Development and Practice of Mediation in the United Kingdom Between 1995 and 2005' in J C Goldsmith, A Ingen-Housz and G H Pointon (eds), *ADR in Business: Practice and Issues Across Countries and Cultures* (Alphen aan den Rijn, Kluwer Law International 2006) 228–31.

[101] See Hopt and Steffek (n 6) 49.

[102] See, e.g., in Australia, Evidence Act 1995 (Cth) s 131(1): 'Evidence is not to be adduced of: (a) a communication that is made between persons in dispute, or between one or more persons in dispute and a third party, in connection with an attempt to negotiate

statutory provisions usually contain exceptions to the general grant of privilege.[103]

In Australia, there is no comprehensive federal law on confidentiality, but a range of statutory privileges. In New South Wales, the privilege applies in relation to any 'tribunal or body', and mediation is defined broadly to include steps taken to arrange mediation meetings or follow-ups to meetings,[104] while in Queensland, privilege is extended to mediation sessions and documents sent to or produced at a Dispute Resolution Centre for the purpose of arranging mediation.[105]

In the USA, rules of evidence, privileges, confidentiality and disclosure statutes and rules are all primary sources of rules governing confidentiality in mediation. Almost every state has adopted a rule of evidence to protect the confidentiality of settlement discussions. The key provision, rule 408 of the Federal Rules of Evidence covering compromise offers and negotiations, is known as the settlement negotiation rule and has been applied to mediations. It has served as the model for many state rules. It is a rule of evidence, rather than a guarantee of confidentiality, and is narrower than a privilege, which can be claimed at the discretion of the privilege holder for any purpose. The purpose of the rule is to prevent a party from using settlement negotiations to gain a litigation advantage by limiting what litigants can offer in evidence in a court proceeding. It does not typically affect what parties or third parties can disclose in any other context, and it has many exceptions. Evidence from the USA suggests that rules of evidence can be difficult to enforce, as parties who evade them ordinarily risk a judicial reprimand at most.[106]

A privilege bars the admission of evidence, regardless of the purpose for which it was offered, and is therefore less subject to evasion than an evidentiary rule such as rule 408. A violation of a privilege can also give rise to a cause of action for damages. While courts almost always apply their own rules of evidence, this is not the case with privileges. Whether a privilege

---

a settlement of the dispute; or (b) a document (whether delivered or not) that has been prepared in connection with an attempt to negotiate a settlement of a dispute.'

[103] See Boulle (n 2) 686. The approach in Australia under the Evidence Act 1995 (Cth) provides more exceptions than the English 'without prejudice' principle: see Briggs (n 52) 506.

[104] Courts Legislation (Mediation and Evaluation) Amendment Act 1994 (NSW) sch 1.

[105] Dispute Resolution Centres Act 1990 (Qld) s 36(b). See also Boulle (n 2) 687.

[106] See N Alexander (n 2) 271; R Korobkin, 'The Role of Law in Settlement' in M Moffitt and R Bordone (eds), *The Handbook of Dispute Resolution* (San Francisco, Jossey-Bass 2005) 269–70; D Golann and J Folberg, *Mediation: The Roles of Advocate and Neutral* (3rd ed, New York, Wolters Kluwer 2016) 330–31.

applies may depend on choice of law principles if the mediation takes place in one state and the case later goes to trial in another, making the outcome difficult to predict. There is no general mediation privilege in US federal proceedings, and federal courts can apply either state or federal privilege rules depending on the claim.[107] This can make it difficult to predict how confidential communications will be treated in federal courts. The rules on what phases of the mediation process are covered by privilege vary from state to state and can be poorly defined. As only those who hold the privilege can invoke it, it leaves the mediator without protection unless a party agrees to protect them from testifying. While the Uniform Mediation Act grants mediators the right to prevent disclosure of their own mediation communications,[108] Californian law goes significantly further, providing that the consent of both the mediator and the parties is required for anyone to testify regarding the content of a mediation, and the mediator may not testify at all.[109]

While neither the US legislature nor the federal courts have provided any general guarantee of mediation confidentiality, provisions exist in specific federal statutes.[110] Section 652(d) of the Alternative Dispute Resolution Act of 1998 (US) requires that federal district courts adopt local rules to provide for the confidentiality of alternative dispute resolution (ADR) processes within their court-connected programmes. Consequently, parties are more likely to find confidentiality protected in federal cases if they mediate under the auspices of a court ADR programme than if they privately mediate the dispute. Mediation programmes in state courts also typically provide similar mediation confidentiality protection, but their rules often do not specify what is meant by confidentiality.[111]

9.4.6.1   The EU Mediation Directive

Under the EU Mediation Directive,[112] EU Member States are required to ensure that, unless the parties agree otherwise, neither mediators nor

---

[107] Federal Rules of Evidence, rule 501.

[108] Uniform Mediation Act, s 4 (discussed in Section 9.4.6.3).

[109] California Evidence Code sections 703.5, 1122. Some states' mediation privileges are absolute, containing no exceptions, although courts may nonetheless create common law exceptions. The Uniform Mediation Act and others permit disclosure in set circumstances: see Golann and Folberg (n 106) 331–32.

[110] See, e.g., Administrative Dispute Resolution Act of 1996 (US) s 574, which generally bars disclosure of communications made in the course of mediating administrative cases.

[111] See Golann and Folberg (n 106) 333.

[112] Directive 2008/52/EC of the European Parliament and the Council of 21 May 2008 on certain aspects of mediation in civil and commercial matters ('EU Mediation Directive').

those involved in the administration of the mediation process will be compelled to give evidence in civil and commercial judicial proceedings or arbitration regarding information arising out of or in connection with a mediation process. Exceptions include circumstances where the information is required to implement or enforce a mediated settlement or where there are overriding reasons of public policy such as child protection or prevention of personal harm.[113]

While the Mediation Directive establishes a privilege for mediators to refuse to testify in subsequent adjudicative proceedings, it is silent on the 'without prejudice' rule. Nor does it address mediation participants such as parties and lawyers and their obligations regarding the admissibility of mediation evidence in subsequent court or arbitral proceedings. While there may be domestic privileges or other legal protections, these may permit potential gaps in, and opportunities for challenges to, confidentiality.

The Directive's confidentiality provision covers 'information arising out of or in connection with a mediation process', which is very broad and seems to cover documentation and conversations about the mediation that occur before, after or between mediation sessions or that are distinct from the mediation sessions themselves. There is still significant diversity in the law of mediation confidentiality within the European Union. Given that this is one of the most litigated aspects of mediation, legal advisors and parties are advised to examine the applicable law on confidentiality before engaging in cross-border mediation.[114]

---

[113] ibid 7(1). This may be contrasted with the Uniform Mediation Act, which gives mediators a higher standard of protection. Section 6(c) of the Uniform Mediation Act provides that a mediator may not be compelled to provide evidence of a mediation communication to prove or disprove a claim or complaint of professional misconduct or malpractice filed against a mediation party, non-party participant or representative of a party based on conduct occurring during a mediation or in a proceeding to prove a claim to rescind or reform, or a defence to avoid liability on, a contract arising out of the mediation.

[114] EU Mediation Directive (n 112) article 7(2) provides that it is open to Member States to enact stricter mediation confidentiality measures: see N Alexander, 'Harmonisation and Diversity in the Private International Law of Mediation: The Rhythms of Regulatory Reform' in Hopt and Steffek (eds) (n 1) 181–82. See also Koo (n 43) 202. There tends to be less judicial development on the issue of mediation privilege in the USA and Australia as those jurisdictions established statutory mediation privileges: see Alexander (n 2) 273–79. Article 7 of the EU Mediation Directive covers confidentiality issues in a similar way to the Uniform Mediation Act, as evidentiary privileges. See also Kulms (n 1) 230.

9.4.6.2   The UNCITRAL Mediation Model Law

The main provision in the Mediation Model Law[115] dealing with the general obligation of confidentiality in mediation is article 10, which states:

> Unless otherwise agreed by the parties, all information relating to the mediation proceedings shall be kept confidential, except where disclosure is required under the law or for purposes of implementation or enforcement of a settlement agreement.

This is preceded by article 9, which protects information entrusted to the mediator in caucus, if the relevant party requires that it not be disclosed to the other side. Article 9 reflects the 'open communication' approach rather than the more commonly used 'in-confidence' approach, reversing the more widely accepted presumption in many jurisdictions.[116] If this law were to act as a framework in a particular jurisdiction,[117] or if parties incorporated its provisions into their agreement to mediate, it would require revision to be made consistent with predominant international practice and reflect the more widely accepted 'in-confidence' presumption that a mediator may only divulge information to a party when explicitly permitted to do so by the party furnishing the information.

The third form of confidentiality, covering the non-disclosure of information in pre-trial discovery or in evidence in arbitral, judicial or similar proceedings is covered by article 11. Hence, confidentiality applies regardless of whether or not the mediated dispute is the same dispute that is subject to the court or arbitral proceedings where the disclosure is being sought, which broadens the scope of confidentiality.[118]

---

[115] UNCITRAL Model Law on International Commercial Mediation and International Settlement Agreements Resulting from Mediation 2018 ('Mediation Model Law').

[116] See Section 9.4.2.2. See also Boulle (n 2) 712; Alexander (n 114) 192. The 'in-confidence' as opposed to the 'open communication' presumption is also the approach adopted in many institutional rules including those of the LCIA and the World Intellectual Property Organization: see Brown and Winch (n 88) 330–31.

[117] See Feehily, 'Confidentiality in Commercial Mediation (Part 2)' (n 10) 734, for a critique of the draft Bill that ultimately became the Irish Mediation Act 2017, which draws heavily upon the Mediation Model Law (n 115).

[118] Boulle (n 2) 712. Similar to section 1119 of the California Evidence Code (discussed in Section 9.4.6.3) and s 131 of Australia's Evidence Act 1995 (Cth) (mentioned at n 102) this is an evidentiary exclusion rather than a privilege and consequently does not attach to mediation participants and cannot be waived. Evidentiary exclusions either list specific information or communications that are subject to confidentiality such as article 11 of the Mediation Model Law (n 115), or comprise a general rule of exclusion, making

While the Mediation Model Law provisions are more comprehensive than the EU Mediation Directive, the confidentiality provisions – like most aspects of the Model Law – are subject to the overarching objective of enhancing party autonomy. Consequently, by mutual agreement the parties can vary the level of confidentiality protection.[119]

9.4.6.3   The Uniform Mediation Act and California's Rule of Evidence

Statutory protection of mediation confidentiality is the solution adopted by a large number of states in the USA, as well as by the drafters of the Uniform Mediation Act.[120] With the growth of mediation, by 2001 there were over 2,500 separate state statutes or rules relating to mediation in the USA. The Uniform Mediation Act was adopted that year by the National Conference of Commissioners on Uniform State Laws to deal with the different provisions relating to mediation across the nation, with the principal purposes of assuring confidentiality and fostering uniformity. While the Uniform Mediation Act is intended to create a baseline or minimum confidentiality standard, it does not supplant more stringent state confidentiality requirements. It provides a mechanism for protecting mediation confidentiality and specifies limited exceptions where other policy considerations take priority.[121]

Privileges regarding confidential professional relationships are common in the USA: examples are the attorney–client and psychiatrist–patient privileges. Many originate from the code of ethics of a professional organisation or statute. They usually include a duty to keep information confidential and an exemption from involuntary testimony. The mediation context is different from other contexts where the duty of confidentiality is imposed on the professional but not on the client; the mediator–disputant privilege created by the Uniform

---

all mediation evidence inadmissible subject to specific exceptions: see Alexander (n 2) 262–63.

[119] See Alexander (n 114) 190.

[120] See Van Ginkel (n 59) 48.

[121] See Sussman (n 5) 36. The Uniform Mediation Act links confidentiality to upholding principles of procedural fairness, process integrity and informed party consent throughout the mediation process. Hence if mediators breach a professional duty, they lose the confidentiality privilege. The Act effectively adopts a regulatory approach to confidentiality that attempts to balance competing interests and provide greater mediation confidentiality certainty both within states and in interstate mediations: see Alexander (n 2) 252, 258.

Mediation Act is imposed on both the mediator and all other mediation participants. Similarly, the other privileges do not necessarily prevent a third party from attempting to compel testimony on these issues, while the mediator–disputant privilege is absolute unless there is an exception or a waiver. In addition, the other privileges do not prevent a client from making voluntary disclosures outside arbitral or judicial proceedings, whereas the mediator–disputant privilege created by the Uniform Mediation Act is intended to prohibit this.[122]

Framing confidentiality as an evidentiary privilege means legislators can clearly define the extent of the privilege regarding the mediation information and activities covered; the people the privilege affects, including who can invoke or waive it and the extent to which this can be done; the subsequent proceedings the privilege will apply to; and the information excepted from the privilege. In maintaining mediation confidentiality this approach can also accommodate the separate, and possibly conflicting, interests of the mediator and participants. This approach has been adopted in sections 4, 5 and 6 of the Uniform Mediation Act. Section 4[123] creates the privileges of the participants in the mediation, section 5[124] details who is permitted to waive the

---

[122] See Van Ginkel (n 59) 48.

[123] Section 4 provides: '[Privilege against disclosure; admissibility; discovery] (a) Except as otherwise provided in Section 6, a mediation communication is privileged as provided in subsection (b) and is not subject to discovery or admissible in evidence in a proceeding unless waived or precluded as provided by Section 5. (b) In a proceeding, the following privileges apply: (1) A mediation party may refuse to disclose a mediation communication, and may prevent any other person from disclosing, a mediation communication. (2) A mediator may refuse to disclose a mediation communication, and may prevent any other person from disclosing a mediation communication of the mediator. (3) A non-party participant may refuse to disclose, and may prevent any other person from disclosing, a mediation communication of the non-party participant. (c) Evidence or information that is otherwise admissible or subject to discovery does not become inadmissible or protected from discovery solely by reason of its disclosure or use in a mediation.'

[124] Section 5 provides: '[Waiver and preclusion of privilege] (a) A privilege under Section 4 may be waived in a record or orally during a proceeding if it is expressly waived by all parties to the mediation and: (1) in the case of the privilege of a mediator, it is expressly waived by the mediator; and (2) in the case of the privilege of a non-party participant, it is expressly waived by the non-party participant. (b) A person that discloses or makes representation about a mediation communication that prejudices another person in a proceeding is precluded from asserting a privilege under Section 4, but only to the extent necessary for the person prejudiced to respond to the representation or disclosure. (c) A person that intentionally uses a mediation to plan, attempt to commit or commit a crime, or to conceal an ongoing crime or ongoing criminal activity is precluded from asserting a privilege under Section 4.'

relevant privileges, and section 6[125] provides the exceptions to the privileges.[126]

The chief purpose of the Uniform Mediation Act is to ensure that mediation communications remain confidential to make mediation a fairer, more effective and more attractive means to settle disputes. Many US states have refused to adopt the Uniform Mediation Act

---

[125] Section 6 provides: '[Exceptions to privilege] (a) There is no privilege under Section 4 for a mediation communication that is: (1) in an agreement evidenced by a record signed by all parties to the agreement; (2) available to the public under [insert statutory reference to open records act] or made during a session of a mediation which is open, or is required by law to be open, to the public; (3) a threat or statement of a plan to inflict bodily injury or commit a crime of violence; (4) intentionally used to plan a crime, attempt to commit or commit a crime, or to conceal an ongoing crime or ongoing criminal activity; (5) sought or offered to prove or disprove a claim or complaint of professional misconduct or malpractice filed against a mediator; (6) except as otherwise provided in subsection (c), sought or offered to prove or disprove a claim or complaint of professional misconduct or malpractice filed against a mediation party, non-party participant, or representative of a party based on conduct occurring during a mediation; or (7) sought or offered to prove or disprove abuse, neglect, abandonment, or exploitation in a proceeding in which a child or adult protective services agency is a party, unless the [Alternative A: [State to insert, for example, child or adult protection] case is referred by a court to mediation and a public agency participates.] [Alternative B: public agency participates in the [State to insert, for example, child or adult protection] mediation]. (b) There is no privilege under Section 4 if a court, administrative agency, or arbitrator finds, after a hearing in camera, that the party seeking discovery or the proponent of the evidence has shown that the evidence is not otherwise available, that there is a need for the evidence that substantially outweighs the interest in protecting confidentiality, and that the mediation communication is sought or offered in: (1) a court proceeding involving a felony [or misdemeanour]; or (2) except as otherwise provided in subsection (c), a proceeding to prove a claim to rescind or reform or a defence to avoid liability on a contract arising out of the mediation. (c) A mediator may not be compelled to provide evidence of a mediation communication referred to in subsection (a)(6) or (b)(2). (d) If a mediation communication is not privileged under subsection (a) or (b), only the portion of the communication necessary for the application of the exception from nondisclosure may be admitted. Admission of evidence under subsection (a) or (b) does not render the evidence, or any other mediation communication, discoverable or admissible for any other purpose.'

Section 6 of the Uniform Mediation Act is effectively an effort to balance competing public policy needs, reflecting a qualified approach to privilege. Only that part of a mediation communication required for applying the exception is disclosed or admitted as evidence, ensuring the principle of proportionality in section 6(d) is observed. Exceptions to confidentiality tend to be interpreted narrowly, with disclosure being proportional to the exception. This is in contrast to the approach adopted in the California Evidence Code, discussed below, and interpreted by the courts in absolute terms: see Alexander (n 2) 281.

[126] See Van Ginkel (n 59) 48–49. See also Alexander (n 2) 276–79; R Kulms, 'Mediation in the USA: Alternative Dispute Resolution Between Legalism and Self-Determination' in Hopt and Steffek (eds) (n 1) 1287–90.

despite its invitation to incorporate existing state laws, largely because existing state mediation laws, particularly those dealing with confidentiality, are already much stronger than the Uniform Mediation Act.[127] California provides an interesting example of a state that has gone considerably further than the Uniform Mediation Act in protecting mediation confidentiality. In California, the first form of confidentiality – where a party shares information with the mediator in caucus – is contained in rule 3.854(c) of the California Rules of Court.[128] Similar to many institutional rules,[129] it provides that the mediator must keep information that was shared in caucus confidential, unless express consent to disclose it to others in the mediation is provided by the person sharing it. The Uniform Mediation Act does not have a corresponding provision.[130]

The second form of confidentiality – the general obligation on the mediator and all participants not to disclose information to any third party – is covered in California by section 1119(c) of the Evidence Code, which provides: 'All communications, negotiations, or settlement discussions by and between participants in the course of a mediation or a

---

[127] See Golann and Folberg (n 106) 346–47.

[128] Rule 3.854(c) provides: '[Confidentiality of separate communications; caucuses] If, after all the parties have agreed to participate in the mediation process and the mediator has agreed to mediate the case, a mediator speaks separately with one or more participants out of the presence of the other participants, the mediator must first discuss with all participants the mediator's practice regarding confidentiality for separate communications with the participants. Except as required by law, a mediator must not disclose information revealed in confidence during such separate communications unless authorised to do so by the participant or participants who revealed the information.'

[129] For example, article 3(h) of the CPR Mediation Procedure (promulgated by the CPR International Institute for Conflict Prevention & Resolution) provides: 'The mediator will not transmit information received in confidence from any party to any other party or any third party unless authorized to do so by the party transmitting the information, or unless ordered to do so by a court of competent jurisdiction'. Article 6.3 of the LCIA Mediation Rules provides: 'Nothing which is communicated to the mediator in private during the course of the mediation shall be repeated to the other party or parties, without the express consent of the party making the communication.' Most of the older mediation rules seem to provide the reverse – that is, that the mediator can share information obtained in caucus from the other mediation participants unless the person revealing the information specifically requests that it be kept confidential: see, e.g., UNCITRAL Mediation Rules (n 84) art 10, which was adopted almost verbatim by article 8 of the UNCITRAL Model Law on International Commercial Conciliation (now article 9 of the UNCITRAL Mediation Model Law (n 115)). See Section 9.4.2.2. See also Van Ginkel (n 59) 47.

[130] Similarly, there is no corresponding provision in rules such as the ICC Mediation Rules (n 84) or the ICDR Mediation Rules. See also Van Ginkel (n 59) 47; Alexander (n 2) 286–87. See also Kulms (n 1) 228–29.

mediation consultation shall remain confidential.' The equivalent provision is section 8 of the Uniform Mediation Act, and was inserted after extensive discussion regarding the usefulness of the provision. The reluctance of the Drafting Committee to adopt it is clear from the text:

> Unless subject to the [insert statutory references to Open Meetings Act and Open Records Act], mediation communications are confidential to the extent agreed by the parties or provided by other law or rule of this State.

Section 8 of the Uniform Mediation Act effectively bars confidentiality of mediation communications unless and to the degree that the parties have agreed to it, or another law or rule of the state provides differently. The mediator's consent is not required. Section 1119(c) of the Evidence Code is at the other end of the spectrum, as it provides for a broad duty of confidentiality from which a departure can only be made under section 1122(a), which effectively requires the express written agreement of all parties and the mediator.[131]

The third form of confidentiality is covered in California by section 1119(a) (for oral communications) and (b) (for writings) of the Evidence Code. These provide in principle that evidence of information disclosed in a mediation is inadmissible, both in pre-trial discovery and in arbitral and non-criminal judicial proceedings.[132] Section 1120(a) of the Code provides the general exception:

---

[131] Section 1122(a) provides: 'A communication or a writing, as defined in Section 250, that is made or prepared for the purpose of, or in the course of, or pursuant to, a mediation or a mediation consultation, is not made inadmissible, or protected from disclosure, by provisions of this chapter if either of the following conditions is satisfied: (1) All persons who conduct or otherwise participate in the mediation expressly agree in writing, or orally in accordance with Section 1118, to disclosure of the communication, document, or writing. (2) The communication, document, or writing was prepared by or on behalf of fewer than all the mediation participants, those participants expressly agree in writing, or orally in accordance with Section 1118, to its disclosure, and the communication, document, or writing does not disclose anything said or done or any admission made in the course of the mediation.' See also Van Ginkel (n 59) 47; Alexander (n 2) 286–87.

[132] Section 1119(a) and 1119(b) provides: 'Except as otherwise provided in this chapter: (a) No evidence of anything said or any admission made for the purpose of, in the course of, or pursuant to, a mediation or a mediation consultation is admissible or subject to discovery, and disclosure of the evidence shall not be compelled, in any arbitration, administrative adjudication, civil action, or other noncriminal proceeding in which, pursuant to law, testimony can be compelled to be given. (b) No writing, as defined in Section 250, that is prepared for the purpose of, in the course of, or pursuant to, a mediation or a mediation consultation, is admissible or subject to discovery, and disclosure of the writing shall not be compelled, in any arbitration, administrative adjudication, civil action, or other noncriminal proceeding in which, pursuant to law, testimony can be compelled to be given.'

> Evidence otherwise admissible or subject to discovery outside of a mediation or a mediation consultation shall not be or become inadmissible or protected from disclosure solely by reason of its introduction or use in a mediation or a mediation consultation.

In addition to this general exception, section 1119(a) and 1119(b) of the Evidence Code, by limiting the protection of mediation communications to non-criminal proceedings, effectively excludes criminal proceedings from the inadmissibility rule. In addition, section 1120(b)[133] provides specific exceptions to the exclusionary rule of section 1119 relating to (1) an agreement to mediate; (2) any agreement not to take a default or to extend time to act in a pending action; and (3) the fact that a particular mediator served or was otherwise involved in a mediation, so that these three elements are admissible in any subsequent proceeding. The provisions of sections 1119 and 1120 are not mandatory, and can be waived by agreement among all participants in the mediation, including the mediator, by section 1122(a) of the Code.[134]

The scope of sections 1119 and 1120 is uncertain, and it can be difficult to distinguish between documents, photographs, etc. that have been 'prepared for the purpose of, in the course of, or pursuant to, a mediation', and evidence otherwise admissible that 'shall not be or become inadmissible or protected from disclosure solely by reason of its introduction or use in a mediation'. This problem was central to *Rojas* v. *Superior Court*.[135] In this case, the California Supreme Court overturned the Court of Appeal's ruling that had devised an exception to mediation confidentiality to help plaintiffs in a subsequent proceeding access documents that the trial court had held, as a non-appealable finding of fact, were created exclusively for the mediation. The Supreme Court held that the confidentiality of mediation communications is absolute as it applies to evidence prepared for the sole and limited purpose of mediation, with the exception being evidence that is expressly specified by statute.[136]

---

[133] Section 1120(b) reads: 'This chapter does not limit any of the following: (1) The admissibility of an agreement to mediate a dispute. (2) The effect of an agreement not to take a default or an agreement to extend the time within which to act or refrain from acting in a pending civil action. (3) Disclosure of the mere fact that a mediator has served, is serving, will serve, or was contacted about serving as a mediator in a dispute.'

[134] Section 1122(a) applies as much to section 1119(a) and 1119(b) as it does to section 1119(c): see Van Ginkel (n 59) 48.

[135] 33 Cal 4th 407 (2004).

[136] See Van Ginkel (n 59) 48. For a discussion of the *Rojas* case, see E Van Ginkel, '*Rojas v Superior Court*: The Battle of Two Opposing Public Policies', IBA Legal Practice Division Mediation Committee Newsletter, April 2005, 31–37.

Before embarking on a specific discussion of *Rojas*, three preceding cases that redefined the relationship between mediators and the courts in California warrant a mention. In *Olam* v. *Congress Mortgage Co*,[137] a federal court ordered a mediator to testify as to whether an agreement signed in mediation was the product of duress or free will. The parties asked that the mediator testify. The judge assumed that the mediator would object, and ruled that, even over such an objection, the mediation privilege was subordinate to the orderly administration of justice.[138]

In *Rinaker* v. *Superior Court*,[139] two juveniles accused of a crime had participated in an earlier mediation during which a witness made statements that would contradict critical testimony he would offer at trial.[140] The trial judge ordered the mediator to testify, and the California Court of Appeals held that the juvenile proceeding was like any other civil matter, but that mediation confidentiality was subordinate to the 'constitutional right to effective impeachment'.[141]

In *Foxgate Homeowners' Association* v. *Bramalea California Inc*,[142] the court ordered mediation and the parties stipulated that the mediation would be a procedure in which experts would debate the merits of the claim. The plaintiff brought nine experts, while the defendant arrived late, bringing none. The mediation ended early. With no progress being made, the mediator filed a report with the court indicating that the defendant had shown bad faith and should be sanctioned. The trial court acknowledged the mediator's report and awarded $30,000 in damages. The defendant appealed and the appellate court ruled that the mediator's report could be considered in a case involving sanctions without infringing unduly on mediation confidentiality.[143] The

---

[137] 68 F Supp 2d 1110 (ND Cal 1999).
[138] ibid 1132. The facts of the case are given in Chapter 8 at Section 8.2.6. The Court believed that the mediator's testimony was the most reliable and probative evidence and that there was no likely alternative source.
[139] 62 Cal App 4th 155 (1998).
[140] ibid 161.
[141] ibid 164. Although a delinquency proceeding is a civil action within the meaning of section 1119 and the confidentiality provisions were consequently applicable, the Court believed that this statutory right must be subordinate to the minors' due process rights to defend themselves and to confront, cross-examine and impeach the witness about the inconsistent nature of his statements. The witness was also the alleged victim. He claimed that the minors had thrown rocks at his car, but in the mediation admitted he had not seen who threw them.
[142] 26 Cal 4th 1 (2001).
[143] *Foxgate Homeowners' Association v Bramalea California* 78 Cal App 4th 653 (2000).

California Supreme Court took a different view and held that confidentiality was to be respected even in a sanctions case.[144]

The case of *Rojas*[145] provides a further example of the dilemma that arises when the policy that requires parties to disclose all relevant evidence conflicts with the policy that supports mediation confidentiality. In this case, the policy of disclosure prevailed in the Court of Appeal, while the policy of mediation confidentiality ultimately prevailed in the Supreme Court.[146]

The background to this case involved Julie Coffin and others who purchased a building complex in Los Angeles in 1994. In December 1996, they filed a construction defect action[147] against the developers, contractors and subcontractors ('developers'). They alleged that water leakage resulted from poor construction work, which caused the presence of toxic moulds and other microbes on the property.[148] The parties mediated the dispute and settled the underlying action in April 1999. As it was in both parties' interests to keep this evidence concealed from the tenants who may have suffered injury by the presence of toxic mould when they lived at the building complex, the parties specifically agreed in their mediated settlement agreement that the defect reports, repair reports and photographs for informational purposes were protected by section 1119[149] of the California Evidence Code and section 1152 – an exclusionary rule relating to negotiations in compromise of litigation – and that the materials and information they comprised would

---

[144] *Foxgate* (2001) (n 142). The Supreme Court distinguished the case from *Rinaker* (n 139), saying this was consistent with its previous recognition – and that of the United States Supreme Court – that due process entitles juveniles to some of the fundamental constitutional rights enjoyed by adults, including the right to confront and cross-examine, but that the plaintiffs in *Foxgate* (2001) had 'no comparable supervening due process based right' to use mediation evidence: at 16.

[145] *Rojas* (2004) (n 135).

[146] See Van Ginkel, '*Rojas v Superior Court*' (n 136) 31. See also Kulms (n 126) 1282–86.

[147] *Coffin v. KSF Holdings* (unreported); see Van Ginkel, '*Rojas v Superior Court*' (n 136) 32.

[148] *Rojas v. Superior Court* 102 Cal App 4th 1062, 1067 (2002).

[149] The relevant parts of section 1119 of the Evidence Code provide: 'Except as otherwise provided in this chapter: (a) No evidence of anything said or any admission made for the purpose of, in the course of, or pursuant to, a mediation or a mediation consultation is admissible or subject to discovery, and disclosure of the evidence shall not be compelled, in any ... civil action ... (b) No writing, as defined in Section 250, that is prepared for the purpose of, in the course of, or pursuant to, a mediation or a mediation consultation, is admissible or subject to discovery, and disclosure of the writing shall not be compelled, in any ... civil action ... (c) All communications, negotiations, or settlement discussions by and between participants in the course of a mediation or a mediation consultation shall remain confidential.'

not be published or disclosed without the prior consent of Coffin or by court order.[150]

In August 1999, Rojas and almost 200 other tenants of the building complex including minors ('Rojas') began an action against Coffin and some of the contractors. They claimed that they had not been aware of the building defects until April of that year, when the remedial work had commenced, and that Coffin and the developers colluded to conceal the defects and microbe infestation from them. The trial court indicated it was concerned about applying the mediation privilege to raw evidence, as the photographs were just fixed representations of the state of a place at a particular time, and that if there was no alternative way for the plaintiff to get the relevant evidence, the mediation privilege was not meant as a device to block such evidence. However, it felt bound by the statutory language and ruled that the materials were protected from discovery, despite the showing of necessity by Rojas.[151]

The Court of Appeal rejected Coffin's reading of sections 1119 and 1120 that all materials introduced at the mediation, or prepared for the mediation, including those of a purely evidentiary nature, are incorporated within the scope of the privilege because they were 'prepared for the purpose of, in the course of, or pursuant to' the mediation. The Court remarked that 'such a reading would render section 1120 complete surplusage and foster the evils it is designed to prevent: namely, using mediation as a shield for otherwise admissible evidence'.[152] The Court of Appeal found that non-derivative material such as raw test data, photographs and witness statements are not protected by section 1119, and, to the extent that any of the materials sought are part of a compilation, they would have to be produced if they could be reasonably separated from the compilation. The Court also noted that, as Rojas had not been joined in the prior lawsuit, and as Coffin's and the developers' remediation works

---

[150] See Van Ginkel, 'Rojas v Superior Court' (n 136) 32.

[151] While the courts often refer to the evidentiary rule regarding mediation confidentiality as a privilege, the California Evidence Code does not create a privilege in the true meaning of the word, such as the mediation privilege created by the Uniform Mediation Act. California's confidentiality protections are stated in the form of an evidence exclusion provision, and have been construed by the courts more like a privilege held by all participants which operates as a bar to compelling disclosure, discovery or testimony without everyone's consent: see Van Ginkel, 'Rojas v Superior Court' (n 136) 32; R Callahan, 'Mediation Confidentiality: For California Litigants, Why Should Mediation Confidentiality Be a Function of the Court in which the Litigation is Pending?' (2012) 12(1) Pepperdine Dispute Resolution Law Journal 63, 94.

[152] Rojas (2002) (n 148) 1076.

had eliminated most, if not all, of the relevant evidence, Rojas had no other means of acquiring this information.[153]

The Supreme Court delivered its opinion confirming 'absolute confidentiality' in July 2004. In reversing the Court of Appeal's decision, which had argued that an interpretation such as the one advocated by Coffin, would render section 1120 'surplusage', Ming Chin J, delivering the opinion for a unanimous Supreme Court, noted that the Court of Appeal's construction of section 1119(a) would mean that section 1119(b) would serve no purpose, and would result in that section being 'essentially useless'. It also found that the Court of Appeal's decision was inconsistent both with the plain meaning of section 1119 and the legislative history of sections 1119 and 1120.[154] Referring to its earlier decision in *Foxgate*,[155] the Supreme Court emphasised that:

> '[C]onfidentiality is essential to effective mediation' because it 'promote[s] a candid and informal exchange regarding events in the past' ... This frank exchange is achieved only if the participants know that what is said in the mediation will not be used to their detriment through later court proceedings and other adjudicatory processes.[156]

The Supreme Court also recalled that in *Foxgate* it had:

> stated that '[t]o carry out the purpose of encouraging mediation by ensuring confidentiality, [our] statutory scheme ... unqualifiedly bars disclosure of specified communications and writings associated with a mediation 'absent an *express statutory* exception'. We also found that the 'judicially crafted exception' to section 1119 there at issue was 'not necessary either to carry out the legislative intent or to avoid an absurd result'. We reach the same conclusion here; as Judge Mohr observed, 'the mediation privilege is an important one, and if courts start dispensing with it by using the (Court of Appeal) ... test you may have people less willing to mediate.'[157]

The Supreme Court's interpretation does not distinguish between writings marked before their introduction into a mediation and writings marked towards the end of the process. The interpretation of sections 1119 and 1120 adopted by the Court does not prevent a party to a mediation in a litigated case declaring certain writings to be 'prepared for mediation' at a time that the parties know they have a settlement, so

---

[153] See Van Ginkel, '*Rojas v Superior Court*' (n 136) 33. See also Alexander (n 2) 254–56.
[154] *Rojas* (2004) (n 135) 416–24.
[155] *Foxgate* (n 142).
[156] *Rojas* (2004) (n 135) 422, quoting *Foxgate* (n 142) 14.
[157] ibid 424 (emphasis in original).

that those writings can be excluded from subsequent proceedings.[158] A practical solution would result in the statute being amended in order that the mediation privilege would attach only to those writings that have been marked 'prepared for mediation' before their introduction into a mediation, and also expressly authorising a trial court to weigh the interests of the two conflicting public policies in a subsequent trial, whether it is between the same parties or involves one or more third parties. With this type of discretionary authority, in appropriate circumstances the court could admit such a writing despite the proposed rule of its subsequent inadmissibility, if the interests of access to evidence in litigation outweighed the interests of keeping it confidential because it had been prepared for mediation; for example, where there is no other way for a party to acquire such evidence as it no longer exists.[159]

Subsequent to *Rojas*,[160] the California Supreme Court appears to have maintained its 'absolute confidentiality' approach. In *Simmons* v. *Ghaderi*,[161] the Supreme Court unanimously reversed the decision of the Court of Appeal and refused to allow evidence of what had transpired in mediation. The parties reached an oral agreement at mediation, but before signing it, Simmons withdrew from the mediation and refused to sign the written agreement that gave effect to the oral agreement. Ghaderi sought to enforce the settlement with a declaration from the mediator outlining events at the mediation. The Supreme Court held that the doctrine of estoppel could not be used to create a judicial exception to the comprehensive scheme of mediation confidentiality. In the course of its judgment, the Supreme Court referred to its disapproval of 'judicially crafted' exceptions[162] to mediation confidentiality statutes it had condemned in *Foxgate*.[163]

In *Cassel* v. *Superior Court*,[164] an action for legal malpractice was taken by a client against his attorneys based on what transpired during the

---

[158] Southern California Mediation Association, Amicus Curiae Brief in Support of Petitioners, *Rojas v Superior Court* 33 Cal 4th 407 (2004), 9. See also Van Ginkel, '*Rojas v Superior Court*' (n 136) 34.

[159] See Van Ginkel, '*Rojas v Superior Court*' (n 136) 34–35.

[160] *Rojas* (2004) (n 135).

[161] 80 Cal Rptr 3d 83 (2008).

[162] ibid 93 (Chin J): 'Judicially crafted exceptions to mediation confidentiality are not appropriate.'

[163] *Foxgate* (n 142).

[164] 51 Cal 4th 113 (2011). See also *Wimsatt* v. *Superior Court* 152 Cal App 4th 137 (2007), a case that involved allegations of legal malpractice where the Court of Appeal adopted a similarly restrictive mediation confidentiality approach, reversing the trial court's decision.

mediation of an underlying lawsuit. It was alleged that bad advice, deception and coercion, on the part of his attorneys, induced him to settle the claim at an undervalue. The trial court granted the defendant's request for a motion, before the malpractice trial, to exclude all evidence of private attorney–client discussions before and during the mediation relating to mediation settlement strategy and efforts to persuade the client to settle during the mediation. The Court of Appeal subsequently reversed the order, on the basis that the statutory regime for mediation confidentiality is intended to prevent the damaging use against a mediation 'disputant' of strategies employed, or opinions and information exchanged during a mediation, and not to protect attorneys from malpractice claims.

The Supreme Court revisited *Foxgate*,[165] *Rojas*[166] and *Simmons*[167] and concluded:

> [T]he plain language of the mediation confidentiality statutes controls our result. Section 1119, subdivision (a) clearly provides that '[n]o evidence of anything said or any admission made for the purpose of, in the course of, or pursuant to, a mediation ... is admissible or subject to discovery' ... Plainly, such communications include those between a mediation disputant and his or her own counsel, even if these do not occur in the presence of the mediator or other disputants.[168]

The Supreme Court also relied on the exceptions in section 1122 of the Evidence Code, which provides for the admissibility of communications where not all mediation participants confirm disclosure of otherwise confidential information, provided the disclosure does not reveal 'anything said or done ... in the course of the mediation'.[169] In addition, the Court rejected the Court of Appeal's focus on 'disputants' noting that '[t]he protection afforded by these statutes is not limited by the identity of the communicator'.[170] Consistent with its well-established doctrine, the Court was unwilling to create a judicially crafted exception to absolute mediation confidentiality outside the express statutory language.

Rojas[171] demonstrated the courts' concern about making mediation evidence inaccessible where a party declares certain writings to be

---

[165] *Foxgate* (n 142).
[166] *Rojas* (2004) (n 135).
[167] *Simmons* (n 161).
[168] *Cassel* (n 164) 128.
[169] ibid 131. Section 1122(a) is set out at n 131.
[170] ibid 130.
[171] *Rojas* (2004) (n 135).

'prepared for mediation' at a time that the parties know they have a settlement, to ensure those writings can be excluded from subsequent proceedings. Laws ostensibly designed to strengthen mediation as a dispute resolution process may also, ironically, reduce constraints on using misrepresentation to create bargaining power within the process. Decisions such as *Foxgate*,[172] *Rojas* and the jurisprudence that has followed demonstrate that the courts' strict interpretation of the California Evidence Code, as providing an absolute privilege for statements made in mediation, strongly suggests that evidence of deceit during the process cannot be introduced into evidence in court for any reason. In jurisdictions that recognise an absolute mediation privilege, contract and tort law may technically limit parties' ability to use deceit to create bargaining power, while evidence law effectively makes these limitations unenforceable.[173]

9.5 Concluding Thoughts

Confidentiality in mediation involves striking a balance between encouraging settlement through a protected process and ensuring that litigants and courts have adequate access to evidence; between supporting mediation and not freezing litigation or upholding illegality. While the principle of sanctity of contract supports maintaining confidentiality where there is an agreement, if it is too wide, it will sterilise too much evidence and seriously undermine the trial process, and if it is too narrow, it will discourage parties from engaging in good faith in mediation. There is often a lacuna between the general perception that complete confidentiality applies to the participants in a mediation, and the more limited protection conferred by the courts. Where the information given to parties at the start of the process does not equate with the legal position if the issue later comes before a court, this will raise concerns about the parties' informed consent.[174] The practical implication of mediation confidentiality's legal complexities is to use caution when promoting and explaining the process to disputants, and to advise them that there may be limits on the extent to which courts will protect communications made during the process.[175]

---

[172] *Foxgate* (n 142).
[173] Korobkin (n 106) 264.
[174] See P Brooker, 'Mediator Immunity: Time for Evaluation in England and Wales?' (2016) 36(3) *Legal Studies* 464, 481.
[175] See Boulle and Nesic (n 16) 505–6; Koo (n 43) 201. As noted in Section 9.4.2, in England, the existence of an agreement to mediate requiring confidentiality has not succeeded in

While the approach of making mediation confidentiality 'absolute' seems to create a straightforward rule suitable to an informal process, experience demonstrates that absolute rules can be an overreaction to the shortcomings of more liberal evidentiary rules, statutes and contractual arrangements. Restricting disclosure to specific circumstances or discrete contexts can cover matters with a veil of privilege that may prove difficult to circumvent where necessary. Many US states have resisted implementing the Uniform Mediation Act on the basis that courts should maintain the right to circumvent the privilege where the interests of justice require it. Some have also suggested that the provisions of the Act go too far in protecting mediators against legitimate state interests. It has also been suggested that some provisions are hostile to the areas of practice that made mediation the popular process it has become, and, while it is reasonable to expect some consistency when participating in the mediation process, mediation must adapt to the needs of the parties and the parameters of the dispute being mediated. Mediation flourished due to the diversity and adaptability of the process; these qualities are inconsistent with absolute rules, and these may, it has been suggested, prove to be incompatible with uniform laws.[176]

An alternative approach in common law countries would involve the creation of a mediation privilege that appreciates the distinct nature of the process and protects mediation evidence including communications made in the course of the mediation.[177] Disclosure of documents and communications within a mediation could be admitted in limited circumstances to be specified by the court on a case-by-case basis. This more generalised formulation – recognising

providing any wider protection than that provided by the 'without prejudice' principle, however a contractual remedy may provide a secure basis to obtain an injunction to restrain a threatened breach of confidentiality: see *Venture Investment Placement Ltd v. Hall* [2005] EWHC 1227 (Ch); *David Instance* (n 37). See also Briggs (n 52) 506.

[176] R Birke and L E Teitz, 'US Mediation in the Twenty-First Century: The Path That Brought America to Uniform Laws and Mediation Cyberspace' in N Alexander (ed), *Global Trends in Mediation* (The Hague: Kluwer Law International 2003) 387–88.

[177] This has been mooted by the English courts: see, e.g., *Brown* (n 19) [20], where Deputy High Court Judge, Mr Stuart Isaacs QC, remarked, 'it may be in the future that the existence of a distinct mediation privilege will require to be considered by either the legislature or the courts'; *Cumbria Waste Management* (n 35) [30], where Kirkham J stated, 'whether on the basis of the without prejudice rule or as an exception to the general rule that confidentiality is not a bar to disclosure, the court should support the mediation process by refusing, in normal circumstances, to order disclosure of documents and communications within a mediation'. See Section 9.4.1.1 for a discussion of both cases.

a distinct mediation privilege – would give clear protection to virtually all mediation communications. On the occasional circumstance when the veil of privilege needed to be dislodged, it could allow the court greater latitude than prescriptive, static exceptions.[178]

This approach could provide the flexibility that the mediation process requires, by dealing with issues on a case-by-case basis, balancing public policy considerations, the requirements of the process and the needs of participants and third parties. Commercial courts will increasingly be panelled with judges who have experience of the mediation process. Continued training and education of the judiciary will help ensure that the courts are familiar with commercial mediation. Specialised judges with experience and expertise in the commercial mediation process gained while in practice as a legal advisor or mediator or both, could be deployed within the commercial courts to deal with mediation-related issues. This would ensure that the judge who decides if an exception to the privilege is justified has knowledge of both the process and its legal limitations.[179] The emerging jurisprudence would give mediators, lawyers and parties clear guidance about the contours of mediation privilege and what they can expect in the jurisdiction where they are mediating.

While mediation privileges bar evidence from being admitted in adjudication, they do not bar disclosure outside court proceedings; consequently, privilege does not equate to comprehensive confidentiality. There is nothing to stop those with information sharing it outside a court proceeding. In the absence of a comprehensive mediation statute, for confidentiality protection the parties must enter into an agreement.[180] Coupled with other forms of regulation, such as statute and common law, contractual terms can be helpful in securing the level and type of confidentiality required. Confidentiality provisions should clearly reflect the scope of confidentiality; who possesses the rights or obligations; what is protected; the temporal coverage, including whether preliminary meetings, interim and follow-up contact is included; and whether any exceptions are required. Contractual confidentiality is also helpful in clarifying the

---

[178] See Feehily, 'Confidentiality in Commercial Mediation (Part 2)' (n 10) 734. The privilege would be tailored according to the commercial mediation process and the public interest in protecting it: see Boulle (n 2) 681–82; Boulle and Nesic (n 16) 497–99.

[179] This already happens in the field of arbitration. For example, Ireland's Commercial Court, a division of its High Court, has a designated Arbitration Judge to hear all arbitration-related matters: see The Courts Service of Ireland, 'Judges of the Commercial Court' <www.courts.ie/judges-commercial-court> accessed 10 May 2022.

[180] See Golann and Folberg (n 106) 331.

existing law and the parties' intentions, especially regarding discretionary law and any lacuna that may appear in existing regulation. For example, neither the EU Mediation Directive nor the Uniform Mediation Act provides for the confidentiality of caucus sessions or the general duty of confidentiality with regard to outside parties, leaving it to the parties, in the absence of supportive domestic legislation, to contract for this protection.[181]

The extent of mediation disclosure is best provided for in the agreement to mediate and any ancillary confidentiality agreements with other mediation participants and support staff. Parties and their advisors should consider how best this can be achieved through appropriate drafting to ensure that all relevant information and individuals are covered. However, contracts that traverse national borders and legal cultures are tempered by national legal culture, domestic public policies and mandatory forms of regulation. The relevant jurisdiction is likely to be where litigation may take place, rather than where the mediation occurred. Effective mediation confidentiality requires an investigation into and analysis of the extent to which national courts recognise contractual confidentiality undertakings in the relevant jurisdictions. Parties should be aware of the extent of confidentiality protection to ensure there are no unintended or commercially harmful disclosures.[182]

Confidentiality in commercial mediation is likely to receive cumulative protection. Commercial parties in most cases will have signed an agreement to mediate. This will be reinforced if the agreement incorporates a set of institutional rules that contain confidentiality provisions. If the

---

[181] Section 4 of the Uniform Mediation Act, set out at n 123 covers privilege against disclosure, admissibility and discovery. Section 8 of the Act covers confidentiality, and provides that mediation communications are confidential to the extent agreed by the parties or provided by other laws or rules of the adopting state. Article 7 of the EU Mediation Directive (n 112) covers confidentiality and provides that neither mediators nor those involved in the administration of the mediation process will be compelled to give evidence in civil and commercial judicial proceedings or arbitration regarding information arising out of or in connection with a mediation process, subject to the exceptions discussed in Section 9.4.6.1, and acknowledging that Member States are not precluded from introducing stricter mediation confidentiality protection. Article 9 of the Mediation Model Law (n 115) protects information entrusted to the mediator in caucus if the relevant party requires that it not be disclosed to the other side. This reflects the 'open communication' approach rather than the more widely accepted 'in-confidence' approach, reversing the more widely accepted presumption in many jurisdictions. Parties to mediation in Model Law jurisdictions where article 9 remains unchanged will need to reflect the 'in-confidence' approach in their agreements to mediate where this is required. See Section 9.4.6.2.

[182] Alexander (n 2) 280–91.

institution administers the mediation, the mediator may be bound by a duty to maintain confidentiality comprised in any standards adopted by the institution. National legislation may also play an essential role where it requires the help of courts in upholding the contractual nature of the confidentiality obligation.[183] While contract offers the best opportunity to tailor confidentiality to specific commercial legal requirements, it is at the mercy of the relevant court in terms of enforcement. In the context of the number of mediations taking place, experience from the USA reveals encouraging evidence that very few cases come before the courts raising confidentiality issues. Those reported cases that do so largely arise from court mediation programmes where parties are compelled to participate, suggesting that there is generally greater compliance where the process is private and voluntary.[184]

---

[183] Brown and Winch (n 88) 330.

[184] Where intentional breaches do occur, the court's remedy is generally to strike out or disregard the offending material. Parties rarely sue for damages, possibly due to the difficulty of proving monetary loss: see Golann and Folberg (n 106) 345–46.

10

Process Controversies

10.1 Introduction

The rule of law requires that the supremacy of the law be applied equally, ensuring that parties are protected against the use of arbitrary power.[1] With suggestions that settlements reached through mediation lack the 'legitimacy' of authoritative judicial decisions, the mediation process has elicited criticism. The development of judicial precedents provides important guidance for acceptable lawful behaviour, and the referral of commercial disputes to mediation gives rise to the understandable concern that mediation could inhibit the development of precedent and, in turn, commercial law. There can also be a fine balance between encouraging mediation and inhibiting access to the courts.[2] The benefit of mediation over litigation and arbitration – its private and informal nature – can also create potential risks; given the absence of judicial due process safeguards, opportunities can exist for manipulative and oppressive behaviour by the parties, their lawyers and the mediator.[3]

The court and tribunal system plays an important role, casting a shadow over the mediation process, as many disputes are resolved or discontinued on the basis of the likely court outcomes. Courts are required to publicly resolve irreconcilable commercial differences; in doing so, they play an important preventative and precedent-setting

---

[1] The elusive term was described by Lord Bingham: '[A]ll persons and authorities within the state, whether public or private, should be bound by and entitled to the benefit of laws publicly made, taking effect (generally) in the future and publicly administered in the courts': Lord Bingham, 'The Rule of Law' (2007) 66(1) *Cambridge Law Journal* 67, 69. For a discussion on the controversies of the mediation process generally from the rule of law perspective, see G Morris and A Shaw, *Mediation in New Zealand* (Wellington, Thomson Reuters 2018) 45–75. See also R Hollander-Blumoff and T R Tyler, 'Procedural Justice and the Rule of Law: Fostering Legitimacy in Alternative Dispute Resolution' (2011) 1 *Journal of Dispute Resolution* 1–19.

[2] See Chapter 7 at Section 7.5 for a discussion on conduct, costs and compulsion.

[3] See Chapter 5 at Sections 5.4 and 5.7 for a discussion on efforts to professionalise mediation, including the development of standards, to address this issue.

role. They also play a crucial role in defining the appropriate limits of the mediation process.[4] The primary controversies relating to the commercial mediation process can be categorised into three groups: substantive fairness, procedural fairness and public interest concerns. Much of the criticism of mediation stems from the fact that many different processes are, regrettably, characterised collectively as 'mediation'. It is critical that the process is clearly characterised and understood. The judicial system and mediation should be viewed as having a symbiotic relationship, with each contributing different principles to an interconnected and increasingly integrated justice framework.

10.2   Areas of Controversy

10.2.1   Substantive Fairness

Varied commercial contexts and various factors such as differences in resources between the parties can often lead to disparities in power (actual or perceived) between the parties in a mediation. Where there is a power imbalance between the parties, it has been suggested that mediation can result in substantively unfair or unjust outcomes.[5] The concern is that weaker parties, particularly where there is a disparity in resources between the parties, may be pressured into accepting offers, such that mediation reflects existing power imbalances, legitimising existing, undesirable power

---

[4] See R Feehily, 'Commercial Mediation: Commercial Conflict Panacea or an Affront to Due Process and the Justice Ideal?' (2015) 48(2) *Comparative and International Law Journal of Southern Africa* 317; K Hopt and F Steffek, 'Mediation: Comparison of Laws, Regulatory Models, Fundamental Issues' in K Hopt and F Steffek (eds), *Mediation: Principles and Regulation in Comparative Perspective* (Oxford, Oxford University Press 2013) 113. A number of the controversies relating to alternative dispute resolution (ADR) in the USA were discussed in an influential article by Owen Fiss, who believed that 'settlement is a capitulation to the conditions of mass society and should be neither encouraged nor praised': O Fiss, 'Against Settlement' (1984) 93(6) *Yale Law Journal* 1073, 1075.

[5] M Cappelletti, 'Alternative Dispute Resolution Processes within the Framework of the World-Wide Access-to-Justice Movement' (1993) 56(3) *Modern Law Review* 282, 288. It has been suggested that this can lead to 'second class justice'. Much of the literature raising second-class justice arguments relates to individuals with claims that are of low value, where the mass processing of files is prioritised over legal rights, leading to a two-track justice system; consequently it is not directly relevant to commercial mediation: see Feehily (n 4) 321–31; R Kulms, 'Mediation in the USA: Alternative Dispute Resolution Between Legalism and Self-Determination' in Hopt and Steffek (eds) (n 4) 1251–53. See also generally R Storrow 'Institutionalised Mediation and Access to Justice in the State Court System in the United States' in A Georgakopoulos (ed), *The Mediation Handbook: Research, Theory, and Practice* (Abingdon, UK, Routledge 2017) 192–99.

structures.[6] Parties may feel pressure or a degree of duress, even where they have voluntarily engaged in the process.[7] The most difficult problem the mediator faces in the context of power relationships is where there is a wide discrepancy between the strength of means of influence. As a result of their commitment to neutrality and impartiality, mediators are ethically barred from direct advocacy for the weaker party but are also ethically obliged to help the parties to reach a mutually acceptable agreement.[8]

Rather than viewing power as a measurable commodity, and that there is an awareness where one party possesses more than the other, power in mediation can be a dynamic and a fluid concept, changing during the course of a mediation depending on the issue being discussed.[9] Power can be both contextual and situational, and this is the reason that a party may appear to be quite powerful in some situations but not in others.[10] The context and relationship between the parties can be critically important. Powerful parties may be unable to use or resist using their power for numerous reasons, such as prioritising an ongoing business relationship, maintenance of reputation or the preservation of confidentiality. An ostensibly weak party may have sources of power other than finances and professional advice. Power can be relational rather than possessory, and the parties' perceptions of their own and each other's power can be as important as actual power realities. A party that is perceived as weak may make an informed choice to mediate, appreciating that no dispute resolution

[6] See Fiss (n 4) 1076–78. Empirical research from Australia indicates that this can be a recurring issue in franchise disputes: see J Giddings and others, 'Understanding the Dynamics of Conflict Within Business Franchise Systems' (2009) 20(1) *Australasian Dispute Resolution Journal* 24, 25–26, 29, 31.

[7] See Chapter 8 at Section 8.2 for a discussion of cases where aggrieved parties alleged oppressive behaviour during mediation.

[8] Effective training and accreditation can help mediators understand such distinctions and learn how best to deal with such ethical issues when they arise in practice. See Chapter 5 at Sections 5.5 and 5.6.

[9] Power may be structural, relating to the legal and practical realities of the dispute, and personal, relating to the characteristics that parties bring to the mediation such as communication skills and resilience. It has been suggested that mediators have more success in influencing personal power relationships: see H Astor, 'Some Contemporary Theories of Power in Mediation: A Primer for the Puzzled Practitioner' (2005) 16(1) *Australasian Dispute Resolution Journal* 30, 31–32. See also B Mayer, *The Dynamics of Conflict Resolution: A Practitioner's Guide* (2nd ed, San Francisco, Jossey-Bass 2012) 67–91.

[10] B Gray, 'Mediation as a Post-Modern Practice: A Challenge to the Cornerstones of Mediation's Legitimacy' (2006) 17(4) *Australasian Dispute Resolution Journal* 208, 212.

process, including litigation, can mitigate all power differences.[11] Various factors can give rise to inequities in relationships of power and mediators must remain mindful of them and respond accordingly throughout the mediation process.[12]

Voluntariness is the characteristic principle of commercial mediation. Whether a settlement is reached rests on the private autonomy of each party. This voluntariness brings with it the expectation of substantive justice and an outcome that benefits both parties, or at least does not leave one worse off. From this perspective, mediation has been characterised as the procedural counterpart of the contract.[13] The principle of voluntariness is inherent to the principle of common control of the process by the parties. As a private, autonomous process, the parties select the mediator; third parties or experts are involved only with the consent of the parties; a mediator may act even if their neutrality is called into question if they are who the parties want; and, ultimately, the decision to settle and the terms of resolution emanate from the parties.[14]

While there may be a degree of compulsion at the initial stage, continued participation in mediation is voluntary and if either party does not like the way the mediation is progressing, they can choose to exit the process. There is a clear distinction between initial engagement and continued engagement. Parties are free to walk away at any stage, as no one is forced to compromise. If parties do not reach an agreement, no adverse consequences will follow.[15] Most commercial mediations will

---

[11] See L Boulle, *Mediation: Principles, Process, Practice* (3rd ed, Chatswood, NSW, LexisNexis 2011) 203–4; Astor (n 9) 31–32. Indeed, it has even been acknowledged by critics of US court-mandated mediation programmes that the traditional litigation process may be no better than mediation in creating a level playing field: see D R Hensler, 'Our Courts, Ourselves: How the Alternative Dispute Resolution Movement is Re-Shaping Our Legal System' (2003) 108(1) *Penn State Law Review* 165, 195.

[12] Astor (n 9) 35. See also C W Moore, *The Mediation Process: Practical Strategies for Resolving Conflict* (4th ed, San Francisco, Jossey-Bass 2014) 149–53, 518–22.

[13] See Hopt and Steffek (n 4) 109.

[14] See ibid. Mediation effectively gives preference to the parties in dispute over those who would prioritise institutional and structural arrangements: see C Menkel-Meadow, 'Whose Dispute Is It Anyway? A Philosophic and Democratic Defense of Settlement (In Some Cases)' (1995) 83(7) *Georgetown Law Journal* 2663, 2669.

[15] The possibility of exiting the process at any stage makes mediation a low-risk dispute resolution option, even when things do not go according to plan: see C H Brower, 'Selection of Mediators' in C Titi and K Fach Gómez (eds), *Mediation in International Commercial and Investment Disputes* (Oxford, Oxford University Press 2019) 301, 320. Over the years, in many jurisdictions, the need for initial engagement to be consensual has been diluted. In England, for example, compulsory mediation is not part of the civil justice landscape, but courts strongly encourage use of the process and parties can receive

have lawyers present. On the occasions when lawyers are absent, if either party is unsure about the legal implications of the proposed settlement agreement, they can make it conditional upon their lawyer's approval. All of the power concerns can also happen in unmediated contexts where power differences can influence procedures and settlements. Mediation has certain advantages over settlement through negotiation in that the mediator can perceive, understand and respond to power imbalances in the process. Mediator strategies have evolved to deal with inequalities of power when they do arise. Mediators can, for example, suggest that a party seek their own legal, taxation or other relevant professional or expert advice.[16]

10.2.2   Procedural Fairness

Concerns about procedural fairness emanate from the perception that mediation lacks process safeguards. This lack of safeguards means that a party can use the process tactically to delay litigation or glean information that might be useful later. The truth of statements made at mediation cannot be tested and one party may conceal information, leading the other party to take a different view of a proposed settlement. Mediation does not provide interlocutory relief or the procedural enforcement

---

a costs sanction if they unreasonably refuse to mediate. In *BPC Hotels* v. *Brooke North* [2014] EWHC 2367, the Court nominated several leading mediators for the parties to consider: see T Allen, *Mediation Law and Civil Practice* (2nd ed, Haywards Heath, Bloomsbury Professional 2019) 97–98.

[16] See Feehily (n 4) 332–35; H Astor and C Chinkin, *Dispute Resolution in Australia* (2nd ed, Chatswood, NSW, LexisNexis Butterworths 2002) 162–63. The mediator does not have a role in looking to the reasons why parties agree on particular commercial terms, provided the agreement is enforceable. In light of their independence and impartiality requirements, mediators are not responsible for the substantive fairness of settlements. However, they do have process obligations of neutrality and impartiality: see Chapter 5 at Section 5.7.3. The management of power relationships is explicitly provided for in some mediator codes of conduct: for example, the Australian National Mediator Accreditation System. Section 6 of the Practice Standards is titled 'Power and safety' and provides: '6.1 A mediator must be alert to changing balances of power in mediation and manage the mediation accordingly. 6.2 A mediator must consider the safety and comfort of participants and where necessary take steps, which may include: (a) agreeing guidelines to encourage appropriate conduct; (b) activating appropriate security protocols; (c) using separate sessions, communication technology or other protective arrangements; (d) having a participant's friend, representative or professional advisor attend mediation meetings; (e) providing participants with information about other services or resources; and (f) suspending or terminating the mediation with appropriate steps to protect the safety of participants.'

measures available in court-based adjudication, such as compulsory production of documentation or other information, or compulsory attendance. There are no guaranteed time frames for preparing a case, and mediation lacks the formal equality of the legal process such as equal rights to present, test and rebut evidence and make legal and factual arguments.

The fairness and natural justice obligations of judges and arbitrators do not apply to mediators; thus, a mediator can meet separately with each party and could spend more time with one party in separate caucus meetings than the other. Confidentiality restrictions mean that mediator behaviour is not systematically reviewed and there are no official records to provide a basis for mediator accountability. In most mediations, there are no procedural justice safeguards and no judicial review mechanisms. Concerns are also raised by the fact that courts in some jurisdictions are empowered to order parties to use a private mediation process, run by private providers, in circumstances that impede public scrutiny, as a condition for seeking access to court; this increases costs for litigants, with a privately selected and privately funded mediator taking the place of a publicly funded and publicly selected judge.[17]

Mediation is based on needs and interests rather than legal rights and duties. While it does not uphold the principles of court-based justice, it is based on an alternative set of values in which formalism is replaced by informality of procedure, and court procedures focussed on fact-finding, evidence and liability are replaced by future-focussed direct-party participation. Mediation presents an alternative conceptualisation of conciliatory justice that can be characterised as 'co-existential justice' or 'mending justice'. Justice through mediation is distinguished by its direct accessibility, which contrasts with the resource impediments to judicial justice, and by its responsiveness to the particular interests and needs of the parties such as the preservation of relationships. Mediation does not promise substantive justice in terms of enforcing court rules. However, the limitations in substantive justice terms can be compensated for by

---

[17] See Hensler (n 11) 192, 195. This has led to concerns that justice is being privatised, where, for example, a commercial party offers favourable terms to keep matters confidential and away from judicial scrutiny: see Boulle (n 11) 193–94, 207–9. Similarly, it is contended that the privatisation of justice to facilitate the cost-effective settlement of cases disregards fundamental principles of a democratic justice system, as the parties are subtly pressured into using the process; this has resulted in confidentiality inhibiting transparency and the evolution of justice being frustrated: see R Kulms, 'Privatising Civil Justice and the Day in Court' in Hopt and Steffek (eds) (n 4) 208, 211, 214, 216, 224.

benefits in procedural justice terms that can make settlements more acceptable, legitimate and qualitatively better, even where they amount to less than could objectively have been achieved in court or arbitration.[18] Mediators can provide checks and balances that correspond to those of the court system and can ultimately terminate the mediation if the process is being abused. Parties can make use of advisors, including lawyers, and settlement agreements can provide for 'cooling off' periods. As a further safeguard, mediation operates in the shadow of the law such that settlements resulting from duress or unconscionable behaviour during the process could be set aside. Procedural fairness concerns raised about mediation largely reflect the risks inherent in any negotiation, and commercial parties make decisions with these factors in mind.[19]

While procedural justice in general terms refers to the fairness of a process by which a decision is reached, in psychological terms it refers to the parties' subjective assessments of the fairness of the process. In mediation, empirical evidence suggests, procedural justice drives the assessment about satisfaction with outcomes. While parties care about the fairness of an outcome, the fairness of a process is an independent driver of satisfaction. Even if parties do not receive what they want or believe they deserve in a mediated settlement, they are nonetheless more likely to comply with those outcomes if they believe they were achieved through a fair process.[20] Indeed, empirical evidence reveals that the parties' sense that justice has been done in mediation is connected more strongly with the course of the process and the resolution of the underlying conflicting interests than the settlement terms.[21] When mediation is perceived as legitimate due to the parties' subjective assessments about fairness, the process is consistent with the objectives – if not necessarily the specific elements – of the rule of law.[22] While parties

---

[18] Parties' perceptions of factors such as 'voice' – the ability to speak and be heard – as well as respect and fairness in the process are instrumental in this regard: see Hollander-Blumoff and Tyler (n 1) 6; C Alkon, 'Lost in Translation: Can Exporting ADR Harm Rule of Law Development?' (2011) 1 *Journal of Dispute Resolution* 165, 171–74.

[19] See Cappelletti (n 5) 289–90; Boulle (n 11) 210–12.

[20] Hollander-Blumoff and Tyler (n 1) 3–5. See also D R Hensler, 'Suppose It's Not True: Challenging Mediation Ideology' (2002) 1 *Journal of Dispute Resolution* 81, 88.

[21] Conversely, justice in court proceedings is assessed primarily by its results, over which the parties have less control when compared to mediation: see Hopt and Steffek (n 4) 106.

[22] It has been suggested that parties' preferences for certain types of ADR are based on their assessments that these processes are procedurally fairer than litigation: see Hollander-Blumoff and Tyler (n 1) 12–13. See also generally D Shestowsky and J Brett, 'Disputants' Preferences for Dispute Resolution Procedures: An Ex Ante and Ex Post Longitudinal Empirical Study' (2008) 41(1) *Connecticut Law Review* 63.

may want to mediate rather than litigate disputes, they still want the rule of law and elements that foster procedural justice. Parties value fairness in the process, and procedural justice helps to bridge the gap between mediation and the rule of law. Hence, to maintain legitimacy in the eyes of the parties, it is important that the mediation process is consistent with the parties' procedural justice needs.[23]

Parties' assessments of procedural justice in mediation are critical in ensuring that mediation exists in harmony with rule of law values, even if mediated outcomes do not result from the rule of law per se. The shift of focus away from rules has related benefits, as parties have increased voice, trust and respect, even if they lose the neutral decision-maker. As a party-empowering process, mediation offers parties enhanced levels of procedural justice, leading to a sense of legitimacy that means it appears consistent with the rule of law even where it facilitates the creation of extra-legal solutions to disputes.[24]

10.2.3   Public Interest Concerns

While court and tribunal decisions resolve disputes, they also act as 'trustees' of the public interest: vindicating rights, ensuring accountability, developing and applying the law, and articulating standards of behaviour that enforce social norms and create precedents that guide future decisions. Through public hearings and decisions, the law is developed, and precedents are created. Precedents are undoubtedly a 'public good', ensuring consistency with previous relevant decisions and providing a degree of certainty for disputants.

There are clearly contexts where it is not in the public interest to use mediation, where the justice system requires authoritative decisions on matters of public interest, social policy or public resource allocation.[25]

---

[23] Hollander-Blumoff and Tyler (n 1) 19.

[24] ibid 2, 15–16.

[25] However, this need not always be a binary choice: it can be a question of assessing those aspects that can be mediated and those that should be adjudicated. In the context of financial disputes, for example, it has been suggested that the scope of mediation should not extend to the financial aspects of transactions, to avoid adversely affecting the rights of third-party creditors. The uncertainty about risk in this context outweighs the benefits of mediation. Again, in the context of a mediation where a party subsequently becomes insolvent, if a mediated settlement is reached that results in the outflow of value from that party (such as the sale of assets at an undervalue), any such arrangement could subsequently be voided by the court, depending on the insolvency law regarding issues such as the preferential treatment of a creditor and the relevant time period in the relevant

While mediation neither observes existing precedents nor provides precedents to guide future disputes, it would only undermine precedents where it involved indeterminate disputes where outcomes are uncertain, but not when it dealt with cases where there were clear existing precedents. Hence, there is a complementary relationship between mediation and the civil justice system: the latter setting precedents, and the former resolving cases where the parties do not require a precedent.[26]

Mediation directly addresses issues of cost and delay, and this enhances both the efficiency of, and access to, the courts. As more disputes are mediated, court lists and judicial workloads are reduced, ensuring that disputes that cannot be mediated have a more efficient route to judicial adjudication.[27] Rather than impeding the creation of

---

jurisdiction. A transaction made by a company is voidable if the transaction is an insolvent transaction entered into within the specified period. A voidable transaction is one that was not necessarily void from the beginning, but which can be either avoided (made void) or affirmed at a later time. The 'specified period' can vary from three to twenty-four months before the date of commencement of liquidation or before the making of the application to the court, depending on the jurisdiction: see J Barrett and R Feehily, *Understanding Company Law* (Wellington, LexisNexis 2019) 272–74. Procedural safeguards would be required in cases involving financial disputes; the courts can provide these, demarcating aspects of financial disputes that are suitable for mediation and those that are not on a case-by-case basis. Those aspects that are not directly connected to financial flows and risk taking (such as improving communication, facilitating the exchange of information and the solving of operational or standardised issues) may be the subject of the mediation, while financial aspects of the transactions would not. Hence, aspects of ongoing proceedings can be mediated, but only those aspects that the 'judicial filter' believes are suitable. A number of jurisdictions have introduced rules that permit debtors to appoint a mediator both in pre-insolvency contexts and after insolvency proceedings have commenced: see I Forestieri and P Paech, 'Mediation of Financial Disputes' in Titi and Fach Gómez (eds) (n 15) 215–22. See also Kulms (n 5) 1299–302.

[26] Boulle (n 11) 205–6. It seems, however, that mediation is sometimes used where settlement may be contrary to the public interest, albeit in non-commercial contexts: see L Mulcahy, 'The Collective Interest in Private Dispute Resolution' (2012) 33(1) *Oxford Journal of Legal Studies* 59, 72–73, 80. It has been suggested that procedural filters could be put in place to identify and promote the cases that would usually be propelled to trial: see Mulcahy at 62. See also H Genn, *Judging Civil Justice* (New York, Cambridge University Press 2010) 74–75. It seems that US programmes on court-connected mediation are predicated on the implicit understanding that they will filter out cases that are likely to settle out of court: see Kulms (n 17) 210. It has even been somewhat controversially suggested that, as judge-made law is created by a very small number of public officials, in response to issues framed by as few as two lawyers, and given that judicial decisions generally go unchecked by other branches of government, judge-made law should be made cautiously and sparingly: see J R Seul, 'Litigation as a Dispute Resolution Alternative' in M Moffitt and R Bordone (eds), *The Handbook of Dispute Resolution* (San Francisco, Jossey-Bass 2005) 351–52.

[27] N Alexander, 'Global Trends in Mediation: Riding the Third Wave' in N Alexander (ed), *Global Trends in Mediation* (The Hague, Kluwer Law International 2003) 9.

precedents, mediation enhances it by freeing up court time and resources for those cases where precedent is required – both for the courts and for the shadow of the law within which mediation operates. Further, the freeing up of court time ensures that the courts, in dealing with those cases that require judicial determination, receive adequate time and resources to apply the law and create precedents effectively. Ultimately, fewer cases does not necessarily mean fewer precedents, as judicial time can be spent dealing with the most important cases.[28]

Other public interest concerns centre on the impact that increased use of mediation has had on young lawyers, as the decline in available trials means that they receive less experience. Clients are also disadvantaged when represented by litigators who fear the prospect of a trial. The dearth of trials also means there is a diminishing framework for lawyers and parties to measure settlement options against. It is claimed that this also deprives mediators of the experience required to help parties assess risks and benefits. It follows that the system of justice is ultimately affected, as the reduction in trials results in a reduction in the quality of advocacy and the ability of lawyers to try cases protecting legal rights. The neutrality of the judiciary could also be compromised by their attempts to promote settlement, and the settlement movement could erode public values inherent in formal adjudication. Instead of providing more options for disputants, the advent of such court-mandated alternatives is responsible for reshaping how judges view the role of the courts, fundamentally transforming the civil justice system.[29] It has been suggested that as the sponsorship of settlement is now the courts' primary responsibility, trial and the delivery of judgments has become a residual solution of last resort, with judges appearing as exemplary ceremonial figures who legitimate other people's decisions.[30]

Contrary to these concerns, increased use of mediation does not necessarily mean fewer trials, as court-sanctioned mediation may attract cases that would otherwise have settled through negotiation.[31] Civil case loads have been declining significantly for some years in courts in many jurisdictions, while there has simultaneously been a dramatic decrease in the fraction of civil cases reaching trial.[32] Empirical evidence from the

---

[28] See Mulcahy (n 26) 74–75.

[29] See Hensler (n 20) 82, 96; Hensler (n 11) 176. See also Feehily (n 4) 327–31.

[30] See S Roberts, '"Listing Concentrates the Mind": The English Civil Court as an Arena for Structured Negotiation' (2009) 29(3) *Oxford Journal of Legal Studies* 457, 458, 479. See also Kulms (n 17) 210.

[31] See Mulcahy (n 26) 61–62.

[32] See Hensler (n 11) 166–67; Roberts (n 30) 476.

USA suggests that a range of factors have contributed to this. The Litigation Section of the American Bar Association compiled a report titled 'The Vanishing Trial: An Examination of Trials and Related Matters in Federal and State Courts'.[33] The report documented that issued cases in federal courts between 1962 and 2002 that reached a conclusion (or 'disposition') increased from 50,320 to 258,876, but the number of civil trials over the same period dropped from 5,802 to 4,569. Hence the civil trial rate in US federal courts (the percentage of federal cases concluded or 'disposed of' by trial) dropped from 11.5 per cent in 1962 to 1.8 per cent in 2002. This means that while the number of civil cases filed actually increased five-fold, US federal courts tried fewer cases in 2002 than they did in 1962.[34] A number of possible causes for the decline are identified in the report. These include the increased technical nature, complexity and expense of litigation and trial; misperceptions of trials due in part to media bias reinforcing the tendency of defendants to be risk averse and settle claims; changing institutional practice or 'managerial judging' that has led to judges being proponents of settlement, with expanded unreviewed discretion as case managers; and increased use of ADR.[35]

---

[33] This seminal examination is set out in M Galanter, 'The Vanishing Trial: An Examination of Trials and Related Matters in Federal and State Courts' (2004) 1(3) *Journal of Empirical Legal Studies* 459. See also M Galanter, 'A World Without Trials?' (2006) 1 *Journal of Dispute Resolution* 7.

[34] The drop in civil trials was not constant over the forty-year period of the study. In the early part of the period there was an increase in trials, peaking at 12,529 in 1985. From then to 2002, the number of trials in federal courts dropped by over 60 per cent and the portion of cases concluded or disposed of by trial dropped from 4.7 per cent to 1.8 per cent: see Galanter, 'The Vanishing Trial' (n 33) 459–63. Galanter remarks at 516: 'We would expect that as the population of claims increases more rapidly than the capacity of the system to provide full treatment, the portion receiving that treatment would decrease.' The phenomenon of vanishing trials continues to be of particular relevance in the USA. The percentage of federal civil cases resolved by jury trial was reported to have shrunk from 5.5 per cent in 1962 to 0.5 per cent in 2015: see New York University School of Law, Civil Jury Project <https://civiljuryproject.law.nyu.edu> accessed 10 May 2022. The decline of the trial has also been observed in Australia: see D Spencer, 'The Decline of the Trial in Australia' (2011) 30(2) *Arbitrator and Mediator* 1; and in Canada and the UK: see H Kritzer, 'Disappearing Trials? A Comparative Perspective' (2004) 1(3) *Journal of Empirical Legal Studies* 735; R Dingwall and E Cloatre, 'Vanishing Trials? An English Perspective' (2006) 1 *Journal of Dispute Resolution* 51. See generally Genn, *Judging Civil Justice* (n 26); H Genn, 'Why the Privatisation of Justice Is a Civil Law Issue', 36th FA Mann Lecture, Lincoln's Inn, 19 November 2012; Allen (n 15) 6–8.

[35] See Galanter, 'The Vanishing Trial' (n 33) 515–20. It has been suggested that all the changes that reduced the trial rate are likely to have increased ADR use, leading courts to

Due to the private and confidential nature of commercial mediation, no studies exist to indicate the impact that settlement through this process has had on the rate of court adjudication. However, research conducted in the USA on court mediation programmes may provide some insights. Resolution Systems Institute (RSI)[36] based in Chicago summarised the results of sixty-two studies that evaluated the effectiveness of more than 100 court mediation programmes.[37] The studies revealed a wide range of programmes varying widely in both effectiveness and structure. Some of the studies examined the impact on the trial rate and, while revealing mixed findings, in most studies, mediation was found to have no impact on the trial rate. Overall, the studies revealed many other ways in which mediation can alter the dispute resolution experience, such as improved settlement rates, greater participant satisfaction with the process or its results, perceptions of enhanced fairness, cost savings, faster resolution, improved or sustained relationships among parties and higher rates of compliance.

While empirical evidence may not reflect a negative correlation between the use of mediation and the trial rate, evidence does suggest that its prevalence in resolving commercial disputes has led to a reduction in the use of arbitration. In 2011, Cornell University's Scheinman Institute on Conflict Resolution, the Straus Institute for Dispute Resolution at Pepperdine University School of Law and the International Institute for Conflict Prevention and Resolution co-sponsored a survey of corporate counsel in Fortune 1,000 companies. The survey presented contrasting pictures of the evolution of the two primary ADR choices: mediation and arbitration. Ninety-eight per cent of respondents indicated that their company had used mediation at least once in the previous three years. More counsel also represented that their company had at least one experience with arbitration in the prior three

---

commit more resources to pre-trial case management and ADR: see J Lande, '"The Vanishing Trial" Report: An Alternative View of the Data' (Summer 2004) *Dispute Resolution Magazine* 19.

[36] Formerly known as The Centre for Analysis of Alternative Dispute Resolution Systems.

[37] See T J Stipanowich, 'ADR and "The Vanishing Trial"' (Summer 2004) *Dispute Resolution Magazine* 7, 7; J Shack, 'Efficiency: Mediation Can Bring Gains, But Under What Conditions?' (Winter 2003) *Dispute Resolution Magazine* 11, which provides general descriptions of surveys that are summarised more specifically on the RSI website <www.aboutrsi.org> accessed 10 May 2022. Much depends on the shape and structure of mediation programmes: see T J Stipanowich, 'ADR and the "Vanishing Trial": The Growth and Impact of "Alternative Dispute Resolution"' (2004) 1(3) *Journal of Empirical Legal Studies* 843, 848–75.

years. However, the increase was modest, from 80 per cent to 83 per cent over the previous fourteen years.[38] More significantly, arbitration usage actually dropped, in some cases precipitously, for most categories of disputes and significantly for commercial/contract disputes. It has been concluded from the findings that they may be remembered as a tipping point in the modern history of mediation and arbitration, as the findings mark the point at which reliance on mediation contributed to a drop-off in arbitration.[39]

10.3 Definitional Issues

Much of the criticism of mediation stems from the fact that many different processes are described as mediation. The use of the term by users with diverse backgrounds, skill sets and practices, often for different purposes and in different contexts, has led to the term acquiring different meanings.[40] This is reflected in the US experience where the definitions and terminology used to describe mediation have varied significantly across the country. For example, what has been termed 'mediation' has often resembled non-binding arbitration, where a third party heard the evidence, did not discuss it with the disputants and rendered an advisory non-binding opinion.[41] Concerns have been

---

[38] The Cornell University Survey Research Institute administered the survey: see T J Stipanowich and J R Lamare, 'Living with ADR: Evolving Perceptions and Use of Mediation, Arbitration and Conflict Management in Fortune 1,000 Corporations' (2014) 19 *Harvard Negotiation Law Review* 1, 41. In 1997 Cornell University conducted an earlier study of ADR use among Fortune 1,000 corporations. Based on responses from more than 600 companies, 87 per cent reported using mediation and 80 per cent reported using arbitration at least once in the previous three years. While other forms of ADR processes were used, mediation was the preferred ADR option across all industries for numerous reasons, but primarily as it saves time and money, allows parties to resolve disputes themselves and results in a more satisfactory process and settlements. See D B Lipsky and R L Seeber, *The Appropriate Resolution of Corporate Disputes: A Report on the Growing Use of ADR by US Corporations* (Ithaca, Institute on Conflict Resolution 1998).

[39] Stipanowich and Lamare (n 38) 45–47. Stipanowich and Lamare further stated (at 52–53) that: 'Mediated resolutions may obviate the need for an arbitration demand, or settle a case along the way to arbitration hearings. This phenomenon alone may account for the observed drop-off in the use of arbitration.' However, when asked for reasons why companies had not used arbitration in disputes, a leading concern of survey respondents was 'not having enough control in arbitration'.

[40] For a discussion on defining commercial mediation, see Chapter 1 at Section 1.10. See also Feehily (n 4) 345–54. For a critique of the many different processes characterised as mediation in South Africa, see Feehily at 335–45.

[41] See Hensler (n 20) 87.

expressed that court-connected mediation programmes in the USA can be less voice-driven and self-deterministic, and look more like litigation, where the mediator, while not imposing a decision, strongly guides it.[42] Empirical observations from US studies of what happened during court-connected mediation reveal that parties were largely not involved in the process and that mediators rarely encouraged integrative negotiation. Mediation resembled a privatised version of the traditional judicial settlement conference.[43] The available empirical evidence reflects that referring to court-mandated settlement as 'mediation' misrepresents the process, and the real target of the criticisms is consequently forms of ADR other than mediation, as it should be used to resolve commercial conflict.[44]

Mediator neutrality and party consent are cornerstones of the mediation process and are viewed as legitimising the profession. The legal systems in some jurisdictions have not come to grips with the theoretical underpinnings of mediation and this is why so many varied approaches and standards have been adopted by courts in their efforts to use the process. In some respects, this has resulted in processes being adopted that fail to resemble how mediation should be practised. While mediation cannot exist in a vacuum and should not be perceived as theoretically static, it is its commitment to empowerment principles that legitimises the profession from a user perspective.[45] When the process is clearly

---

[42] Characterised as 'muscle mediation', some court-connected mediators engage in very aggressive evaluations of parties' cases and settlement options, where the goal is winning a settlement, rather than helping the parties exercise self-determination: see N A Welsh, 'The Thinning Vision of Self-Determination in Court-Connected Mediation: The Inevitable Price of Institutionalization?' (2001) 6 *Harvard Negotiation Law Review* 1, 5. See also N Welsh, 'Making Deals in Court-Connected Mediation: What's Justice Got to Do with It?' (2001) 79(3) *Washington University Law Quarterly* 787, 788–816. It is suggested that the institutionalisation of procedural justice in such programmes to enhance voice, respect and fairness in the process, could resolve these issues: see N A Welsh, 'Disputants' Decision Control in Court-Connected Mediation: A Hollow Promise Without Procedural Justice' (2002) 1 *Journal of Dispute Resolution* 179, 191; N A Welsh, 'Do You Believe in Magic? Self-Determination and Procedural Justice Meets Inequality in Court-Connected Mediation' (2017) 70(3) *SMU Law Review* 721, 750–61.

[43] In the USA, judicial settlement conferences often involved the judge evaluating the likely outcome should the case go to trial, and helping the lawyers negotiate a compromise. Such involvement from the judge could signal to lawyers who resisted settlement that they would face obstacles at trial. Judicial settlement conferences were also erroneously described by some as mediation: see Hensler (n 11) 175, 192.

[44] See Hensler (n 20) 82; Shack (n 37) 11 (providing general descriptions of surveys that are summarised more specifically on the RSI website <www.aboutrsi.org> accessed 10 May 2022.).

[45] See Gray (n 10) 219; Astor and Chinkin (n 16) 160–61.

understood as reflecting these principles, where a mediator actively helps parties work towards a negotiated agreement of a dispute or difference, with the parties in ultimate control of the decision to settle and of the terms of resolution, many of the above criticisms are moot.

10.4 The Symbiotic Character of the Modern Justice System

Civil litigation across the common law world involves a large group of claimants at point of entry into the system that narrows progressively towards final judgment.[46] In the vast majority of cases that enter the judicial system, disputing parties neither expect nor want their dispute to go to trial or ultimately an appeal court. Of the cases that do proceed to trial, many lack precedent-setting potential, while few raise broader issues or even involve much law. Hence the precedent-setting cases are a very small proportion of justiciable disputes.[47] It has been suggested that the debate should move away from the relative merits of adjudication, mediation and settlement and towards the more critical issue of determining how the common law needs to be developed.[48]

Many settlements take place under time or financial constraints or under pressure from lawyers at various stages of the litigation process, without judicial or public scrutiny. Viewed from a practical perspective, substantive and procedural fairness and public interest concerns may appear largely academic in a context where settlement is the dominant way in which disputes are concluded globally.[49] As indicated from the empirical evidence available, the claim that mediation has a negative impact on the trial rate or the creation of precedent is not factually substantiated. The greater threat to judicial decisions and access to justice

---

[46] See Roberts (n 30) 476.
[47] See Mulcahy (n 26) 63.
[48] See ibid 80.
[49] See, e.g., Productivity Commission, *Access to Justice Arrangements: Report*, vol 1 (Commonwealth of Australia, 2014) 394: 'Courts deal with a significant proportion of disputes entering the formal civil justice system. However, most matters that reach courts are resolved prior to final judgement. For example, judicial determination generally accounts for less than three per cent of all civil finalisations in state and territory supreme and district courts.' The most common way of concluding civil cases in the UK and in many other jurisdictions is settlement: see Genn, *Judging Civil Justice* (n 26) 21, 124–25. Settlement negotiations have been characterised as a textbook case of bilateral monopoly, where a successful outcome is based on a quid pro quo transaction in which the claimant receives an acceptable settlement and in return promises not to pursue the trial to final judgment: see R Posner, *Economic Analysis of Law* (8th ed, Austin, Wolters Kluwer 2011) 597. See also Kulms (n 17) 220.

generally appears to centre on high legal costs and court fees and, in some jurisdictions, delay.[50] Hence, settlement appears to be an inevitable component of civil justice systems, and this was the case long before mediation developed as a widely available form of ADR. A civil justice system should ensure that mediation is considered at appropriate intervals to save parties unnecessary expense, and the court system unnecessary demands. This is the rationale underpinning the approach in many jurisdictions to use mediation to incorporate settlement organically into civil justice systems, whether in the form of costs sanctions under the Civil Procedure Rules in England or as a mandatory pre-trial step in the USA and Australia, or across the European Union stimulated in part by the EU Mediation Directive.[51] Justice systems exist to deliver outcomes to parties who need and want them, and access to justice should be viewed in broad terms, not as something only the courts can provide.[52]

Justice according to law is often characterised as a set of transparent legal rules and principles applied in particular circumstances by an independent judiciary to all parties equally through an impartial process where the outcomes result from objective application of general legal norms which ensures final and enforceable outcomes. Associated with the rule of law and the principles of constitutional democracy, this characterisation of justice according to law overlooks the ambiguous nature of many legal rules and principles; the discretionary nature of judgments in interpreting statutes and precedents; the conflicts and inconsistencies between potentially applicable legal rules, standards and principles; and the difficulties parties face when taking a court action, such as following court procedures and technicalities. Assumptions about the objectivity of legal norms and procedures ignore the idiosyncratic human dimensions of justice according to law. The characterisation is also predicated on assumptions about the accessibility of this form of justice, in terms of parties' ability to afford it, comprehend it and feel comfortable with it.[53] The result is that the basic principle of the rule of law – that we are all equal before the law – is more a façade than a reality,

---

[50] From the perspective of procedural fairness, it matters little whether trials are not a viable option due to budget cuts resulting in delays or due to a party's inability to finance litigation. For many litigants, mediation is often the only opportunity to obtain procedural justice, where budget cuts and intolerable court delays obstruct access to justice: see Kulms (n 17) 229, 231.

[51] Directive 2008/52/EC of the European Parliament and the Council of 21 May 2008 on certain aspects of mediation in civil and commercial matters ('EU Mediation Directive').

[52] Allen (n 15) 14–23. See also Mulcahy (n 26) 76–77.

[53] See Boulle (n 11) 190.

and has led to supplementing the law with alternatives such as mediation to help make justice fair and accessible.[54]

There is a tendency by some commentators to adopt an extreme position as either an 'adjudication romanticist' or a mediation 'zealot'.[55] However, a divisive approach is irreconcilable with the reality that modern civil justice systems have embedded mediation as a central instrumental feature. Mediation and judicial adjudication are integral parts of the civil justice system, each serving a distinct but complementary and essential function within it. Rather than viewing the roles of mediation and judicial adjudication in binary terms, the focus should be on assessing the best means of achieving settlement, and the extent to which the courts should promote or facilitate it.[56]

Mediation should not be viewed as competing with, or undermining, the judicial process. These distinct and separate processes have a symbiotic relationship as they each benefit the other.[57] Some disputes require adjudication and others mediation; each fulfils a function the other cannot. There are some disputes that the judicial system was not designed to resolve and lacks the capacity to resolve, and these would remain unaddressed without alternatives such as mediation. For example, mediation is better suited to complex commercial disputes involving parties across numerous jurisdictions and can provide a wider range of remedies and more flexible outcomes than the bilateral adversarial framework of the judicial process.[58] Similarly, judicial adjudication provides a justice function that mediation cannot, including the clarification and development of the law and creation of precedent. Consequently, there is an interdependence between the two processes, and mediation and judicial adjudication contribute to each other in support of the justice system. This involves expanding the traditional understanding of the justice concept to encompass judges promoting the use of mediation in appropriate cases and mediation, in turn, supporting the functioning of the justice system.

---

[54] Cappelletti (n 5) 294–96.
[55] See Mulcahy (n 26) 79; Genn (n 26) 83.
[56] See Allen (n 15) 5; Genn (n 26) 125. It seems that for two centuries or so, Western civilisations 'glorified the ideal of fighting for one's rights' failing to recognise that an alternative approach, 'co-existential justice might be preferable and better able to assure access to justice': see Cappelletti (n 5) 287.
[57] See Astor and Chinkin (n 16) 44.
[58] See ibid 69.

While the rule of law is traditionally associated with trial and judgment, it now provides legitimacy for a very different process as the courts sponsor settlement.[59] The judicial architect of the Civil Procedure Rules in England made this point explicitly by claiming that justice may be achieved through settlement.[60] To ensure procedural justice in the mediation process, it is important that expectations are clearly established from the outset about the type of mediation that the parties will participate in. While mediated settlements are not a product of the rule of law, they can co-exist harmoniously with the rule of law system, provided the mediation process is procedurally just. Where parties have a voice, are treated with respect and believe the process is fair, mediation will be viewed as consistent with rule of law values and in turn be more successful through increased acceptance and adherence to outcomes.[61]

Public policy, and in turn judicial policy towards mediation has changed significantly in many jurisdictions as it has become embedded in many civil justice systems. The future focus of the courts in such contexts is likely to be issues such as the admission of mediation evidence, the contours of mediator liability and the enforcement of agreements to mediate and settlement agreements. Justice cannot be equated with one system, and the judicial system and mediation should be viewed as each contributing different principles to an interconnected and increasingly integrated justice framework.[62]

[59] See Roberts (n 30) 478.
[60] In *Access to Justice: Interim Report*, vol 2 (1995), Lord Woolf prescribed 'case management' and identified its overall purpose as 'to encourage settlement of disputes at the earliest appropriate stage; and, where trial is unavoidable, to ensure that cases proceed as quickly as possible to a final hearing which is itself of strictly limited duration': 5, 16. See also Roberts (n 30) 478.
[61] Hollander-Blumoff and Tyler (n 1) 15–18.
[62] See Boulle (n 11) 213–18.

BIBLIOGRAPHY

Abramson, H. *Mediation Representation* (2nd ed, Oxford: Oxford University Press 2011).

Abramson, H. *Mediation Representation: Advocating as a Problem-Solver (In Any Country or Culture)* (Louisville: National Institute for Trial Advocacy 2010).

Abramson, H. 'Mediation Representation: Representing Clients Anywhere' in A. Ingen-Housz (ed), *ADR in Business: Practice and Issues Across Countries and Cultures*, vol 2 (Alphen aan den Rijn: Kluwer Law International 2011), pp. 293–312.

Abramson, H. 'Mining Mediation Rules for Representation Opportunities and Obstacles' (2004) 15(1) *American Review of International Arbitration* 103.

Abramson, H. 'New Singapore Convention on Cross-Border Mediated Settlements: Key Choices' in C. Titi and K. Fach Gómez (eds), *Mediation in International Commercial and Investment Disputes* (Oxford: Oxford University Press 2019), pp. 360–88.

Ahmed, M. 'Implied Compulsory Mediation' (2012) 31(2) *Civil Justice Quarterly* 151.

Alexander, N. 'Global Trends in Mediation: Riding the Third Wave' in N. Alexander (ed), *Global Trends in Mediation* (The Hague: Kluwer Law International 2003), pp. 1–36.

Alexander, N. 'Harmonisation and Diversity in the Private International Law of Mediation: The Rhythms of Regulatory Reform' in K. Hopt and F. Steffek (eds), *Mediation: Principles and Regulation in Comparative Perspective* (Oxford: Oxford University Press 2013), pp. 131–204.

Alexander, N. *International and Comparative Mediation: Legal Perspectives* (Austin: Wolters Kluwer 2009).

Alexander, N. 'The Mediation Metamodel: Understanding Practice' (2008) 26(1) *Conflict Resolution Quarterly* 97–123.

Alexander, N. and Chong, S. *The Singapore Convention on Mediation: A Commentary* (Alphen aan den Rijn: Kluwer Law International 2019).

Alexander, N., Gottwald, W. and Trenczec, T. 'Mediation in Germany: The Long and Winding Road' in N. Alexander (ed), *Global Trends in Mediation* (2nd ed, The Hague: Kluwer Law International 2006), pp. 223–58.

Alexander, N. and LeBaron, M. 'The Alchemy of Mediation' in I. Macduff (ed), *Essays on Mediation: Dealing with Disputes in the 21st Century* (Alphen aan den Rijn: Wolters Kluwer 2016), pp. 249–269.

Alkon, C. 'Lost in Translation: Can Exporting ADR Harm Rule of Law Development?' (2011) 1 *Journal of Dispute Resolution* 165.

Allen, T. 'A Binding Settlement (or Not?): The Mediator's Dilemma' (Blog Archive: Mediation Law Developments, CEDR Publications 2014) <www.cedr.com/a-binding-settlement-or-not-the-mediators-dilemma> accessed 10 May 2022.

Allen, T. *Mediation Law and Civil Practice* (2nd ed, Haywards Heath: Bloomsbury Professional 2019).

Allen, T. 'Should Mediators (and Mediation) Be Trusted?' (2012) 162 *New Law Journal* 842.

Almoguera, J. 'Arbitration and Mediation Combined: The Independence and Impartiality of Mediators' in M. A. Fernandez-Ballesteros and D. Arias Lozano (eds), *Liber Amicorum Bernardo Cremades* (Madrid: Le Lay 2010), pp. 101–30.

American Bar Association (ABA) Standing Committee on Ethics and Professional Responsibility, Formal Opinion 06–439 'Lawyer's Obligation of Truthfulness When Representing a Client in Negotiation: Application to Caucused Mediation' (12 April 2006).

American Bar Association Section of Dispute Resolution, Resolution on Good Faith Requirements for Mediators and Mediation Advocated in Court Mandated Mediation Programs (7 August 2004).

American Bar Association Section of Dispute Resolution, 'Resolution on Mediation and the Unauthorized Practice of Law' (2002) < https://americanbar .org/content/dam/aba/administrative/dispute_resolution/dispute_resolution/ resolution2002.pdf> accessed 10 May 2022.

Antaki, N. N. 'Cultural Diversity and ADR Practices in the World' in J. C. Goldsmith, A. Ingen-Housz and G. H. Pointon (eds), *ADR in Business: Practice and Issues Across Countries and Cultures* (Alphen aan den Rijn: Kluwer Law International 2006), pp. 265–303.

Antrobus, M. and Sutherland, R. 'Some ADR Techniques in Commercial Disputes: Prospects for Better Business' in P. Pretorius (ed), *Dispute Resolution* (Cape Town: Juta 1993), pp. 163–75.

Apter, I. and Muchnik, C. H. 'Reservations in the Singapore Convention: Helping to Make the New York Dream Come True', Singapore Mediation Convention Reference Book (2019) 20(4) *Cardozo Journal of Conflict Resolution* 1267–81.

Armstrong, F. 'Business Litigation and the Litigation Business: Getting to Settlement through Mediation' (2004) *Public Affairs Ireland* 4.

Armstrong, F. 'Lost in Translation' (August/September 2004) *Law Society Gazette* 26.

Astor, H. 'Some Contemporary Theories of Power in Mediation: A Primer for the Puzzled Practitioner' (2005) 16(1) *Australasian Dispute Resolution Journal* 30–39.

Astor, H. and Chinkin, C. *Dispute Resolution in Australia* (2nd ed, Chatswood, NSW: LexisNexis Butterworths 2002).

Auerbach, J. S. *Justice Without Law?* (New York: Oxford University Press 1983).

Australian National Mediator Accreditation System. Section 6 Practice Standards, 'Power and Safety' <https://msb.org.au/themes/msb/assets/documents/national-mediator-accreditation-system.pdf> accessed 10 May 2022.

Barrett, J. and Feehily, R. *Understanding Company Law* (Wellington: LexisNexis 2019).

Bartlet, M. 'Mediation Secrets "In the Shadow of the Law"' (2015) 34(1) *Civil Justice Quarterly* 112–26.

Baruch Bush, R. A. and Folger, J. *The Promise of Mediation: The Transformative Approach to Conflict* (San Francisco: Jossey-Bass 2005).

Bazerman, M. H. and Neale, M. A. 'Improving Negotiation Effectiveness Under Final Offer Arbitration: The Role of Selection and Training' (1982) 67(5) *Journal of Applied Psychology* 543–48.

Bazerman, M. H. and Shonk, K. 'The Decision Perspective to Negotiation' in M. Moffitt and R. Bordone (eds), *The Handbook of Dispute Resolution* (San Francisco: Jossey-Bass 2005), pp. 52–65.

Berzon, M. 'Beyond Altruism: How I Learned to Be a Better Lawyer by Being a Pro Bono Neutral' (Summer 2004) *Dispute Resolution Magazine* 27.

Binder, P. *International Commercial Arbitration and Mediation in UNCITRAL Model Law Jurisdictions* (4th ed, Alphen aan den Rijn: Kluwer Law International 2019).

Bingham, T. 'The Rule of Law' (2007) 66(1) *Cambridge Law Journal* 67–85.

Birke, R. and Teitz, L. E. 'US Mediation in the Twenty-First Century: The Path That Brought America to Uniform Laws and Mediation Cyberspace' in N. Alexander (ed), *Global Trends in Mediation* (The Hague: Kluwer Law International 2003), pp. 359–96.

Blake, S., Browne, J. and Sime, S. *A Practical Approach to Alternative Dispute Resolution* (5th ed, Oxford: Oxford University Press 2018).

Blake, S., Browne, J. and Sime, S. *The Jackson ADR Handbook* (2nd ed, Oxford: Oxford University Press 2016).

Bok, D. C. 'A Flawed System of Law Practice and Training' (1983) 33(4) *Journal of Legal Education* 570–85.

Bond, G. and Wall, C. *International Commercial Mediation Training Role-Plays: Cases from the ICC International Commercial Mediation Competition* (Paris: International Chamber of Commerce 2015).

Bordone, R. C., Moffitt, M. L. and Sander, F. E. 'The Next Thirty Years: Directions and Challenges in Dispute Resolution' in M. Moffitt and R. Bordone (eds), *The Handbook of Dispute Resolution* (San Francisco: Jossey-Bass 2005), pp. 507–20.

Born, G. B. *International Commercial Arbitration* (3rd ed, Alphen aan den Rijn: Kluwer Law International 2020).

Boulle, L. *Mediation: Principles, Process, Practice* (3rd ed, Chatswood, NSW: LexisNexis Butterworths 2011).

Boulle, L. and Alexander, N. *Mediation: A How To Guide* (Chatswood, NSW: LexisNexis Butterworths 2015).

Boulle. L. and Field, R. *Mediation in Australia* (Chatswood, NSW: LexisNexis Butterworths 2018).

Boulle, L. and Nesic, M. *Mediation: Principles, Process, Practice* (Haywards Heath: Butterworths Law 2001).

Boulle, L. and Teh, H. H. *Mediation: Principles, Process and Practice* (Singapore: Butterworths 2000).

Bowling, D. and Hoffman, D. 'Bringing Peace into the Room: The Personal Qualities of the Mediator and their Impact on the Mediation' (2000) 16(1) *Negotiation Journal* 5–28.

Brigg, M. 'Mediation, Power and Cultural Difference' (2003) 20(3) *Conflict Resolution Quarterly* 287–306.

Briggs, M. 'Mediation Privilege?' (2009) 7364 *New Law Journal* 550–51.

Brooker, P. 'Mediator Immunity: Time for Evaluation in England and Wales?' (2016) 36(3) *Legal Studies* 464–90.

Brower, C. H. 'Selection of Mediators' in C. Titi and K. Fach Gómez (eds), *Mediation in International Commercial and Investment Disputes* (Oxford: Oxford University Press 2019), pp. 301–20.

Brown, C. and Winch, P. 'The Confidentiality and Transparency Debate in Commercial and Investment Mediation' in C. Titi and K. Fach Gómez (eds), *Mediation in International Commercial and Investment Disputes* (Oxford: Oxford University Press 2019), pp. 321–41.

Brown, H. and Marriott, A. *ADR: Principles and Practice* (London: Sweet & Maxwell 2018).

Bruneau, J. and Feehily, R. 'The Transatlantic Trade and Investment Partnership: A Threat to the International Trading System or the Panacea for the Economic Predicaments Faced by the EU and the USA?' (2017) 33(1) *Connecticut Journal of International Law* 43–92.

Buhring-Uhle, C., Kirchhoff, L. and Scherer, G. *Arbitration and Mediation in International Business* (2nd ed, Alphen aan den Rijn: Kluwer Law International 2006).

Burger, W. 'Our Vicious Legal Spiral' (1977) 16(4) *Judges Journal* 23–24, 48–49.

Cairns, D. J. A. 'Mediating International Commercial Disputes: Differences in US and European Approaches' (2005) 60(3) *Dispute Resolution Journal* 62–69.

Calkins, R. M. and Lane, F. *Lane & Calkins Mediation Practice Guide* (New York: Aspen Publishers 2006).

Callahan, R. 'Mediation Confidentiality: For California Litigants, Why Should Mediation Confidentiality Be a Function of the Court in which the Litigation is Pending?' (2012) 12(1) *Pepperdine Dispute Resolution Law Journal* 63–96.

Cappelletti, M. 'Alternative Dispute Resolution Processes Within the Framework of the World-Wide Access-to-Justice Movement' (1993) 56(3) *Modern Law Review* 282–96.

Carroll, E. 'The Future Belongs to Mediation and its Clients' in C. Newmark and A. Monaghan (eds), *Butterworths Mediators on Mediation: Leading Mediator Perspectives on the Practice of Commercial Mediation* (Haywards Heath: Tottel Publishing 2005), pp. 397–408.

CEDR, 'Mediation Training' <www.cedr.com/skills/individuals/mediationtrain ing/advocacy> accessed 10 May 2022.

CEDR, *Model Mediation Procedure: 2020 Edition* <www.cedr.com> accessed 10 May 2022.

Center for Professional Responsibility, *Annotated Model Rules of Professional Conduct* (9th ed, Chicago: American Bar Association 2019).

Chern, C. *International Commercial Mediation* (London: Informa 2008).

Chern, C. *The Commercial Mediator's Handbook* (London: Informa 2015).

Chong, S. and Steffek, F. 'Enforcement of International Settlement Agreements Resulting from Mediation under the Singapore Convention: Private International Law Issues in Perspective' (2019) 31 *Singapore Academy of Law Journal* 448, 452, 456.

Christie, N. 'Conflicts as Property' (1977) 17(1) *British Journal of Criminology* 1–15.

Clark, B. and Sourdin, T. 'The Singapore Convention: A Solution in Search of a Problem?' (2020) 71(3) *Northern Ireland Legal Quarterly* 481.

Clarke, D. C. 'Dispute Resolution in China' in T. V. Lee (ed), *Contract, Guanxi, and Dispute Resolution in China* (New York: Garland 1997), pp. 369–420.

Clarke, T. 'The Future of Civil Mediation' (2008) 74(4) *Arbitration* 419–23.

Coben, J. R. 'Evaluating the Singapore Convention through a US-Centric Litigation Lens: Lessons Learned from Nearly Two Decades of Mediation Disputes in American Federal and State Courts' in Singapore Mediation Convention Reference Book (2019) 20(4) *Cardozo Journal of Conflict Resolution* 1063–1102.

Coben, J. R. and Thompson, P. N. 'Disputing Irony: A Systematic Look at Litigation About Mediation' (2006) 11 *Harvard Negotiation Law Review* 43.

Coe, J. J. 'Concurrent Co-Mediation: Toward a More Collaborative Centre of Gravity in Investor–State Dispute Resolution' in C. Titi and K. Fach Gómez (eds), *Mediation in International Commercial and Investment Disputes* (Oxford: Oxford University Press 2019), pp. 61–79.

Cohen, J. R. 'A Taxonomy of Dispute Resolution Ethics' in M. Moffitt and R. Bordone (eds), *The Handbook of Dispute Resolution* (San Francisco: Jossey-Bass 2005), pp. 244–53.

Cole, L. 'Exploring International Mediation, Past, Present and Beyond' in A. Georgakopoulos (ed), *The Mediation Handbook: Research, Theory, and Practice* (Abingdon, UK: Routledge 2017), pp. 315–23.

Collins, R. and Albornoz, M. M. 'On the Dwindling Divide Between Public and Private: The Role of Soft Law Instruments in Global Governance' in V. R. Abou-Nigm, K. McCall-Smith and D. French, *Linkages and Boundaries in Private and Public International Law* (Oxford: Hart Publishing 2018), pp. 105–20.

Commission for Conciliation Mediation and Arbitration (CCMA), 'Guidelines on Conciliation Proceedings', GN 896, GG 18936, June 1998.

Comte-Sponville, A. *A Short Treatise on the Great Virtues: The Uses of Philosophy in Everyday Life* (London: Heinemann 2002).

Cornes, D. 'Mediator Fails to Have Witness Summons Set Aside: *Farm Assist Ltd v Secretary of State for the Environment Food and Rural Affairs (No 2)*' (2009) 75 (4) *Arbitration* 582–89.

Courts Service of Ireland, 'Judges of the Commercial Court' <www.courts.ie /judges-commercial-court> accessed 10 May 2022.

Crawford, D. K. and Bodine, R. J. 'Youths, Education and Dispute Resolution' in M. Moffitt and R. Bordone (eds), *The Handbook of Dispute Resolution* (San Francisco: Jossey-Bass 2005), pp. 471–86.

Cremades, B. M. 'Overcoming the Clash of Legal Cultures: The Role of Interactive Arbitration' (1998) 14(2) *Arbitration International* 157–72.

Creo, R. A. 'Business and Practice Issues of US Mediators' in C. Newmark and A. Monaghan (eds), *Butterworths Mediators on Mediation: Leading Mediator Perspectives on the Practice of Commercial Mediation* (Haywards Heath: Tottel Publishing 2005), pp. 309–39.

Crown, C. H. 'Are Mandatory Mediation Clauses Enforceable?' (2010) 29(2) *Litigation Journal* 3.

Davies, P. S. 'Negotiating the Boundaries of Admissibility' (2011) 70(1) *Cambridge Law Journal* 24.

De Palo, G. and Canessa, R. 'Sleeping? Comatose? Only Mandatory Consideration of Mediation Can Awake Sleeping Beauty in the European Union' (2014) 16(3) *Cardozo Journal of Conflict Resolution* 713.

De Palo, G. and Carmeli, S. 'Mediation in Continental Europe: A Meandering Path Toward Efficient Regulation' in C. Newmark and A. Monaghan (eds), *Butterworths Mediators on Mediation: Leading Mediator Perspectives on the Practice of Commercial Mediation* (Haywards Heath: Tottel Publishing 2005), pp. 340–55.

De Palo, G., D'Urso, L., Trevor, M., Canessa, R., Cawyer, B., Regan Florence, L. '"Rebooting" the Mediation Directive: Assessing the Limited Impact of Its Implementation and Proposing Measures to Increase the Number of Mediations in the EU' (Luxembourg: European Parliament 2014).

De Vera, C. 'Arbitrating Harmony: Med-Arb and the Confluence of Culture and the Rule of Law in the Resolution of International Commercial Disputes in China' (2004) 18(1) *Columbia Journal of Asian Law* 149.

Deason, E. E. 'Procedural Rules for Complementary Systems of Litigation and Mediation – Worldwide' (2005) 80(2) *Notre Dame Law Review* 553.

Deason, E. E. 'What's in a Name? The Terms "Commercial" and "Mediation" in the Singapore Convention on Mediation', Singapore Mediation Convention Reference Book (2019) 20(4) *Cardozo Journal of Conflict Resolution* 1149–72.

Deekshitha, S. and Saha, A. 'Amalgamating the Conciliatory and the Adjudicative: Hybrid Processes and Asian Arbitral Institutions' (2014) 3(1) *Indian Journal of Arbitration Law* 76.

del Ceno, J. S. 'Case Comment: Mediated Settlements and Enforceable Settlements: *Frost v Wake Smith*' (2013) 79(4) *Arbitration* 467–69.

Dingwall, R. and Cloatre, E. 'Vanishing Trials? An English Perspective' (2006) 1 *Journal of Dispute Resolution* 51–70.

Donahey, M. S. 'Seeking Harmony: Is the Asian Concept of the Conciliator/Arbitrator Applicable in the West?' (1995) 50(2) *Dispute Resolution Journal* 74.

Dyson, J. 'A Word on Halsey v Milton Keynes' (2011) 77(3) *Arbitration* 337–41 (3rd Annual Mediation Symposium of the Chartered Institute of Arbitration, London, October 2010)

Dyson, J. 'Halsey 10 Years On: The Decision Revisited' in *Justice: Continuity and Change* (Oxford: Hart Publishing 2018), pp. 379–94.

Edwards, H. T. 'Alternative Dispute Resolution: Panacea or Anathema?' (1985–1986) 99(3) *Harvard Law Review* 668.

Eijsbouts, A. J. A. J. 'Mediation as a Management Tool in Corporate Governance' in A. Ingen-Housz (ed), *ADR in Business: Practice and Issues Across Countries and Cultures*, vol 2 (Alphen aan den Rijn: Kluwer Law International 2011), pp. 67–80.

Ervasti, K. 'Past, Present and Future of Mediation in Nordic Countries' in A. Nylund, K. Ervasti and L. Adrian (eds), *Nordic Mediation Research* (Cham: Springer 2018), pp. 225–68.

European Commission, 'EU Overview on Mediation' (18 January 2019) <https://e-justice.europa.eu/content_eu_overview_on_mediation-63-en.do> accessed 10 May 2022.

European e-Justice, 'Mediation in Member States: Sweden' (18 March 2013) <https://e-justice.europa.eu> accessed 10 May 2022.

Fach Gómez, K. 'The Role of Mediation in International Commercial Disputes: Reflections on Some Technological, Ethical and Educational Challenges' in C. Titi and K. Fach Gómez (eds), *Mediation in International Commercial and Investment Disputes* (Oxford: Oxford University Press 2019), pp. 3–20.

Feehily, R. 'An Alternative Approach to Postgraduate Legal Education' in R. Feehily and S. Seeparsad (eds), *Governance, Globalisation and Dispute Resolution* (New Delhi: Star Publications 2017), 46–64.

Feehily, R. 'Commercial Mediation Agreements and Enforcement in South Africa' (2016) 49(2) *Comparative and International Law Journal of Southern Africa* 305.

Feehily, R. 'Commercial Mediation and the Costs Conundrum' (2019) 23(1) *Vindobona Journal of International Commercial Law and Arbitration* 1.

Feehily, R. 'Commercial Mediation: Commercial Conflict Panacea or an Affront to Due Process and the Justice Ideal?' (2015) 48(2) *Comparative and International Law Journal of Southern Africa* 317.

Feehily, R. 'Confidentiality in Commercial Mediation: A Fine Balance (Part 1)' (2015) 3 *Journal of South African Law/Tydskrif vir die Suid-Afrikaanse Reg* 516.

Feehily, R. 'Confidentiality in Commercial Mediation: A Fine Balance (Part 2)' (2015) 4 *Journal of South African Law/Tydskrif vir die Suid-Afrikaanse Reg* 719–37.

Feehily, R. 'Costs Sanctions: The Critical Instrument in the Development of Commercial Mediation in South Africa' (2009) 126(2) *South African Law Journal* 291.

Feehily, R. 'Creeping Compulsion to Mediate: The Constitution and the Convention' (2018) 69(2) *Northern Ireland Legal Quarterly* 127.

Feehily, R. 'Learning to Think Like a Lawyer' (2018) 9(1) *Mauritius Institute of Education, Journal of Education* 23.

Feehily, R. 'Mediation as an Instrument of Transitional Justice', Harvard Law School Symposium on Restorative Justice, Harvard University, USA, 5–8 February 2019.

Feehily, R. 'Neutrality, Independence and Impartiality in International Commercial Arbitration: A Fine Balance in the Quest for Arbitral Justice' (2019) 7(1) *Penn State Journal of Law and International Affairs* 88.

Feehily, R. 'Problem Based Learning and International Commercial Dispute Resolution in the Indian Ocean' (2018) 52(1) *The Law Teacher* 17–37.

Feehily, R. 'Separability in International Commercial Arbitration: Confluence, Conflict and the Appropriate Limitations in the Development and Application of the Doctrine' (2018) 34(3) *Arbitration International* 355–83.

Feehily, R. 'The Certainty of Settlement' (2016) 27(1) *Stellenbosch Law Review* 25.

Feehily, R. 'The Contractual Certainty of Commercial Agreements to Mediate in Ireland' (2016) 6(1) *Irish Journal of Legal Studies* 59–105.

Feehily, R. 'The Development of Commercial Mediation in South Africa in View of the Experience in Europe, North America and Australia' (PhD thesis, University of Cape Town 2008).

Feehily, R. 'The Legal Status and Enforceability of Mediated Settlement Agreements' (2013) 12(1) *Hibernian Law Journal* 1–26.

Feehily, R. 'The Role of the Commercial Mediator in the Mediation Process: A Critical Analysis of the Legal and Regulatory Issues' (2015) 132(2) *South African Law Journal* 372.

Feehily, R. 'The Role of the Lawyer in the Mediation Process: A Critical Analysis of the Legal and Regulatory Issues' (2016) 133(2) *South African Law Journal* 352.

Feehily, R. and Tiong, R. *An Introduction to the Law of Contract in New Zealand* (Wellington: Thomson Reuters 2018).

Feehily, R. and Tiong, R. *Commercial Law and the Legal System* (Wellington: Thomson Reuters 2020).

Fiechter, E. 'Mediation: Confidentiality and Enforcement Issues and Solutions', IBA Legal Practice Division Mediation Committee Newsletter, April 2005.

Filler, E. A. (ed), *Commercial Mediation in Europe: An Empirical Study of the User Experience*, Global Trends in Dispute Resolution, Book 5 (Alphen aan den Rijn: Kluwer Law International 2012).

Fisher, W. and Ury, R. *Getting to Yes: Negotiating Agreement Without Giving In* (New York: Penguin 1981) updated and most recently revised in 2012 (London: Business Books).

Fiss, O. 'Against Settlement' (1984) 93(6) *Yale Law Journal* 1073–90.

Fiss, O. 'Out of Eden' (1985) 94(4) *Yale Law Journal* 1669–73.

Forestieri, I. and Paech, P. 'Mediation of Financial Disputes' in C. Titi and K. Fach Gómez (eds), *Mediation in International Commercial and Investment Disputes* (Oxford: Oxford University Press 2019), pp. 207–22.

Fortún, A. and Iglesia, A. 'Mediation and Other ADR in International Construction Disputes' in C. Titi and K. Fach Gómez (eds), *Mediation in International Commercial and Investment Disputes* (Oxford: Oxford University Press 2019), pp. 278–99.

Frenkel, D. N. and Stark, J. H. *The Practice of Mediation* (2nd ed, New York: Wolters Kluwer Law & Business 2012).

Fuller, L. 'Mediation: Its Form and Functions' (1971) 44(2) *Southern California Law Review* 305.

Fuller, L. and Winston, K. 'The Forms and Limits of Adjudication' (1978) 92(2) *Harvard Law Review* 353–409.

Galanter, M. 'A World Without Trials?' (2006) 1 *Journal of Dispute Resolution* 7.

Galanter, M. 'Reading the Landscape of Disputes: What We Know and Don't Know (and Think We Know) About our Allegedly Contentious and Litigious Society' (1983) 31(1) *UCLA Law Review* 4.

Galanter, M. 'The Vanishing Trial: An Examination of Trials and Related Matters in Federal and State Courts' (2004) 1(3) *Journal of Empirical Legal Studies* 459–570.

Genn, H. *Judging Civil Justice* (New York: Cambridge University Press 2010).

Genn, H. 'Why the Privatisation of Justice Is a Civil Law Issue', 36th FA Mann Lecture, Lincoln's Inn, 19 November 2012.

Georgakopoulos, A., Coleman, H. and Storrow, R. 'Organisational Conflict Management Systems, The Emergence of Mediators as Conflict Resolution Professionals' in A. Georgakopoulos (ed), *The Mediation Handbook: Research, Theory, and Practice* (Abingdon, UK: Routledge 2017), pp. 153–63.

Gibson, K., Thompson, L. and Bazerman, M. H. 'Shortcomings of Neutrality in Mediation: Solutions Based on Rationality' (1996) 12(1) *Negotiation Journal* 69–80.

Giddings, J., Frazer, L., Weaven, S. and Grace, A. 'Understanding the Dynamics of Conflict Within Business Franchise Systems' (2009) 20(1) *Australasian Dispute Resolution Journal* 24–32.

Golann, D. and Folberg, J. *Mediation: The Roles of Advocate and Neutral* (3rd ed, New York: Wolters Kluwer 2016).

Goldberg, S. B. 'Mediating the Deal: How to Maximise Value by Enlisting a Neutral's Help At and Around the Bargaining Table' (2006) 24(9) *Alternatives to the High Cost of Litigation* 147.

Goldberg, S. B., Sander, F. E. A., Rogers, N. H., Rudolph Cole, S. *Dispute Resolution: Negotiation, Mediation, Arbitration, and Other Processes* (7th ed, New York: Wolters Kluwer 2020).

Gray, B. 'Mediation as a Post-Modern Practice: A Challenge to the Cornerstones of Mediation's Legitimacy' (2006) 17(4) *Australasian Dispute Resolution Journal* 208.

Guillemin, J. F. 'Reasons for Choosing Alternative Dispute Resolution' in J. C. Goldsmith, A. Ingen-Housz and G. H. Pointon (eds), *ADR in Business: Practice and Issues Across Countries and Cultures* (Alphen aan den Rijn: Kluwer Law International 2006), pp. 21–52.

Hanks, M. 'Perspectives on Mandatory Mediation' (2012) 35(3) *University of New South Wales Law Journal* 929–52.

Hartley, T. *International Commercial Litigation: Text, Cases and Materials on Private International Law* (3rd ed, Cambridge University Press 2020).

Hensler, D. R. 'Our Courts, Ourselves: How the Alternative Dispute Resolution Movement is Re-Shaping our Legal System' (2003) 108(1) *Penn State Law Review* 165.

Hensler, D. R. 'Suppose It's Not True: Challenging Mediation Ideology' (2002) 1 *Journal of Dispute Resolution* 81.

Her Majesty's Stationery Office, 'Access to Justice: Interim Report to the Lord Chancellor on the Civil Justice System in England and Wales', Vol 2 (London 1995).

Hill, J. 'The Exercise of Judicial Discretion in Relation to Applications to Enforce Arbitral Awards under the New York Convention 1958' (2016) 36(2) *Oxford Journal of Legal Studies* 304.

Hinshaw, A. 'Regulating Mediators' (2016) 21(2) *Harvard Negotiation Law Review* 163.

Hollander-Blumoff, R. and Tyler, T. R. 'Procedural Justice and the Rule of Law: Fostering Legitimacy in Alternative Dispute Resolution' (2011) 1 *Journal of Dispute Resolution* 1–19.

Hopt, K. and Steffek, F. 'Mediation: Comparison of Laws, Regulatory Models, Fundamental Issues' in K. Hopt and F. Steffek (eds), *Mediation: Principles and*

Regulation in Comparative Perspective (Oxford: Oxford University Press 2013), pp. 3–130.

Howard, A. *EU Cross-Border Commercial Mediation: Listening to Disputants – Changing the Frame; Framing the Changes* (Alphen aan den Rijn: Kluwer Law International 2021).

Hughes, S. H. 'The Uniform Mediation Act: To the Spoiled Go the Privileges' (2001) 85 *Marquette Law Review* 9.

IMI, 'Certify' <https://imimediation.org/practitioners/certify> accessed 10 May 2022.

Ingen-Housz, A. (ed), *ADR in Business: Practice and Issues Across Countries and Cultures*, vol 2 (Alphen aan den Rijn: Kluwer Law International 2011).

International Bar Association, 'Guidelines on Conflicts of Interest in International Arbitration' (2014) <https://ibanet.org/MediaHandler?id=e2fe5e72-eb14-4bba-b10d-d33dafee8918> accessed 10 May 2022.

Jackson, R. *Review of Civil Litigation Costs: Final Report* (Ministry of Justice, December 2009).

Jacobs, P. 'Confidentiality in Mediation: Right or Risk', IBA Legal Practice Division Mediation Committee Newsletter, September 2006.

Jarrosson, C. 'Legal Issues Raised by ADR' in A. Ingen-Housz (ed), *ADR in Business: Practice and Issues Across Countries and Cultures*, vol 2 (Alphen aan den Rijn: Kluwer Law International 2011), pp. 157–82.

Jarrosson, C. 'Legal Issues Raised by ADR' in J. C. Goldsmith, A. Ingen-Housz and G. H. Pointon (eds), *ADR in Business: Practice and Issues Across Countries and Cultures* (Alphen aan den Rijn, Kluwer Law International 2006), pp. 111–33.

Jones, D. 'Various Non-Binding (ADR) Processes' in A. J. van den Berg (ed), *New Horizons in International Commercial Arbitration and Beyond* (The Hague: Kluwer Law International 2005) (ICCA Congress Series vol 12), pp. 367–414.

Jones, T. 'Using Costs to Encourage Mediation: Cautionary Tales on the Limits of Good Intentions', IBA Legal Practice Division Mediation Committee Newsletter, September 2006.

Kadayifci-Orellana, S. A. 'Religion and Mediation, Strange Bedfellows or Natural Allies?' in A. Georgakopoulos (ed), *The Mediation Handbook: Research, Theory, and Practice* (Abingdon, UK: Routledge 2017), pp. 369–78.

Kallipetis, M. 'Singapore Convention Defences Based on Mediator's Misconduct: Articles 5.1(e) and (f)', Singapore Mediation Convention Reference Book (2019) 20(4) *Cardozo Journal of Conflict Resolution* 1197–1207.

Kallipetis, M. and Ruttle, S. 'Better Dispute Resolution: The Development and Practice of Mediation in the United Kingdom Between 1995 and 2005' in J. C. Goldsmith, A. Ingen-Housz and G. H. Pointon (eds), *ADR in Business: Practice and Issues Across Countries and Cultures* (Alphen aan den Rijn: Kluwer Law International 2006), pp. 191–248.

Katz, N. H. 'Mediation and Dispute Resolution Services in Higher Education' in A. Georgakopoulos (ed), *The Mediation Handbook: Research, Theory, and Practice* (Abingdon, UK: Routledge 2017), pp. 170–78.

Koo, A. K. C. 'Confidentiality of Mediation Communications' (2011) 30(2) *Civil Justice Quarterly* 192–203.

Koo, A. K. C. 'Exploring Mediator Liability in Negligence' (2016) 45 *Common Law World Review* 165.

Koo, A. K. C. 'Ten Years after Halsey' (2015) 34(1) *Civil Justice Quarterly* 77.

Koo, A. K. C. 'Unreasonable Refusal to Mediate: The Need for a Principled Approach: PGF II' (2014) 33(3) *Civil Justice Quarterly* 261.

Korobkin, R. 'The Role of Law in Settlement' in M. Moffitt and R. Bordone (eds), *The Handbook of Dispute Resolution* (San Francisco: Jossey-Bass 2005), pp. 254–76.

Kovach, K. K. 'Mediation' in M. Moffitt and R. Bordone (eds), *The Handbook of Dispute Resolution* (San Francisco: Jossey-Bass 2005).

Kovach, K. K. and Love, L. 'Mapping Mediation: The Risks of Riskin's Grid' (1998) 3 *Harvard Negotiation Law Review* 71.

Kritzer, H. 'Disappearing Trials? A Comparative Perspective' (2004) 1(3) *Journal of Empirical Legal Studies* 735–54.

Kronke, H. 'Introduction: The New York Convention Fifty Years On: Overview and Assessment' in H. Kronke and others (eds), *Recognition and Enforcement of Foreign Arbitral Awards: A Global Commentary on the New York Convention* (Alphen aan den Rijn: Kluwer Law International 2010) pp. 1–18.

Kronke, H., Nacimiento, P., Otto, D. and Port, N. C. (eds), *Recognition and Enforcement of Foreign Arbitral Awards: A Global Commentary on the New York Convention* (Alphen aan den Rijn: Kluwer Law International 2010).

Kronman, A. *The Lost Lawyer: Failing Ideals of the Legal Profession* (Cambridge, MA: Harvard University Press 1995).

Kulms, R. 'Mediation in the USA: Alternative Dispute Resolution Between Legalism and Self-Determination' in K. Hopt and F. Steffek (eds), *Mediation: Principles and Regulation in Comparative Perspective* (Oxford: Oxford University Press 2013), pp. 1245–1328.

Kulms, R. 'Privatising Civil Justice and the Day in Court' in K. Hopt and F. Steffek (eds), *Mediation: Principles and Regulation in Comparative Perspective* (Oxford: Oxford University Press 2013), pp. 205–44.

Kupfer Schneider, A. 'Public and Private International Dispute Resolution' in M. Moffitt and R. Bordone (eds), *The Handbook of Dispute Resolution* (San Francisco: Jossey-Bass 2005), pp. 438–54.

Lande, J. '"The Vanishing Trial" Report: An Alternative View of the Data' (Summer 2004) *Dispute Resolution Magazine* 19.

Lappi-Seppälä, T. and Storgaard, A. 'Nordic Mediation: Comparing Denmark and Finland' (2015) 27 *Neue Kriminalpolitik* 136–47.

Lau, K. 'Mediation in a Cross-Cultural Setting: What a Mediator Should Know' (2014) 25(4) *Australasian Dispute Resolution Journal* 221.

Law Council of Australia, *Guidelines for Lawyers in Mediations* (2011).

Law Society Code of Practice, Civil and Commercial Mediation Accreditation Scheme (England and Wales, 2011).

Law Society of New South Wales, *Dispute Resolution Kit* (2012).

Lax, D. and Sabenius, J. *3-D Negotiation: Powerful Tools to Change the Game In Your Most Important Deals* (Boston: Harvard Business School Press 2006).

Leach, P. *Taking a Case to the European Court of Human Rights* (3rd ed, Oxford: Oxford University Press 2012).

Leff, A. A. 'Law and . . . ' (1978) 87(5) *Yale Law Journal* 989–1011.

Leoveanu, A. and Erac, A. 'ICC Mediation: Paving the Way Forward' in C. Titi and K. Fach Gómez (eds), *Mediation in International Commercial and Investment Disputes* (Oxford: Oxford University Press 2019), pp. 81–100.

Lewicki, R. J., Barry, B. and Saunders, D. *Essentials of Negotiation* (6th ed, New York: McGraw Hill 2016).

Lightman, G. 'In My Opinion . . . CEDR Mediation Training for a Judge' (CEDR Publications, 27 November 2007).

Lightman, G. 'Mediation: An Approximation to Justice' (2007) 73(4) *Arbitration* 400–2.

Lipsky, D. B. and Seeber, R. L. *The Appropriate Resolution of Corporate Disputes: A Report on the Growing Use of ADR by US Corporations* (Ithaca: Institute on Conflict Resolution 1998).

Lopez, G. A. 'Conclusion: The Future of Mediation in a Changing World' in A. Georgakopoulos (ed), *The Mediation Handbook: Research, Theory, and Practice* (Abingdon, UK: Routledge 2017).

Lorcher, G. 'Enforceability of Agreed Awards in Foreign Jurisdictions' (2001) 17(3) *Arbitration International* 275.

Love, L. 'The Top Ten Reasons Why Mediators Should Not Evaluate' (1997) 24(2) *Florida State University Law Review* 937.

Lovenheim, P. and Guerin, L. *Mediate, Don't Litigate: Strategies for Successful Mediation* (Berkeley: Nolo 2004).

Ludwig, E. V. 'A Judge's View: The Trial/ADR Interface' (Summer 2004) *Dispute Resolution Magazine* 13.

Macfarlane, J. *The New Lawyer: How Clients Are Transforming the Practice of Law* (2nd ed, University of British Columbia Press 2017).

Mackie, K., Miles, D., Marsh, W. and Allen, T. *The ADR Practice Guide: Commercial Dispute Resolution* (3rd ed, Haywards Heath: Tottel Publishing 2007).

Main, T. O. 'ADR: The New Equity' (2005) 74 *University of Cincinnati Law Review* 329.

Marchisio, G. 'A Comparative Analysis of Consent Awards: Accepting Their Reality' (2016) 32(2) *Arbitration International* 331.

Marsh, B. 'The Development of Mediation in Central and Eastern Europe' in C. Newmark and A. Monaghan (eds), *Butterworths Mediators on Mediation: Leading Mediator Perspectives on the Practice of Commercial Mediation* (Haywards Heath: Tottel Publishing 2005), pp. 384–94.

Mattl, C., Prokop-Zischka, A. and Ferz, S. 'Mediation in Austria' in N. Alexander (ed), *Global Trends in Mediation* (2nd ed, The Hague: Kluwer Law International 2006), pp. 65–82.

Mayer, B. *Beyond Neutrality: Confronting the Crisis in Conflict Resolution* (San Francisco: Jossey-Bass 2004).

Mayer, B. *The Dynamics of Conflict Resolution: A Practitioner's Guide* (2nd ed, San Francisco: Jossey-Bass 2012).

McCormick, K. and Ong, S. S. M. 'Through the Looking Glass: An Insider's Perspective into the Making of the Singapore Convention on Mediation' (2019) 31 *Singapore Academy of Law Journal* 520.

McFadden, D. 'The Growing Importance of Regional Mediation Centres in Asia' in C. Titi and K. Fach Gómez (eds), *Mediation in International Commercial and Investment Disputes* (Oxford: Oxford University Press 2019), pp. 160–81.

McRedmond, P. *Mediation Law* (Dublin: Bloomsbury Professional 2018).

Menkel-Meadow, C. 'Is Mediation the Practice of Law?' (1996) 14(5) *Alternatives to the High Costs of Litigation* 57.

Menkel-Meadow, C. *Mediation and Its Application for Good Decision Making and Dispute Resolution* (Cambridge, UK: Intersentia 2016).

Menkel-Meadow, C. 'Roots and Inspirations: A Brief History of the Foundations of Dispute Resolution' in M. Moffitt and R. Bordone (eds), *The Handbook of Dispute Resolution* (San Francisco: Jossey-Bass 2005), pp. 13–32.

Menkel-Meadow, C. 'The Future of Mediation Worldwide: Legal and Cultural Variations in the Uptake of Resistance to Mediation' in I. Macduff, *Essays on Mediation: Dealing with Disputes in the 21st Century* (Alphen aan der Rijn: Wolters Kluwer 2016), pp. 29–46.

Menkel-Meadow, C. 'Whose Dispute Is It Anyway? A Philosophic and Democratic Defense of Settlement (In Some Cases)' (1995) 83(7) *Georgetown Law Journal* 2663.

Merrills, J. G. *International Dispute Settlement* (6th ed, Cambridge: Cambridge University Press 2017).

Mills, A. 'Variable Geometry, Peer Governance, and the Public International Perspective on Private International Law' in H. Muir Watt and D. P. Fernández Arroy (eds), *Private International Law and Global Governance* (Oxford: Oxford University Press 2014), pp. 245–61.

Ministry of Justice, *Solving Disputes in the County Courts: Creating a Simpler, Quicker and More Proportionate System – A Consultation on Reforming Civil Justice in England and Wales – The Government Response* (Cm 8274, February 2012).

Mistelis, L. A. 'ADR in England and Wales: A Successful Case of Public Private Partnership' in N. Alexander (ed), *Global Trends in Mediation* (2nd ed, Alphen aan den Rijn: Kluwer Law International 2006), pp. 139–80.

Mnookin, R. M. and Kornhauser, L. 'Bargaining in the Shadow of the Law: The Case of Divorce' (1979) 88(5) *Yale Law Journal* 950.

Moffitt, M. 'Casting Light on the Black Box of Mediation: Should Mediators Make Their Conduct More Transparent?' (1997) 13(1) *Ohio State Journal on Dispute Resolution* 1.

Moffitt, M. 'Disputes as Opportunities to Create Value' in M. Moffitt and R. Bordone (eds), *The Handbook of Dispute Resolution* (San Francisco: Jossey-Bass 2005), pp. 173–88.

Moffitt, M. 'Ten Ways to Get Sued: A Guide for Mediators' (2003) 8 *Harvard Negotiation Law Review* 81.

Moore, C. W. 'Mediation Within and Between Organisations' in A. Georgakopoulos (ed), *The Mediation Handbook: Research, Theory, and Practice* (Abingdon, UK: Routledge 2017), pp. 139–52.

Moore, C. W. *The Mediation Process: Practical Strategies for Resolving Conflict* (4th ed, San Francisco: Jossey-Bass 2014).

Morris, G. and Shaw, A. *Mediation in New Zealand* (Wellington: Thomson Reuters 2018).

Morris-Sharma, N. Y. 'The Singapore Convention is Live, and Multilateralism, Alive!' in Singapore Mediation Convention Reference Book (2019) 20(4) *Cardozo Journal of Conflict Resolution* 1009.

Mowatt, J. G. 'Mediation and Chinese Legal Theory' (1989) 106(2) *South African Law Journal* 349.

Mulcahy, L. 'The Collective Interest in Private Dispute Resolution' (2012) 33(1) *Oxford Journal of Legal Studies* 59.

National Mediator Accreditation System, 'National Mediator Accreditation Standards', <https://msb.org.au/themes/msb/assets/documents/national-mediator-accreditation-system.pdf> accessed 10 May 2022.

Neuberger, D. 'Equity, ADR, Arbitration and the Law: Different Dimensions of Justice', The Fourth Keating Lecture, 2010.

New York University School of Law, Civil Jury Project, <https://civiljuryproject.law.nyu.edu> accessed 10 May 2022.

Newmark, C. and Hill, R. 'Can a Mediated Settlement Agreement Become an Enforceable Arbitration Award?' (2008) 16(1) *Arbitration International* 81.

Nigmatullina, D. *Combining Mediation and Arbitration in International Commercial Dispute Resolution* (New York: Routledge 2018).

Nitschke, F. 'ICSID Conciliation Rules in Practice' in C. Titi and K. Fach Gómez (eds), *Mediation in International Commercial and Investment Disputes* (Oxford: University Press 2019), pp. 121–43.

Nolan-Haley, J. M. 'Mediation Exceptionality' (2009) 78(3) *Fordham Law Review* 1247–64.

Nolan-Haley, J. M. 'Mediation: The Best and Worst of Times' (2015) 16(3) *Cardozo Journal of Conflict Resolution* 731.

Nylund, A., Ervasti, K. and Adrian, L. 'Introduction to Nordic Mediation Research' in A. Nylund, K. Ervasti and L. Adrian (eds), *Nordic Mediation Research* (Cham: Springer 2018).

Otto, D. and Elwana, O. 'Article V(2)' in H. Kronke and others (eds), *Recognition and Enforcement of Foreign Arbitral Awards: A Global Commentary on the New York Convention* (Alphen aan den Rijn: Kluwer Law International 2010), pp. 345–414.

Ozoke, V. 'From Peers to Community, Transferring Peer Mediation Skills from School to Community' in A. Georgakopoulos (ed), *The Mediation Handbook: Research, Theory, and Practice* (Abingdon, UK: Routledge 2017), pp. 243–50.

Patton, B. 'Negotiation' in M. Moffitt and R. Bordone (eds), *The Handbook of Dispute Resolution* (San Francisco: Jossey-Bass 2005), pp. 279–303.

Pauwelyn, J., Wessel, R. A. and Wouters, J. (eds), *Informal International Lawmaking* (Oxford: Oxford University Press 2012).

Pepper, R. 'Contract Formation in Imperfect Markets: Should We Use Mediators in Deals?' (2004) 19(2) *Ohio State Journal on Dispute Resolution* 283.

Phillips, N. 'Alternative Dispute Resolution: An English Viewpoint' (2008) 74(4) *Arbitration* 406–18.

Pirie, A. 'The Lawyer as Mediator: Professional Responsibility Problems or Profession Problems?' (1985) 63(2) *Canadian Bar Review* 378.

Plapinger, E. and Stienstra, D. *ADR and Settlement in the Federal District Courts: A Sourcebook for Judges and Lawyers* (Washington DC: Federal Judicial Center 1996).

Poorooye, A. and Feehily, R. 'Confidentiality and Transparency in International Commercial Arbitration: Finding the Right Balance' (2017) 22(2) *Harvard Negotiation Law Review* 275.

Posner, R. *Economic Analysis of Law* (8th ed, Austin: Wolters Kluwer 2011).

Pretorius, P. 'Introduction and Overview' in P. Pretorius (ed), *Dispute Resolution* (Cape Town: Juta 1993), pp. 1–11.

Pretorius, P. 'Commercial Mediation in the Southern African Development Community', Arbitration Workshop, Mauritius, April 2007.

Productivity Commission, *Access to Justice Arrangements: Report*, vol 1 (Commonwealth of Australia, 2014).

Pryles, M. 'Multi-Tiered Dispute Resolution Clauses' (2001) 18(2) *Journal of International Arbitration* 159–76.

Purnell, S. 'The Attorney as Mediator: Inherent Conflict of Interest?' (1985) 32(5) *UCLA Law Review* 986.

Queensland Law Society, *Standards of Conduct for Solicitor Mediators* (1996).

Rampall, Y. and Feehily, R. 'The Sanctity of Party Autonomy and the Powers of Arbitrators to Determine the Applicable Law: The Quest for an Arbitral Equilibrium' (2018) 23(2) *Harvard Negotiation Law Review* 345.

Resnik, J. 'Managerial Judges' (1982) 96(2) *Harvard Law Review* 374.

Richbell, D. 'Mediating Multi-Party Disputes' in C. Newmark and A. Monaghan (eds), *Butterworths Mediators on Mediation: Leading Mediator Perspectives on the Practice of Commercial Mediation* (Haywards Heath: Tottel Publishing 2005), pp. 229–38.

Riskin, L. 'Retiring and Replacing the Grid of Mediator Orientations' (2003) 21(4) *Alternatives to the High Cost of Litigation* 69–76.

Riskin, L. 'Understanding Mediators' Orientations, Strategies and Techniques: A Grid for the Perplexed' (1996) 1 *Harvard Negotiation Law Review* 7.

Roberts, S. '"Listing Concentrates the Mind": The English Civil Court as an Arena for Structured Negotiation' (2009) 29(3) *Oxford Journal of Legal Studies* 457–79.

Roberts, S. *Order and Dispute: An Introduction to Legal Anthropology* (2nd ed, Louisiana: Quid Pro Books, 2013).

Roberts, S. and Palmer, M. *Dispute Processes: ADR and the Primary Forms of Decision-Making* (revised ed, Cambridge: Cambridge University Press 2005).

Roebuck, D. *Ancient Greek Arbitration* (Oxford, Holo Books: Arbitration Press 2001).

Roebuck, D. 'The Myth of Modern Mediation' (2007) 73(1) *Arbitration* 105–16.

Roebuck, D. and de Loynes de Fumichon, B. *Roman Arbitration* (Oxford, Holo Books: Arbitration Press 2004).

Rogers, N., Bordone, R. C., Sander, F. E. A. and McEwen, C. A. *Designing Systems and Processes for Managing Disputes* (2nd ed, New York: Wolters Kluwer 2019).

Runesson, E. and Guy, M. L. *Mediating Corporate Governance Conflicts and Disputes* (International Finance Corporation, World Bank Group 2007), available at <www.ifc.org> accessed 10 May 2022.

Rycroft, A. 'Settlement and the Law' (2013) 130(1) *South African Law Journal* 187.

Sander, F. 'Varieties of Dispute Processing: Address Before the National Conference on the Causes of Popular Dissatisfaction with the Administration of Justice' (1976) 70 *Federal Rules Decisions* 79.

Sander, F. and Goldberg, S. 'Fitting the Forum to the Fuss: A User-Friendly Guide to Selecting an ADR Procedure' (1994) 10(1) *Negotiation Journal* 49.

Sander, F. and Rozdeiczer, L. 'Selecting an Appropriate Dispute Resolution Procedure: Detailed Analysis and Simplified Solution' in M. Moffitt and R. Bordone (eds), *The Handbook of Dispute Resolution* (San Francisco: Jossey-Bass 2005), pp. 386–406.

Sanders, P. 'UNCITRAL's Model Law on International Commercial Conciliation' (2007) 23(1) *Arbitration International* 105.

Scanlon, K. M. and Bryan, K. A. 'Will the Next Generation of Dispute Resolution Clause Drafting Include Model Arb-Med Clauses?' in A. W. Rovine (ed), *Contemporary Issues in International Arbitration and Mediation: The Fordham Papers* (Leiden: Brill 2010), pp. 429–35.

Schnabel, T. 'Implementation of the Singapore Convention: Federalism, Self-Execution, and Private Law Treaties' (2019) 30(2) *American Review of International Arbitration* 265.

Schnabel, T. 'Recognition by any Other Name: Article 3 of the Singapore Convention on Mediation' in Singapore Mediation Convention Reference Book (2019) 20(4) *Cardozo Journal of Conflict Resolution* 1181.

Schnabel, T. 'The Singapore Convention on Mediation: A Framework for the Cross-Border Recognition and Enforcement of Mediated Settlements' (2019) 19(1) *Pepperdine Dispute Resolution Law Journal* 1.

Seul, J. R. 'Litigation as a Dispute Resolution Alternative' in M. Moffitt and R. Bordone (eds), *The Handbook of Dispute Resolution* (San Francisco: Jossey-Bass 2005), pp. 336–57.

Shack, J. 'Efficiency: Mediation Can Bring Gains, But Under What Conditions?' (Winter 2003) *Dispute Resolution Magazine* 11.

Shaffer, T. L. and McThenia, A. W. 'For Reconciliation' (1985) 94(7) *Yale Law Journal* 1660–68.

Shestack, J. 'Introduction' in J. R. Van Winkle, *Mediation: A Path for the Lost Lawyer* (Chicago: American Bar Association 2001), pp. vii–xii.

Shestowsky, D. and Brett, J. 'Disputants' Preferences for Dispute Resolution Procedures: An Ex Ante and Ex Post Longitudinal Empirical Study' (2008) 41(1) *Connecticut Law Review* 63.

Shipman, S. 'Compulsory Mediation: The Elephant in the Room' (2011) 30(2) *Civil Justice Quarterly* 163.

Shipman, S. 'Waiver: Canute Against the Tide?' (2013) 32(4) *Civil Justice Quarterly* 470.

Shub, O. 'Evidence Act Trumps Confidentiality Clause of Mediation Agreement', IBA Legal Practice Division Mediation Committee Newsletter, April 2005.

Singapore Mediation Convention Reference Book (2019) 20(4) *Cardozo Journal of Conflict Resolution*.

Smith, R. *Textbook on International Human Rights* (5th ed, Oxford: Oxford University Press 2012).

Sourdin, T. 'Mediation in Australia: Impacts on Litigation' in N. Alexander (ed), *Global Trends in Mediation* (2nd ed, The Hague: Kluwer Law International 2006), pp. 37–64.

South African Law Commission, *Project 94: Domestic Arbitration Report* (2001).

Southern California Mediation Association, Amicus Curiae Brief in Support of Petitioners, *Rojas v Superior Court* 33 Cal 4th 407 (2004).

Spencer, D. 'The Decline of the Trial in Australia' (2011) 30(2) *Arbitrator and Mediator* 1.

Spencer, D. 'Uncertainty and ADR Clauses: The Victorian View' (2001) 12(4) *Australasian Dispute Resolution Journal* 214–18.

Spencer, D. 'Uncertainty and Incompleteness in Dispute Resolution Clauses' (1995) 2 *Commercial Dispute Resolution Journal* 23–40.

Spencer, D. and Brogan, M. *Mediation Law and Practice* (Melbourne: Cambridge University Press 2007).

Steele, B. L. 'Enforcing International Commercial Mediation Agreements as Arbitral Awards Under the New York Convention' (2007) 54(5) *UCLA Law Review* 1385.

Steffek, F. 'Mediation' in J. Basedow, K. Hopt, R. Zimmerman and A. Stier (eds), *The Max Planck Encyclopedia of European Private Law*, vol 2 (Oxford: Oxford University Press 2012), p. 1163.

Steffek, F. 'Principled Regulation of Dispute Resolution: Taxonomy, Policy, Topics' in F. Steffek, H. Unberath, H. Genn, R. Greger and C. Menkel-Meadow (eds), *Regulating Dispute Resolution: ADR and Access to Justice at the Crossroads* (Oxford: Hart Publishing 2013), pp. 33–61.

Steffek, F., Unberath , H. and others, 'Guide for Regulating Dispute Resolution (GRDR): Principles' in F. Steffek and others (eds), *Regulating Dispute Resolution: ADR and Access to Justice at the Crossroads* (Oxford: Hart Publishing 2013), pp. 3–11.

Steffek, F., Unberath, H. and others, 'Guide for Regulating Dispute Resolution (GRDR): Principles and Comments' in F. Steffek and others (eds), *Regulating Dispute Resolution: ADR and Access to Justice at the Crossroads* (Oxford: Hart Publishing 2013), pp. 13–32.

Sternlight, J. R. 'Creeping Mandatory Arbitration: Is it Just?' (2005) 57(5) *Stanford Law Review* 1631.

Stipanowich, T. J. 'ADR and "The Vanishing Trial"' (Summer 2004) *Dispute Resolution Magazine* 7.

Stipanowich, T. J. 'ADR and the "Vanishing Trial": The Growth and Impact of "Alternative Dispute Resolution"' (2004) 1(3) *Journal of Empirical Legal Studies* 843.

Stipanowich, T. J. and Lamare, J. R. 'Living with ADR: Evolving Perceptions and Use of Mediation, Arbitration and Conflict Management in Fortune 1,000 Corporations' (2014) 19 *Harvard Negotiation Law Review* 1–68.

Stone, R. *Textbook on Civil Liberties and Human Rights* (10th ed, Oxford: Oxford University Press 2013).

Storrow, R. 'Institutionalised Mediation and Access to Justice in the State Court System in the United States' in A. Georgakopoulos (ed), *The Mediation Handbook: Research, Theory, and Practice* (Abingdon, UK: Routledge 2017), pp. 192–99.

Straw, B. M. 'The Escalation of Commitment to a Course of Action' (1981) 6(4) *Academy of Management Review* 577.

Street, L. 'Commentary on Some Aspects of the Advent and Practice of Mediation in Australia' in C. Newmark and A. Monaghan (eds), *Butterworths Mediators on Mediation: Leading Mediator Perspectives on the Practice of Commercial Mediation* (Haywards Heath: Tottel Publishing 2005), pp. 356–83.

Street, L. 'Mediation and the Judicial Institution' (1997) 71(10) *Australian Law Journal* 794.

Street, L. 'Note on the Detachment of Judges to Mediation' (2006) 17(4) *Australasian Dispute Resolution Journal* 188.

Strong, S. I. 'Applying the Lessons of International Commercial Arbitration to International Commercial Mediation: A Dispute System Design Analysis' in C. Titi and K. Fach Gómez (eds), *Mediation in International Commercial and Investment Disputes* (Oxford: Oxford University Press 2019), pp. 39–60.

Strong, S. I. 'Realizing Rationality: An Empirical Assessment of International Commercial Mediation' (2016) 73(4) *Washington and Lee Law Review* 1973.

Stulberg, J. B. 'The UMA: Some Roads Not Taken' (2003) 1 *Journal of Dispute Resolution* 221.

Summers, R. 'Good Faith in General Contract Law and Sales Provisions of the Uniform Commercial Code' (1968) 54(2) *Virginia Law Review* 195–267.

Susskind, L. E. 'Consensus Building and ADR: Why They Are Not the Same Thing' in M. Moffitt and R. Bordone (eds), *The Handbook of Dispute Resolution* (San Francisco: Jossey-Bass 2005), pp. 358–70.

Sussman, E. 'A Brief Survey of US Case Law on Enforcing Mediation Settlement Agreements over Objections to the Existence or Validity of Such Agreements and Implications for Mediation Confidentiality and Mediator Testimony', IBA Legal Practice Division Mediation Committee Newsletter, April 2006.

Sussman, E. 'A Path Forward: A Convention for the Enforcement of Mediated Settlement Agreements' (2015) 6 *Transnational Dispute Management* 1.

Sussman, E. 'Combinations and Permutations of Arbitration and Mediation: Issues and Solutions' in A. Ingen-Housz (ed), *ADR in Business: Practice and Issues Across Countries and Cultures*, vol 2 (Alphen aan den Rijn: Kluwer Law International 2011), pp. 381–98.

Sussman, E. 'Developing an Effective Med-Arb/Arb-Med Process' (2009) 2(1) *New York Dispute Resolution Lawyer* 71.

Sussman, E. 'Med-Arb: An Argument for Favouring ex parte Communications in the Mediation Phase' (2013) 7(2) *World Arbitration and Mediation Review* 1.

Sussman, E. 'The New York Convention through a Mediation Prism' (2009) 15(4) *Dispute Resolution Magazine* 10.

Sussman, E. 'The Singapore Convention: Promoting the Recognition and Enforcement of International Mediated Settlement Agreements' (2018) 3 *ICC Dispute Resolution Bulletin (Paris)* 42.

Symeonides, S. C. *Choice of Law, The Oxford Commentaries on American Law* (New York: Oxford University Press 2016).

Taelman, P. and Van Severen, C. *Civil Procedure in Belgium* (Alphen aan den Rijn: Kluwer Law International 2018).

Tapper, C. *Cross and Tapper on Evidence* (13th ed, Oxford: Oxford University Press 2018).

Thanki, B. (ed), *The Law of Privilege* (3rd ed, Oxford: Oxford University Press 2018).

Tirado, J. and Vincente Maravall, E. 'Codes of Conduct for Commercial and Investment Mediators' in C. Titi and K. Fach Gómez (eds), *Mediation in International Commercial and Investment Disputes* (Oxford: Oxford University Press 2019), pp. 342–59.

Titi, C. 'Mediation and the Settlement of International Investment Disputes: Between Utopia and Realism' in C. Titi and K. Fach Gómez (eds), *Mediation in International Commercial and Investment Disputes* (Oxford: Oxford University Press 2019), pp. 21–38.

Trollip, A. T. *Alternative Dispute Resolution in a Contemporary South African Context* (Durban: Butterworths 1991).

Tuchmann, E., Frisch, T. B., Micheli, G. and Quiroz, Y. 'The International Centre for Dispute Resolution's Mediation Practice and Experience' in C. Titi and K. Fach Gómez (eds), *Mediation in International Commercial and Investment Disputes* (Oxford: Oxford University Press 2019), pp. 101–20.

Tumbridge, J. 'Mediators: Confidentiality and Compulsion to Give Evidence' (2010) 21(4) *International Company and Commercial Law Review* 144.

UK Civil Justice Council, *Compulsory ADR* (June 2021) 29 < https://judiciary.uk/wp-content/uploads/2021/07/Civil-Justice-Council-Compulsory-ADR-report.pdf> accessed 10 May 2022.

UK Civil Mediation Council, Guidance Note No 1 'Mediation Confidentiality' (8 July 2009).

UK Civil Mediation Council, Guidance Note No 2, 'The Obligations of Mediators under the Proceeds of Crime Act 2002'.

UNCITRAL, 'Report of Working Group II (Arbitration and Conciliation) on the Work of its Sixty-Seventh Session' (Vienna, 2–6 October 2017), A/CN.9/929 (11 October 2017).

UNCITRAL, 'Report of Working Group II (Dispute Settlement) on the Work of its Sixty-Eighth Session (New York, 5–9 February 2018)', A/CN.9/934 (19 February 2018).

UNCITRAL Secretariat, *Settlement of Commercial Disputes: Enforceability of Settlement Agreements Resulting from International Commercial Conciliation/ Mediation*, A/CN.9/WG.II/WP.187 (27 November 2014).

UNCITRAL Secretariat, *Settlement of Commercial Disputes: Enforcement of Settlement Agreements Resulting from International Commercial Conciliation/ Mediation: Compilation of Comments by Governments*, A/CN.9/846 (27 March 2015).

Ury, W., Brett, J. and Goldberg, S. *Getting Disputes Resolved: Designing Systems to Cut the Cost of Conflict* (San Francisco: Jossey-Bass 1988).

Van Ginkel, E. 'Mediation Under National Law: United States of America', IBA Legal Practice Division Mediation Committee Newsletter, August 2005.

Van Ginkel, E. '*Rojas v Superior Court*: The Battle of Two Opposing Public Policies', IBA Legal Practice Division Mediation Committee Newsletter, April 2005.

Van Riemsdijk, A. M. 'An International Mediator Perspective' in A. Ingen-Housz (ed), *ADR in Business: Practice and Issues Across Countries and Cultures*, vol 2 (Alphen aan den Rijn: Kluwer Law International 2011), pp. 60–66.

Van Winkle, J. R. *Mediation: A Path for the Lost Lawyer* (Chicago: American Bar Association 2001).

Vandekerckhove, K. 'Mediation of Cross-Border Commercial Disputes in the European Union' in C. Titi and K. Fach Gómez (eds), *Mediation in International Commercial and Investment Disputes* (Oxford: Oxford University Press 2019), pp. 182–205.

Wallgren, C. 'ADR and Business' in J. C. Goldsmith, A. Ingen-Housz and G. H. Pointon (eds), *ADR in Business: Practice and Issues Across Countries and Cultures* (Alphen aan den Rijn: Kluwer Law International 2006), pp. 3–19.

Walsh, N. A. 'Institutionalisation and Professionalisation' in M. Moffitt and R. Bordone (eds), *The Handbook of Dispute Resolution* (San Francisco: Jossey-Bass 2005), pp. 487–506.

Wanis-St John, A. 'Cultural Pathways in Negotiation and Conflict Management' in M. Moffitt and R. Bordone (eds), *The Handbook of Dispute Resolution* (San Francisco: Jossey-Bass 2005), pp. 118–34.

Weldon, E. M. and Kelly, P. W. 'Prelitigation Dispute Resolution Clauses: Getting the Benefit of your Bargain' (2011) 31(1) *Franchise Law Journal* 28.

Welsh, N. A. 'Disputants' Decision Control in Court-Connected Mediation: A Hollow Promise Without Procedural Justice' (2002) 1 *Journal of Dispute Resolution* 179.

Welsh, N. A. 'Do You Believe in Magic? Self-Determination and Procedural Justice Meets Inequality in Court-Connected Mediation' (2017) 70(3) *SMU Law Review* 721.

Welsh, N. A. 'Making Deals in Court-Connected Mediation: What's Justice Got to Do with It?' (2001) 79(3) *Washington University Law Quarterly* 787.

Welsh, N. A. 'The Thinning Vision of Self-Determination in Court-Connected Mediation: The Inevitable Price of Institutionalization?' (2001) 6 *Harvard Negotiation Law Review* 1.

Wilensky, H. J. 'The Professionalisation of Everyone' (1964) 70(2) *The American Journal of Sociology* 137.

Wiwen-Nilsson, T. 'Conciliation: Enforcement of Settlements', *Modern Law for Global Commerce: Proceedings of the UNCITRAL Congress*, Vienna, 9–12 July 2007.

Wollgast, H. and de Castro, I. 'WIPO Mediation: Resolving International Intellectual Property and Technology Disputes Outside the Courts' in C. Titi and K. Fach Gómez (eds), *Mediation in International Commercial and Investment Disputes* (Oxford: Oxford University Press 2019), pp. 259–77.

World Bank Group, *Alternative Dispute Resolution Guidelines* (Washington DC, 2011).

Zelizer, C. and Chiochetti, C. 'Mediation Career Trends Through Time, Exploring Opportunities and Challenges' in A. Georgakopoulos (ed), *The Mediation Handbook: Research, Theory, and Practice* (Abingdon, UK: Routledge 2017), pp. 9–19.

INDEX

additional dispute resolution, 7
adjudication, 5, 14
Africa, traditional forms of dispute
 resolution, 30
alternative dispute resolution
 adjudicative options, 13–14
 context of, 6–8
 hybrid options, 15–16
 and litigation, 9–10
 methods, 11
 non-adjudicative options, 11–13
 process selection and design, 17–19
appropriate dispute resolution, 7
arbitral awards, 216–17, *See also*
 New York Convention
arbitration, 13, 31
arb-med, 15–16
Asia, historical use of mediation, 30
assisted deal-making, 101
Australia
 conduct, costs and confidentiality,
 194–5
 definitions of mediation, 22
 mediated settlement agreements,
 201, 205, 206, 208, 210
 protection of mediation
 confidentiality, 272
Austria, regulation of mediation, 47

Canada, mediated settlement
 agreements, 201, 203
capacity, 208
Centre for Effective Dispute Resolution
 definition of mediation, 25–6
China, historical use of mediation, 30
civil law countries, mediation in, 35–7
coercion, 206–7

commercial contracts. *See also*
 mediation clauses in contracts
 dispute resolution provisions, 54
commercial dispute resolution
 processes, 27–8
commercial disputes
 effect on relationship between
 parties, 18
 recurrence, 18–19
 remedies provided by legal
 system, 4–5
 resolution, 27–8
 satisfaction with outcomes, 18
 transaction costs, 17
commercial interests, legal rights
 and, 3–4
commercial mediation. *See also*
 international commercial
 mediation
 agreements to mediate. *See* future
 agreements to mediate
 benefits of mediated solutions,
 98–100
 confidentiality in, 246–8
 consent to, 182
 as costs containment device, 162–4
 defining, 20–5
 historical background, 29–33
 in non-contentious transactional
 settings, 101
 process. *See* commercial mediation
 process
 voluntariness in, 296–7
commercial mediation models, 83–4
 evaluative mediation, 84–6
 facilitative mediation, 84–6
 mixed process, 87–8

334

For EU product safety concerns, contact us at Calle de José Abascal, 56–1°,
28003 Madrid, Spain or eugpsr@cambridge.org.